Programming the IBM® User Interface   Using Turbo Pascal®

Many of the designations used by manufacturers and sellers to
distinguish their products are claimed as trademarks. Where
those designations appear in this book, and Addison-Wesley
was aware of a trademark claim, the designations have been
printed in initial caps or all caps. LogiTech C7 Mouse and
LogiMouse are trademarks of LogiTech, Inc.

Library of Congress Cataloging-in-Publication Data

Ezzell, Ben.
    Programming the IBM user interface : using Turbo Pascal /
Ben Ezzell.
        p.   cm.
    Includes index.
    ISBN (invalid) 1-201-15009-3
    1. IBM Personal computer—Programming. 2. Pascal
(Computer program language) 3. Turbo Pascal (Computer
program) 4. User interfaces (Computer systems) I. Title.
    QA76.8.I2594E99 1989   005.265—dc19   88-20968

Copyright © 1989 by Ben Ezzell

009-3
-HA-898
December 1988

Programming the IBM® User Interface
USING TURBO PASCAL®

BEN EZZELL

ADDISON-WESLEY PUBLISHING COMPANY, INC.

Reading, Massachusetts   Menlo Park, California   New York
Don Mills, Ontario   Wokingham, England   Amsterdam   Bonn   Sydney
Singapore   Tokyo   Madrid   San Juan

Dedication

Respectfully dedicated to my parents, Ben who
showed me that I could learn anything, and Nancy
who taught me the importance of words, and
puns, and all manner of communication; to a
veritable legion of teachers, professors, programmers, and others who have shared unstintingly
their own hard-won knowledge; and — far from
least — to Mary who, for more than half a
lifetime, has aided and abetted (and instigated) all
manner of educational adventuring.

Contents

CONTENTS

Introduction

This book is an attempt to define methods and practices for producing a smoothly operating interface between two computational systems.

A casual expansion of this first statement may suggest an interface between two computers or between a human operator and a computer, but beware such simplification — the interface in question here is the interrelation between *you*, the human programmer, and your *customer*, the also human, end-user of your program.

If your programs are designed and intended to speak *only* to the computer, you may stop reading right now, put this book down, and turn off your monitor. A computer is only the medium; it is not the message!

The interfacing described here should be viewed as part of a chain linking a human (a programmer) via a medium (a computer using Turbo Pascal 3.x or 4.x) with another human (an end-user). Although the topics being discussed will center heavily on the medium (the computer), keep in mind that all the programs, demonstrations, and techniques covered in this book are aimed firmly at the two humans on each end of the chain. Programs are written and constructed for the convenience of humans (primarily the users) and not for the convenience of the computer.

A program is nothing more than a communication vehicle and should be designed first for the convenience of the user. The convenience of the computer is important only if and when it contributes to this primary objective. It is always tempting to do something simply because the computer can do it — like climbing mountains because they are there — without regard to the actual needs of the program and the convenience or applications for the user. For instance, you can write a subprogram to translate Pig Latin, but please don't feature it in my word processor — ecausebay Iway illway owthray itway outway, astfay!

This Is Not a Cookbook

I am not offering you *Papa Ben's Secret Compendium of Ultimate Programming Recipes*. You may think of this as a course of instruction providing a variety of useful tools, but these are not straight-from-the-kitchen-to-the-table-in-ten-minutes recipes for instant gourmet programming. These are tools, techniques, and suggestions that you are free to tear apart — and I sincerely hope you will — examine the works, reassemble or revise for new purposes, discard as inapplicable and create your own, curse me for missing your own favorite trick (tell me about it), and use.

I am not attempting to define rigid structures which must be followed in all circumstances. Instead, I offer guidelines and tools for general programming practices. I have tried to make these tools sufficiently broad in scope to fit with most applications. But if these do not fit your application as written, feel free to rewrite them to suit your needs.

Since these utilities are written as guides and teaching devices rather than use-as-is drop-ins, extensive explanations and notes are included in the program listings as well as in the text. I have attempted to explain both the *why* and *why not* as well as the *how*. In some cases, I suggest experiments which will demonstrate techniques and effects that cannot be easily described in English.

Many of the later programs and demos in this book use include files that have been described earlier. If you skip around in your reading, you may need to search earlier chapters to find referenced material. All of the programs and utilities are included on the program disk(s), which may be purchased to accompany this book. (See the coupon at the back.) In some cases and particularly in the later sections, brief program procedures are illustrated which have not been used in any specific program or demo and therefore are not included on the disk.

Notes and Changes — Version 3.x versus 4.0

Version 4.0 of Turbo Pascal has a number of conventions, syntax changes, and new functions and procedures that are not totally compatible with and/or are not included in earlier versions. In most cases, these changes permit more efficient programming, so version 4.0 will be the standard used in this book. (If you wish to convert existing source code from version 3.x to 4.0, refer to your Turbo Pascal 4.0 manual and the Upgrade utility distributed with 4.0.) Where practical, notes or conversion suggestions are included as comments in the source code. A few items, however, are so common that complete notation would be excessive (and confusing). Some of these common differences are described in the following list.

1. The instruction uses `Crt, Dos, etc;` will appear in most source listings for version 4.0 immediately following the program name. If you are using version 3.x, simply delete this line as inapplicable.

2. The predefined variable type string in version 4.0 is not supported by version 3.x and should be replaced by declaring an equivalent as follows:

```
type
    LongStr : string[255];
```

and by changing all variables of type string to type LongStr.

3. Interrupt calls have two principal differences. First, in the declaration of type Registers, version 4.0 uses word values, whereas version 3.x uses integer values.

version 4.0	version 3.x
Registers = record case Integer of	Registers = record case Integer of
1: (AX ... Flags : word);	1: (AX ... Flags : integer);

For version 4.0, the Registers type is predeclared in the Dos unit. You will still need to declare a variable `Reg` of type Registers. All programs shown here include the type declaration for Registers even though this is not required.

Second, when calling an interrupt, different formats are used.

version 4.0	version 3.x
intr($xx,Dos.Registers(Reg));	intr($xx,Reg);

In all other respects, the interrupt calls are the same.

4. Two procedures, Inc and Dec, are new to version 4.0; earlier versions used the succ and pred procedures, respectively.

version 4.0	version 3.x
inc(IntVar);	IntVar := succ(IntVar);
dec(IntVar);	IntVar := pred(IntVar);

As an alternative, you might create your own Inc and Dec procedures as follows:

```
procedure Inc( var IntVar: Integer);
begin
    IntVar := succ(IntVar);
end;
```

In some cases, however, such procedures may remain incompatible because version 4.0's **Inc** and **Dec** procedures allow an optional second argument (inc(IntVar,5)) for the amount by which the variable is increased or decreased.

5. In Turbo 4.0, a new function **ReadKey** is provided as a replacement for the earlier read(kbd,Ch). For version 3.x, I suggest creating the **ReadKey** function as follows:

```
function ReadKey: char;
   var
      Ch : char;
   begin
      read(kbd,Ch);
      ReadKey := Ch;
   end;
```

Conventions and Comments

In general, most preexisting procedures and functions (that is, those built in in versions 3.x and 4.0) appear in lowercase only. New functions and procedures, which are being created or introduced here, are capitalized and use an Underscore_Separator for readibility, for example, **Open_File**, **Change_Case**, **Swap_If**.

Likewise, most variables and constants begin with capital letters and may have additional capitalized characters to provide ease of recognition, for example, FileName, ListFile, or StringLen.

In all cases, procedure, function, constant, and variable names are chosen to be effectively self-identifying and self-documenting as well as easily remembered.

Program Listing Conventions

Program listings use stepped indentation for easy reading. Although a single-space indent is often used to save disk space, I have used a three-space indent step for greater clarity.

In the printed listings, comments and notes appear within curly brackets with **boldface** used occasionally for emphasis. The program instructions themselves are in regular monospace type.

The program listings on disk omit boldface and italics, of course, but will otherwise duplicate the printed listings (with a few exceptions). (See the coupon in the back of the book for information on purchasing the program disk.)

Numbers and Characters

Some programmers insist that all enumeration should appear in the familiar decimal format, whereas others can be just as stubborn about employing only hexadecimal notation in their programs. I have mainly used hexadecimal notation. Thus, all values passed to interrupt calls and/or registers and all values used in bit-wise operations appear in hexadecimal form. Similarly, hexadecimal values are used to represent a character as a numerical reference.

However, if a loop is set for a value greater than 9, the notation normally appears as for I := 1 to 100 (decimal), and not as for I := 1 to $100 (hexadecimal, equals 256 decimal) nor as for I := 1 to $64 (hexadecimal, equals 100 decimal). All other values not directly connected with bit operations appear in conventional decimal form.

My reasons for this dichotomy of notation are neither arbitrary nor capricious, and may be summed up in the Danish phrase: *"For os der taler alle sprog er det jo ingen sag."* Literally translated, this states "For we who speak all languages, there is no problem."

In Germany, the *Wandervölker* (hippies of the early twentieth century) greeted friends with the expression *"Grüss Gott,"* which did not mean "Hello" or even the more common *"Guten Morgen"* (Good morning). Literally it meant "Greet God" and was an expression rooted in a philosophy and way of life that differed from the popular culture. If you did not understand the language and relied only on a rough translation, you did not understand the people.

With computers, the problem is further complicated because the "culture" — the actual machine-level binary workings of the computer — is so different from our own familiar thought patterns. We can, however, make an effort to understand the computer's language and, therefore, understand its "culture" and behavior.

Being human, I do find it difficult to readily recognize binary phrases such as 10001111, while the hexadecimal 8Fh is at least a passable pidgen binary and one that I can read relatively easily. More importantly, I can relate the hexadecimal representation directly to the computer's binary operations.

For example, the computer can recognize the decimal value in the instruction Select_Color(143) as an instruction to set blinking white characters.

However, I find it much more convenient to say Select_Color($8F)[1] because I can mentally translate the hexadecimal character F to 1111 (binary), which turns on all three color guns for the foreground color while setting the high intensity flag, thus producing intense white. I can also recognize the hexadecimal 8 as 1000, which tells me that the background color is black (all color guns flagged off) and the seventh bit (the 1) sets the blink flag on. This same instruction could have been passed as binary (10001111) and this information would have been recognizable, but not as readily. Turbo also allows you to say Select_Color(White+Blink), which is even clearer English but gives less of an idea of what the computer is seeing and thinking and understanding. The computer's viewpoint is important — vitally important — to the computer programmer.

Setting a loop using hexadecimal value would also work but it makes it less convenient to recognize how many times the loop is being told to execute. For example, if I want to use a loop to repeat a four-character string twenty times to fill the width of the screen, using 14h is as acceptable to the computer as using the decimal 20 and accomplishes the same task. However, since I grew up with decimal notation and thus find the 20 far easier to recognize than 14h. I will, again, suit my own convenience (and I hope yours) in the choice of notation.

Pascal does not recognize the common notation 7Fh to indicate hexadecimal. I have used this form in the text, notes, and comments but the form $7F is used in the program instructions. Pascal does recognize $7F.

The pound or number sign (#) is used by Pascal to denote that a value is to be treated as a character and not as a number. For example, the character A = #65 (decimal) = #$40 (hexadecimal). Where the actual character cannot be entered conveniently (for instance, because of keyboard limitations), the latter hexadecimal form will be employed exclusively.

In any other instances of hexadecimal versus decimal notation, you may simply attribute the choice of notation to my own personal idiosyncracies.

Using the Program Listings in This Book

One or more demo programs are used in most chapters to illustrate the topics and practices discussed. For the most part, these demo programs are not intended to be complete, stand-alone utilities designed for immediate practical

---

1. The **Select_Color** procedure does not appear in any version of Turbo Pascal and is used here for illustration purposes only. See also the TextAttr variable in version 4.0. A similar procedure, **SetColor**, is included in version 4.0's Graph Unit to select graphics palette color.

applications (aside from the application of demonstrating a program practice). The demo programs may contain the listings for one or more include files, which may also be needed by other demo programs or may contain references to include files which appear with the demo programs in previous chapters.

If you have purchased the program disks available to accompany this book, the include files have already been created separate from the demo programs and may be used directly. Otherwise, it would be good programming practice to enter the indicated sections of each listing as separate include files, using the filenames as they appear in the comment fields at the beginning of the segment.

In some cases, and particularly in the chapter on pointer structures, the code structure shown may be less than theoretically optimum. In most cases, this has been done to make the code statements clearer to the reader even though an experienced programmer might choose a more concise format to achieve essentially the same results. As long as the compiled results do not differ materially in performance, all source code has been structured for the reader's convenience, not for the computer's.

In other cases, functions or techniques have been demonstrated that are generally obsolete with the current introduction of version 4.0. This is not an oversight. Simply because a particular DOS interrupt function is better handled — *in most cases* — by functions or procedures supplied by Turbo Pascal, this does not mean that the interrupt function should be ignored or forgotten entirely. You may find circumstances or applications where a direct handle to the interrupt function offers an advantage. Power saws are wonderful, but I still have my hand saws and my pocket knife.

Using Include Files — Version 3.x versus 4.0

In earlier versions of Turbo Pascal (versions 3.x and before), any include file was compiled in its entirety, even if most or none of the procedures in the file were actually used by the program. Beginning with version 4.0, this is no longer the case and only those procedures or functions that are actually used by the program will be included in the final compilation. This feature offers a significant improvement and great convenience to the programmer. Instead of pondering which procedures and functions actually need to be provided in include files, you can now put a variety of desired functions and procedures into a standard set of include files that you can reference as your programming needs dictate. When your program compiles, only the code actually needed is created; the excess and any uncalled functions and procedures do not appear in the product.

Nested include files (that is, an include file containing references to further include files) are now allowed. For example, a library include reference might be employed in your main program as follows:

```
{$I StdEdLib.Lst}  (* include Standard Edit Library *)
```

where StdEdLib.Lst only contains reference to a series of other include files such as:

```
(* StdEdLib: Standard Edit Library list *)
{$I C:\TURBO\LIBRARY\GEN_UTIL.INC}  (* General Utilities *)
{$I C:\TURBO\LIBRARY\EDT_UTIL.INC}  (* Editor Utilities  *)
{$I C:\TURBO\LIBRARY\BOX_UTIL.INC}  (* Box Creation      *)
{$I C:\TURBO\LIBRARY\SPEC_EFF.INC}  (* Special Effects   *)
```

Warning!!! Nested include files present a very subtle danger and must be used with care and consideration. Since one include file can call another, it becomes very easy for a program to have two or even more include references to the same file *without being obvious*. The compiler will not necessarily flag this as an error, but the resulting compiled product *may* produce unexpected results which can be very difficult to track down. Use nested include files carefully — very carefully!

New with Turbo 4.0 is the Uses declaration. This is rather like the standard library inclusion mentioned above, and it is a provision allowing your program to reference a number of Units (precompiled include files) such as **Crt** or **Dos**. As with the regular include files, only those portions of the uses reference that are actually needed will appear in your finished program and these may be employed freely without adding excess code. The Uses reference is explained in detail (including how to create your own Units) in the Turbo 4.0 manual.

1

Programming the Computer/User Interface

Folk wisdom holds that a thin line divides genius and insanity. The division, however, between a good programmer and a great programmer is not marked by a line but (pardon a mixed metaphor) by a vast chasm filled with a maze of twisted, winding passages, obscured by a thick fog of uncertainty, and shrouded within an enigma. (The descriptions of Colossal Cave in the early computer game **Adventure** were hardly accidental in their imagery.)

There are several hallmarks by which a good programmer can be distinguished. When he or she completes a task, the resulting code runs without crashing, accomplishes the designed task with a minimum of effort, accepts input smoothly and as necessary, produces the required output cleanly and neatly, and, last but not least, does not leave the system tied in knots on exiting. (There are other desirable characteristics but these are the principal categories.) Being a good programmer requires an understanding of the computer and its operations, a thorough knowledge of the programming language, and careful planning and debugging of the product.

Being a great programmer, however, requires a less easily defined knowledge and skill. In some respects, a great programmer must combine the diverse talents of efficiency expert, psychologist, teacher, and — without insult to either you or your end-users — an expert babysitter[1].

---

1. I strongly recommend reading *Design for the Real World* by Victor Papanek. Although this book has nothing to do with computer programming, it has everything to do with good design and, therefore, with good programming design. The cover blurb reads "Why the Things You Buy Are Expensive, Badly Designed, Unsafe and Usually Don't Work!" This is immediately and directly applicable to too much of the computer software sold today.

Both computers and computer programs are difficult products to sell. Since many purchasers know little or nothing about what they are buying, both products may be sold on the basis of packaging. Most computer ads feature fancy color graphics (with or without skits and pantomime by famous stars), whereas computer programs are marketed in fancy four-color boxes (usually large enough to hold several hundred floppy disks) showing elaborate, windowed color displays.

For both the novice and the experienced programmer, these computing frills and flourishes, including windows, color, pop-ups, and moving displays, are virtually irresistible attractions. I am no more immune than you; I love them too. After all, the computer *is* the ultimate toy!

But these are not the hallmarks of a great programmer. These flourishes *may* be the tools of a great programmer, but the true hallmark isn't that simple, nor is it anything obvious which can be splashed across a four-color wrapper. The true hallmark of a great programmer consists of a multitude of small concerns, which should also be invisibly unobtrusive to the end user. These are difficult elements to define, but having offered my excuses (and this caveat), I will attempt a brief definition that is subject, of course, to later correction, expansion, and annotation:

> The true hallmark of a great programmer lies in his or her ability to anticipate accurately the needs and expectations of the users.

The first element of my definition is to *anticipate*. Anticipation is at once the most difficult of tasks as well as the basic intent of any program. The value of doing so *accurately* should be obvious.

The next element is *needs*. The needs of the user are multiple and vary greatly depending on the intentions and purpose of your program. If users knew what their needs actually were, the two preceding elements could be disposed of, but such is rarely the case. Instead, your task as programmer begins with defining exactly what these needs are and which can be provided with solutions.

The last element is *expectations*. Expectations are like the fabled "wealth beyond dreams of avarice." Such dreams have no limits and neither do the expectations of the users. As a programmer, your best hope is to select a reasonable subset of expectations and attempt to fulfill these in a concise manner. Otherwise, your program will never be completed.

Fulfilling this definition of a great programmer is no small challenge, but it is a task worthy of accomplishment.

Every program begins with the same first step. The user types the program name for the first time and waits expectantly to see what happens. But the program name itself is not always enough, and many programmers rely on command line parameters to specify external files for use, to indicate which of several tasks are desired, or to provide other needed specifications. The command line parameter can be anything. If you've ever entered the DOS command **TYPE READ.ME** to view a file on screen, you've used a command line parameter (in this case, to specify the filename).

Using the Command Line Parameter

The command line parameter might be a single filename, a series of filenames, a series of switch specifications, some combination of these, or almost any type of string passing instructions to a program. For example, I've designed a simple program to list my own Pascal source codes (see the **PLIST.PAS** demo program at the end of this chapter) and would like to be able to call the program with the syntax PLIST MYPROG.PAS, or simply with PLIST. I might want to be able to call PLIST \TURBO\MYPROG \TURBO\MYPROG2.INC \UTILITY\MYUTIL.INC and have three files formatted and sent to the printer. I should also consider whether I want to enter Plist MyProg.pas or plist myprog or any other combination of uppercase and/or lowercase letters. In any case, I don't want **PLIST** to come back and beep at me with an error message or, worse, to sit there and blink while waiting for some undefined input.

Three possible conditions require response:

1. No command line parameter is present.

2. A command line parameter is present.

3. More than one parameter has been passed by the command line.

The first step is to check Turbo's **ParamCount**.

The ParamCount Function

ParamCount is an integer function that returns a count of the number of parameters passed in the command line buffer — space or tab characters act as delimiters or separators between parameters.

In the procedure **OpenMainFile**, if **ParamCount** returns a value of zero (0), only the program name was entered and **PLIST** should prompt for the name of a file to list:

```
if ParamCount = 0 then
begin
    write('Enter filename: ');
    readln(MainFileName);
end  ...
```

In the second case, if **ParamCount** is not zero (that is, a filename was included in the command line), the **OpenMainFile** procedure omits the prompt and extracts the MainFileName variable directly using the ParamStr(1) function as follows:

```
...  else MainFileName := ParamStr(1);
```

The ParamStr Function

ParamStr is a second function provided by Turbo for handling the command line buffer. Calling **ParamStr(N)** returns the nth element passed to the command line buffer, assuming that such an element exists.

Turbo version 3.x
```
var I: byte; { or integer }
begin
    for I   := 1 to ParamCount do
        writeln(ParamStr(I));
end;
```

Turbo version 4.0
```
var I: word; { word value expected }
begin           { by ParamStr          }
    for I := 1 to ParamCount do
        writeln(ParamStr(I));
end;
```

For instance, if the command line said PLIST MYPROG MYPROG2 MYPROG3, **ParamCount** would return a value of 3, **ParamStr(1)** would return MYPROG, **ParamStr(2)** return MYPROG2 and **ParamStr(3)** MYPROG3.

Notes of Caution

If you expect to read three parameters from the command line, first test using the function **ParamCount** to see how many exist. If **ParamCount** returns a value of 2, *don't* try to read a third parameter — ask for it directly instead. Attempting to read a nonexistent parameter may return a string, but it isn't likely to be the string you expected.

Always read *all* of the command line parameters at the start of your program. If you won't need them until later, assign them to global string variables for storage, but don't expect to be able to retrieve them from the command line buffer later. This is especially true if you are expecting a command line longer than 32 characters because *any subsequent reads or writes will shorten the command line to the default length of 32.* Yes, the first 32 bytes *will* remain for your use, but it's still bad programming.

Programmer's Rule Number I: Bad programming remains bad programming... no matter how you disguise it!

Using MS-DOS, it is very difficult to type a command line that is more than 80 characters long. Although **ParamStr** can handle a longer string (maximum length of 127 characters), the user cannot — except with great difficulty and excessive possibilities for error. If longer or complex inputs are required, definitely provide alternate input options.

Although not precisely a caution, this next item is still worth your consideration. The elements passed via the command line buffer must be delimited by either a space (20h) or a tab (09h) character. For example, if you want to pass command line inputs in the form:

    PLIST MYPROG,MYPROG2,PROG3, etc.

ParamStr(1) will return the entire string MYPROG,MYPROG2,PROG3, etc. To use commas, slash marks, or other delimiters, you will have to provide a subroutine to parse these separately. Note that a delimiting space was still used between PLIST and MYPROG.

Although the preceding example was trivial (that is, there was no reason to use commas instead of spaces or tabs), there are occasions when it would be a reasonable strategy. For example, suppose I want to pass a variable number of file references to **PLIST**, and I want to include separate handling instructions for each file. (The sample program **PLIST** is not written to accommodate such commands, but another program might well be.) For such a case, I might enter the following command line:

    MYPROG FILENAME/A/L FILENAM2/A FILENAM3/J/L/K

In this case, **ParamStr(1)** would return FILENAME/A/L; **ParamStr(2)**, FILENAM2/A; and **ParamStr(3)**, FILENAM3/J/L/K. After storing each of these as string variables, I could use a separate procedure, **Parse__Command**, to extract the actual filename and to test the various instruction flags passed for each file.

For this type of application, using **Parse__Command** has several advantages over passing a command string in the form `MYPROG FILENAME A L FILENAM2 A FILENAM3 J L K`. Using slash marks (or commas or other delimiters), the filenames and the applicable flags are conveniently grouped both for the user inputting them and for the program. If instead each element were separated as above, the program would have to read each ParamStr(N) for N := 1 to ParamCount, test the contents of the string, and then decide if it was a filename or a flag and, if so, which filename each flag belongs to. If this sounds simple to program, just think about it for a minute.

Programmer's Rule Number II: There's always a harder way to do it ... but why use it?

Uppercase Versus Lowercase

Before getting too far afield with alternate command input structures, recall that earlier I mentioned being able to choose to enter `Plist MyProg.pas` or `plist myprog` or any other combination of uppercase and/or lowercase letters. This option is simple to provide and therefore it is puzzling that so many presumably capable programmers refuse to recognize the possibility that some users may not permanently lock their keyboards in CAPS. Which is to say, their programs respond to uppercase only. Heaven help users who foolishly expect a well-behaved program to respond both to uppercase and lowercase inputs.

Programmer's Rule Number III: KISS: Keep It Simple, Stupid ... it works better that way!

Adding the line `MainFileName := Cased(MainFileName);` to **PLIST** is a convenient assist for the user (even if the program is only for my own use), which is exactly why and how **PLIST** was originally written.

The **Cased** function does nothing other than accept a string and, using Turbo's **UpCase** function return the equivalent uppercase string. This routine should be a standard utility function in your box of programming tools.

Turbo version 3.x

```
type
    WorkString = string[255];
function Cased(WorkStr: WorkString): WorkString;
    var
        I : integer;     TempStr :  WorkString;
    begin
        TempStr := '';
        for I := 1 to length(WorkStr) do
            TempStr := TempStr+upcase(copy(WorkStr,I,1));
        Cased := TempStr;
    end;
```

Turbo version 4.0

```
function Cased(WorkStr: string): string;
    var
        I : integer;
    begin
        for I := 1 to length(WorkStr) do
            WorkStr[I] := upcase(WorkStr[I]);
        Cased := WorkStr;
    end;
```

In the case of a single input character such as a Y/N question, instead of **Cased**, it's simpler to use the **UpCase** function directly:

```
if UpCase(keychar) = 'Y' then ...
```

Now, you've seen how a command line parameter works and, unless you've led a very insular life around computers, you've used a variety of programs that accepted command line inputs and, probably some that insist on these. This is a favorite tool of many, if not most, programmers. It's efficient and convenient, but it can also create a bad impression if end users do not know what you, the programmer, expected when they called your program. If the results resemble INCORRECT SYNTAX or even a simple ?, you've created a bad *first* impression, no matter how good the program may appear later.

Some programmers avoid this possibility by designing their program structures around alternative setup utilities, input prompts, or anything rather than contending with command line inputs. However, this is often like using nails instead of screws because you don't like screwdrivers, not because it's the best solution. Sometimes a command line parameter is not only the best solution, but it may also be the only reasonable solution.

Prompting the User

In the preceding examples, one unstated assumption was present — an assumption that is usually not only unstated but also often unrecognized. This missing assumption — that the user *knows* what input is expected on the command line — is very simple but *very* critical. Usually but unfortunately not always, some form of the user documentation hints at the expected input, but users are just as notorious for not reading the documentation as programmers are for failing to document fully.

Possibly one of the best examples of the *proper* way to handle user command line input is found in the popular share-ware program ARC (Archive utility from System Enhancement Associates). If you are not familiar with ARC, instead of hunting for documentation, simply enter the command ARC<cr> (or ARC ?<cr>) and a complete list will appear showing the input command syntax and explaining each command flag.

```
Usage: ARC (amufdxerplvtc)[bswn][g<password>] <archive> [<filename>...]
Where:    a   = add files to archive
          m   = move files to archive

          .           .
          .           .

          .           .
          g   = Encrypt/decrypt archive entry
Please refer to the program documentation for complete instructions.
```

This display does not purport to be a complete set of instructions, but it does provide everything the average user needs when employing ARC.

Even if I had reproduced the entire ARC display, the ? option would not have appeared in the list, but if you've gotten this far, you hardly need it. Without disassembling ARC to check this hypotheses, a few simple tests suggest that the ARC program has been written to provide this option list as a default *in any case in which a command line parameter cannot be recognized or cannot be parsed intelligently.*

This is sensible and intelligent programming, and I offer a tip of the hat to System Enhancement Associates. Remember that imitation is not only the sincerest form of flattery but also the most sensible course.

Precisely *how* this should be accomplished depends on your specific application and requirements, but consider the following general decision structure for this purpose:

```
if ParamCount = 0 then           { see if anything's entered        }
   Options_Message else          { nothing was, show options        }
   begin
```

```
case ExtractOption of
    Option_1: Execute_1;          { test each option to act          }
         .   :    .   .
    Option_N: Execute_N;
    else Options_Message;         { if no match, show options        }
  end; {case}
end; {else}
```

In the preceding structure, each command line parameter is acted on in turn. If several tasks have been specified, each will be executed until (and unless) one is not recognized. At this point, the **Options__Message** procedure takes over and, by assumption, shows the incorrect command parameter and the acceptable command options. At this point, you might want to abort further action, ask for corrections before proceeding, or simply skip forward to the next (if any) task.

On the other hand — and a more common circumstances — if several command parameters are needed to define the requested action, the following structure would be preferable:

```
if ParamCount = 0 then              { see if anything's entered        }
   Options_Message else             { nothing was, show options        }
   begin
      for I := 1 to ParamCount do   { otherwise, begin a loop          }
         if not Parse_Option(I) then { and test each command           }
         begin
            Options_Message;        { command failed, show options     }
            halt;                   { and stop right here              }
         end;
      Execute_Task;                 { everything passed, proceed       }
   end;
```

In many cases, you may want to use a more specific prompt. For example, you might revise **PLIST** to require two command parameters, (a filename and a printer port or device) because you have three printers (a dot matrix, a laser printer, and port device to another computer, which will need special handling if selected).

Suppose you had only typed PLIST MYFILE, forgetting to add the listing device. In this case, a suitable prompt display might read:

```
Usage: PLIST Filename[.PAS <.Ext>] Dev{Prn,Lpt1,Lpt2,Com1}
                         ↑          ↑        ↑
                                          (device options; PRN is default)

                              (another extension may be specified)

             (default filename extension)
```

or

```
Usage: PLIST Filename[.PAS <.Ext>] Dev{Epson,LaserJet,CommLink}
                              ↑              ↑         ↑
                        (names are easier to remember)
```

Alternatively, asking for the entire input line to be repeated might not be necessary. A friendlier structure could begin by checking the parameters that *were* passed, decide if it is an existing filename, and if so, ask which listing device should be used for output. If the filename passed did not exist, but the listing device had been specified, **PLIST** could simply ask for a new filename.

In either case, there should always be a way out as well as a way to continue. When prompting for a new filename or new listing device, if a null string (simply a **CR**) is returned, the simplest method is to exit. Never insist that the user continue — he or she might not want to.

Programmer's Rule Number IV: If a mistake is possible ... it doesn't require a fool to make it!

To conclude, never assume the user knows what you (the programmer) expected.

PLIST.PAS Demo Program

```
program Pascal_Source_Lister;
uses   Crt,  Dos;              { version 3.x — omit this line              }

    const
        PrintLength = 55;      { length set for letter-size paper          }
          PageWidth = 95;      { width set for Elite typeface              }
        PathLength = 65;       { maximum allowed path length               }
        VertTabLen = 2;
          FormFeed = #$0C;

    type
      { word = integer; }       { declare for version 3.x only! }
      STR65 = string[65];
      STR20 = string[20];
       STR5 = string[5];
      Regs = record case Integer of
             1: (AX, BX, CX, DX, BP, SI, DI, DS, ES, Flags : word);
             2: (AL, AH, BL, BH, CL, CH, DL, DH             : byte);
          end;
    var
        Page, CurRow, I, Hor, Ver : integer;      MainFile : text;
                  InitPrinter : boolean;              Reg : Regs;
```

```
        BoldOn, BoldOff, ItalicOn, ItalicOff : STR20;
                             Search1, Search2 : STR5;
                MainFileName, IncludeFileName : STR65;

procedure Test_Printer_Status;
    { optional test for printer status reports — some fast computers    }
    { have minor troubles talking to printers with slower clocks —      }
    { other times, there can be more serious problems — use as needed   }
    begin
        if Hor = 0 then Hor := WhereX;
        if Ver = 0 then Ver := WhereY;
        with Reg do
        if (AH and $E9) <> $00 then     { expected result = 1110 1001 = $E9  }
        begin                           { printer status is in AH register   }
            gotoxy(Hor,Ver);
            write('Printer Status: ');
            if (AH and $01) = $01 then write(' timed-out ');
            if (AH and $02) = $02 then write(' 1! {not used} ');
            if (AH and $04) = $04 then write(' 2! {not used} ');
            if (AH and $08) = $08 then write(' I/O error ');
            if (AH and $10) = $00 then write(' NOT selected ');
            if (AH and $20) = $20 then write(' out of paper ');
            if (AH and $40) = $40 then write(' acknowledge ');
            if (AH and $80) = $80 then write(' not busy ');
            writeln;
        end;
    end;

procedure Write_String(TextString: string);
    begin
        for I := 1 to length(TextString) do
        begin
            Reg.AL := ord(TextString[I]);
            Reg.AH := $00;                   { function 0 — write char to printer  }
            Reg.DX := $00;                   { printer number — 0-2 for port #     }
            intr($17,Dos.Registers(Reg));
            Test_Printer_Status;             { optional test for printer response  }
        end;
    end;
procedure PrintLn(TestString: string);
    begin
        Write_String(TestString+#$0D+#$0A);    { add CR / LF to line }
    end;

procedure Print(TestString: string);
    begin
        Write_String(TestString);                   { no CR / LF          }
    end;
```

```
procedure SetPrinter(Key: string);
    begin
        CurRow := 0;                              { start things off right          }
        Page := 1;                               { with default values             }
        IncludeFileName := ";                     { for the variables               }
        BoldOn := ";   BoldOff := ";              { initialize these to nulls, then }
        ItalicOn := "; ItalicOff := ";            { reset if applicable for printer }
        if Key = 'EPSON' then
        begin
            BoldOn := #$1B+'G';                   { Esc-G }
            BoldOff := #$1B+'H';                  { Esc-H }
            ItalicOn := #$1B+'4';                 { Esc-4 }
            ItalicOff := #$1B+'5';                { Esc-5 }
            Write_String(#$1B+'@');               { reset printer to default state, }
            Write_String(#$1B+'M');               { then select elite typeface ...  }
        end else
        if Key = 'HP' then
        begin                                     { settings for J-Cartridge fonts  }
            BoldOn := #$1B+'(OU'+#27+'(s0p12h10v0s3b8T';
            BoldOff := #$1B+'(OU'+#27+'(s0p12h10v0s0b8T';
            ItalicOn := #$1B+'(OU'+#27+'(s0p12h10v1s0b8T';
            ItalicOff := BoldOff;
            Write_String(BoldOff); { selects 12 cpi USASCII & Prestige Elite }
            Write_String(#$1B+'&195F'); { w/ 95 character width            }
            Write_String(#$1B+'&a10L'); { and 10 col indent                }
        end;
    end;

procedure Close_Printer;
    begin
        if length(BoldOn) > 5
            then Write_String(#27+'(s10H')        { reset to 10 cpi Courier }
            else Write_String(#27+'P');           { reset to 10 cpi Pica    }
    end;

procedure Initialize;
    begin
        Hor := 0;   Ver := 0;
        with Reg do                               { initialize parallel port }
        begin
            AH := $01;   DX := $00;               { DX = port number (0-2)  }
            intr($17,Dos.Registers(Reg));
            Test_Printer_Status;
        end;
        SetPrinter('HP');                         { change to 'EPSON' as applicable ... }
        InitPrinter := true;
        clrscr;
        Search1 := '{$'+'I';                      { these are so PLIST can list itself }
        Search2 := '(*$'+'I';                     { without tripping over it's own     }
    end;                                          { search strings ...                 }
```

```pascal
function Change Case(WorkStr: string): string;
    var
        I: integer;      TempStr: string;
    begin
        TempStr := '';
        for I := 1 to length(WorkStr) do
            TempStr := TempStr+ upcase(WorkStr[I]);
        Change_Case:= TempStr;
    end;


procedure Check_Extension(var FileName: STR65);
    var
        I : integer;
    begin
        I := pos('.',FileName);              { see if the file has an extension  }
        if I = 0 then FileName := FileName+'.PAS';   { if not, add default   }
    end;                                       { remember — this is for .PAS files  }


function Open_File(var ListFile: text; FileName: STR65): Boolean;
    var
        Test : Boolean;
    begin
        assign(ListFile,FileName);
        {$I-}  reset(ListFile);  {$I+}
        Test := IOresult = 0;                { if it's okay, leave it open;    }
        if not Test then close(ListFile);    { otherwise, close the file...    }
        Open_File := Test;                   { return the test results         }
    end;


procedure Open_Main;
    begin
        if ParamCount = 0 then
        begin
            writeln('Enter [d:\path\] FILENAME <.PAS> as');
            write('  filename for listing: ');
            readln(MainFileName);
        end else MainFileName := ParamStr(1);
        MainFileName := Change_Case(MainFileName);    { check the case   }
        Check_Extension(MainFileName);                { and the extension }
        if not Open_File(MainFile,MainFileName) then  { see if file exists  }
        begin                                         { if it doesn't, then }
            writeln('ERROR -- File not found: ', MainFileName);
            halt;                                     { stop right here   }
        end;
    end;


procedure Vertical_Tab;
    var
        I : integer;   TempStr : STR5;
```

```
      begin
        str(Page,TempStr);
        Print(BoldOn+'        Page #'+TempStr+'    |    '+MainFileName+'    |
        if IncludeFileName <> '' then PrintLn(IncludeFileName+'  |  ')
                          else PrintLn('');

        Print(BoldOff);
        Page := succ(page);
        for I := 1 to VertTabLen do PrintLn('');
      end;

procedure Process_Line(PrintStr: string);
    begin
      CurRow := Succ(CurRow);
      if length(PrintStr) > PageWidth then CurRow := succ(CurRow);
      if CurRow > PrintLength then
      begin
        Print(FormFeed);
        Vertical_Tab;
        CurRow := 1;
      end;
      PrintLn(PrintStr);
    end;

procedure Process_File;
    var
      TestLine, LineBuffer: string;

    function Include_In(var CurStr: string): Boolean;
        var
          ChkChar: char;        Column: integer;
        begin
          ChkChar := '-';
          Column := pos(Search1,CurStr);       { looking for '{' + '$I'    }
          if Column <> 0 then ChkChar := CurStr[Column+3] else
          begin
            Column := pos(Search2, CurStr);    { looking for '(*' + '$I'   }
            if Column <> 0 then ChkChar := CurStr[Column+4];
          end;
          if ChkChar in ['+','-'] then Include_In := False
                              { if it isn't $I+ or $I- then              }
                          else Include_In := True;
                              { it must be an include listing            }
    end; { Include_In }

procedure Process_Include_File(var IncStr: string);
    var
      NameStart, NameEnd: integer;
          IncludeFile: text;
```

```
function Parse(IncStr: string): string;
  begin
    NameStart := pos('$I',IncStr)+2;
    while IncStr[NameStart] = ' ' do NameStart := succ(NameStart);
    NameEnd := NameStart;
    while (not (IncStr[NameEnd] in ['"','}','*']))
                        { we're looking for flag characters in the line     }
        and ((NameEnd - NameStart) <= PathLength)
                        { and testing the permissible string length         }
          do NameEnd := Succ(NameEnd);
                        { while we increment the length counter             }
    NameEnd := pred(NameEnd);
                        { now set it back one place                         }
    Parse := copy(IncStr,NameStart,(NameEnd-NameStart+1));
                        { and return the path and filename                  }
  end;


begin {Process_Include_File}
                        { it looks like an include file so                  }
  IncludeFileName := Change_Case(Parse(IncStr));
                        { ... get the path and filename                     }
  if not Open_File(IncludeFile,IncludeFileName) then
                        { and see if it exists                              }
  begin
    LineBuffer := ItalicOn + '$I' + IncludeFileName +
                  ' (* ERROR -- Include file not found! *)' +
                  ItalicOff;
    Process_Line(LineBuffer);
                        { report errors in the listing and on screen        }
    writeln(' ERROR -- Include file ',IncludeFileName,' not found!');
  end else
  begin
    LineBuffer := ItalicOn + '$I' + IncludeFileName + ItalicOff;
    Process_Line(LineBuffer);
                        { put header in listing and report on screen        }
    writeln(' Including ',IncludeFileName);
                        { now we open and list the include file             }
                        { note: version 4.0 allows nested include files,    }
                        { which are not provided for here, but              }
                        { even though they are allowed, they remain bad     }
                        { programming practice and should be avoided!       }
    while not eof(IncludeFile) do
    begin
      Readln(IncludeFile,LineBuffer);
      Process_Line(LineBuffer);
    end;           { but, if you insist on using nested includes,      }
                        { you could make this procedure recursive           }
                        { carefully                                         }
    close(IncludeFile);
```

```
            Process_Line(ItalicOn + '(******************** END OF ' +
                         + IncludeFileName + ' ********************)'
                         + ItalicOff);
         end;
         IncludeFileName := '';
      end;


begin   { Process_File }
    Vertical_Tab;                        { space headers according to personal taste  }
    writeln('Printing ... ',MainFileName);
    while not eof(MainFile) do                          { while not End-of-File }
    begin
        readln(MainFile,LineBuffer);                    { read from the file    }
        TestLine := Change_Case(LineBuffer);
            { the flags we're looking for might be $I or $i so we'll             }
            { test an uppercase version of the program line but keep             }
            { the original program text to print in the listings                }
        if Include_In(TestLine)                { if it lists an include          }
           then Process_Include_File(LineBuffer)   { file, treat accordingly    }
           else Process_Line(LineBuffer);       { else process the line         }
    end;
    close(MainFile);                     { always close files when done          }
    Print(FormFeed);                     { and eject the sheet                   }
  end;


begin { main program }
    Initialize;                          { set up system and variables           }
    Open_Main;                           { open the main listing file            }
    Process_File;                        { and get to work                       }
    Close_Printer;                       { done — clean it up                    }
  end.
```

2

Tailoring Your Program To Fit the User

Many programs do not require command line input and many others can either accept command line parameters or execute without them (for example, Microsoft's Multiplan might be called as MP BANKFILE or simply called as MP with BANKFILE accessed after the program was already active). This is fine. Command line input is useful, maybe even essential in some cases, but hardly universal in application.

What is universal in application is fitting your program to the end user as opposed to forcing the user to fit your program. Programming is a commercial endeavor every bit as much as making shoes or building cars. If customers don't feel comfortable using your product, they'll buy another program (or pair of shoes or car) from another manufacturer — and quite rightly so.

When the first microcomputers bearing a certain three-letter trademark appeared on the market, heralded by a massive public marketing campaign, hundreds of thousands of customers discovered the joys of owning a personal computer. Very quickly, these novices discovered the tremendous advantages of word processors over typewriters, spreadsheets over ledger pages and adding machines, and electronic mail over the conventional post office.

What these novices were so enthusiastic about were the improvements in electronic convenience, speed, handling, and production over the older manual methods. Since they had no previous computer experience as a basis for comparison, they were quite enthusiastic over a very mediocre product. After all, if you've been riding a mule to work every day, a model A can seem wonderful if you've never driven a sports car.

The essential point is that the early users were quite as unsophisticated as those first PCs (and many remain essentially "computer illiterate"), but the number of raw novices is decreasing quickly while the general level of sophistication is rising even faster. Programs that once seemed wonderful to novices now do not look so impressive. (A program like Lotus may seem wonderful if you've been using paper and pencil until you try a real spreadsheet like Multiplan or Quattro.)

The contemporary programmer must accommodate the users, even though it was once possible (and common) to force users to accommodate the programmer. The programmer's main goal is to *anticipate* what the users are going to want, how they are going to want to enter data, what they are going to expect as results, and what the best ways are to provide this — and do it *before* they ask for it. The seller's market is vanishing fast, and the buyer's market is a whole different ballgame — a demanding one!

Structured Input and Error Correction

Programmer's Rule Number V: To err is human . . . but it's no excuse for being stupid!

As a general rule, a program will ask the user for three types of data: alphanumerical (text), numerical only (values and operands), and screen position (cursor) selection. Taking these in order (since this is also the order of simplicity of handling), I'll demonstrate a simple calculation sheet that supports input and editing for text comments, numerical data, and cursor key selection of items.

Reading the Keyboard

To perform any functions with text, numerical data, or the cursor, the first step is simply to be able to read the keyboard. You need to be able to recognize when a key has been pressed, which key has been pressed, and what it should mean.

When any key is pressed, two events are generated. The first is that the keyboard uses a scan code to decide which *physical* key has been pressed. Once this has been discovered, an evaluation of the Shift, Caps-Lock, Number-Lock, Control, and Alternate keys determines what character value (if any) should be returned.

On earlier computer systems, this was a relatively straightforward procedure with a keyboard decoder chip deciphering the scan results and passing ASCII data, control characters, or ESCape sequences back to the system. (ASCII data, control characters, and ESCape sequences are discussed in the next section.)

With the contemporary keyboard, even the full 8-bit code set is not enough to provide separate codes for each key and key condition (including all ALTernate, Shifted, un-Shifted, and Control combinations). To simplify matters, the present keyboards return scan codes to identify which physical key has been pressed and char codes to identify, if applicable, which character was intended.

With the enhanced or expanded keyboard, two (or more) keys may be intended to return the same ASCII character (the 1, Key-Pad-1, and End keys can each return the ASCII character 31h) even though the scan codes identify these as separate keys.

Now, to further confuse matters, the function keys may return different scan codes depending on whether the Shift, Alt, or Control keys were pressed at the same time. However, the right and left Shift keys each return separate scan codes, and the right and left Alt and right and left Control keys (found on enhanced keyboards) each return the same scan code.

Programmer's Rule Number VI: No matter how simply you design it, Somebody can find a way to make it complicated.

For the moment, however, the subject is user input, and I'll leave the more elaborate methods of reading the keyboard as a later topic (see the **ShowKey.Pas** demo program for a more exhaustive handling procedure).

In its simplest state, the **Check_Kbd** procedure will serve to capture two keyboard events and is sufficient for most purposes. Check_Kbd assumes two variables, Ch and KCh, which are global in scope. The ASCII code, if any, is returned in Ch and the scan code (when Ch is null) is returned in KCh.

```
var
   Ch, KCh: char;              { Ch and KCh are global variables }
procedure Check_Kbd;           { ASCII values are returned in Ch and }
   begin                       { Scan codes in KCh if extended code key }
      Ch := readkey;           { check keyboard for input }
```

```
                    {  v3.x use  read(kbd,Ch);  and  read(kbd,KCh);        }
                    {  and use  if  Ch = #27 (ESCape) instead of #00 (null)  }
           if  Ch = #00                             { if it's an extended key, }
              then  KCh := readkey                  { read the second key code; }
              else  KCh := #00;                     { otherwise, set second null }
       end;
```

Note: A slightly different version of **Check_Kbd** is shown in the Turbo Pascal manual in which, when the key code is returned as null (#$00), a Boolean variable, FunctKey, is set; and the scan code is returned in Ch. Either method works, but I believe that returning separate scan and key codes provides greater flexibility in programming structure and fewer opportunities for (programmer's) errors and/or confusion. This also simplifies independent testing of such codes as Ctrl-C (Ctrl Break).

Control Codes, ASCII Characters, and ESCape Sequences

In keeping with the venerable tradition that ontogeny recapitulates phylogeny (that is, each organism repeats its evolutionary history as it forms), the ASCII character set reflects a long history of development that began with teletype and baudot devices. In these historical relics, the first 32 binary codes (00h through 1Fh) were machine control codes or signals. The code 05h, for example, meant ENQuiry ("Are you there? Is anybody ready to receive?"), and the code 06h meant ACKnowledge.

Similarly, 07h was used to ring a bell to get an operator's attention, 15h was NegativeAcKnowledge ("I'm busy — try later"), 04h was End Of Transmission, 09h was (and still is) Horizontal Tab, and 0Bh was a Vertical Tab (and faster than a string of line feeds, which were 0Ah). Also, many of these earlier machines were limited to uppercase characters only (BAUDOT) and used only 6 bits of information (versus 7 for conventional ASCII and 8 for the extended character set).

With the advent of computers and video teminals, most of the original control characters no longer fit any of the now-necessary tasks (some were and still are used for printer controls), and a host of new codes were needed to control new functions and capabilities. At this time, with computers operating on 8-bit buses, the eighth bit was commonly used for error checking and ports were only expected to effectively handle 7-bit communications (ignoring the high bit except for checking). Thus the ESCape codes were born.

An ESCape sequence was a series of two or three characters beginning with hexcode 1B and followed by one or two ASCII characters, and these generally acted to produce machine-specific results. For example, ESC-E on most systems was the clear screen command. Since these were firmware operations, software would also use the ESCape commands to exercise system control.

On contemporary systems, the 7-bit restriction is no longer deemed necessary, and 8-bit characters are commonly used to provide character graphics for display while the keyboard is permitted to return 8-bit codes. Now, instead of ESCape sequences issued by the special function, cursor control, and command keys, most of these return extended ASCII codes (hex codes between 80h and FFh).

An exception remains in the control codes, which continue to use the first 32 binary codes (00h through 1Fh), though these are no longer used for their original purposes. Control codes are commonly represented as Ctrl-@ through Ctrl-__ (underscore) with the character's ASCII codes 64 higher (40h) than the actual code returned. Thus Ctrl-A refers to a binary code of 01 (41h minus 40h or 65 minus 64 decimal), and Ctrl-M is 13 decimal (or 0Dh) which corresponds to the Carriage__Return code.

Editing Text Strings

The next step is edited text input. Note that the following procedure is not intended for a general text editor. This is only designed for text items such as on a spreadsheet, a forms package, or other line item entries, which still covers the majority of applications in general programming.

Edit__String provides both for intial input as well as for editing and revising existing text string data. **Edit__String** is called with screen- (or window relative-) coordinates for the origin, the maximum permissible string length (which *is not* the size of the TextStr variable), and the variable parameter TextStr.

Since TextStr is declared as a string of length 255, Pascal requires that all strings passed to **Edit__String** also be declared as length 255, which is obviously inefficient memory usage but is controlled by the compiler's default type checking {$V+} on all strings passed as variable parameters. (Formal and actual parameters must be identical string types, that is, identical lengths.) The optimum choice in such situations is to use the { $V- } directive, which permits any string length variable to be passed as the actual parameter.

Note: The formal parameter in the called procedure should still be equal to or larger than the largest actual string length expected to be passed as a variable. If the formal parameter is smaller than the parameter passed, the passed parameter will be truncated.

Edit__String begins by writing the TextStr variable to the screen, setting CursorOfs to the actual length of TextStr and positioning the cursor at the end of the displayed string. Next, **Check__Kbd** is called to wait for input. If Ch is returned as null (#$00), one of the special keys has been pressed and the value returned in KCh is tested for cursor positioning, exit keys, and so on. If additional option keys (non-ASCII) are required such as F1 for a help prompt, these would be included in the case KCh of list. The Insert key (#$52) is also tested and **Insert__Status** called to test the insert condition setting and update the display.

Otherwise, check Ch for action keys. These include Ctrl-C (#$03), Tab (#$09) and CR (#$0D) for exit, and Backspace (#$08) for cursor control and delete before cursor position. Last, the displayable ASCII characters are checked (#$20 through #$7E, that is, space through tilde). If a match is made, **Add__Text** is called to insert the character at the appropriate position in the string.

Notes: When a value is preceded by the number sign (#80), the value is indicated as a character (P) with the ordinal value shown (80 decimal). If, however, a dollar sign precedes the value (#$50), the value is hexadecimal rather than decimal even though the same character (P) is represented. Thus capital A could be shown as #64 (decimal) or #$40 (hex).

The ordinal values 00 through 09 are the same whether represented as $09 (hex) or 09 (decimal) but, for all higher values, the hex and decimal notations will not be the same.

For consistency, only hexadecimal notation will be used when referring to scan and char codes, system register values, and so on.

Add__Text, as a subprocedure within **Edit__String**, does not require any passed parameters but does make several tests. First, since the user should be permitted to add text anywhere on the line, the cursor position is tested, and if it is beyond the end of the existing string, blanks are added to fill the string to the cursor position and the new character appended.

Note: Simply because a string is defined as a particular length does not mean that a character can be inserted anywhere within this length. If a string variable is *declared* as length 40 but contains only 10 characters, the actual length of the string is 11 bytes, with the first element (TextStr[0]) containing the value for the length. For a string containing 12 characters, TextStr[0] contains the value (character) #$0C.

Pascal supports several string-handling operations. A character or string can be inserted within the existing string, for example, insert(NewStr, TextStr,Position). An existing element can be changed, for example, TextStr[Position] := Character. However, an element beyond the existing length of the string cannot be reassigned (or directly referenced in any fashion) because it does not exist. For this reason, the only option is to append a new element (or a new string) to the end of the existing string, that is, TextStr := TextStr + NewStr;. (See also the **Concat** function.)

If the cursor is not beyond the end of the existing string, the Boolean function **Insert__Status** is tested to determine whether to overwrite existing characters or to insert new characters within the existing string. In either case, the cursor position is incremented (unless this would exceed the limits set by StrLen).

Last, TextStr is truncated to the length specified by StrLen, that is, since TextStr has a length of 255, there may be characters beyond the set length (especially if anything has been inserted within an existing string) that need to be cut before **Add__Text** exits.

One other subprocedure, **Write__String**, is provided for screen output. Simply positioning the cursor and writing the string to the screen is fine as long as nobody cares what the display looks like.

For an edited input, however, a bit more care is required and, if the new string display is any shorter than the previous display, the addition of blanks is required to pad out the display (and to overwrite characters that would otherwise remain on the screen). Thus, copy(TextStr+' ':80,1,StrLen) is used first to pad TextStr and then to truncate the result to StrLen before writing the screen. Alternative strategies would be either to use **ClrEol** (CLeaR__to__End__Of__Line), which would erase more than was wanted, or to pad all strings with their blanks to their maximum length, which would both waste memory and slow program execution.

For similar considerations, **Write__Real** and **Write__Integer** are used to handle numeric display. For example, to print (display) a number showing seven places left of the decimal and two places to the right, the appropriate instruction would be as follows:

```
write(Number:TotalFieldWidth:DecimalWidth)
```
or
```
write(Number:10:2)
```

This is not, however, compatible with the way the requirements were stated (nor with the way we would normally think of our layout). For this reason, individual values for integer width and decimal width are passed to **Write__Real**, and TotalFieldWidth is calculated from these. (And, since a subprocedure is being used anyway, it becomes convenient to pass the x/y coordinates and allow **Write__Real** to handle the screen positioning at the same time. **Write__Integer** operates in a similar fashion.

Editing Numerical Values

Programmer's Rule Number VII:* There are nine and sixty ways, Of asking what the keyboard says, And almost all of them are right . . . sometimes.
(*With apologies to R. Kipling, who said it somewhat better.)

There are three basic ways to edit numerical values. The first way is to replace the original value with an entirely new numerical entry. However, most users would, quite rightly, consider this an annoying option. The second way is to use a formatted numerical display (as used in **Write__Real** and **Write__Integer**), control the cursor position, and, after reading the keyboard, calculate the change in the number value. Although possible, and, if done well, effectively transparent to the user, this method is difficult. The third way, as used in **Edit__Number**, is to convert the number value to a string, edit the string, and then reconvert the string to a numerical value. The first step, of course, is to provide the correct string representation of the number value and two subroutines, **Read__Real** and **Read__Integer**, which are used to convert real and integer values to strings and reconvert strings to reals and integers, respectively.

Once the appropriate string is created, the **Edit_Number** procedure is somewhat more complex than **Edit_String** for several reasons. One reason is that the string representing the number must be presented as right justified or, for real numbers, decimal justified, whereas the others are simply a matter of controlling the cursor position appropriately and keeping the correct number of leading spaces in the string to maintain the appropriate justification.

A few other considerations must be accounted for: when editing a number string, the cursor is not allowed to move further than the first blank left of the number (no white space is allowed in the string) and all blanks (leading or trailing) must be removed before reconversion. Also, remember, in **Edit_String**, all ASCII characters were accepted as valid string elements while, in **Edit_Number**, only 0 through 9 are valid for inclusion and the period character is used for cursor positioning. The handling for each of these provisions is shown in the listing for the **Edit_Number** procedure.

In the **Edit_Number** procedures, several items have not been included that might be quite appropriate to various applications. For instance, what about the + and − characters? Thus far, all values have been assumed to be positive, but if these procedures were incorporated in a checkbook utility, such a restricted entry option would be a prime error in program design.

Incorporating a minus sign (allowing the plus sign to remain understood) could be accomplished with a few minor revisions. The first step would be in the main **Edit_Number** procedure, allowing for acceptance of both the + and − characters as follows:

```
#$2B, #$2D,                     { include plus, minus, and   }
#$30..#$39: Make_Change(Ch);    { numerical change string    }
```

Even though the plus sign is allowed to remain understood, if the negative is permitted and will be acted on, allowance must be made for the opposite change instruction.

Naturally, the minus sign should only be permitted to appear at the left end of the number string, so a further revision will be required in the **Make_Change** procedure so that entry of a plus characer changes to positive if it had previously been negative. This is accomplished as follows:

```
procedure Make_Change;
   var
      I, J : integer;
   begin
      case Ch of     { if the character is a plus or minus then ... }
```

```
'-': begin
        for I := 1 to LimitSize do Move_Cursor_Left;
        NumStr[CursorOfs] := '-';
```
{ since Move__Cursor__Left (see following) will stop when it finds   }
{ either a space or a minus sign, if there's already a minus at the   }
{ left end of the string, nothing really changes   }
```
     end;
'+':   begin  J := pos('-',NumStr);
                  if J > 0 then NumStr[J] := ' ';    end;
```
                    { if it's already minus, change it; otherwise, do nothing }
```
     else
     begin              { else it's only a number so handle per normal }
        if Insert_On then
```
                 .

                 .

                 .

```
       end;
     end;
  end; {case Ch}
  Write_String(XAxis,YAxis,LimitSize,NumStr);
end;
```

A minor change in **Move__Cursor__Left** will finish the immediate task:

```
procedure Move_Cursor_Left;
  begin
    if NumStr[CursorOfs+1] <> ' ' and     { if not on leader space    }
       NumStr[CursorOfs+1] <> '-' then     { or minus sign,            }
       dec(CursorOfs);                     { move left one position    }
    if CursorOfs < 0 then CursorOfs := 0{ and check for left limit  }
  end;
```

Both the **Read__Real** and **Read__Integer** subprocedures will append a left minus sign when converting negative numbers to strings and, on reconversion, will accept a minus sign to return a negative value, so no revisions are needed here.

One other item should be taken into account. What happens if the value string length is already equal to the permitted field length when a minus sign is entered? What happens and where does the minus sign fit? (And I'll leave this minor conundrum for your consideration, experimentation, and solution.

Screen Position (Cursor) Selection

The third type of data that a program might expect from the user is screen position (cursor) selection, that is, selecting an entry field or menu item by using cursor control keys (or a mouse) to move the cursor to the appropriate position.

In both the **Edit__Number** and **Edit__String** procedures, the Ctrl-C, Down, Return (Enter), Shift-Tab, Tab, and Up keys were defined as exit keys, that is, keys that caused **Edit__Number** or **Edit__String** to exit from their repeat . . . until loops, passing control back to the calling procedure. In the case of **Edit__Number**, the calling procedure was either **Read__Integer** or **Read__Real**, but in either case, these procedures require no further input to finish their tasks and also terminate, passing control back to the main program.

Returning to the main program body, the program is again in a repeat loop (but not the same repeat used in the edit procedures). At this point, however, the program is no longer interested in editing a string. The intention now is to allow the user to select a new active cell on the data sheet or, if Ctrl-C was entered, to exit entirely. If by some programming error none of the expected key values were found (in either Ch or KCh, the main repeat loop would simply reenter the last cell edited (probably too quickly for the user to notice) and wait for further input.

On the other hand, you might want to include a key to force recalculation of the results (when editing a numerical cell) without requiring the user to exit the current cell. In Multiplan, the ! (exclamation key) is used to force immediate recalculation, and a similar feature can be implemented here with a slight revision in the **Edit__Number** procedure:

```
procedure Edit_Number
       .
       .
       .
    begin  {Edit_Number }
         .
         .
         .
      case Ch of
         .
         .
         .
  { ! }    #$21: Complete := true;    { Exit for recalculation }
```

```
        end; {case Ch}
    until Complete;
```

.

.

.

To forestall future confusion, the following notation should also be made in the main program:

```
begin {main}
    .

    .

    .

    repeat
        .

        .

        .

        case Ch of
            .

            .

            .

            #$21: { exit key forces recalculation };
        end; {case Ch}
    until Demo_Complete;
end. {main}
```

The fact that the case constant (#$21) has no statement following it is immaterial (syntax, however, does require the closing semicolon). If this case constant were not present, the program would execute as described earlier, but if an else option were included in the case statement, providing this null option would prevent the else option from being executed by an exclamation entry.

In the demo program INPUT.PAS, several options were selected:

1. To use the Tab and Shift-Tab keys for lateral movement between cells (reserving the right and left arrow keys for use within a cell).

2. To use the Return (Enter) key identical to the Tab (move right).

3. To allow movement right and left to wrap across the screen.

4. To use the up and down arrow keys for straight vertical selection without wrapping.

In the case of a display larger than a single screen or of multiple screen pages (which may or may not be similar displays), the Page__Up and Page__Down keys would be the logical candidates for extended movements, but any of the function keys (F1 through F12 with or without Alt, Ctrl, and Shift) as well as Ctrl__Page__Up and Ctrl__Page__Down might also have been implemented. With a further elaboration, the shifted arrow, Home, and End keys (which would normally be read as numbers) could also be brought into service. When required, an even wider range of controls, including Alt-A through Alt-Z, are available. (See the discussion of **ShowKey** in Section x-ref for further details on trapping keyboard inputs.)

Quiz

1. In the **Edit__String** procedure, instead of providing a definite case option, `#$20..#$7E: Add_Text;`, to cover the standard ASCII character set, why would an `else Add_Text;` not have provided the same results? Under what circumstances would using `else Add_Text;` have provided acceptable results?

2. Why might a real value (using version 3.x) be used with the **Read__Integer** procedure?

3. In the **Edit__Number** and **Edit__String** procedures, two different statements were used to implement the Home key.

   In **Edit__Number:** `for I := 1 to LimitSize do`
   `Move_Cursor_Left;`

   In **Edit__String:** `CursorOfs := 0;`

   Why were different Home key procedures used?

4. In the demo program, calculations are made only on exit from the **Edit__Number** procedure (and, in forcing a recalculation, a exit is also required, followed by reentry to **Edit__Number**). Why isn't a recalculation procedure called directly from within the **Edit__Number** procedure?

Solutions

1. Using the `else Add_Text` statement would allow the (attempted) inclusion in the `TextStr` variable of any keycode that wasn't previously specified in the case statement. Although this would not necessarily affect

your display, it would allow the string to be filled with accidental characters (including control codes). For a demonstration of the exact results, I suggest modifying the source code and trying it.

On the other hand, permitting inclusion of the extended ASCII characters (the graphics character set) might be desired in some circumstances. If so, however, it would still be best to provide a specific case selection and statement and to reserve use of the else condition for circumstances where all else *is* intended.

2. A real value might be preferred over integer values (using version 3.x) for the same reason that the longint declaration was used with version 4.0 to allow for larger integer values. (Note: integer values are limited to −32768 . . . +32767.) If the **Edit_Number** has a field width greater than 4, values not compatible with integer conversion become possible and therefore, become probable.

Murphrey's Law: If somethinw can go wrong, it gill!

---

3. In **Edit_String,** acting on the Home key to set the cursor full left is okay, but if this were done in **Edit_Number,** the cursor could be placed left of the beginning of the number string (which is *always* right justified). Instead, the subprocedure **Move_Cursor_Left** is already written to limit movement to one place left of the beginning of the string — no further! This precaution helps avoid accidentally creating a number string containing white space, which would further compound the error when the program attempted to change the string back to a numerical value. (See Murphrey's Law.)

4. A recalculation could be called directly, but unless the working string were first reconverted to a number value and passed back to the proper numerical variable, the recalculation would not reflect any changes. The easiest way to accomplish this is by using the existing exit procedures and then reentering for further editing. (See also Programmer's Rules II and III.)

INPUT.PAS Demo Program

```
program Keyboard_Input_Demo_1;   {INPUT.PAS}

{$V-}     { relax string length type-checking for more efficient memory usage     }
   uses   Crt, Dos;
```

```
const
   MinRow = 1;    MaxRow = 9;    MinCol = 1;    MaxCol = 3;
type
   Regs = record case integer of
 { v3.x }  { 0:  (AX, BX, CX, DX, BP, SI, DI, DS, ES, Flags : integer);          }
 { v4.0 }    0:  (AX, BX, CX, DX, BP, SI, DI, DS, ES, Flags : word);
             1:  (AL, AH, BL, BH, CL, CH, DL, DH            : byte);   end;


   RecType    = (StringData,RealData,IntegerData);
   DataRecord = record            XAxis, YAxis : byte;
                   case DataType : RecType of
                      StringData : ( DataStr : string[40];
                                     StrLen  : integer    );
                        RealData : ( RValue  : real;
                                     IntSizR,
                                     DecSize : byte       );
                     IntegerData : ( IValue  : longint;
```
{ v3.x use either integer or real types   ------------^---^   }
```
                                     IntSize : byte       );end;  {record}
```
{ v3.x declare type LongStr : string[255]; and   }
{   use Search & Replace function to change string; to LongStr;   }
```
   var
        Reg : Regs;              Demo_Complete : Boolean;
    Ch, KCh : char;  I, Active_Col, Active_Row : integer;
  DataArray : array[1..10,1..4] of DataRecord;
```

GEN__UTIL.INC — General Utility Procedures

```
function Insert_Status: Boolean;
   begin
      Reg.AH := $02;
      intr($16,Dos.Registers(Reg));                    { v3.x  - > intr($16,Reg); }
      Insert_Status := (Reg.AL and $80) = $80;
   end;


procedure Beep;
   begin
      write(chr(7));                 { a little audio feedback helps but don't over do it }
   end;


procedure Check_Kbd;                           { Ch and KCh are global variables}
            { returns ASCII values in Ch, Scan codes in KCh if extended code key }
   begin
   Ch := readkey;       { v3.x read(kbd,Ch); } { check keyboard for input          }
   if Ch = #00          { v3.x if Ch = #27   } { if it's an extended key,          }
      then KCh : readkey                       { read the second key code;         }
      else KCh := #00;                         { otherwise, set null               }
end;
```

EDT__UTIL.INC — Utilities Used With Edit__String and Edit__Number Procedures

```
procedure Write_Real(XAxis,YAxis,IntSize,DecSize: byte; Value: real);
   begin
      gotoxy(XAxis,YAxis);
      write(Value:IntSize+1+DecSize:DecSize);
end;            {  |     |    |      ^---width of decimal display        }
                {  |<--- |<---|<---- TOTAL width of number display       }
                {  |     |    ^----  places right of decimal point       }
                {  |     ^---- one space for decimal point               }
                {  ^---- places left of decimal point                    }

procedure Write_Integer(XAxis,YAxis,IntSize: integer; Value: longint);
   begin                      {              v3.x use integer or real --^   }
      gotoxy(Xaxis,YAxis);
      write(Value:IntSize);   { if real, then write(Value:IntSize:0)        }
   end;

procedure Write_String(XAxis, YAxis, StrLen: integer; TextStr: string);
   const
      BlankStr = '                            ';
   begin
      gotoxy(XAxis,YAxis);
      write( copy(TextStr+BlankStr,1,StrLen) );
   end;

procedure Check_Insert;                      { it helps if you don't have    }
   begin                                     { to guess whether insert is    }
      gotoxy(70,1);                          { turned on or off - use it      }
      if Insert_Status then write('INSERT ON')
                 else write('OverWrite');
   end;
                        { Edit__String subroutine provides edited text input and display }

procedure Edit_String(XAxis,YAxis,StrLen: integer; var TextStr: string);
   var
      Complete: Boolean;  CursorOfs: integer;

   procedure Add_Test;
      const
      BlankStr = '                                                    ';
   begin
      if CursorOfs >= length(TextStr)
         then TextStr := copy(TextStr+BlankStr,1,CursorOfs)+Ch
      else if Insert_Status then insert(Ch,TextStr,CursorOfs+1)
      else TextStr[CursorOfs+1] := Ch;
      if CursorOfs+1 < StrLen then inc(CursorOfs);
                                   { v3.x CursorOfs := succ(CursorOfs); }
      TextStr := copy(TextStr,1,StrLen);
   end;
```

```
      begin
        Complete := false;
        CursorOfs := length(TextStr);        { start cursor at end of string      }
        repeat
          Write_String(XAxis,YAxis,StrLen,TextStr);
          gotoxy(XAxis+CursorOfs,YAxis);     { use cursor for visual feedback     }
          Check Kbd;                         { first, see what key was pressed    }
          case Ch of
            #$00: case KCh of                    { if Ch is null, act on KCh      }
{ left    }        #$4B: if CursorOfs > 0 then dec(CursorOfs);
                         { v3.x then CursorOfs := pred(CursorOfs);               }
{ right   }        #$4D: if CursorOfs < StrLen then inc(CursorOfs);
                         { v3.x then CursorOfs := succ(CursorOfs);               }
{ home    }        #$47: CursorOfs := 0;
{ end     }        #$4F: CursorOfs := length(TextStr);
{ insert  }        #$52: Check_Insert;
{ Sh-Tab  }        #$0F,                           { Exit on Sh-Tab,             }
{ up      }        #$48,                           {           Up,               }
{ down    }        #$50: Complete := true;  {        or Down keys               }
{ delete  }        #$53: delete(TextStr,CursorOfs+1,1);
                 end; {case KCh}
            #$08: if CursorOfs > 0 then
                    begin
                      delete(TextStr,CursorOfs,1);
                      dec(CursorOfs);
                      { v3.x CursorOfs := pred(CursorOfs); }
                    end;
          #$03,#$09,#$0D: Complete := true;              { exit on Ctrl-C, TAB or CR }
            #$20..#$7E: Add Text;                        { use all ASCII characters  }
              end; {case Ch}
          until Complete;
      end;
        { Edit_Number subroutine provides edited numerical inputs, formatted display }

procedure Edit_Number( XAxis, YAxis: byte;                  { display position    }
                    IntSize, DecSize: byte;             {  IntSize.DecSize        }
                        var NumStr: string );           {    working number       }
      var
        I, CursorOfs, LimitSize: integer;    Complete: Boolean;

procedure Move_Cursor_Left;
    begin
      if NumStr[CursorOfs+1] <> ' ' then             { if not on leader space,    }
        dec(CursorOfs);                              { move left one position     }
        { v3.x CursorOfs := pred(CursorOfs); }
      if CursorOfs < 0 then CursorOfs := 0;          { and check for left limit   }
    end;
```

```
procedure Move_Cursor_Right;
  begin
    inc(CursorOfs);                                    { move right one position  }
    { v3.x CursorOfs := succ(CursorOfs); }
    while CursorOfs > LimitSize-1 do                   { check right limit         }
      dec(CursorOfs);
      { v3.x CursorOfs := pred(CursorOfs); }
  end;


procedure Make_Change;
  begin
    if Insert_Status then                              { test insert status flag   }
    begin
      if CursorOfs < IntSize then                      { if cursor left of decimal }
      begin
        if NumStr[1] = ' ' then                        { any leader space?         }
        { v3.x if copy(NumStr,1,1) = }
        begin
            delete(NumStr,1,1);                         { delete left space         }
            insert(Ch,NumStr,CursorOfs+1);             { then insert number        }
        end else Beep;                                 { no space - raspberry      }
      end else
      if CursorOfs > IntSize then        { if cursor right of decimal              }
      begin
        insert(Ch,NumStr,CursorOfs+1);                 { insert number             }
        NumStr := copy(NumStr,1,LimitSize);            { trim string length        }
        Move_Cursor_Right;
      end else
      begin                              { if cursor at decimal point              }
        if NumStr[1] = '' then                         { any leader space?         }
        begin
          delete(NumStr,1,1);                          { delete left space         }
          insert(Ch,NumStr,CursorOfs);                 { insert to left            }
        end;
      end;
    end else
    begin                                { insert is off / use overwrite           }
      if CursorOfs = IntSize
        then Move_Cursor_Right;          { move right off decimal point            }
      NumStr[CursorOfs+1] := Ch;         { overwrite character at cursor           }
    {-------------------------------------------------------------------}
    {   Turbo v3.x -- delete previous line, substitute following        }
    {           delete(NumStr,CursorOfs,1);                             }
    {           insert(Ch,NumStr,CursorOfs);                           }
    { ----------------------------------------------------------------- }
      Move_Cursor_Right;
    end;
    Write_String(XAxis,YAxis,LimitSize,NumStr);
  end;
```

```
procedure Delete_Left;
   begin
      if CursorOfs < IntSize+1 then
      begin                                  { cursor is left of decimal         }
         if CursorOfs > 1 then               { is there space to the left?       }
         begin
            delete(NumStr,CursorOfs,1);
            insert(' ',NumStr,1);            { pad with space at left            }
         end else Beep;
      end
      else                                   { cursor is right of decimal        }
      if CursorOfs > IntSize+1 then          { is there a number at left?        }
      begin
         delete(NumStr,CursorOfs,1);
         NumStr := NumStr+'0';               { pad the decimal at right          }
         Move_Cursor_Left;
      end
      else Move_Cursor_Left;                 { move off of decimal point         }
      Write_String(XAxis,YAxis,LimitSize,NumStr);
   end;

procedure Delete_At_Cursor;
   begin
      if CursorOfs <> IntSize then           { do nothing at decimal point       }
      begin
         delete(NumStr,CursorOfs+1,1);       { delete char at cursor             }
         if CursorOfs < IntSize              { if cursor left of decimal         }
            then insert(' ',NumStr,1)        { then pad NumStr with space        }
            else NumStr := NumStr+'0';       { else pad decimal at right         }
         Write_String(XAxis,YAxis,LimitSize,NumStr);
      end;                                   { and don't move the cursor         }
   end;

begin { Edit_Number }
   Complete := false;
   LimitSize := IntSize;
   if DecSize > 0 then                       { don't forget to include           }
      LimitSize := LimitSize+DecSize+1;      { space for the decimal             }
   Write_String(XAxis,YAxis,LimitSize,NumStr);
   CursorOfs := IntSize;                     { start cursor left of decimal      }
   repeat
      gotoxy(XAxis+CursorOfs,YAxis);         { use cursor for visual feedback    }
      Check_Kbd;                             { first, see what key was pressed   }
{ Note: only numbers, period and cursor controls will be accepted as input       }
      case Ch of
      #$00: case KCh of                      { if Ch is null, act on KCh         }
{ left  }    #$4B: Move_Cursor_Left;
{ right }    #$4D: Move_Cursor_Right;
{ home  }    #$47: for I := 1 to LimitSize do Move_Cursor_Left;
```

```
{ end    }    #$4F: CursorOfs := LimitSize-1;
{ insert }    #$52: Check_Insert;
{ Sh-Tab }    #$0F,                              { Exit on Sh-Tab,              }
{ up     }    #$48,                              {        Up and                }
{ down   }    #$50: Complete := true;            {       Down keys              }
{ delete }    #$53: Delete_At_Cursor;            { Note: delete char (7Fh) is   }
            end; {case KCh}                      { not supported by PCDOS kbd   }
       #$08: Delete_Left;                        {           backspace          }
   #$03,#$09,#$0D: Complete := true;             {      Exit on Ctrl-C, TAB, CR }
             #$20: Move_Cursor_Right;            {      space bar moves right   }
             #$2E: CursorOfs := IntSize+1;       {      decimal sets cursor     }
       #$30..#$39: Make_Change;                  {    numerical, change string  }
            end; {case Ch}
       until Complete;
       while NumStr[1] = ' ' do delete(NumStr,1,1);
     end;
```

```
{                    Intermediate routines used to call Read__Number            }
{                                                                               }
{     Integer and real values require different handling before being           }
{ passed to the Edit__Number subroutine and separate handling on exit to        }
{ return the correct integer and real values to the calling routines.           }
{ Rather than duplicating the Edit subroutine (once for real numbers,           }
{ once for integers), it's more efficient to use two entry procedures,          }
{ providing the appropriate string conversions and reconversions.               }
```

```
procedure Read_Real(XAxis,YAxis,IntSize,DecSize: byte; var Value: real);
   var
      Result: integer;   TempStr: string;
   begin
      str(Value:IntSize+3:DecSize,TempStr);               { change to string    }
      Edit_Number(XAxis,YAxis,IntSize,DecSize,TempStr);   { edit the string     }
      val(TempStr,Value,Result);                          { return new value    }
   end;

procedure Read_Integer(XAxis,YAxis,IntSize: integer; var Value: longint);
   var                                        { v3.x integer or real ---^ }
      Result: integer;   TempStr: string;
   begin
      str(Value:IntSize,TempStr);                         { change to string    }
 { v3.x > str(Value:IntSize:0,TempStr); use if Value: real }
      Edit_Number(XAxis,YAxis,IntSize,0,TempStr);         { edit the string     }
      val(TempStr,Value,Result);                          { return new value    }
   end;

{ end include file EDT__UTIL.INC }
```

```
{                The following routines are for Demo purposes only              }
{                                                                               }
{      If this demo sheet seems useless from an application standpoint,         }
{  you've missed the point of the demonstration. This demo is simplified        }
{  to emphasize handling and input methods and, for most practical              }
{  applications, the defined arrays used with this procedure should be          }
{  replaced with pointer arrays — a topic that will be discussed in             }
{  detail later in this book. You may also wish to study the MicroCalc          }
{  program, which uses similar, if more elaborate, procedures and               }
{  handling and which may be found on your Turbo Pascal distribution            }
{  disks.                                                                       }

procedure Calculate_Totals;
    var
        I : integer;   Count : longint;
    begin
        for I := 1 to 9 do
            DataArray[I,4].RValue :=
                DataArray[I,2].IValue * DataArray[I,3].RValue;
        with DataArray[10,2] do
        begin   IValue := 0;
                for I := 1 to 9 do
                    IValue := IValue+DataArray[I,2].IValue;      end;
        with DataArray[10,4] do
        begin   RValue := 0.0;
                for I := 1 to 9 do
                    RValue := RValue+DataArray[I,4].RValue;      end;
        with DataArray[10,3] do
        begin   RValue := 0.0;   Count := 0;
                for I := 1 to 9 do
                    if ( DataArray[I,2].IValue > 0 ) and
                       ( DataArray[I,3].RValue > 0 ) then
                            Count := Count+DataArray[I,2].IValue;
                if Count > 0 then
                    RValue := DataArray[10,4].RValue/Count;      end;
    end;

procedure Show_Setup;
    var
        I, J : integer;
    begin
        for I := 1 to 10 do
        for J := 1 to 4 do
            with DataArray[I,J] do
                case DataType of
                    StringData : Write_String(XAxis,YAxis,StrLen,DataStr);
                    IntegerData : Write_Integer(XAxis,YAxis,IntSize,IValue);
                     RealData : Write_Real(XAxis,YAxis,IntSizR,DecSize,RValue);
                end; {case}
    end;
```

```
procedure Initialize_Array;
   var
      I : integer;
   begin
      for I := 1 to 10 do
      begin
         with DataArray[I,1] do
         begin      XAxis := 1;           YAxis := I+8;
                Data Type := StringData;
                   DataStr := '';           StrLen := 38;      end;
         with DataArray[I,2] do
         begin      XAxis := 40;          YAxis := I+8;
                DataType := IntegerData;
                   IntSize := 6;           IValue := 0;      end;
         with DataArray[I,3] do
         begin      XAxis := 50;          YAxis := I+8;
                DataType := RealData;   RValue := 0.0;
                   IntSizR := 7;           DecSize := 2;      end;
         with DataArray[I,4] do
         begin      XAxis := 65;          YAxis := I+8;
                DataType := RealData;   RValue := 0.0;
                   IntSizR := 10;          DecSize := 2;      end;
      end;
      for I := 1 to 4 do with DataArray[10,I] do YAxis := YAxis+1;
```

{ initial values for demo only — not a good way to set up by any standard   }

```
         DataArray[ 1,1].DataStr := 'This is the first data line (cell)';
         DataArray[ 2,1].DataStr := 'and a second data cell';
         DataArray[10,1].DataStr := 'and a line for Total/Average/Total -->';
         DataArray[ 1,2].IValue   := 3435;
         DataArray[ 2,2].IValue   := 1;
         DataArray[ 1,3].RValue   := 12345.6789;
         DataArray[ 2,3].RValue   := 679.3;
      end;


begin {main}
   clrscr;
   Demo_Complete := false;
   Ch := #$00;
   KCh := #$00;
   Active_Col := 1;
   Active_Row := 1;
   Check_Insert;
   Initialize_Array;
```

{ demo calculator with simple product/sum/average displays }

```
gotoxy(10,4);   write('Use Ctrl-C to exit!        Simple demo calculator
gotoxy(4,7);    write('Comments or other string data    Items  $ Values
repeat
Calculate_Totals;
Show_Setup;
with DataArray[Active_Row,Active_Col] do
   case DataType of
       StringData: Edit_String( XAxis, YAxis, StrLen, DataStr );
      IntegerData: Read_Integer( XAxis, YAxis, IntSize, IValue );
         RealData: Read_Real( XAxis, YAxis, IntSizR, DecSize, RValue );
   end; {case}
```

{ The current Ch and KCh were used before (in either Edit__String or   }
{ Edit__Number) to exit from those procedures; now the same values   }
{ can be used again to determine the next step: which cell to   }
{ make active or, if Ch = Ctrl-C, to exit from the program   }

```
      case Ch of
          #$00: case KCh of
{Sh-Tab}      #$0F: if Active_Col > MinCol then dec(Active_Col)
```
                            { v3.x then Active__Col := pred(Active__Col)   }
```
                      else
                      if Active_Row > MinRow then
                      begin
                          dec(Active_Row);
```
                          { v3.x Active__Row := pred(Active__Row); }
```
                          Active_Col := MaxCol;
                      end;
{up     }     #$48: if Active_Row > MinRow then dec(Active_Row);
```
                            { v3.x then Active__Row := pred(Active__Row); }
```
{down   }     #$50: if Active_Row < MaxRow then inc(Active_Row);
```
                            { v3.x then Active__Row := succ(Active__Row); }
```
              end; {case KCh}
{Ctrl-C} #$03: Demo_Complete := true;    { demo program exits on Ctrl-C }
{Tab   } #$09,
{CR    } #$0D: if Active_Col < MaxCol then inc(Active_Col)
```
                            { v3.x then Active__Col := succ(Active__Col)   }
```
                else if Active Row < MaxRow then
                      begin   inc(Active_Row);
```
                            { v3.x Active__Row := succ(Active__Row);   }
```
                          Active_Col := MinCol;            end;
      end; {case Ch}
   until Demo_Complete;
end.
```

3

Tiny Boxes and Other Attentions

Even when graphic video cards and VGA-resolution color monitors become universally standard equipment (currently, these remain far from common in the general market), there will still be applications and uses for the extended (graphic) character set if programmers will only recognize their usefulness.

I love working with bit-mapped graphics and, unfortunately, sometimes spend entirely too much time getting a particular appearance, fine tuning delay/response characteristics, or simply enjoying the visual effects achieved by some serendipitous interaction. Unfortunately, none of these activities significantly helps me achieve the principal objective, which always remains to complete a working program.

Although a fancy display has definite attractions for the programmer (they're fun and impressive) and for the end user (they do look impressive), the graphics characters offer an intermediate choice between the elaborate and time-consuming bit graphics and the easy but unimpressive plain-text displays. More important, graphics characters provide for faster design, are easier to trouble-shoot and alter, and, not least, offer effectively universal compatibility.

In most cases, users will not be aware of any discrepancy. Between a program using bit graphics and character graphics (except in cases requiring visual simulation such as Ventura Publisher or Shuttle-Lander) key impressions will be formed on the basis of execution, clarity of information displayed, and ease of use rather than on the methods used to create the display.

The principal use of the graphics characters lies in creating borders and boxes that can be used to gather or emphasize blocks of information or even to set off a single information field for immediate recognition or emphasized input.

> For example: I particularly want you to notice this paragraph — and since I have put it in a box, your attention was drawn to it immediately when you turned to this page . . . wasn't it? . . . right!

I didn't have to use color or bit-mapped graphics to achieve my goal. Think back for just a moment. Did your eye travel first to the words "For example" or did your gaze leap to "immediately" because it was also boxed within the box?

Using Graphics Characters

Although when compared to bit graphics, graphics characters are easier to use, no keyboards offer keys for graphics character sets and few editors (including the Turbo program editor) support convenient entry of these characters. Many editors are positively reluctant to allow their use except by the program itself, which makes them even less convenient.

Using the graphics characters directly, however, is not the only route possible. The routines provided in the **Box__Utility** demo program offer methods for creating, adding to, and altering borders, boxes, and outlines without wasting time reinventing the wheel (in this case a square wheel, but the principle remains). In addition to boxes, **Box__Utility** demonstrates the basics of handling screen colors, of recognizing characters already on the screen, and of retrieving color attributes.

The Box__Line Procedure

The first step is draw a box on the screen using the **Box__Line** procedure. **Box__Line** contains the graphics elements (graphics characters) to construct screen boxes with either single or double line sides while the **H__Line** and **V__Line** procedure (discussed following) provide horizontal and vertical lines within an existing box.

Box_Line is called with eight parameters; the first four (XAxis1, YAxis1, XAxis2 and YAxis2) providing the corner coordinates, the next two selecting line styles (single or double lines) for the top and sides of the box and the final two parameters selecting foreground and background colors.

Box_Line does not test the values passed as coordinates. Since this is a utility for use by programmers, it would be redundant — and maybe a bit insulting — to question these parameters beyond the simple **Swap_If** test. **Swap_If** insures that the XAxis1 and YAxis1 parameters are less than XAxis2 and YAxis2 respectively and verifies that each of Style parameters are limited to values 1 or 2 since only single and double lines are provided and single lines are the default. (I'll come back to the FColor and BColor parameters and **SetTextColor** in a moment.) Thus, if your coordinates lie beyond the screen's (or window's) limits, no validity checks are made.

In operation, **Box_Line** begins with the Style1 and Style2 parameters, creating a six character string composed of the graphics characters required to 'draw' the selected box style, sets the cursor position according to the X and Y coordinates, then writes the appropriate box elements to the screen. If desired, **Box_Line** can be called with calculated parameters to fit special applications such as allowing the end user to size a box using cursor keys as input or to have a formula or algorithm determining the necessary size for an application and setting parameters accordingly. There you have it, a simple provision for boxes.

The H_Line and V_Line Procedures

Simple boxes are sometimes less than needed and sometimes more. Therefore, to make the display more flexible, the **H_Line** and **V_Line** procedures can add independent vertical and horizontal lines, which can be used to subdivide boxes, join boxes, or simply used alone for column dividers, rule lines, and so on.

H_Line and **V_Line** are called with screen coordinates for placement, a style flag (as with **Box_Line**), and color attributes. When called, these procedures draw lines using graphics characters. Rather than simply drawing a single or double line, however, the **H_Line** and **V_Line** procedures look at the existing screen image at each character location and, if a graphics box character is recognized, use the appropriate characters to fit together with the existing display.

Special options have been provided here for the background and foreground colors. If either (or both) color bytes are passed with a value of −1, the preexisting foreground or background (or both) colors will be retained when the new character is written. (If both colors are set to zero, this option will also be used.) Alternatively, both (or either) foreground and background colors may be assigned new value (run the **Box__Utility** demo program for an example).

Text Color Handling Procedure

In text modes, the system's video memory stores two bytes of information for each character: a character value and a video attribute. The character value is simply the ordinal value of the character: that is, the character A is stored for screen display as 41h (65 decimal) and the character ⊐ is B8h (184 decimal).

The video attribute, again stored as a single byte, is actually three segments of information: bits 0-3 contain the value for the foreground (character) color, bits 4-6 contain the background color, and bit 7 (the left-most bit) is used to store the blink flag (see Figure 3-1).

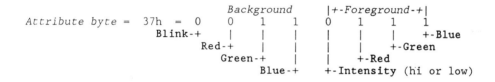

```
                              Background     |+-Foreground-+|
Attribute byte =   37h  =  0     0   1   1    0   1   1   1
                     Blink-+     |   |   |    |   |   |   +-Blue
                        Red-+    |   |    |   |   +-Green
                       Green-+   |    |   +-Red
                         Blue-+     +-Intensity (hi or low)
```

Figure 3-1 The Attribute Byte

Each bit of the attribute byte is a flag: bit 0 (at the right) turns the blue color gun on or off; bit 1 controls the green; bit 2 the red. Thus the value 7 for the foreground color turns on the blue, green and red guns (leaving the intensity low) to produce LightGray. If the value is changed to 15 (changing bit 3), the intensity is set high to produce White.

The background color is determined in the same fashion by bits 4, 5, and 6 with the difference that there is no intensity bit for background colors and these are limited to low intensity values only. In Figure 3-1, with bits 4 and 5 set True, the green and blue guns are enabled to produce a background color of Cyan.

The remaining bit (bit 7), instead of setting background color intensity, is used to set the foreground Blink characteristic (as True or False).

Note: Intensity for each gun can be controlled separately and high-intensity background colors can be created through direct control of the video system, but this requires procedures not implemented in Turbo Pascal and will not be covered here.

Turbo Pascal (in common with several other languages) provides two separate procedures for setting the default screen color attributes: **TextColor** and **TextBackground**. Each accept byte value arguments. You cannot, however, pass the **TextColor** procedure a complete attribute byte to set both the foreground and background colors. Instead, **TextColor** accepts the low four bits (0-3) as the color value and interprets any of the high four bits (4-7) as an intensity bit. Thus any value above 0Fh (15 decimal) turns on the blink characteristic.

In a similar manner, the **TextBackground** procedure accepts only bits 0 through 2 to set the background color and ignores any higher values. Thus a value of FFh (255 decimal) would be interpreted as 07h and would set LightGray as the background color.

In Turbo version 4.0, three other text attribute commands offer limited redundancy in video aspect controls:

1. **HighVideo** sets the high-intensity bit for all colors, mapping the low colors (values 0-7) to high (values 8-15), changing LightGray to White, and so on. In version 3.x, **HighVideo** selects yellow on black (or white on black for monochrome modes).

2. **NormVideo** selects the original text attribute read from the cursor position when your program started (in version 3.x, **NormVideo** was identical to **HighVideo**).

3. **LowVideo** clears the high-intensity bit for all colors, mapping the high colors (values 8-15) to low (values 0-7). In version 3.x, **LowVideo** selects only LightGray on Black.

Also, the **Crt** unit includes the byte variable TextAttr, which can be used to set the color attribute directly.

The Read_Screen Procedure

Both versions 3.x and 4.0 of Turbo Pascal offer a variety of text screen control procedures, but the only option offered for seeing what is on the screen is looking at it from the front, which is a bit difficult for a program to accomplish.

(Turbo version 4.0 does offer the graphics function **GetPixel**, which could be used to decipher a screen characer, but before trying this, refer back to Programmer's Rules Numbers II and VI.)

MS-DOS, however, can read a location in video memory and return the values found. This capability offers several useful options, the first of which is the **Read_Screen** procedure.

Note: Attempting to use **Read_Screen** in a graphics mode returns uncertain but definitely confusing results. This is for use with text modes only.

The **Read_Screen** procedure is called with specified *X/Y* screen coordinates and returns two variables containing the character and attribute values at that location. Within **Read_Screen**, the first step is to set the cursor to the location to be read and, in the example, after setting DH and DL to the screen coordinates, this is done with a call to interrupt 10h, function 2 (Set Cursor Position).

In text modes, Turbo Pascal supports only page zero of screen memory. (Depending on the graphics video adapter in use, as many as four pages of screen memory may be available.) The BH register is used to set the active memory page to zero.

Since the coordinates used by interrupt 10h, function 2, are absolute screen coordinates (beginning with 0,0 at the upper left corner), both the X and Y values passed must be decremented by one (X-1,Y-1) to match the coordinate system used by Turbo Pascal (which begin with 1,1 as the upper left corner). Also, if windowing is in use, a direct call to the **Set Cursor Position** interrupt will not take the window coordinates into account. In such cases, using Turbo's **GotoXY** procedure will avoid the necessity of calculating offsets.

Once the cursor position is set, a call to interrupt 10h, function 8, returns with the ordinal value of the screen character in the AL register and the attribute byte in the AH register. Both values could be returned as byte values, but for convenience in use, converting the character from a byte to a char value is preferable.

The Set_Text_Color Procedure

Set_Text_Color is passed the screen attribute byte (ScrAttr) retrieved by the **Read_Screen** procedure as well as the foreground (FColor) and background (BColor) values originally sent to either **H_Line** or **V_Line**.

If *both* FColor and BColor are zero, both are ignored and the existing attribute byte continues to govern both the foreground and background color attributes and the Blink byte.

If either (or both) FColor or BColor has a value of -1, the preexisting color value for the foreground and/or background remains in effect. If either (or both) FColor and BColor has a nonzero value (that is, not -1), *both* the FColor and BColor values are used to set the new color value. Now, if this sounds confusing, the flaw lies in the language (English), which lacks the syntax to cleanly say what a logic-based language (Pascal) can say quite concisely. The confusion might be better alleviated by reading the source code.

A final caution: if both FColor and BColor are passed as 0s or –1s *and* the variable Attr has not been set by a call to **Set__Text__Color**, the resulting video attributes will be almost anything.

Programmer's Rule Number VIII: If an error is possible, someone will find a way to cause it.

Corollary A, Rule Number VIII: Only a fool believes *every* error can be error-trapped. And only a bigger fool tries.

In the **H__Line**, **V__Line** and **Set__Text__Color** procedures, FColor and BColor have been declared as short int, whereas the other attributes were passed as byte values. (If you are using version 3.x — change all of these to integer values.) Byte values are an *unsigned* 8 bits and allow only positive integers (0..255). Short int values are also 8 bits, but the eighth bit is used for sign and permits negative integers (-128..127), which are necessary before a -1 can be passed.

The Cap__Line Procedure

Cap__Line provides a convenient method of inserting text into an existing character/graphics line or box or simply writing a new line to the screen while keeping the established color attributes. As with the **H__Line** and **V__Line** procedures, you can specify any color attributes, but you also have the option of matching the existing attributes at the area written without having to *know* what attributes are in effect.

Cap__Line also looks to see if the inserted text will begin or end on a graphics character line or box, and it provides a suitable graphics character on each end of inserted text. The color attribute for the insert is taken from the end position, but you could easily modify this procedure to test the color attribute at each point along the text line and set the color characteristics accordingly.

More Screen Tricks

Boxes and bars are not the only devices for getting the user's attention. Blinking characters, reverse video (on B/W systems), or bright colors (with EGA systems) all serve quite well and can be quite conveniently included in your program using the **Video_Shift**, **Reverse_Video**, and **Blink_On_Off** procedures. Typical uses might be to set new colors to highlight an error or a paragraph of text, to clarify a cursor position, or to indicate an active block or input cell.

The Video_Shift Procedure

Video_Shift is called with four coordinates (for the corners of the desired block) and foreground and background colors. These colors will be set for all characters within the designated area *without* otherwise changing the displayed text. The mechanism for this is quite simple.

First, the variable NColor is given the desired color attribute (NColor := FColor and $0F + BColor shl 4;).

Second, using loops for the X and Y ranges specified, Turbo's **GotoXY** procedure is used to position the cursor and interrupt 10h, function 8, is called and returns the indicated character value in the AL register. Since the value in AL is right where it will be required next, nothing else is done with it. Also, at this point, the AH register contains the old color attribute value, but it will not be needed for this procedure and can be simply ignored.

Third, preparation for interrupt 10h, function 9, requires that the function value (9) be placed in the AH register, the active page (zero) in the BH register, and the new color attribute (NColor) in BL. Also, the CX register accepts a value for replication (repeating) the character in AL. Because the intention is to write a single character, CX is given the value one.

Last, interrupt 10h is called and the same character that was read from this position is returned but with the new color attributes. The loop continues until the specified range has been given the new color attributes. All very simple — and very fast.

The Reverse__Video Procedure

The **Reverse__Video** procedure is equally simple. Corner coordinates are passed to specify a region. Within the region, the foreground and background colors are swapped. At the same time, the blink and intensity flags for each character remain unchanged. In other words, if a character is set to Blink, it remains blinking; and if a foreground color is high intensity, the new foreground color (the old background color) becomes high intensity and the new background color (the old foreground) changes to low intensity.

Reverse__Video operates in almost exactly the same way as **Video__Shift** with one difference. No values are passed for foreground and background colors. Instead, after calling interrupt 10h, function 8, the old attribute byte in the AH register (OColor := Reg.AH;) is saved for further operations.

Next, using OColor, start by pasing the blink and intensity bits (bits 7 and 3) directly to NColor. Then take the foreground color bits (bits 0-2 without the intensity bit) and shift-left four places to establish the new background color. The old background color bits (bits 6-4) are shifted-right four places to become the new foreground color.

Now, the new value in NColor is assigned to the BL register and interrupt 10h, function 9, is called as before to rewrite the character value and the new color attribute to the screen buffer. Thus the loop continues.

The Blink__On__Off Procedure

Blink__On__Off, like the previous two procedures, uses interrupt 10h, functions 8 and 9, to read and write the character and attribute at the cursor position. In this instance, however, instead of changing the colors in the attribute byte, only the blink byte is changed.

In this procedure, NColor gets the old color attribute from the AH register *plus 80h*. This last instruction is the key that forces the blink bit to be reversed.

Basic Binary Arithmetic

In both the **Reverse__Video** and **Blink__On__Off** procedures, binary or bitwise operations were executed on byte variables to change specific bits in the simplest possible manner. Unfortunately, if you are neither a mathematician nor heavily into assembly language, the details of the operations used may have been a bit obscure. Since the details of the operations were exactly where the hat-trick occurred, here's a look inside.

For demonstration, the instruction NColor := OColor AND $88 + OColor AND $07 shl 4 + OColor AND $70 shr 5; can be broken down to a series of simpler operations.

```
OColor AND $88                          { save blink and intensity bits    }
   OColor  = 5Bh =    0 1 0 1 1 0 1 1   { in a bit-wise AND operation       }
           AND 88h =  1 0 0 0 1 0 0 0   { only if both bits are ones        }
   equals    08h =    0 0 0 0 1 0 0 0   { does a one appear in the result   }


OColor AND $07 shl 4                    { move foreground bits to back      }
   OColor  = 5Bh =    0 1 0 1 1 0 1 1   { if either bit is zero, the        }
           AND 07h =  0 0 0 0 0 1 1 1   { result is also zero               }
   equals    03h =    0 0 0 0 0 0 1 1
```

{ the shift left operation moves }
{ all bits one place to the left, }
{ adding a zero to the right. }
{ And, after four shifts to the }

```
   shl 4   = 30h =    0 0 1 1 0 0 0 0   { left, here's the result           }


OColor AND $70 shr 4;                   { move background bits to fore      }
   OColor  = 5Bh =    0 1 0 1 1 0 1 1
           AND 70h =  0 1 1 1 0 0 0 0
   equals    50h =    0 1 0 1 0 0 0 0
```

{ the shift right operation moves }
{ all bits to the right, adding }
{ a zero to the left }

```
   shr 4   = 05h =    0 0 0 0 0 1 0 1   { and produces this result          }


Finally:    08h =     0 0 0 0 1 0 0 0
        +   30h =     0 0 1 1 0 0 0 0
        +   05h =     0 0 0 0 0 1 0 1
produces := 3Bh =     0 0 1 1 1 1 0 1   { which give us a new color         }
                                        { attribute with the foreground and }
                                        { background colors swapped         }
```

In the **Blink__On__Off** procedure, a simpler operation, NColor :=
Reg.AH+$80;, was possible. Assuming the previous initial color attribute:

```
Reg.AH  = 5Bh =   0 1 0 1 1 0 1 1
        + 80h =   1 0 0 0 0 0 0 0
becomes   DBh =   1 1 0 1 1 0 1 1   { and the blink bit is set          }
```

If the blink bit had been set before:

```
Reg.AH  = 5Bh =    1 1 0 1 1 0 1 1
        + 80h =    1 0 0 0 0 0 0 0
becomes   DBh = 1 0 1 0 1 1 0 1 1  { with the blink bit off        }
                  ^- - - - - - - - - - - - - - - - { while the overflow is dropped!  }
```

Doing this with simple binary addition was a whole lot easier (and faster) than accomplishing the same task with an if...then...else... structure or any other type of decision mechanism.

Although it's a whole world of difference not to have to depend on direct binary operations to accomplish everyday tasks, it is also important not to forget entirely about these useful, low-level operations.

Quiz

1. Several references have been made to using Turbo's **GotoXY** procedure instead of interrupt 10h, function 2, to avoid needing to calculate offset positions when windows were in use. Why would using the interrupt call be disadvantageous? What problems would in calculating offsets, and, aside from calculations, why would **GotoXY** make matters easier?

2. In the preceding utilities, interrupt 10h was used to read and write the screen buffer. Why were Turbo's existing procedures such as **TextColor** and **TextBackground** not used for these tasks?

3. The **Blink_On_Off** procedure reverses each existing blink bit, producing a blink where the display was normal and turning off a blinking display. In other cases, it might be preferable to have separate **Blink_On** and **Blink_Off** procedures. What changes would be necessary in the existing procedure to create each of these?

4. Instead of the shr and shl operators, could some other operation have been used to accomplish the tasks illustrated in the **Reverse_Video** procedure? If so, what operators would be used and how? If not, why not?

5. Instead of the complicated bit-wise manipulation used in the **Reverse_Video** procedure, what video effects could be produced by executing a straight **shift-left** or **shift-right** operation on the video attributes?

6. In **Set_Text_Color**, the instruction TextColor(ScrAttr and $8F); was used. Since only bits 0-3 are needed to set the text color, why was and 8Fh used instead of and 0Fh?

1. In a sense, this is a trick question and was designed to emphasize certain realities of programming. If you are going to use windows, two choices present themselves: either to use only direct interrupt calls (cf interrupt 10h, function 6, initialize window / scroll window up) for all window handling and keep complete track of the window coordinates and limits *or* to use the supplied Turbo functions and procedures that keep track of the active window coordinates without your special attention. The point is simple: if you can use existing utilities, *don't reinvent the wheel!* On the other hand, if it's snowing and you need skis, then go ahead.

2. **TextColor** and **TextBackground**, together with a Write(Ch) can accomplish the same task as calling interrupt 10h, function 9. However, handling each element as a separate task requires several additional lines of code to assign the various elements (the foreground and background colors and the character) to the several procedures and, overall, results in longer code and a slower execution.

Note: Since Turbo does not supply means to read the character and attribute from the screen buffer, this is *not* a case of reinventing the wheel. In this case our new "wheel" is a unique tool designed for a specific task that could not otherwise have been accomplished and, by not attempting to call on other, existing tools, has been produced in an elegant and streamlined form.

---

3. There are several alternatives here. A single procedure might be created which, acting on a flag, could accomplish all three versions of the task. For purposes of illustration, however, I will assume a separate procedure for each, even though these differ in only one line of code.

    Blink__On__Off uses the instruction NColor := Reg.AH + $80h; to reverse the existing blink bit.

    Instead, to turn on the blink bit, using a binary (or bit-wise) AND $7F in the instruction NColor := Reg.AH AND $7F; forces the eighth bit (left-most bit) to zero if it was one or leaves it unchanged if it was already zero. For example,

```
        1 x x x x x x x                      0 x x x x x x x
    AND 0 1 1 1 1 1 1 1 (7Fh)          AND 0 1 1 1 1 1 1 1 (7Fh)
becomes 0 x x x x x x x             becomes 0 x x x x x x x
```

To accomplish the reverse, that is, to *turn on* all blink bits, is essentially the same but uses `or $80` in the instruction `NColor := Reg.AH or $80;`. For example,

	1 x x x x x x x			0 x x x x x x x
OR	1 0 0 0 0 0 0 0 (80h)		OR	1 0 0 0 0 0 0 0 (80h)
becomes	1 x x x x x x x		becomes	1 x x x x x x x

4. The **shift-left 4** and **shift-right 4** operations could have been replaced with, respectively, multiplication (`* 10h`) or division (`DIV 10h`). Both of these operators, however, accomplish their own tasks using the `shl` and `shr` operators. Thus, the change would be redundant as well as producing slightly longer code and increasing the possibility of error in writing the code.

    Once you understand these operators, using the shift functions for bit-wise manipulation becomes much simpler and a thousand times clearer than attempting to accomplish the same task by more devious means. Remember, that you may want to (be able to) read your own code later.

5. This is another trick question, but this time the trick would be to describe the effects that are, to phrase it mildly, unusual. Thus, a brief demo is recommended (VGA/EGA/color preferred).

    Remember that using the `shl` operator discards the left-most bit and adds a zero as the right bit. After a maximum of 7 shifts, this would quickly leave both the foreground and background colors black, which wouldn't be much of a display. If, however, the procedure shown in **Blink__On__Off** is modified to `NColor := (Reg.AH shl 1) + (Reg.AH shr 7)`, the bits are shifted cyclically instead of being lost.

    Depending on the original attribute byte, the precise effects will vary, and you may find it helpful to add a time delay to make this easier to see, but try looping a display block using this operation. (The suggested procedure is included in the demo listing as Shift__Attribute.)

6. If Turbo's **TextColor** were passed only bits 0-3 of `ScrAttr` (using `AND 0Fh`), the blink bit would remain off at all times. **TextColor** uses the low four bits to set the foreground color and intensity, but if *any* of the high four bits (7-4) are set, **TextColor** also sets the blink attribute. Thus, if `ScrAttr` were passed without the `and 8Fh` filter, any background color except black (000) would cause the blink attribute to be turned on *regardless of the blink bit actually passed.*

```pascal
program Box_Utility_Demo;     { BOX.PAS }

uses Crt, Dos, Graph;

   type
     Regs = record case integer of
                 0: (AX, BX, CX, DX, BP, SI, DI, DS, ES, Flags : word);
                 1: (AL, AH, BL, BH, CL, CH, DL, DH           : byte); end;
   var
     Reg : Regs;
```

SPEC__EFF.INC — Special Effect Utilities (Video Effects)

```pascal
procedure Swap_If(var LoNum, HiNum: byte);
   var   Temp: byte;
   begin                              { just to make sure that paired    }
       if LoNum > HiNum then          { values are correctly ordered     }
       begin
          Temp  := LoNum;
          LoNum := HiNum;
          HiNum := Temp;
       end;
   end;


procedure Video_Shift(XAxis1, YAxis1, XAxis2, YAxis2, FColor, BColor: byte);
   var
       X, Y, NColor: byte;
   begin
       NColor := FColor and $0F + BColor shl 4;
       Swap_If(XAxis1,XAxis2);
       Swap_If(YAxis1,YAxis2);
       for Y := YAxis1 to YAxis2 do
          for X := XAxis1 to XAxis2 do
          begin
              gotoxy(X,Y);                        { see comments re Read__Screen }
              Reg.AH := 8;                        { function 8 -- read character }
              Reg.BH := 0;                        { select active page 0         }
              intr($10,Dos.Registers(Reg));       { read screen buffer           }
                 { Reg.AL now contains the character value - so we'll just        }
                 { leave it there ... ( the old attribute byte is in AH)          }
              Reg.AH := 9;                        { function 9 -- write character }
              Reg.BH := 0;                        { select active page 0          }
              Reg.BL := NColor;                   { set new screen attribute      }
              Reg.CX := 1;                        { set replication factor at one }
              intr($10,Dos.Registers(Reg));       { and write to screen buffer    }
          end;
   end;
```

```
procedure Reverse_Video(XAxis1, YAxis1, XAxis2, YAxis2: byte);
    var
        X, Y, NColor, OColor: byte;
    begin
        OColor := 0;                              { start both color values at zero   }
        NColor := 0;
        Swap_If(XAxis1,XAxis2);                   { check the coordinates             }
        Swap_If(YAxis1,YAxis2);
        for Y := YAxis1 to YAxis2 do
            for X := XAxis1 to XAxis2 do
            begin
                gotoxy(X,Y);                      { see comments re Read_Screen }
                Reg.AH := 8;                      { function 8 -- read character      }
                Reg.BH := 0;                      { select active page 0              }
                intr($10,Dos.Registers(Reg));     { read screen buffer                }
                { now AL contains the character - so just leave it there              }
                OColor := Reg.AH;                 { but get the attribute byte        }

                NColor := OColor and $88          { save blink and intensity bits }
                        + OColor and $07 shl 4    { move foreground bits to back }
                        + OColor and $70 shr 4;   { move background bits to fore }

                Reg.AH := 9;                      { function 9 -- write character     }
                Reg.BH := 0;                      { select active page 0              }
                Reg.BL := NColor;                 { set new screen attribute          }
                Reg.CX := 1;                      { set replication factor at one     }
                intr($10,Dos.Registers(Reg));     { and write to screen buffer        }
            end;
    end;

procedure Blink_On_Off(XAxis1, YAxis1, XAxis2, YAxis2: byte);
    var
        X, Y, NColor: byte;
    begin
        NColor := 0;
        Swap_If(XAxis1,XAxis2);
        Swap_If(YAxis1,YAxis2);
        for Y := YAxis1 to YAxis2 do
            for X := XAxis1 to XAxis2 do
            begin
                gotoxy(X,Y);                      { see comments re Read_Screen }
                Reg.AH := 8;                      { function 8 -- read character      }
                Reg.BH := 0;                      { select active page 0              }
                intr($10,Dos.Registers(Reg));     { read screen buffer                }
                { now AL contains the character - so just leave it there              }
                NColor := Reg.AH + $80;           { but get the attribute byte        }
                                                  { and reverse the blink bit         }
                Reg.AH := 9;                      { function 9 -- write character     }
                Reg.BH := 0;                      { select active page 0              }
                Reg.BL := NColor;                 { set new screen attribute          }
```

```
                Reg.CX := 1;                 { set replication factor at one   }
                intr($10,Dos.Registers(Reg)); { and write to screen buffer      }
            end;
        end;


procedure Shift_Attribute(XAxis1, YAxis1, XAxis2, YAxis2: byte);
    var
        X, Y, NColor: byte;
    begin
        NColor := 0;
        Swap_If(XAxis1,XAxis2);
        Swap_If(YAxis1,YAxis2);
        repeat
            for Y := YAxis1 to YAxis2 do
                for X := XAxis1 to XAxis2 do
                begin
                    gotoxy(X,Y);                 { see comments re Read_Screen }
                    Reg.AH := 8;                 { function 8 -- read characer    }
                    Reg.BH := 0;                 { select active page 0           }
                    intr($10,Dos.Registers(Reg)); { read screen buffer             }
                    { now AL contains the character - so just leave it there ...   }

                    NColor := Reg.AH shl 1 +     { but get the attribute byte     }
                              Reg.AH shr 7;      { and reverse the blink bit      }

                    Reg.AH := 9;                 { function 9 -- write character  }
                    Reg.BH := 0;                 { select active page 0           }
                    Reg.BL := NColor;            { set new screen attribute       }
                    Reg.CX := 1;                 { set replication factor at one  }
                    intr($10,Dos.Registers(Reg)); { and write to screen buffer     }
                end;
            delay(100);
        until keypressed;
    end;

{ end include SPEC_EFF }
```

BOX_UTIL.INC — Graphics-Character Box Creation Utilities

```
procedure Read_Screen(XAxis, YAxis: byte; var Ch: char; var Attribute: byte);
    begin

{ before a character and attribute can be read from the screen, the screen       }
{ position has to be assigned -- this could be done with Turbo's GotoXY          }
{ procedure but calling interrupt 10, function 2 accomplishes the same task      }
{ if you are using windows, however, the GotoXY procedure will set window-       }
{ relative coordinates without needing offset conversion                         }

        with Reg do
        begin
```

```
      AH := 2;              { function 2 -- set cursor position           }
      BH := 0;              { select active page 0                        }
      DH := YAxis-1;        { vertical position, top of screen is zero    }
      DL := XAxis-1;        { horizontal position, left of screen is zero }
   end;
   intr($10,Dos.Registers(Reg));
```

{ now the cursor is positioned, call interrupt 10, function 8 (and select   }
{ page zero as active) -- the ordinal value of the character at this screen }
{ position is returned in the AL register and the color attributes in AH   }

```
      Reg.AH := 8;          { function 8 -- read character                }
      Reg.BH := 0;          { select active page 0                        }
      intr($10,Dos.Registers(Reg));
      Ch := chr(Reg.AL);    { convert value in AL to a character          }
      Attribute := Reg.AH;
   end;
```

```
procedure Set_Text_Color) ScrAttr: byte; FColor, BColor: shortint );
   begin
```

{ if neither Foreground or Background colors were assigned, the current   }
{ screen attribute will be used as default.   }

```
      if (FColor <> 0) and (BColor <> 0) then
      begin
```

{ if either Foreground or Background colors are assigned as -1, the   }
{ current Foreground or Background attribute will be retained. If either   }
{ or both colors are assigned values, the new attributes will be   }
{ assigned to the screen cell. See also the Change__Attribute procedure. }

```
         if FColor > -1 then
            ScrAttr := (ScrAttr and $F0) + (FColor and $0F);
         if BColor > -1 then
            ScrAttr := (ScrAttr and $0F) + (BColor shl 4);
      end;
```

```
      TextAttr := ScrAttr;                 { v4.0 only - v3.x substitute following: }
(*
```
{ in Turbo v3.x, separate procedures are used to set Fore- & Background   }
{ color attributes, even though the system stores these as a single byte. }
{ This passes the values in the manner expected by Turbo.   }

```
      TextColor(SctAttr and $8F);
```

{ TextColor gets bits 0-3 for the color value and bit 7 which holds the   }
{ blink attribute -- TextBackground only gets bits 4-6 for color but   }
{ these must be shifted four places right (to bits 0-2) before passing   }

```
      TextBackground(ScrAttr and $70 shr 4);
                                                                      *)
   end;
```

TINY BOXES AND OTHER ATTENTIONS

```pascal
procedure Box_Line(XAxis1, YAxis1, XAxis2, YAxis2,
                   StyleH, StyleV, FColor, BColor: byte);
  var
    Attr, Position : byte;      Box_Str : string[6];
  begin
    Attr := FColor + BColor shl 4;
    Set_Text_Color(Attr,FColor,BColor);
    if StyleH <> 2 then StyleH := 1;
    if StyleV <> 2 then StyleV := 1;
    Swap_If(XAxis1,XAxis2);
    Swap_If(YAxis1,YAxis2);
    case StyleH of

      1: case StyleV of   { ┌   ─   ┐   │   ┘  └            }
           1: Box_Str := #$DA+#$C4+#$BF+#$B3+#$D9+#$CO;
                           { ╓   ─   ╖   ║   ╜  ╙            }
           2: Box_Str := #$D6+#$C4+#$B7+#$BA+#$BD+#$D3;    end;
      2: case StyleV of   { ╞   ═   ╡   │   ┘  └            }
           1: Box_Str := #$D5+#$CD+#$B8+#$B3+#$BE+#$D4;
                           { ╞   ═   ╒   ║   ╜  ╚            }
           2: Box_Str := #$C9+#$CD+#$BB+#$BA+#$BC+#$C8;    end;
    end; {case}
                       { BEGIN WITH TOP OF THE BOX }
    Position := 1;
    gotoxy(XAxis1,YAxis1);
    write(Box_Str[1];
    if XAxis2 > XAxis1+1 then
       for Position := XAxis1+1 to XAxis2-1 do
          write(Box_Str[2]);
    write(Box_Str[3]);
                       { ADD THE SIDES OF THE BOX }
    if YAxis2 > YAxis1+1 then
    for Position := YAxis1+1 to YAxis2-1 do
    begin
       gotoxy(XAxis1,Position);
       write(Box_Str[4]);
       gotoxy(XAxis2,Position);
       write(Box_Str[4]);
    end;
                       { ADD THE BOTTOM OF THE BOX }
    Position := 1;
    gotoxy(XAxis1,YAxis2);
    write(Box_Str[6]);
    if XAxis2 > XAxis1+1 then
       for Position := XAxis1+1 to XAxis2-1 do
          write(Box_Str[2]);
    write(Box_Str[5]);
  end;
```

```
procedure H_Line(XAxis1, YAxis, XAxis2, StyleH: byte; FColor, BColor: shortint);
  var
    Ch: char;    Attr, Position: byte;
  begin
    if StyleH <> 2 then StyleH := 1;
    Swap_If(XAxis1,XAxis2);
```
              { BEGIN WITH LEFT END OF LINE }
```
    Read_Screen(XAxis1,YAxis,Ch,Attr);
    Set_Text_Color(Attr,FColor,BColor);
    case StyleH of
      1: case Ch of
           #$D4,#$C0,#$D5,#$DA,              {  ⌊  L  F  ⌈  ⌊⌊  ⌊⌊          }
           #$C8,#$D3,#$C9,#$D6: write(Ch);   {  ⌐⌐  ⌐⌐  no change           }
           #$C7,#$BA,#$CC: write(#$C7);{  ⊩  |  ⊩  :  ⊩    }
           #$C3,#$B3,#$C6: write(#$C3);{  ⊢  |  ⊢  :  ⊢    }
           #$B9,#$CE: write(#$B9);{  ⊣|  ⊣⊢  :  ⊣|   }
           #$B4,#$C5: write(#$C5);{  ⊣  +  :  +    }
           #$B6,#$D7: write(#$D7);{  ⊣|  ⊩⊩  :  ⊩⊩   }
           #$B5,#$D8: write(#$B5);{  ⊣  +  :  ⊣    }
           #$D9,#$BE: write(#$C1);{  ⌟  ⌟  :  ⊥    }
           #$BF,#$B8: write(#$C2);{  ⌐  ⌐  :  ⊤    }
           #$BD,#$BC: write(#$CA);{  ⊩⊩  ⌟⌟  :  ⊥⊥   }
           #$B7,#$BB: write(#$CB);{  ⊤⊤  ⌐⌐  :  ⊤⊤   }
         else                      write(#$C4);{  —  }  end;    {case Ch}
      2: case Ch of
           #$D4,#$C0,#$D5,#$DA,              {  ⌊  L  F  ⌈  ⌊⌊  ⌊⌊          }
           #$C8,#$D3,#$C9,#$D6: write(Ch);   {  ⌐⌐  ⌐⌐  no change           }
           #$C7,#$BA,#$CC: write(#$CC);{  ⊩  ||  ⊩  :  ⊩    }
           #$C3,#$B3,#$C6: write(#$C3);{  ⊢  |  ⊢  :  ⊢    }
           #$B9,#$CE: write(#$B9);{  ⊣|  ⊩⊩  :  ⊩⊩   }
           #$B4,#$C5: write(#$B4);{  ⊣  +  :  ⊣    }
           #$B6,#$D7: write(#$D7);{  ⊣|  ⊩⊩  :  ⊣|   }
           #$B5,#$D8: write(#$B5);{  ⊣  +  :  +    }
           #$D9,#$BE: write(#$CF);{  ⌟  ⌟  :  ⊥    }
           #$BF,#$B8: write(#$D1);{  ⌐  ⌐  :  ⊤    }
           #$BD,#$BC: write(#$CA);{  ⊤⊤  ⌟⌟  :  ⊥⊥   }
           #$B7,#$BB: write(#$CB);{  ⊤⊤  ⌐⌐  :  ⊤⊤   }
         else                      write(#$CD); { = }   end; {case Ch}
    end; {case StyleH}
```
              { FILL THE LINE }
```
    if XAxis2 > XAxis1+1 then
    for Position := XAxis1+1 to XAxis2-1 do
    begin
      Read_Screen(Position,YAxis,Ch,Attr);
      Set_Text_Color(Attr,FColor,BColor);
      case StyleH of
        1: case Ch of          {  ||  ⊩  ⊩  ⊣|  ⊩⊩  ⊣|  ⊩⊩  :  ⊩⊩  }
             #$BA,#$CC,#$C7,#$B9,#$CE,#$B6,#$D7 : write(#$D7);
                               {  |  ⊢  ⊢  ⊣  +  ⊣  +  :  ⊢  }
```

```
              #$B3,#$C3,#$C6,#$B4,#$C5,#$B5,#$D8 : write(#$C5);
                        #$D4,#$C0,#$D9,#$BE : write(#$C1);
                        #$D5,#$DA,#$BF,#$B8 : write(#$C2);
                        #$C8,#$D3,#$BD,#$BC : write(#$D0);
                        #$C9,#$D6,#$B7,#$BB : write(#$D2);
          else write(#$C4); { ─ }              end;  {case Ch}
    2: case Ch of              { ‖ ╟ ╠ ╢ ╬ ╣ ╫  :  ╪ }
        #$BA,#$CC,#$C7,#$B9,#$CE,#$B6,#$D7 : write(#$CE);
                                 { │ ├ ╞ ┤ ┼ ╡ ╪  :  ╪ }

         #$B3,#$C3,#$C6,#$B4,#$C5,#$B5,#$D8 : write(#$D8);
                        #$D4,#$C0,#$D9,#$BE : write(#$CF);
                        #$D5,#$DA,#$BF,#$B8 : write(#$D1);
                        #$C8,#$D3,#$BD,#$BC : write(#$CA);
                        #$C9,#$D6,#$B7,#$BB : write(#$CB);
          else write(#$CD); { = }             end;  {case Ch}
    end;  {case StyleH}
end;
```

{ AND FINISH THE RIGHT END OF LINE }

```
Read_Screen(XAxis2,YAxis,Ch,Attr);
Set_Text_Color(Attr,FColor,BColor);
case StyleH of
  1: case Ch of
        #$D9,#$BE,#$BF,#$B8,              { ┘ ╛ ╕ ╪ ╨ ╝      }
        #$BD,#$BC,#$B7,#$BB: write(Ch);   { ╜ ╗ no change    }
     #$B6,#$BA,#$B9,#$CE,#$CC: write(#$B6);{ ╢ ‖ ╣ ╬ ╟  :  ╢ }
                  #$C3,#$C5: write(#$C5);{        ├ ┼  :  ┼ }
     #$B5,#$B3,#$B4,#$C6,#$D8: write(#$B4);{ ╡ │ ┤ ╞ ╪  :  ┤ }
                  #$C7,#$D7: write(#$D7);{        ╞ ╪  :  ╫ }
                  #$D4,#$C0: write(#$C1);{        ╙ ╚  :  ╨ }
                  #$D5,#$DA: write(#$C2);{        ╒ ╔  :  ╤ }
                  #$C8,#$D3: write(#$D0);{        ╘ ╙  :  ╨ }
                  #$C9,#$D6: write(#$D2);{        ╓ ╔  :  ╥ }
          else   write(#$C4); { ─ }                end; {case Ch}
  2: case Ch of
        #$D9,#$BE,#$BF,#$B8,              { ┘ ╛ ╕ ╪ ╨ ╝      }
        #$BD,#$BC,#$B7,#$BB: write(Ch);   { ╜ ╗ no change    }
     #$B6,#$BA,#$B9,#$C7,#$D7: write(#$B9);{ ╢ ‖ ╣ ╞ ╫  :  ╣ }
                  #$CE,#$CC: write(#$CE);{        ╬ ╞  :  ╬ }
     #$B5,#$B3,#$B4,#$C3,#$C5: write(#$B5);{ ╡ │ ┤ ├ ┼  :  ╡ }
                  #$C6,#$D8: write(#$D8);{        ├ ╪  :  ╪ }
                  #$D4,#$C0: write(#$CF);{        ╙ ╚  :  ╨ }
                  #$D5,#$DA: write(#$D1);{        ╒ ╔  :  ╤ }
                  #$C8,#$D3: write(#$CA);{        ╘ ╙  :  ╨ }
                  #$C9,#$D6: write(#$CB);{        ╓ ╔  :  ╥ }
          else   write(#$CD); { = }               end; {case Ch}
    end; {case StyleH}
end;
```

TINY BOXES AND OTHER ATTENTIONS

```pascal
procedure V_Line(XAxis, YAxis1, YAxis2, StyleV: byte; FColor, BColor: shortint);
  var
    Ch: char;   Attr, Position: byte;
  begin
    if StyleV <> 2 then StyleV := 1;
    Swap_If(YAxis1, YAxis2);
                            { TOP END OF LINE }
    Read_Screen(XAxis, YAxis1, Ch, Attr);
    Set_Text_Color(Attr, FColor, BColor);
    case StyleV of
      1: case Ch of
              #$BF, #$B7, #$B8, #$BB,                       { ┐ ┐ ┐ ┐ ┌ ┌      }
              #$D6, #$DA, #$C9, #$D5: write(Ch);  { ╟ ╓ no change         }
         #$CD, #$CB, #$D1, #$CE, #$CA: write(#$D1); { = ╥ ╤ ╬ ╩ : ╤ }
                          #$D8, #$CF: write(#$D8); {        ╟ ╨ : ╟ }
         #$C4, #$C2, #$D2, #$D7, #$D0: write(#$C2); { ─ ┬ ╥ ╫ ╨ : ┬ }
                          #$C5, #$C1: write(#$C5); {     ┼ ┴ : ┼ }
                          #$D9, #$BD: write(#$B4); {     ┘ ╜ : ┤ }
                          #$BE, #$BC: write(#$B5); {     ╛ ╝ : ╡ }
                          #$D3, #$C0: write(#$C3); {     ╙ └ : ├ }
                          #$C8, #$D4: write(#$C6); {     ╚ ╘ : ╞ }
              else   write(#$B3); { │ }                          end; {case Ch}
      2: case Ch of
              #$BF, #$B7, #$B8, #$BB,                       { ┐ ┐ ┐ ┐ ┌       }
              #$D6, #$DA, #$C9, #$D5: write(Ch);  { ╟ ╓ no change          }
         #$CD, #$CB, #$D1, #$D8, #$CF: write(#$CB); { = ╥ ╤ ╫ ╨ : ╥ }
                          #$CE, #$CA: write(#$CE); {     ╬ ╩ : ╬ }
         #$C4, #$C2, #$D2, #$C5, #$C1: write(#$D2); { ─ ┬ ╥ ┼ ┴ : ╥ }
                          #$D7, #$D0: write(#$D7); {     ╫ ╨ : ╫ }
                          #$D9, #$BD: write(#$B6); {     ┘ ╜ : ╢ }
                          #$BE, #$BC: write(#$B9); {     ╛ ╝ : ╣ }
                          #$D3, #$C0: write(#$C7); {     ╙ └ : ╟ }
                          #$C8, #$D4: write(#$CC); {     ╚ ╘ : ╫ }
              else   write(#$BA); { ║ }                          end; {case Ch}
    end; {case StyleV}
                            { DRAW THE LINE }
    if YAxis2 > YAxis1+1 then
    for Position := YAxis1+1 to YAxis2-1 do
    begin
      Read_Screen(XAxis, Position, Ch, Attr);
      Set_Text_Color(Attr, FColor, BColor);
      case StyleV of
        1: case Ch of        { = ╥ ╤ ╬ ╩ ┼ ┴ : ┼ }
             #$CD, #$CB, #$D1, #$CE, #$CA, #$D8, #$CF  : write(#$D8);
                             { ─ ┬ ╥ ┼ ┴ ╫ ╨ : ┼ }
```

```
        #$C4,#$C2,#$D2,#$C5,#$C1,#$D7,#$D0 : write(#$C5);
                    #$BF,#$B7,#$D9,#$BD : write(#$B4);
                    #$B8,#$BB,#$BE,#$BC : write(#$B5);
                    #$D6,#$DA,#$D3,#$C0 : write(#$C3);
                    #$C9,#$D5,#$C8,#$D4 : write(#$C6);
        else   write(#$B3); { │ }                          end; {case Ch}
    2: case Ch of              {  ═  ╤  ╥  ╪  ╨  ╫  ╧  :  ╪  }
        #$CD,#$CB,#$D1,#$CE,#$CA,#$D8,#$CF : write(#$CE);
                                 {  ─  ┬  ╥  ┼  ┴  ╫  ╨  :  ╫  }
        #$C4,#$C2,#$D2,#$C5,#$C1,#$D7,#$D0 : write(#$D7);
                    #$BF,#$B7,#$D9,#$BD : write(#$B6);
                    #$B8,#$BB,#$BE,#$BC : write(#$B9);
                    #$D6,#$DA,#$D3,#$C0 : write(#$C7);
                    #$C9,#$D5,#$C8,#$D4 : write(#$CC);
        else   write(#$BA); { ║ }                          end; {case Ch}
    end; {case StyleV}
end;
```

{ BOTTOM END OF LINE }

```
    Read_Screen(XAxis,YAxis2,Ch,Attr);
    Set_Text_Color(Attr,FColor,BColor);
    case StyleV of
      1: case Ch of
            #$D9,#$BD,#$BE,#$BC,                { ┘ ╜ ╛ ╝ ╚ ╙      }
            #$D3,#$C0,#$C8,#$D4: write(Ch)       { ╘ ╚  no change    }
            #$CD,#$CA,#$CF,#$CB,#$CE : write(#$CF); { ═ ╩ ┴ ╤ ╪ : ┴ }
                    #$D8,#$D1 : write(#$D8); {          ╪ ╤ : ╪ }
            #$C1,#$C4,#$D0,#$D2,#$D7: write(#$C1); { ┴ ─ ╨ ╥ ╪ : ┴ }
                    #$C2,#$C5: write(#$C2); {          ┬ ┼ : ┼ }
                    #$BF,#$B7: write(#$B4); {          │ ─ ╖ : ┤ }
                    #$B8,#$BB: write(#$B5); {          ╕ ╗ : ╡ }
                    #$D6,#$DA: write(#$C3); {          ╟ ╓ : ├ }
                    #$C9,#$D5: write(#$C6); {          ╟ ╔ : ╞ }
        else   write(#$B3); { │ }                 end; {case Ch}
    2: case Ch of
            #$D9,#$BD,#$BE,#$BC,                { ┘ ╜ ╛ ╝ ╚ ╙      }
            #$D3,#$C0,#$C8,#$D4: write(Ch)       { ╘ ╚  no change    }
            #$CD,#$CA,#$CF,#$D8,#$D1 : write(#$CA); { ═ ╩ ┴ ╪ ╤ : ╩ }
                    #$CB,#$CE : write(#$CE); {          ╤ ╪ : ╪ }
            #$C1,#$C4,#$D0,#$C2,#$C5: write(#$D0); { ┴ ─ ╨ ┬ ┼ : ╨ }
                    #$D2,#$D7: write(#$D7); {          ╥ ╪ : ╪ }
                    #$BF,#$B7: write(#$B6); {          ╖ ╗ : ╢ }
                    #$B8,#$BB: write(#$B9); {          ╕ ╗ : ╣ }
                    #$D6,#$DA: write(#$C7); {          ╟ ╓ : ╠ }
                    #$C9,#$D5: write(#$CC); {          ╟ ╔ : ╠ }
        else   write(#$BA); { ║ }                 end; {case Ch}
    end; {case StyleV}
end;
```

```
procedure Cap_Line( XAxis,YAxis: byte;
                     Cap_Str: string; FColor,BColor: shortint );
  var
    Ch, LCh, RCh : char;    Attr : byte;
  begin
    if XAxis > 1 then
       Read_Screen(XAxis,YAxis,Ch,Attr);
    case Ch of
      #$B6,#$BA,#$B3 : LCh := Ch;    { ⊣ ‖ │  no change          }
           #$CE,#$B9 : LCh := #$B9;  {   ╫ ⊣ : ⊣                  }
           #$CD,#$B5 : LCh := #$B5;  {   = ⊣ : ⊣                  }
      #$C4,#$C5,#$B4 : LCh := #$B4;  { ─ + ⊣ : ⊣                  }
         else          LCh := ' ';
    end;
    Read_Screen(XAxis+length(Cap_Str)+1,YAxis,Ch,Attr);
    case Ch of
      #$C7,#$BA,#$B3 : RCh := Ch;    { ⊢ ‖ │  no change          }
           #$CE,#$CC : RCh := #$CC;  {   ╫ ⊢ : ⊢                  }
           #$CD,#$C6 : RCh := #$C6;  {   = ⊢ : ⊢                  }
      #$C4,#$C5,#$C3 : RCh := #$C3;  { ─ + ⊢ : ⊢                  }
         else          RCh := ' ';
    end;
    Set_Text_Color(Attr,FColor,BColor);
    gotoxy(XAxis,YAxis);
    write(LCh+Cap_Str+RCh);
  end;

{ end include BOX__UTIL }
procedure Prompt(XAxis,YAxis : byte; PStr : string);
  begin
     gotoxy(XAxis,YAxis);
     ClrEol;
     Write(PStr);
     readln;
  end;
begin
  TextColor(15)
  TextBackground(0);
  ClrScr;

{ Box__Line( X1, Y1, X2, Y2, StyH, StyV, FColor, BColor );   }

  Box_Line( 1, 1, 5, 3, 2, 1, 0, 9);
  Box_Line(10, 1,20, 3, 2, 2, 1, 7);
  Box_Line(25, 1,45, 3, 1, 2, 2, 6);
  Box_Line(50, 1,80, 3, 1, 1, 3, 5);
```

```
   Box_Line( 1, 5, 5, 8, 1, 2, 4,13);
   Box_Line(10, 5,20, 8, 1, 1, 5,11);
   Box_Line(25, 5,45, 8, 2, 1, 6, 2);
   Box_Line(50, 5,80, 8, 2, 2, 7, 1);

   Box_Line( 1,10, 5,15, 2, 2, 8, 0);
   Box_Line(10,10,20,15, 2, 1, 9, 0);
   Box_Line(25,10,45,15, 1, 1,10, 0);
   Box_Line(50,10,80,15, 1, 2,11, 0);

   Box_Line( 1,17, 5.23, 1, 1,12, 0);
   Box_Line(10,17,20,23, 1, 2,13, 0);
   Box_Line(25,17,45,23, 2, 2,14, 0);
   Box_Line(50,17,80,23, 2, 1,15, 0);

   Prompt(1,24,' Enter RETURN for Horizontal Lines ');
{ H_Line( X1, Y, X2, StyH, FColor, BColor );  }
   H_Line(1,20,80,2,-1,-1);
   H_Line(1, 7,80,1,-1,-1);

   Prompt(1,24,' Enter RETURN for Vertical Lines ');
{ V_Line( X, Y1, Y2, StyV, FColor, BColor );  }
   V_Line(15,1,23,2,-1,-1);
   V_Line(75,1,23,1,-1,-1);

   Prompt(1,24,' Enter RETURN for Notes ');
{ Cap_Line( X, Y, String, FColor, BColor );  }
   Cap_Line(19, 4,' In addition to Drawing Boxes, ',7,12);
   Cap_Line(10, 7,' I can add line captions! ',-1,-1);
   Cap_Line(27,17,'Box Labels',-1,-1);
   Cap_Line(52,18,'and Inside Box Labels',-1,-1);

   Prompt(1,24,' Enter RETURN for Special Effects ');

   Blink_On_Off(19,4,50,4);       { Blink_On_Off( X1, Y1, X2, Y2 );            }
   DELAY(1000);
   Reverse_Video(10,7,37,7);      { Reverse_Video(X1, Y1, X2, Y2 );            }
   DELAY(1000);
   Video_Shift(27,17,38,17,5,3);  { Video_Shift(X1,Y1,X2,Y2,FColor,BColor);    }
   DELAY(1000);
   Blink_On_Off(52,18,74,18);
   Prompt(1,24,' And now enter RETURN to reverse the entire screen ');
   Reverse_Video(1,1,80,24);

   Prompt(1,24,' And once more to demonstrate Shift Attribute');
   Shift_Attribute(1,1,80,24);
   ClrScr;
end.
```

4

Popups and Other Aids

Computer people tend to be relatively undemanding sorts. They are perfectly satisfied as long as they can have more memory, faster CPUs, and bigger displays. No, this is not a put-down. I began with 16K RAM and an 8-bit Z-80 CPU operating HDOS at 2 MHz with an 80×25 monochrome screen and a single 90K floppy disk drive. Now I find myself content with a mere 10 Meg, 0 wait-state system with 640K RAM (plus 2.5 MB), enhanced keyboard, fast 60 MB hard disk, an 80×43 EGA monitor (high-resolution color, of course) and a few other enhancements. I'm perfectly content — for today.

Today, CPUs are faster, memories are larger, disk storage is both, but 80×25 screens are still standard. (I do not consider 80×25 an improvement over the 40×16 TV monitor standard, which was simply a temporary example of de-evolution and properly deserves to be forgotten.) However, a few things can be done about the 80×25 limit.

Without physically adding monitors for secondary displays or converting to EGA or VGA video cards and monitors, additional display windows can be superimposed over an existing display. They can be used for menus, help displays, warnings, special features, bar graphs, and so on and then deleted, leaving the original display and information untouched. This is the next best thing to a second monitor (and, in many cases, is even better).

EGA and VGA video cards (in text modes) can support multiple pages of video memory, allowing fast switching between active pages. But this is not the approach suggested here because these enhanced video cards are not standard and Turbo Pascal does not offer user access beyond page zero of the video memory, in text modes, anyway. (For those who would like to access these additional video pages, alternate techniques will be covered in Chapter 10.)

Popup Features

The popup video displays discussed here, however, are compatible with all standard monochrome and color video systems since they do not rely on the video-card RAM except for the active screen display.

Note: Recall that video RAM (in text modes) uses 2 bytes for each screen character position (see Figure 10-1). The first byte contains the video attributes for the character; the second byte holds the ASCII value of the displayed character. Thus, a complete screen image requires 4000 bytes ($80 \times 25 \times 2$), or slightly less than 4 Kbytes, of RAM. Under Turbo Pascal and without using any special tricks, this would permit 16 pages of screen image to be saved. (Don't forget the 64K memory limit on a data block.)

Video Tests

Of course, the first trick is to know where the video image is located (and I don't mean on the screen). For monochrome video cards, the video memory address segment begins at B000:0000h, and for color (CGA, EGA, and so on) it begins at B800:0000h. Thus it helps to know which video card is in use.

One simple approach is to use interrupt 10h, function 0Fh (**Get Current Display Mode**), to determine if the active video mode is black and white or color. (See Appendix A.) This is a quick and dirty test, but it reports only what video setting is presently enabled and fails to report precisely what the video system is capable of. Although some video cards can emulate several otherwise incompatible video modes, **Get Current Display Mode** only reports which mode is currently being used but offers no information about other possible modes that might be preferable (see also Turbo version 4.0's LastMode).

Several methods have been devised to attempt to determine current video system capabilities. Unfortunately, none of these have been universally satisfactory.

The **CheckColor** procedure uses

```
ColorVideo := (mem[$0000:$0410] and $30) <> $30;
```

to test for the presence of a color system, and it sets the ScreenSegment (address) accordingly. This procedure operates effectively on most computers, but it occasionally fails to correctly identify the video card in use. Another test, which fails under similar circumstances, is:

```
ColorVideo := (mem[$0000:$0449] <> $07);
```

If the two tests are combined as follows:

```
ColorVideo :=  ( mem[$0000:$0410] and $30 ) <> $30
          and( mem[$0000:$0449]             <> $07);
```

the odds for failure do improve somewhat, but apparently there are still systems that fail to correctly identify the video card in use. Unfortunately, I have not been able to test any of these failures first hand and personally have not found any systems that were not compatible with the preceding tests, but I have received several reports of failure (4, actually). (I would also be pleased to hear of any informative experiences you may have had with this test.)

If you absolutely need a more reliable test, however, Turbo version 4.0 offers the **Graph** unit, which includes the **InitGraph** and **DetectGraph** procedures. Calling **InitGraph** initializes the graphics system and the appropriate graphics driver and then selects a graphics mode. This will require a subsequent call to **CloseGraph** to get back to text mode. The **DetectGraph** procedure could be used, however, to call the system and determine which GraphDriver and GraphMode would be appropriate. Given this information, the type of video card incorporated in the system should be obvious.

Fortunately, if you're using version 4.0, there is a simpler solution. When Turbo initializes, the *predefined* word variable LastMode (in the Crt unit) is initialized with the currently active video mode. This permits a very simple test:

```
ColorVideo := (LastMode <> Mono);
```

in which the value in LastMode is compared with the constant Mono (= 7) to determine if the system was in a monochrome or color mode when called.

Note: This still tells you nothing about which, if any, graphics capabilities may be present in the system or if a color monitor is actually being used (it could be only a black and white monitor using a color video adapter). It does tell you which screen segment address is valid, which is the one piece of information you want to know at the moment.

_____

Save and Restore Screen Procedures

Now that the video card is identified (well, the memory address anyway), what can be done with it?

The first trick is the **Save__Screen** procedure:

```
type
   Screen_Line = array[1..80] of word;
   Screen = array[1..25] of Screen_Line;
                    {this type of declaration could also appear as:}
                    {Screen = array[1..25,1..80] of word;}
var
   KeepScreen : Screen;
procedure Save_Screen;
   begin
      if ColorVideo then KeepScreen := ColorScreen
                    else KeepScreen := MonoScreen;
   end;
```

This procedure creates a duplicate image of the video memory *at this time.* Now, I can write anything I like to the screen or even erase it entirely, and I still have a duplicate of the original image that I can recover with a simple call to **Restore__Screen**.

```
procedure Restore_Screen;
   begin
      if ColorVideo then ColorScreen := KeepScreen
                    else  MonoScreen := KeepScreen;
   end;
```

With minor modifications, these two procedures can also be used to save and recover multiple screen images (or snapshots, if you prefer) as follows:

```
var
   KeepScreen : array[1..10] of Screen;
```

```
procedure Save_Screen( ScreenNumber: byte);
    begin
      if ColorVideo then KeepScreen[ScreenNumber] := ColorScreen
                    else KeepScreen[ScreenNumber] := Monoscreen;
    end;
procedure Restore_Screen;
    begin
      if ColorVideo then ColorScreen := KeepScreen[ScreenNumber]
                    else  MonoScreen := KeepScreen[ScreenNumber];
    end;
```

These screen images can be redisplayed in any sequence (or could be stored as binary disk files), and once the image is returned to the screen buffer, they can be read and altered using the procedures demonstrated in the **Box__Utility** demo program in this book.

Actually, once you have the **Save__Screen** and **Restore__Screen** procedures, there isn't a whole lot left to say in terms of hard programming. The **Pop__Up__Screens** demo program uses procedures from the **Box__Util** include file for box drawing and is otherwise quite straightforward. Although these utilities will be used extensively in subsequent demo programs and should find quite a number of applications in your programs, there seems little point in duplicating explanations that have appeared in previous chapters.

Designing Basic Menus

The **Pop__Menu__Screen** demo program adds a simple, cursor-directed menu with comment lines and a simple response feature. I will not attempt to create a universal menu feature for several reasons:

1. Because several Pascal enhancement packages already offer universal menu creation features, none of which have, in review, proven to even approach universal flexibility.

2. Because a thorough attempt would be so extensive as to preclude inclusion here (and would also be entirely too extensive to include in your programs).

3. Because the best of these required more work to use than creating the program directly.

4. Because menus are so simple to design and implement directly, and when they are tailored to the specific tasks, look much better and operate smoother and faster than anything created by programming utilities.

To put it bluntly, don't look for a substitute for good programming.

If your menus are few and simple (that is, fewer than a hundred items or choices), the simplest approach is to build your menus directly into your program. On the other hand, if you are providing for large number of menus and submenus with extensive choices, text comments, and special features, you should consider creating an external file structure to contain this data. Also, if the user will be altering or adapting the menu, an external file containing the control structure data is the only choice. (For an excellent example of this latter type of menu program design, see HOT Menu from Executive Systems, Inc.)

In the sample menu, **Pop__Menu.PAS**, two columns of five items were displayed with the current selection presented in reverse video. As the cursor keys are used to change the selected item, a comment line for each item appears below the main display. The Left and Right Arrow keys, Tab, and Shift-Tab keys each move the item selection by five (by column), whereas the Up and Down Arrows change the selection by single items. For a very lengthy display, the Page Up and Page Down keys might also have been used for paging the display, with the Home and End keys (as they do now) moving to the first or last item on the list.

Another popular feature for menu selection is the highlighting or setting off of the first letter (or the first capital letter) of each menu item so that selections can be made by striking the appropriate key. This is not difficult to arrange. The key-character highlighting can be an automatic feature that searches for the first capital letter (that is, the first character in the range 41h–5Ah), displaying this in a contrasting or intense color. Then, having provided a visual indicator, if you enter an uppercase search character a simple check is made against the menu prompts (making comparisons only with the first *capital* letter in each). There are problems and choices here. If, as often happens, more than one menu item has the same first letter (see the **Pop__Menu.PAS** demo), which one should be chosen? Should your test begin at the top of the list? Should it begin from the currently highlighted item and run down? Should you show all items matching the selection and provide a prompt for additional specification?

If you choose to begin at the first (top) of the list and there is any likelihood of multiple matches, a good logic would be to highlight the first match *but do not execute this item* unless a CR (ENTER key) is sent. Then, if the same character is repeated, move to the next match and highlight and so on.

If you choose to begin the search with the current item and run down, you might also use this same strategy, but you must also provide for reaching the end of the list and returning to the top *and do so without allowing the search to continue in an indefinite loop if no match is found.*

The last choice mentioned was to show multiple items and provide a prompt for additional specifications. This type of selection is especially excellent when you are dealing with long lists such as address files, stock lists, or autodialers. A program example using this type of search entry appears in Chapter 5.

Which of these systems you choose to implement will be dictated by your applications, your programming style, and by the types of lists used. There are no hard, fast rules that say "this is the only way to do it." There is one key point that you must keep in mind, however! How will the end user see your choices? Will they be pleased or only confused? Will this create a convenience or an irritant? Think it over before you decide on a method, and then think it over again after you create the menu. Don't be afraid to change what doesn't work.

Providing Help Features

Good pop-up help screens are one of the possible hallmarks of a great programmer. Not all programs need help screens and not all programs should have them, but many that should don't.

Unfortunately, it has become virtually axiomatic that the quality of the documentation varies inversely with the quality of the program being documented. Pop-up help screens, when done even moderately well, do a great deal to alleviate such documentation problems. The reasons for this are twofold. First, pop-up screens impose limitations on the amount of information that can be displayed. As a direct result, the information provided tends to be straightforward and to the point. Second, the information is immediately available. The user does not have to stop, look for the manual, and then search through the manual to find the relevant material (by which time, he has probably forgotten just what the question was).

Designing help screens, however, is an art for which there are no fixed rules. The help screens depend entirely on the program in which they appear and on the intentions of the program and programmer. I will offer, however, several guidelines and a few suggestions.

Context-Sensitive Help

The help screens in Turbo 4.0 are examples of context sensitive help — the help screens that appear are determined by where you are or what you are doing in Turbo when help is called. A couple of approaches to this are possible. One good method is to set a variable, HelpType, when different procedures are called. For example,

```
type
   HelpTypes = (Files, Calculate,...);
var
   HelpType : HelpTypes;
procedure Select_File;               procedure Calculate_Result;
   begin                                begin
     HelpType := Files;                   HelpType := Calculate;
       .                                    .
       .                                    .
       .                                    .

         procedure Help_Display;            .
            begin
               case HelpType of
                   Files : ...
                Calculate : ...
            .
            .
            .
```

This type of loose "flag" structure offers several advantages. The items and range do not have to be determined in advance. Instead, a new help flag can be created at any time. The flag can also be self-identifying, which makes it much easier for you to match the proper help text to the proper flag.

Menu-Selected Help

With menu-selected help, the Help key pops up a help menu displaying a list of topics that can be selected in much the same manner as the demo menu. These menus are simple to create and convenient to revise and/or edit later. They also let the user see which topics have help available.

Key Word Help

With key word help, a word or phrase can be selected (usually by highlighting) and used to call up the appropriate help text. This type of help selection often resembles menu-selected help in program structure but with the keywords appearing within a text rather than in a list. In such cases, some method of indicating which words are keyed for further help should be used, usually by highlighting or lowlighting (or underlining on monochrome systems).

Error Help

With error help, an error code or error condition triggers the appropriate help text. These might be system-generated errors or your own internal error conditions (or both).

Note: All four of these types of help are used by Turbo 4.0 in various combinations, and they offer good examples of the various selection techniques.

Help Files Considerations

The text files for the help features, unless these are very brief, are usually maintained as an external text or coded-text file that is keyed for random access or accessed by sequential key search. Unless the help texts are extremely lengthy (more than 5–10 Kbytes in length), there is rarely any occasion for access more elaborate than a simple key search, but arranging the entries in order of probability of need does speed access time.

Screen placement of help texts should also be considered. If possible (and relevant), help texts should not cover up the item for which help is requested. If circumstances do not permit this type of selective screen placement, another approach would be to note the cursor position (when help was first requested) and to place the help window appropriately. To present a lengthy help file, rather than creating a large window for display, using a smaller window with scrolling is usually better. For examples of display control, see Chapter 5.

Help files should be carefully checked, both for what you intended to say *and* for correct spelling, syntax, and good English. I strongly suggest that your help texts be checked by someone else (or by several other people). If they do not understand what you are saying, don't argue or explain — just rewrite the offending help file until it becomes crystal clear. This help file is your emissary to a vast number of others who will not be able to question you directly. Make certain that it speaks clearly and to the point.

This is also the point at which another type of error (a sometimes subtle one) appears. If you find that you cannot create a clear explanation, maybe your program isn't clear. Sometimes the solution may be not to rewrite the help file but to correct the program itself. Never, under any circumstances, attempt to hide the problem. (See Programmer's Rule Number I.) Anything you attempt to cover up is going to stick out like a sore thumb in the end.

If you have been around computers for any length of time, you probably have encountered the infamous "undocumented feature." Sometimes these undocumented features are features that the programmer has created for use while testing the program or utility but has simply not troubled to include in the documentation because they are very specialized or would require excessive explanation or because they reference elements of the program structure that are not intended to be visible or to be accessed by the user. Sometimes these features are useful, but other times they are simply errors that the programmer forgot, was unable or unwilling to correct, did not test correctly in the development, or tried *unsuccessfully* to cover up.

For example, the popular Ventura Publisher program contains a warning message of a fatal system error that concludes with instructions for a last ditch recovery and restart to minimize losses. This is fair and correct and allows the user to start over with a minimum of disruption. If the warning were not given, however, this would be a considerable irritant and major flaw in programming practice. They do, however, have another undocumented feature that is not mentioned: Ventura has a tendency to leave fragments of files on your hard disk — fragments that occupy disk space but do not have directory listings and can only be removed using a **ChkDsk** utility. This *is* a flaw and bad programming (in an otherwise impressive program).

If you absolutely cannot get rid of a bug, cannot fix it, and cannot correct it, be fair to your users. The bug exists and somebody will eventually find it, but *warn them first* before they discover it for themselves.

POP__UP Demo Programs

POP__UP.INC

```
type
   Screen_Line = array[1..80] of word;
   Screen = array[1..25] of Screen_Line;
var
   ScreenSegment : word;               { video memory segment address : two bytes }
      MonoScreen : Screen absolute $B000:$0000;
     ColorScreen : Screen absolute $B800:$0000;
      KeepScreen : Screen;
      ColorVideo : boolean;

procedure CheckColor;
   begin
      ColorVideo := (LastMode <> Mono);
```

```
(*      v3.x use:
            ColorVideo := (mem[$0000:$0410] and $30) <> $30;
    *)

              if ColorVideo then ScreenSegment := $B800
                        else ScreenSegment := $B000;        end;
procedure Save_Screen;
    begin    if ColorVideo then KeepScreen := ColorScreen
                        else KeepScreen := MonoScreen;      end;

procedure Restore_Screen;
    begin    if ColorVideo then ColorScreen := KeepScreen
                        else  MonoScreen := KeepScreen;     end;

procedure Set_Color(Color: byte);          { here color is passed as one byte        }
    begin
      if not ColorVideo and                { is this system monochrome ?             }
         (Color and $80 = $80) then        { is the blink turned on? if yes, then    }
         Color := $70;                     { instead of blink, use black on white    }
      TextAttr := Color;                   { v4.0 - v3.x use following statements     }
(*
      TextColor( Color and $8F );                     { set the foreground and blink }
      TextBackground( Color and $70 shr 4 );          { set the background color      }
*)
    end;

procedure Box_Window( XAxis1, YAxis1, XAxis2, YAxis2, FColor, BColor: byte);
    begin
      Window(1,1,80,25);               { reset to full screen before drawing the box }
      Box_Line( XAxis1, YAxis1, XAxis2, YAxis2, 2, 2, FColor, BColor);
      Window( XAxis1+1, YAxis1+1, XAxis2-1, YAxis2-1 );
                                       { create the new window inside the border      }
      clrscr;                          { and erase new window                         }
    end;

procedure Clr_Line( XAxis, YAxis, Limit: byte );
    var                                { an alternative to ClrEol for compatiblity    }
      I : integer;                     { with the custom windowing used here          }
    begin
      gotoxy(XAxis,YAxis);
      for I := 1 to Limit-XAxis+1 do write(' ');
      gotoxy(XAxis,YAxis);
    end;

procedure Center_Line( XAxis, YAxis, Limit: byte; CenterStr: string);
    var
      OffSet : byte;
    begin
      OffSet := ( Limit-XAxis+1 - length(CenterStr) ) div 2;
      Clr_Line( XAxis, YAxis, Limit );
      gotoxy( XAxis+OffSet, YAxis );
      write(CenterStr);
    end;
```

```
procedure Title_Window(XAxis1,YAxis1,XAxis2,YAxis2,FColor,BColor: byte;
                                          WindowTitle: string);
   begin
      Window(1,1,80,25);           { reset to full screen before drawing the box      }
      Box_Line( XAxis1, YAxis1, XAxis2, YAxis2, 2, 2, FColor, BColor );
      H_Line( XAxis1, YAxis1+2, XAxis2, 1, FColor, BColor );
      Center_Line (XAxis1+1, YAxis1+1, XAxis2-1, WindowTitle);
      Window( XAxis1+1, YAxis1+3, XAxis2-1, YAxis2-1 );
      clrscr;
   end;
```

NUMB_CHK.INC Used by POP_UP and POP_MENU Demos

```
procedure Swap_If(var Number1, Number2: byte );

   var TempNum: byte;

   begin
      if( Number1 > Number2 )then
      begin
         TempNum := Number1;
         Number1 := Number2;
         Number2 := TempNum;
   end;
end;
```

POP_UP.PAS

```
program Pop_Up_Screens;

uses Crt, Dos;

type
   Regs = record case integer of
             0: (AX, BX, CX, DX, BP, SI, DI, DS, ES, Flags : word);
             1: (AL, AH, BL, BH, CL, CH, DL, DH           : byte);   end;
var
   I : byte;   Ch : char;     Reg : Regs;

{$I NUMB_CHK.INC}
{$I BOX_UTIL.INC}
{$I POP_UP.INC}

procedure Pop_Window(WindowNumber: byte);
   var
      I : byte;                { local variables are preferred for loops      }
   begin
      case WindowNumber of
         1: begin  Box_Window(40,1,60,15,7,8);
```

```
                            for I := 1 to 30 do write('Pop_Up_Screen ');              end;
            2: begin  Box_Window(5,10,45,20,10,2);
                            for I := 1 to 30 do write('This might be a menu ');    end;
            3: begin  Box_Window(40,15,80,24,4,2);
                            for I := 1 to 30 do write('Or a warning screen ');     end;
            4: begin  Box_Window(20,15,50,25,12,0);
                            for I := 1 to 30 do write('Or almost anything! ');     end;
            5: begin  Box_Window(20,5,65,20,1,7);
                            for I := 1 to 30 do write(' Pop_Ups are useful! ');    end;
        end; {case}
        Set_Color(White+Blink);          { the predeclared values can still be used      }
        writeln;
        write(' (',WindowNumber,') strike ENTER for original screen ');
        delay(2500);
        Restore_Screen;
    end;

begin
    CheckColor;
    Set_Color($6E);
    ClrScr;
    write(' ');
    for I := 1 to 78 do write(' This is a background screen for Pop_Up \');
    Save_Screen;
    I := 1;
    repeat
        Pop_Window(I);
        if I < 4 then I := 1
                    else inc(I);
    until keypressed;
    Ch := readkey;
end.
```

POP__MENU.PAS

```
program Pop_Menu_Screen;    { POP_MENU.PAS }

uses Crt, Dos;

type
    Regs = record case integer of
            0: (AX, BX, CX, DX, BP, SI, DI, DS, ES, Flags : word);
            1: (AL, AH, BL, BH, CL, CH, DL, DH            : byte);  end;
var
        Reg : Regs;    I : byte;
    Ch, KCh : char;                   { Ch and KCh are global variables for Chk__Kbd }
```

```
{$I  NUMB_CHK.INC}
{$I  BOX_UTIL.INC}
{$I  GEN_UTIL.INC}
{$I  POP_UP.INC}

procedure Pop_Menu;
   var
   FColor, BColor, Item : byte;
   MenuItem : array[1..10] of string[20];
    Comment : array[1..10] of string[35];
       Done : boolean;

procedure Assign_Menu;
   begin
       { when extensive menus are used, MenuItems are best read from an      }
       { external reference file rather than being assigned thus:            }
       MenuItem[1]  := 'Roast Beast';
        Comment[1]  := 'Served with fur-blood gravy';
       MenuItem[2]  := 'Baked Hands';
        Comment[2]  := 'A ten-finger delight, special sauce';
       MenuItem[3]  := 'Ogre Stew';
        Comment[3]  := 'A real treat for the hungry gourmet';
       MenuItem[4]  := 'Frog''s Ears';
        Comment[4]  := 'A rare delicacy in special sauce';
       MenuItem[5]  := 'Green Salad';
        Comment[5]  := 'Season''s finest green caterpillars';
       MenuItem[6]  := 'Blue Salad';
        Comment[6]  := 'Fresh blues with special dressing';
       MenuItem[7]  := 'Karat Salad';
        Comment[7]  := 'A crunchy delight - gem of the menu';
       MenuItem[8]  := 'Spuds Mack';
        Comment[8]  := 'Spotted dog in the height of style';
       MenuItem[9]  := 'Flied Lice';
        Comment[9]  := 'Piping hot and crunchy';
       MenuItem[10] := 'Desserts';
        Comment[10] := 'Our hot and sandy special';
       { granted, the preceding items are frivolous but you can always       }
       { change these to suit your own tastes}
   end;

procedure Write_Item(Item: byte);
   begin
      if Item < 5 then gotoxy(23,Item-4)
                  else gotoxy( 5,Item+1);
      write(' ',MenuItem[Item],' ');
   end;

procedure Select_Item(Item: byte);
   var
```

```
                  CenterStr : string;
              begin
                case Item of
                  1..9: CenterStr := ' Sorry, we''re out of '+MenuItem[Item];
                    10: CenterStr := ' Sorry, no dessert till you eat dinner';
                end;
                Center_Line(1,10,38,CenterStr);              { procedure in POP_UP.INC }
                Beep;    delay(2000);    Beep;
              end;


          begin
            Done := false;
            Assign_Menu;                                 { create an active menu       }
            Save_Screen;                                 { save the current screen     }
            FColor := 15;
            BColor := 1;
            Title_Window(20,3,60,16,FColor,BColor,'Pop_Up Menu Title');
                                                         { procedure in POP_UP.INC     }
            { remember: a window is now active - use window coordinates              }
            for Item := 1 to 10 do Write_Item(Item);     { setup menu in the window    }
            Item := 1;                                   { initialize current item     }
            repeat
              Set_Color( BColor + FColor shl 4 );        { reverse colors              }
              Write_Item(Item);                          { highlight current item      }

              Set_Color( FColor + BColor shl 4 );        { restore original colors     }
              Center_Line(1,8,38,Comment[Item]);         { put up the comment line     }
              Center_Line(1,10,38,'Select Item or Ctrl-C to exit ');

              Check_Kbd;                                 { procedure in GEN_UTIL.INC }
              Write_Item(Item);                          { restore item to normal      }

              case Ch of                                 { now test the key pressed    }
                #$00: case KCh of
                        #$0F: dec(Item,5);               { Sh-Tab }
                        #$4B: dec(Item,5);               { left   }
                        #$48: dec(Item);                 { up     }
                        #$4D: inc(Item,5);               { right  }
                        #$50: inc(Item);                 { down   }
                        #$47: Item := 1;                 { home   }
                        #$4F: Item := 10;                { end    }
                        else Beep;          end;         { case KCh }
                #$03: Done := true;                      { Ctrl-C }
                #$09: inc(Item,5);                       { Tab    }
                #$0D: Select_Item(Item);                 { CR     }
                else Beep;                  end;         { case Ch }
              if Item > 10 then dec(Item,10);            { check valid range }
              if Item < 1  then inc(Item,10);            { check valid range }
            until Done;
```

```
   window(1,1,80,25);                 { restore screen size }
   Restore_Screen;                    { and original image }
end;

begin
   CheckColor;
   Set_Color($6E);
   ClrScr;
   for I := 1 to 82 do write(' Background screen for Pop_Menu Demo! /');
   Pop_Menu;
end.
```

5

Directory Pop-Up Assistance

Second only to command menus, the most often needed help feature in general programming is access to the disk directory. If you could perfectly recollect all the files on your disk, you would be all set. However, very few of us are so prenaturally blessed, and the next best thing is a pop-up directory.

Pop-Up Features

Before going into directory access, however, I'd like to begin by defining a set of criteria: a list of items or features that would be generally desirable. I'm not trying to suggest that all directory pop-ups must have all of these features (which you want will vary with your application), but this will provide a starting point.

The first item obviously is the list itself.

With a hard disk (or even without), a file list can be pretty long. Therefore the second feature should be a way to limit the actual display to a manageable portion of the list so that we can move through this list conveniently and find a desired item. Our second feature will be a cursor-driven display.

A third feature would be the ability to use DOS's familiar wildcard file specification.

Fourth, what about directory trees? It would probably help to be able to see which entries are files and which are root or subdirectory listings. Since the file attribute flags are what will be needed here, we might as well show the attributes for nondirectory files as well. Sometimes it can be very handy to know which files have been backed up (the Archive attribute), which are Read-Only, and which are Hidden and/or System files.

File size, file date, and time stamps are the fifth feature.

Since it can be pretty hard to write to a full disk, we should make the free space on the disk, the total size of the files in the current directory, and the total disk space in use the sixth feature.

The number of files and the number of directories/subdirectories can be the seventh feature.

The eighth feature can be the available free memory because it's always nice to know when memory is running short before it actually disappears.

Here's the wish list so far:

1. List of files

2. Cursor-driven display

3. Select by file specification (wildcards)

4. Identify root, subdirectories, attributes, etc.

5. Show file size, file date, and time

6. Show free space on drive, total files, total space, etc.

7. Show number of files and directories

8. Show available free memory (RAM)

That looks like a pretty good start but I'm not done yet. The information on the list sounds like a good display, but thus far it's only a display and it only checks the currently used drive and path. So, maybe a few other features would be helpful.

The ninth item should allow stepping through the directory tree. Let's be able to move from one directory to another conveniently.

What about changing drives? I have four: two floppies and a partitioned hard disk for C: and D:. So the tenth item becomes the ability to log a new drive.

What if I'm out of space on a drive? Being able to free up some space can be vital at times, so the eleventh item can be a delete feature.

There's one more item I've always wanted: to be able to search a list quickly, for example, to be able to jump through a long list of files to find the P's because I'm looking for POP-UP.PAS. So let's make the alphabetical keys hot keys for a quick search.

These four additional features complete a round dozen items:

9. Directory tree access

10. Log new drive

11. Delete file(s)

12. Quick search on hot key

However, I'm going to add a help feature to make this a baker's dozen:

13. Help menu

   Now that I have a list of features (and I've already assumed that this will be a pop-up display), the next consideration is how to display the information.

Displaying Information

Figure 5-1 is a sample display for the directory pop-up feature.

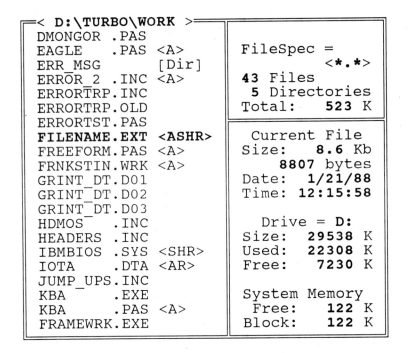

Figure 5-1 Pop-Up Directory Display

   The current path is shown at the top and the files displayed in the left column are scrolled by the arrow and page keys with the current item either highlighted or in color. File attributes are shown in brackets by each filename. To the right (above) are the FileSpec, the File and Directory counts, and the total size for all files listed. To the right (below) are the size, date, and time for the selected file, followed by the drive size and free space and the system memory usage.

Many of the thirteen items on the list we made in the preceding section were display features. Although they've pretty much taken care of themselves for the moment, I still need a way to select item 3 and items 10 through 13.

Item 12, the quick search by alphabetical key, requires the use of most of the regular keys (and, for search purposes, uppercase and lowercase letters are treated alike). This leaves the function keys as likely prospects, but personally, I've always hated trying to remember dozens of different function key assignments for different programs and utilities.

The F1 key has acquired some degree of standardization as a popular Help key, so I'll assign it again to this use. As for the other functions, some form of mnemonic key assignment is preferable and a few control keys can provide this:

Key Assignment	Function
^F	File specification
^L	Log new drive
^D	Delete file(s)
^Q	Quit

For the quit function, I could also use ^X, which would match the Turbo Pascal interface, or I could allow both.

In summary, the alphabetical keys provide quick search, the F1 key pops up a help feature, and four control characters select my other features. Now I can create a help screen to fit with the main display as shown in Figure 5-2.

```
 ERRORTRP.OLD          Total:     523 K
 ERRORTST.PAS
 FILENAME.EXT <ASHR>        Commands
 FREEFORM.PAS <A>
 FRNKSTIN.WRK <A>        ^Attributes*
 GRINT_DT.D01           ^Delete
 GRINT_DT.D02           ^File-spec
 GRINT_DT.D03           ^Log drive
 HDMOS   .INC           ^Print*
 HEADERS .INC           ^Quit
 IBMBIOS .SYS <SHR>     ^Sort*
 IOTA    .DTA <AR>       or enter
 JUMP_UPS.INC          <L>etter for
 KBA     .EXE           fast search
 KBA     .PAS <A>
 FRAMEWRK.EXE          * not in demo

       F1 = Help
```

Figure 5-2 Directory Pop-Up with Help List

The key elements on the help screen are highlighted (reverse video for monochrome systems). Three new options appear in the list: ^Attributes, ^Print, and ^Sort, with an end note that these are not included in the demo. There are several reasons for not including these features at the moment — primarily because these are not immediately relevant — but Sort routines are discussed in Chapter 8. Attributes can be changed using interrupt 21h, function 43h (see Appendix C) and are discussed later in this chapter. The Print option — if desired — is easily devised. A Help prompt is added at the bottom of the frame.

This planned display is 40×25 (a half screen) and will include a horizontal offset variable to allow placing the display either to the right or left (or in between) as seems appropriate. Other layouts are possible, but for demonstration purposes, it seems practical to show as much system information as reasonable.

I will not go into the use of the pointer structures in any detail here. These will be discussed at greater length in Chapters 7 and 8. For now, simply consider these as an array of data records.

Accessing the Disk Directory

The first step in getting information from the disk drive is to know where I am. I'm not about to ask the user what drive and directory I'm on — not when I can get a more reliable answer faster by calling the **Check_Drive** function.

Calling interrupt 21h, function 19h, returns a byte value in the AL register identifying the currently logged drive.

```
function Check_Drive: integer;
   begin
      Reg.AH := $19;
      intr($21,Dos.Registers(Reg));
      Check_Drive := Reg.AL+1;
   end;
```

This call returns a value of 0 for drive A, 1 for B, 2 for C, and so on in the AL register. Most other functions, however, will require a value of 1 for A, 2 for B, and so on, with the value of 0 reserved to indicate the default drive (the drive that is currently logged). Thus, the value returned by the **Check_Drive** function is the AL register value *plus 1*. Doing this here is simply good programming, and it avoids having to remember later that the drive value must be incremented when calling another function or procedure.

Having identified the current drive, what about the current directory path? For this task, Turbo Pascal (both versions 3.x and 4.0) has already provided the **GetDir** function, but this must be called with a value specifying the drive and will return the directory path in a string variable as follows:

```
GetDir(Drive: byte; var Path: string);
```

where drive A: = 1, B: = 2, and so on. A value of 0 calls the default drive.

These two bits of information, the current drive and current path, are stored as the string Original_Path, and the string Dir_Path is created for immediate use. Original_Path is reserved until exiting so that the system can be reset to the original drive and pathway, which is simply proper behavior for any well-crafted program (unless you have a deliberate reason for leaving the system in a different state).

The next step, before reading the disk directory, is a bit of housekeeping. This includes setting the First_Item, Mark_Item, and Last_Item as nulls; setting Dir_Count, File_Count, and Total_Size to zero; and using Mark (HeapTop) so that the memory used by the pointers can be released when I'm done (more on this later). Also, since the Dir_Path string will not automatically end with a backslash character (but may have one already depending on how **Read__Directory** was called), one will need to be added:

```
if Dir_Path[length(Dir_Path)] <> '\' then Dir_Path := Dir_Path + '\';
```

Now Dir_Path and FileSpec can be concatenated and terminated with a null character to create Dir_Spec:

```
Dir_Spec := Dir_Path+FileSpec+#$00;
```

The Read__Directory Procedure

Now I'm almost ready to call DOS to get some information. First, I have to tell DOS where it can put the information I want:

```
Reg.DX := ofs(Data_Array);          { Set Disk Transfer Address }
Reg.DS := seg(Data_Array);
Reg.AX := $1A00;
msdos(Dos.Registers(Reg));
```

Data_Array is a 44-byte array that will be the buffer for the directory information. When using interrupt calls, instead of asking for large blocks of data to be transferred via the registers, the **OFf**Set and **SEG**ment values (the address) of a buffer are used. The AX register has the value for the function requested (1Ah) and the msdos(...) call is the same as saying intr($21...).

```
Reg.DX := ofs(Dir_Spec[1]);                      { Find First Match }
Reg.DS := seg(Dir_Spec[1];
Reg.CX := $3F;
Reg.AX := $4E00;
msdos(Dos.Registers(Reg));
```

I've told DOS *where* to put the information, so now I tell DOS *what* I want. Again the ofs and seg values are passed, but this time pointing to Dir_Spec (the wildcard file specification). However, the file mask is not the only item I need to specify. Reg.CX is given a mask value for the attribute byte. The attribute byte is essentially a set of binary flags that operates as follows:

ReadOnly = 01h = 0000 0001   VolumeID = 08h = 0000 1000
  Hidden = 02h = 0000 0010   Directory = 10h = 0001 0000
 SysFile = 04h = 0000 0100   Archive = 20h = 0010 0000

Therefore, an attribute flag of $3F (0011 1111) will cover all values and all files.

Finally, the AX register takes the function value (4Eh, Find First Match), and DOS hunts for the first file (directory entry) matching the file specification and attribute. If the file is found, DOS returns the directory listing in the buffer area (Data_Array).

In Turbo Pascal version 4.0, the DOS Unit provides the **FindFirst** procedure, which accomplishes the same task as calling interrupt 21h, functions 1Ah and 4Eh. **FindFirst** is called with the same Dir_Spec parameter (the Directory, Path, and FileSpec concatenated as an ASCIIZ string), an Attribute parameter, and the variable parameter FileData (the equivalent of the Data_Array buffer).

In version 4.0, if the path is not found or if no matching file is found, Dos Error returns a nonzero value (02h — Directory Not Found or 12h — No More Files).

In version 3.x, using an interrupt call, the AX register returns the error value 12h if no match is found. Or, if everything proceeded correctly, the value in the AX register will be zero. Thus a loop is created:

```
while lo(Reg.AX) = 0 do                           { while not error }
begin
    Add_Item;                    { take care of the current directory listing }
```

and DOS gets the next item

```
Reg.DX := ofs(Data_Array);                       { Search for Next Match }
Reg.DS := seg(Data_Array);
Reg.AX := $4F00;
msdos(Dos.Registers(Reg));
```

using interrupt 21h, function 4Fh, which is otherwise identical to the earlier call for functional 1Ah. When no further matching file is found, the AL register returns a nonzero value.

For version 4.0, after **FindFirst** has found the first file directory entry matching the criteria, the **FindNext** function, which does not require repeating the parameters, is used to find all subsequent matching entries. Again, DosError returns a nonzero value when no further match is found.

When the loop exits (no match was found or no further matches are found), the First_Item pointer is tested:

```
if First_Item = nil then Null_Pointer;
```

because, if this pointer is nil, a call to the **Null_Pointer** procedure is necessary.

Null_Pointer is a precautionary device. If no data file entries have been made, several pointers (not just First_Item) remain without assigned values. (Note that an undefined pointer is an invitation to catastrophe.)

Assuming a minimum of one directory entry was found, each time an entry *was* returned, the **Add_Item** procedure and the **Dir_Listing** function are used to decipher the information in FileData (in version 3.x, in Data_Array).

The FileData/Data_Array Contents

Now that DOS has transferred a directory listing from the disk to the FileData (or Data_Array) buffer area, the next step is to convert this information into a usable form and place it in (semi-)permanent storage. Remember that the next access to the disk directory is going to overwrite the Data_Array buffer with new information.

Before proceeding, an explanation of the structure of the directory listing is in order. Since, in version 4.0, the information in the FileData buffer is already partially "massaged" by the call to **FindFirst** or **FindNext**, the version 3.x Data_Array will be used to show how the file directory information is arranged. (See Figures 5-3 and 5-4.)

Data_Array Contents
```
[ 01..21 ]  — reserved for system use [1]
[      22 ]  — attribute byte
[ 23..24 ]  — file time
[ 25..26 ]  — file date
[ 27..30 ]  — file size
[ 31..43 ]  — file name
```

Figure 5-3 Data Array Contents (Abbreviated)

96

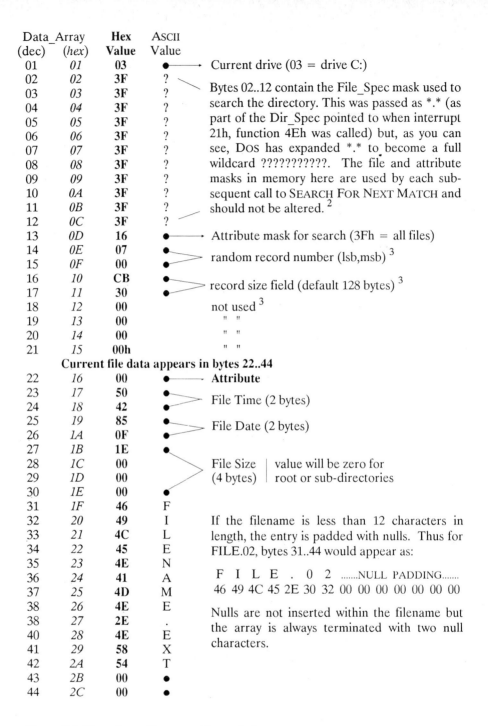

Data_Array (dec)	(hex)	Hex Value	ASCII Value	
01	01	03	●——→	Current drive (03 = drive C:)
02	02	3F	?	
03	03	3F	?	Bytes 02..12 contain the File_Spec mask used to search the directory. This was passed as *.* (as part of the Dir_Spec pointed to when interrupt 21h, function 4Eh was called) but, as you can see, Dos has expanded *.* to become a full wildcard ??????????. The file and attribute masks in memory here are used by each subsequent call to SEARCH FOR NEXT MATCH and should not be altered. [2]
04	04	3F	?	
05	05	3F	?	
06	06	3F	?	
07	07	3F	?	
08	08	3F	?	
09	09	3F	?	
10	0A	3F	?	
11	0B	3F	?	
12	0C	3F	?	
13	0D	16	●——→	Attribute mask for search (3Fh = all files)
14	0E	07	●	random record number (lsb,msb) [3]
15	0F	00	●	
16	10	CB	●	record size field (default 128 bytes) [3]
17	11	30	●	
18	12	00		not used [3]
19	13	00		" "
20	14	00		" "
21	15	00h		" "

Current file data appears in bytes 22..44

22	16	00	●——→	**Attribute**
23	17	50	●	File Time (2 bytes)
24	18	42	●	
25	19	85	●	File Date (2 bytes)
26	1A	0F	●	
27	1B	1E	●	
28	1C	00		File Size | value will be zero for
29	1D	00		(4 bytes) | root or sub-directories
30	1E	00	●	
31	1F	46	F	If the filename is less than 12 characters in length, the entry is padded with nulls. Thus for FILE.02, bytes 31..44 would appear as:
32	20	49	I	
33	21	4C	L	
34	22	45	E	
35	23	4E	N	
36	24	41	A	F I L E . 0 2 ......NULL PADDING......
37	25	4D	M	46 49 4C 45 2E 30 32 00 00 00 00 00 00 00
38	26	4E	E	
38	27	2E	.	Nulls are not inserted within the filename but the array is always terminated with two null characters.
40	28	4E	E	
41	29	58	X	
42	2A	54	T	
43	2B	00	●	
44	2C	00	●	

Figure 5-4 Data Array Contents (Expanded)

The **Dir__Listing** function uses the information in the `Data_Array` to return a string containing the filename and file attributes. This begins by setting the string variable `Temp` equal to the first element of the filename, which is the thirty-first element of `Data_Array`, and then adding each next element until a null, 00h, is found. To make the filenames easier to read, spaces (not nulls) are inserted as padding before the period and extension, and finally the finished string is padded again with spaces for a total length of 13.

```
Temp := chr(Data_Array[31]);
I := 32;
repeat
   case Data_Array[I] of
           $00 : I := 43; { that's the end of the name, cancel loop }
         $21..$2D,
         $2F..$7E : Temp := Temp + chr(Data_Array[I]);
             $2E : begin   Temp := copy(Temp+'        ',1,8);
   { one more test here: since the root directory appears as '.' or '..';  }
   { it helps to check for this before inserting an extra period at the end }
   { of the padding spaces (which would create a string display)           }
                              if Temp[1] <> '.'
                                then Temp := Temp+'.'
                                else Temp := '.'+Temp;     end;
      end; {case}
      inc(I);
   until I > 43;
   Temp := copy(Temp+'            ',1,13);
```

For convenience, the next step is to translate the attribute bytes into an attribute string (separate from the filename). This is a simple looped mask and compare operation except that, if bits 3 or 4 (values 8 or 16) are set, any previous attribute flags will be wiped out (they'd be invalid anyway).

```
Attr_Str := '>      ';
J := 1;
for I := 0 to 5 do
begin
   if (Data_Array[22] and J) = J then
   case J of
      1: Attr_Str := 'R' + Attr_Str;
      2: Attr_Str := 'H' + Attr_Str;
      4: Attr_Str := 'S' + Attr_Str;
      8: Attr_Str := '[Vol] ';
```

```
      16: Attr_Str := '[Dir] ';
      32: Attr_Str := 'A' + Attr_Str;
    end; {case}
    J := J shl 1;
  end;
```

The last steps are to check Attr_Str, increment the directory or file counts, and return the combined filename string (Temp) and Attr_Str.

```
  if Attr_Str = '>         ' then    Attr_Str := '        ';
  if (Attr_Str <> '        ')
  and (Attr_Str[1] <> '[')
     then Attr_Str := '<'+Attr_Str;
  if Attr_Str[1] = '['
     then inc(Dir_Count)
     else inc(File_Count);
  Dir_Listing := ' '+Temp+Attr_Str;
end;
```

This takes care of the string elements in the filename; the size, date, and time items require a bit different handling as shown in the **Add_Item** procedure.

```
    File_Size := Data_Array[27]
              + Data_Array[28] * 256.0
              + Data_Array[29] * 65536.0
              + Data_Array[30] * 16777216.0;
  File_Time := Data_Array[23] + Data_Array[24]*256;
  File_Date := Data_Array[25] + Data_Array[26]*256;
end;
Total_Size := Total_Size + New_Item^.File_Size;
```

The pointer sort routines that follow will be covered fully in Chapter 7.

Turbo Version 4.0 Alternate Directory Access

Although the preceding routines will work in either versions 3.x or 4.0, version 4.0 has now provided virtually identical procedures (with the exception of the **Check_Drive** function). However, my decision was to begin with the interrupt calls in order to show the workings of the directory access from the inside.

Turbo version 4.0 provides the predefined variable type SearchRec for use with the **FindFirst** and **FindNext** procedures to scan directories.

```
type
   SearchRec = record
                   Fill: array[1..21] of byte;
                   Attr: byte;
                   Time: longint; { 4 bytes, contains both date and time }
                   Size: longint;
                   Name: string[12];        end;
```

In a variable of type SearchRec, Time contains both the filedate and filetime fields as a packed value and an UnpackTime procedure is provided to extract the individual values. Otherwise, this variable type can be used instead of the Data_Array and, with **FindFirst** and **FindNext**, could be incorporated in the **Read_Directory** procedure, replacing the interrupt calls now used. (Modifications to use version 4.0 procedures and features are included in the program listing.)

Changing File Specifications

This option is pretty straightforward. Simply ask the user for a string entry with a blank string defaulting to the *.* wildcard and no error checks or any other type of restriction. There seems to be little point (none, actually) in attempting to check the validity of the user's input since an invalid filespec will simply do nothing (and, if this happens, a single keystroke will restore the default wildcard).

When **Change_FileSpec** is called, however, the global FileSpec is not changed immediately. Instead, a local variable, New_Spec is read and, only if New_Spec and FileSpec differ, FileSpec is replaced and the **Change_FileSpec** function returns True.

Change_FileSpec is created as a Boolean function (as are **Change_Drive** and **Check_Selection** in order to return a control flag to the **Display_Directory** procedure. If any of these three functions return True, the loop in **Display_Directory** exits, passing control back to the entry loop in **Pop_Directory** so that new sets of files can be read (disk access is repeated for each applicable change).

Logging a New Drive

The **Change_Drive** function accepts a single character entry (A through Z) and then calls the **Log_Drive** function, which is responsible for determining if the selected drive actually exists and if it is ready for access. These could have been created as a single function, but by making **Log_Drive** a separate function, the opportunity exists to use the IOresult variable (if not returned as zero) to provide information about the drive accessed. (Error trapping will be covered in detail in Chapters 12 and 13.)

Deleting Files

Both Turbo versions 3.x and 4.0 offer the **Erase** procedure for deleting disk files and the **RmDir** procedure for subdirectories. For the current directory utility, however, I prefer creating a single procedure that will act according to the type (file or subdirectory).

The first step, since this procedure is called by a ^D (Ctrl-D) from the directory display, is to get the proper filename:

```
Del_File_Str := copy(Current_Ptr^.Dir_Item,1,13);
```

and then delete any blanks in the string:

```
while pos(' ',Del_File_Str) > 0 do
   delete(Del_File_Str,pos(' ',Del_File_Str),1);
```

leaving Del_File_Str holding the complete file or subdirectory name but without any superfluous blanks (which were used to improve the display) and without the attribute string.

Now, checking Dir_Item for the presence of the bracket character ([) identifies the entry as either a subdirectory or a disk file. In either case, a prompt will query for a Y/N response before actual deletion, but this is a good point to use separate prompts and to remind the user if the entry is a subdirectory (or any other conditions that seem appropriate), for example, Read Only or System flags, special reserved file extensions, and deletion allowed only for certain extensions. If confirmed, then

```
{$I-} RmDir(Dir_Path+Del_File_Str); {$I+}
```

Using {$I-} disables the normal error interrupt handling when **RmDir** is called. Then {$I+} restores the default condition, but now, instead of an error on the **RmDir** call interrupting the program, the IOresult variable can be tested to display a warning message without aborting:

```
if IOresult <> 0 then
begin
   writeln(' ',Del_File_Str);
   writeln(' must be empty');
   writeln('before deletion');
   while not KeyPressed do;
end;
```

The warning message (which covers only one possibility of many) is popped up in the same box where confirmation was previously requested.

If no error occurs, the subdirectory is assumed to have been deleted. Therefore, Dir_Count is decreased and the Remove flag is set (this is used to signal an update of the pointers, removing the listing here also without needing to clear everything and reread the directory).

If the requested deletion is not a subdirectory, confirmation is again requested. Given an affirmative response, instead of using the **Erase** procedure, interrupt 21h, function 41h, will be employed. (No, there is nothing wrong with **Erase**; this is just another route to the same end.)

First, make Del_File_Str a complete path/file string and terminate the string with a null (#$00).

```
Del_File_Str := Dir_Path+Del_File_Str+chr(0);
```

Next, the DX and DS registers are given the OFS and SEG addresses for the first character in Del_File_Str. (As long as DOS knows where to find the start, the null character tells it when to end.) Then interrupt 21h is called to erase the file, and a result value is returned in the low byte of the AX register.

```
with Reg do
begin
    DX := ofs(Del_File_Str[1]);
    DS := seg(Del_File_Str[1]);
    AX := $4100;
    msdos(Dos.Registers(Reg));
    Result := lo(Reg.AX);
    Remove := (Flags and $01) = 0;
end;
```

The result code is not precisely an error code. It does tell you something about the operation, but to find out if the file was deleted correctly, the

```
Remove := (Flags and $01) = 0;
```

statement is the applicable test. If Remove is True, Total_Size (of all listed files) and the File_Count are decreased accordingly.

```
if Remove then
begin
    Total Size := Total_Size-Current_Ptr^.File_Size;
    dec(Filc_Count),
end;
```

If Remove is False (Flags held a value other than 1), the two probable errors are covered as follows:

```
    else
  begin
    writeln(' <',Current_Ptr^.Dir_Item,'>');
    case Result of
      2 : begin   writeln(' is flagged as');
                  writeln(' a directory!');    end;
      5 : begin   writeln(' is Read Only -');
                  writeln('change Attribute');
                  writeln(' before delete!');   end;
    end;                                          {case}
  end;
```

There are other possible errors, such as, if someone had removed or changed floppy disks. (Error traps will be covered in Chapters 12 and 13.)

If the file count has reached zero, the last task is to set up a **Null__Pointer**. If other files remain, **Remove__Item** is called to update the pointer list.

```
  if File_Count = 0
    then Null_Pointer
    else if Remove then Remove_Item;
  Side_Bar;
  Set_Window(2);
end;
```

The Remove__Item and Update__Screen Procedures

The **Remove__Item** and **Update__Screen** procedures are pointer manipulation utilities. The **Remove__Item** procedure creates links bypassing the item to be removed. The removed item is still present in memory but is no longer linked to the list structure and is now effectively lost in the memory.

The **Update__Screen** procedure works quite simply by creating a temporary pointer equivalent to `Current_Ptr`, beginning at the current screen row and rewriting the list from here down.

If you understand pointers, these procedures should be self-explanatory. But, if you do not, detailed explanation will be given in Chapters 7 and 8.

The Fast__Search Procedure

The **Fast__Search** procedure is simplicity itself. This begins by testing the `Key` character (the alpha key entered at the keyboard) against the first letter of the current filename to select a forward or backward search.

For a forward search, as long as the `Key` character is greater than the current filename *and* we have *not* reached the bottom of the list, the list is stepped down as follows:

```
if Key > Current_Ptr^.Dir_Item[2] then
    while ( (Current_Ptr^.Next <> nil) and
       (Key > Current_Ptr^.Dir_Item[2]) )
          do Dn_Line
```

Otherwise, (the Key is either less than *or equal to* the first character of the current filename) the pointer is moved up through the list until the top of the list is reached *or* until the key is *greater than* the preceding item in the list.

```
else
   repeat
      Done := ( Current_Ptr^.Prior = nil );
      if Key > Current_Ptr^.Prior^.Dir_Item[2] then Done := true;
      if not Done then Up_Line;
until Done;
```

The Check_Selection Function

The **Check_Selection** function handles a multiplex task. **Check_Selection** is called when the Enter or Return key is pressed in the main **Display_Directory** procedure. It determines what the appropriate action should be according to the currently highlighted entry and returns a Boolean value used by **Display_Directory**.

The first step is to set Check_Val to a default value of False and to save a working copy of the current directory item as Path_Str:

```
Check_Val := False;
Path_Str := Current_Ptr^.Dir_Item;        { get current item }
```

Next, a decision must be made as to what the directory item is. If the second character is a period (remember that the first character of the string is always a space), this could be either a root directory or a null pointer because the list is empty.

Some assumptions have been made here. If the list is empty, it is assumed this has happened because File_Spec is not a wildcard (*.*). The other half of the assumption is that, if File_Spec were set as a wildcard, there would be something left in the directory, even if it is only the root directory entries. Therefore the appropriate action is to reset File_Spec as a wildcard:

```
if (Path_Str[2] = '.') then
begin
   if copy(Path_Str,2,4) = '....' then
   begin
```

```
      FileSpec  := '*.*';
      Check_Val := true;
    end;
```

Depending on your application and expected circumstances (that is, a *completely* empty root directory) a different assumption and another check and choice of actions might be preferable, but this is your decision.

If the entry is not the null pointer, it must be the root directory (both the single and double periods are assumed to be the same and to refer to the immediate root of the current directory). Therefore, the current path is copied to the Old File variable and the Dir_Path variable is truncated, one character at a time, until the previous backslash is reached. Thus Dir_Path now refers to the root of the presently active directory:

```
else
begin
    Old_File := Dir_Path;
    Check_Val := true;
    repeat
        delete(Dir_Path,length(Dir_Path),1);
    until ( Dir_Path[length(Dir_Path)] = '\' );
```

Now, using the truncated length of Dir_Path, Old_File becomes the current subdirectory name (but don't forget to take the backslash off of the end):

```
Old_File := copy(Old_File,length(Dir_Path)+1,11);
delete(Old_File,length(Old_File),1);
```

The Old_File variable will be used, in a moment, when stepping back up the directory tree, to move the pointer (the highlighted item) to this entry. When moving up the directory tree, pointing back to the branch just left is a courtesy to the user. Thus, if the action was an error, they do not have to hunt for the previous subdirectory but can jump directly back to where they were before.

Programmer's Rule Number IX: Small courtesies pay large dividends.

If the current item was neither the root directory nor null pointer, the next check is to determine if the current item is a subdirectory by checking for a flag (the substring [D should be enough). If this is found, the name is extracted from the entry listing as Path_Str, any spaces within Path_Str are deleted, and Path_Str is appended to Dir_Path together with a terminating backslash (\) to create a revised directory path specification.

```
if (pos('[D',Path_Str) > 0) then
begin
    Check_Val := true;
    Path_Str := copy(Path_Str,1,13);
    while pos(' ',Path_Str) > 0 do
        delete(Path_Str, pos(' ',Path_Str), 1);
    Dir_Path := Dir_Path+Path_Str+'\';
end;
```

As a final step, the Boolean Check_Val must be returned.

```
Check_Selection := Check_Val;
```

Have you noticed a missing condition? What happens if the current file entry is not a null pointer nor a root directory nor a subdirectory? If, instead, it's just a plain old ordinary file?

You might wish to incorporate other checks or features here, but this would be determined by the needs of your application program. For the moment, **Check__Selection** has no provision for any action in such a circumstance, but, on return to **Display__Directory**, a response does become appropriate.

The Display__Directory Procedure

Display__Directory begins by clearing the Select_File variable, displaying the current directory list, and then waiting for instructions from the keyboard (that is, the user). When a key is entered, if a pop-up help screen has been displayed, the original directory screen is restored before any further action is taken.

```
procedure Display_Directory;
    var
        Done : Boolean;     I : integer;
    begin
        Done := false;
        Select_File := ' ';
        Write_List;
        repeat
            i   not PopUp then Hi_Light_Current;
            Check_Kbd;
            if PopUp then
            begin   Restore Screen(1);
                    PopUp := false;    end;
```

The key response (Ch and KCh) is checked first for cursor, screen control, and F1 keys:

```
case upcase(Ch) of
   #$00 : begin
            Lo_Light_Current;
            case KCh of
            #$4B,#$49: for I := 1 to 21 do Up_Line;      { left, pgup }
            #$4D,#$51: for I := 1 to 21 do Dn_Line;     { right, pgdn }
               #$50: Dn_Line;                                { down }
               #$48: Up_Line;                                  { up }
               #$47: First_Of_List;                          { home }
               #$4F: End_Of_List;                             { end }
               #$3B: begin   Command_Help;                    { F1 }
                             PopUp := true;    end;
            end; {case}
         end;
```

Then it is tested for control characters or normal alpha characters (using Ch) if it wasn't a screen control key or the Help key:

```
   #$04: Delete_Current_File;                              { ^D }
   #$06: Done  := Change_FileSpec;                         { ^F }
   #$0C: Done  := Change_Drive;                            { ^L }
   #$0D: if not Check_Selection then                       { CR }
         begin
            Select_File := copy(Current_Ptr^.Dir_Item,2,13);
            while pos(' ',Select_File) > 0 do
               delete(Select_File, pos(' ',Select_File), 1);
            Select_File := Dir_Path+Select_File;
            Complete := true;
         end else Done := true;
   #$11: begin   Select_File := ' ';
                 Complete := true;    end;
 'A'..'Z': Fast_Search(upcase(Ch));
end; {case}
```

If any of the called functions returning Boolean flags are True, Done is set True to allow an exit from the current repeat loop. This sends the program back to **Pop_Directory** (the main procedure) but without exiting from the outer loop. This way, a new directory is read and then displayed.

If **Check_Select** returns as False, the assumption is that the currently highlighted item is a filename to be returned to the calling program. Thus the Select_File variable is given the appropriate information from Current_Ptr^.Dir_Item, deleting any blanks (spaces) within the string and Complete is set True for exit.

```
until Done or Complete;
Release(Heap_Top);
```

Finally, `Release(Heap_Top)` returns the memory used by the pointer heap to the system. `Select_File` must get the current item information before this because, once **Release** is called, the pointer array no longer exists in memory.

The Pop__Directory Function

Pop__Directory begins by calling `Save_Screen(0)` to save a copy of the screen image *as it exists when **Pop__Directory** is first called.* Next, the current drive and path are saved and several variables initialized.

```
Save_Screen(0);
CurDrive := Check_Drive;
GetDir(CurDrive,Original_Path);
Dir_Path := Original_Path;
PopUp := false;
Complete := false;
FileSpec := '*.*)(;        '*.*';
Old_File := '';
```

The present setup is suitable for most applications, but, if required, other defaults are possible. Depending on your application, `FileSpec` might be initialized to select only files matching some default criteria, `Dir_Path` set for a subdirectory (but add an error check in case the path doesn't exist), or `Old_File` could be initialized to point out one specific file (be careful here — if the file doesn't exist, what happens?).

The main control loop comes next:

```
repeat
    Frame_Screen;
    Read_Directory;
    Display_Directory;
until Complete;
```

It operates by beginning with an empty frame, reading the current directory (as set by the `Dir_Path` and `FileSpec` criteria), and then calling the display. When the `FileSpec`, `Dir_Path`, or active drive is changed, the loop in **Display__Directory** is exited to allow the main loop to repeat with a fresh frame, new directory, and display.

Finally, if `Complete` is set `True` (in **Display__Directory**), **Pop__Directory** is passed the string `Select_File`, the system is restored to `Original_Path`, and the entry screen image is restored before exiting.

```
Pop_Directory := Select_File;
ChDir(Original_Path);
Restore_Screen(0);
```

One big consideration here is whether you want to restore the original path and drive or you want **Pop_Directory** to set a new drive and path. In the latter case, it would be best to have your main program determine the entry drive and path and be prepared to restore these on exit. Not only is this a matter of courtesy to the users, but it can also save a lot of angry reboots.

On the other hand, if the person using your application will be (or even might be) calling a series of files, it would be helpful for the application program, when **Pop_Directory** is called, to return the last file and path called so that the user does not have to search back through the directory tree for their previous position.

This pretty well wraps up the directory access demo (except for pointers, which will be covered later). Try it out and see how it works. Many of the features here are intended for hard disk systems, but they function nicely with floppy disks (and also with RAM disks).

Other Features and Options

In the Help display, two items are listed that do not appear in the actual demo program: Attributes and Sort (Sort routines are covered in Chapter 8). Also, one other feature, which might be required by many applications, has not been mentioned at all.

Attributes

The attribute flags are used for various purposes. The **System** attribute is intended to identify a file belonging to the operating system (for example, IBMBIO.SYS or IBMDOS.SYS), and, conventionally, DOS does not permit access to the System attribute flag. Essentially, this is intended to be a "hands-off" flag, protecting the flagged files from direct access by the user.

The **Hidden** flag is designed for a similar purpose: to hide files from conventional directory access. Many directory utilities will not list any file that has either of these attributes set, including DOS's **DIR** command.

Because sophisticated directory programs such as XTree are common, both of these flags seem somewhat redundant. Still, the **Hidden** flag can be used to mask files from casual appearance on directory listings, thus reducing clutter. I do not advise extensive use of this flag because any attempt to restrict access/appearance is quite likely to be more of a headache than a help. Essentially, both of these flags are rather vestigial; they're there but nobody's really sure why.

Next is the **R**ead-Only flag, which does have definite uses. As long as a file is flagged **R**ead-Only, the file cannot be erased (unless the flag is reset). More relevant, in version 3.x of Turbo Pascal (and to a lesser degree in version 4.0), **R**ead-Only files could not be read because Turbo does not open files on a restricted basis. (In Basic, files could be opened for read or opened for write but not for both purposes; thus a **R**ead-Only file could be read without any conflicts.)

The **A**rchive flag is the flag that has the greatest real use in modern systems, especially on hard disk systems. When a backup is created (using the DOS **BACKUP** or **XCOPY** utilities or using other utility programs such as FASTBACK), the Archive flags of the backed-up files are set off (or **–A** in DOS's terminology). After this, any time a file is rewritten (even if there is no change in the actual contents), the Archive flag is turned on again. In this way, backup utilities can identify which files have been changed since the last backup was made.

Note: To manipulate the Read-Only (R) and Archive (A) attribute flags, the DOS **ATTRIB** function can also be used.

Attribute Flag	*Abbreviation*	*Mask*	*Purpose*
Read-Only	R	01h	Read only, no changes permitted
Hidden	H	02h	Hide file from directory
System	S	04h	System use only
Volume__Label	none	08h	Optional label intended for floppy disks
Directory	none	10h	Identifies directory or subdirectory
Archive	A	20h	File has been changed since last backup

Two remaining attribute flags are the **D**irectory and Volume-Label flags. These should not be tampered with except by the DOS calls that set up subdirectories or assign disk volume-labels.

Changing Attribute Flags

To read or set a file's attribute flags, interrupt 21h, function 43h, is available. Thus, to read a file's attribute byte, use:

```
with Reg do
begin
    AH : $43;
    AL := $00;                { select read attribute function      }
    DX := ofs(Dir_Spec[1]);   { set offset and segment address      }
    DS := seg(Dir_Spec[1]);   { for directory specification         }
end;
int($21,Dos.Registers(Reg));
AttrByte := CX;               { returns current attribute byte      }
```

To set a new file attribute, use:

```
with Reg do
begin
    AH := $43;
    AL := $01;                { select write attribute function     }
    CX := AttrByte;           { set attribute byte in CX            }
    DX := ofs(Dir_Spec[1]);   { set offset and segment addresses    }
    DS := seg(Dir_Spec[1]);   { for directory specification         }
end;                          { Dir_Spec must end with null char    }
int($21,Dos.Registers(Reg));
```

In either case (reading or writing a file attribute), the AX register returns an error code if the function fails. The error codes are as follows:

1. function code invalid

2. file not found

3. path not found

4. — n/a —

5. attribute cannot be changed

An error value of 4 is never returned by this function because the flag for 4 is never set without also setting the 1 flag — in effect, saying the function code is invalid because the file attribute in question cannot be legally altered.

Also, attempts to pass invalid attribute codes will return an error code without changing the file attribute. The simple test if (Attrbyte or $27) = $27 then ... can be used to pass the Read-Only (01h), Hidden (02h), System (04h), or Archive (20h) attribute flags, while blocking any accidental attempt to set the Volume Label (08h) or Sub-Directory (10h) flags.

The remaining option is fairly simple but still deserves consideration. **Pop__Directory** allows the user to move through a disk directory and directory tree, to change drives and to return a filename to the calling program. However, you may not always want a filename returned. Sometimes it might be more useful to be able to select a directory path *without* a file specification. Thus a **Path__Only** option responding to a ^P becomes a useful feature (as long, of course, as the calling program can recognize which is which).

This second criterion — that the calling program be capable of recognizing whether the string returned includes a file specification or is only a directory path — can be satisfied fairly simply by insuring the returned string is terminated with a backslash (D:\PATH1\PATH2\etc\) for a directory path only. This way, the calling program can check the last character of the returned string and, if the last character is a backslash, know that no file has been specified.

There is a potential conflict here. When selecting a PathName to pass to **ChDir** (or to interrupt 21h, function 3Bh, **Set Current Directory**), the PathName string must not end with a backslash, with one exception: when changing to the root directory, the PathName string *should* end with a backslash. Depending on your application, you might continue to use the terminating backslash as a flag when returned by **POP__DIR**. However, before changing directory paths, if the path string is longer than three characters (D:\ = root directory) remove the terminal backslash character.

What about a function key for this? A simple CR is already used to step down (or up) through the directory tree and to specify a file. However, something a bit different is needed to give the instruction to return a file path only. My personal suggestion would be to use Ctrl-P (^P, ASCII 10h) and to change the Help screen to read ^Path only in place of the unused ^Print, but you may have a different key/prompt that would better fit with your application. The following modifications will handle the programming task very nicely. In the **Display__Directory** procedure, add:

```
    case UpCase(Ch) of
  .
  .
  .
{ ^L }    #$0C: Done := Change_Drive;
{ CR }       #$0D: if not Check_Selection then
          begin
             Select_File := copy(Current_Ptr^.Dir_Item,2,13);
             while pos(' ',Select_File) > 0 do
```

```
            delete(Select_File, pos(' ',Select_File), 1);
         Select_File := Dir_Path+Select_File;
         Complete := true;
      end else Done := true;
{ ^P }   #$10: begin    Select_File := Dir_Path;
         Complete := true;                    end;
   .
   .
   .

end; {Case}
```

Another programming choice would be to use the PageUp and PageDown keys to step through the directory tree (let PageUp step back one directory level at any time and PageDn step down only if a subdirectory is highlighted) and allow CR to return a file__path__only if a subdirectory is highlighted. This structure can, however, be somewhat more confusing.

Quiz

1. In the **Display__Directory** procedure, the following statement appears:

```
case upcase(Ch) of
   . . . . . .
   'A'..'Z': Fast_Search(upcase(Ch));
end; {case}
```

What is wrong with this statement? Why?

2. The utility call Save_Screen(#) is called to save the *entire* screen image before popping up the directory display (which only fills half the screen) and again before popping up the help display or prompt displays (which occupy even less of the screen). Why waste memory saving an entire screen instead of creating a utility to save only the smaller portion that is actually being overwritten?

3. The ^L key allows logging a new drive. What happens if an invalid drive is specified? If the requested drive is not ready (that is, therre is no disk in drive A:) or the drive is malfunctioning? If an unformatted disk is placed in the drive? If a high-density disk is placed in a standard drive?

4. What advantages, if any, are there in using the functions supplied by version 4.0 instead of the interrupt calls shown as alternatives? What advantages are there in using the interrupt calls?

Solutions

1. Actually, nothing is wrong with the statement except that a few uncommon but valid filenames cannot be accessed by the **Fast__Search** procedure. Normally, all filenames are expected to begin with an alpha character, but there are 23 other valid characters:

```
Valid characters:  ! # $ % & ( ) 0..9 @ A..Z ^ _ { } ~
Invalid characters: sp '' ' * + , - . [ / ] : ; < = > ? ' \ |
```

2. It is possible to create a utility to read only a portion of the screen (see Chapter 2) and to write it back to the screen again. This would save some memory, but it would also be relatively slow. For a very small screen segment, a byte-by-byte replacement can be fast enough to make the savings in memory usage worthwhile. Using the straight equivalence call (Screen := Color_Screen) wastes a small portion of memory but presents a virtually instantaneous change on the screen, which, in most cases, outweighs any waste of memory.

3. Unless the called drive is malfunctioning in such a way as to produce a valid response of some kind, the call to ChDir(New_Dir) will return a nonzero IOresult, and the current drive and directory will remain active. This will happen if there is no disk in the drive or, in most cases, if the drive malfunctions. If an unformatted disk is in the drive, oddly enough, the results may show an empty directory and a close (but not quite) correct disk size. The one real error I have been able to find was with a HD (high-density) disk in a 360K drive. The drive continually tried to read the disk. These are hardly circumstances worth any elaborate error trapping, but additional drive information and error traps will be shown in Chapter 12.

4. Where essentially the same functions are available either by procedures and functions supplied by Turbo version 4.0 or by direct interrupt calls, there is little to choose between, except that using the Turbo calls may provide easier transport to other types of machines (such as an Apple) if and when compatible versions of Turbo Pascal are created for these systems. In other cases, there are useful capabilities that can be accessed by interrupt calls but not by Turbo procedures. The best choice is to be aware of both and to use each appropriately.

POP_DIR.INC Include File

```
{ begin include file POP_DIR.INC here }
{ listing shown is for v3.x or v4.0      }
{ notes show revisions for v3.x only     }
function Pop_Directory(OffSet: byte): string;
    type
        STR80 = string[80];    STR20 = string[20];    STR12 = string[12];
        STR2 = string[ 2];     STR6 = string[ 6];
        Record_Ptr = ^Item_Rec;
      Item_Rec = record        Dir_Item : STR20;
                    File_Date, File_Size : longint;
                            Next, Prior : Record_Ptr;
            end; {record}

(* v3.x change Item_Rec . . . .          *)
(*     Item_Rec = record                 *)
(*                Dir_Item : STR20;      *)
(*             Next, Prior : Record_Ptr; *)
(*             File_Size : real;         *)
(*     File_Date, File_Time : integer;   *)
(*             end; {record}             *)


    var
        FileData : SearchRec;                      Heap_Top : ^integer;
(* v3.x  Data_Array : array[1..44] of byte;       Heap_Top : ^integer;   *)
        FileSpec : STR12;                          PopUp, Complete : boolean;
        Total_Size : real;      First_Item, Last_Item, Current_Ptr : Record_Ptr;
                    CurDrive, Dir_Count, File_Count, Row, I : integer;
            Selected_File, Original_Path, Old_File, Dir_Path : STR80;
```

{ this keeps all the color settings in one convenient location }
```
procedure Accent_Video;
    begin  TextAttr := Red + LightGray shl 4;       end;

procedure Normal_Video;
    begin  TextAttr := Yellow + Black shl 4;        end;

procedure Border_Video;
    begin  TextAttr := LightBlue + Black shl 4;     end;

procedure Border_Accent;
    begin  TextAttr := Red + Black shl 4;           end;

procedure SideBar_Video;
    begin  TextAttr := Blue + LightGray shl 4;      end;

procedure SideBar_Accent;
    begin  TextAttr := Red + LightGray shl 4;       end;
```

```
{ and keeps the window settings together and easy to work with }
procedure Set_Window(WindowNumber: byte);
   begin
      case WindowNumber of
         1:  Window( 1+OffSet, 1,40+OffSet,25);   { Main Window          }
         2:  Window( 2+OffSet, 2,22+OffSet,23);   { Listing Window       }
         3:  Window(24+OffSet, 2,39+OffSet, 7);   { SideBar Window Top    }
         4:  Window(24+OffSet, 9,39+OffSet,23);   { SideBar Window Bottom }
         5:  Window(24+OffSet,11,39+OffSet,23);   { Pop-Up Window         }
      end; {case}
   end;


(* v3.x add                                  *)
(*    function Pad( Pad_Str: STR2 ): STR2;   *)
(*    begin                                  *)
(*       if copy(Pad_Str,1,1) = ' ' then     *)
(*       begin                               *)
(*          delete(Pad_Str,1,1);             *)
(*          Pad_Str := '0'+Pad_Str;          *)
(*       end;                                *)
(*       Pad := Pad_Str;                     *)
(*    end;                                   *)


   procedure Write_Date(File_Date: longint);
      var
         DateRec : datetime;
      begin
         unpacktime(File_Date,DateRec);
         with DateRec do
            write( Month:2,'/',Day:2,'/',(Year-1900):2 );
      end;


(* v3.x use                                                        *)
(*    procedure Write_Date(File_Date: integer);                    *)
(*       var                                                       *)
(*          D_Str, M_Str, Y_Str: string[2];                        *)
(*       begin                                                     *)
(*          str( ( lo(File_Date) and $1F ):2, D_Str);              *)
(*          str( ( lo(File_Date) shr 5 +                           *)
(*                ( hi(File_Date) and $01 shl 3 ) ):2, M_Str);     *)
(*          str( ( hi(File_Date) shr 1 + 80 ):2, Y_Str);           *)
(*          write( Pad(M_Str) + '/' + Pad(D_Str) + '/' + Pad(Y_Str) );  *)
(*       end;                                                      *)


   procedure Write_Time(File_Date: longint);
      var
         DateRec : datetime;
      begin
         unpacktime(File_Date,DateRec);
         with DateRec do
         begin
```

```
                    write( Hour:2,':' );
                  if Min > 9 then write(Min:2,':')
                                  else write('0',Min:1,':');
                  if Sec > 9 then write(Sec:2)
                                  else write('0',Sec:1);
              end;
          end;

(* v3.x use                                                                    *)
(*    procedure Write_Time(File_Time: integer);                                *)
(*       var                                                                   *)
(*          H_Str, M_Str, S_Str: string[2];                                    *)
(*       begin                                                                 *)
(*          str( ( hi(File_Time) shr 3 ):2, H_Str );                           *)
(*          str( ( lo(File_Time) shr 5 +                                       *)
(*               ( hi(File_Time) and $07 shl 3 ) ):2, M_Str);                  *)
(*          str( ( lo(File_Time) and $1F shl 1 ):2, S_Str );                   *)
(*          write( Pad(H_Str) + ':' + Pad(M_Str) + ':' + Pad(S_Str) );         *)
(*       end;                                                                  *)

procedure Frame_Screen;                             { frame for directory pop-up    }
    var
        I : integer;
    begin
        Set_Window(1);
        Border_Video;
        clrscr;
        Box_Line(  1,       1, 40,      24, 2, 2, LightBlue, Black );
          V_Line( 23+offset, 1,         24,    2, LightBlue, Black );
          H_Line( 23+offset, 8, 40+offset,   2,    LightBlue, Black );
        gotoxy(4,1);
        write('< ');
        Border_Accent;
        write(Dir_Path);
        Border_Video;
        write(' >');
        Border_Accent;
        gotoxy(7,25);
        write(' F1 = Help ');
    end;

procedure Side_Bar_2;             { fill in the facts on the current file      }
    begin
        Set_Window(4);
        SideBar_Video;
        gotoxy( 3,1);  write('Current File');
        gotoxy( 2,2);  write('Size:        Kb');
        gotoxy( 8,3);  write('  bytes');
        gotoxy( 2,4);  write('Date:');
        gotoxy( 2,5);  write('Time:');
        with Current_Ptr^ do
```

```
          begin
             SideBar_Accent;
             gotoxy(1,3);
             if pos('[Dir]',Dir_Item) = 0 then
             begin
                gotoxy(1,3);
                write(File_Size:9);
(* v3.x       write(File_Size:9:0);                *)
                gotoxy(7,2);
                write( (File_Size/1024):6:1 );
(* v3.x       write( (File_Size/1024.0):6:1 );     *)
             end else
             begin
                gotoxy(2,2);
                write('Directory or  ');
                gotoxy(2,3);
                write('Sub-Directory ');
             end;
             gotoxy(8,5);  Write_Time(File_Date);
(* v3.x  gotoxy(8,4);  Write_Date(File_Date);      *)
(* v3.x  gotoxy(8,5);  Write_Time(File_Time);      *)
          end;
       end;

procedure Side_Bar;                   { main display for directory pop-up     }
    var
       DskFree, DskSize : integer;
    begin
       Set_Window(3);
       SideBar_Video;
       clrscr;
       gotoxy( 2,2); write('FileSpec =');
       gotoxy( 5,4); write('Files');
       gotoxy( 5,5); write('Directories');
       gotoxy( 2,6); write('Total:        K');
       SideBar_Accent;
       gotoxy( 14-length(FileSpec),3); write('<',FileSpec,'>');
       gotoxy( 1,4); write(File_Count:3);
       gotoxy( 1,5); write(Dir_Count:3);
       gotoxy( 8,6); write( (Total_Size/1024.0):6:0 );
       DskFree := DiskFree(CurDrive) div 1024;
       DskSize := DiskSize(CurDrive) div 1024;
       Set_Window(4);
       SideBar_Video;
       clrscr;
       gotoxy( 4,7); write('Drive = ');
       gotoxy( 2,8); write('Size:        K');
       gotoxy( 2,9); write('Used:        K');
       gotoxy( 2,10); write('Free:        K');
       gotoxy( 3,12); write('System Memory');
```

```
            gotoxy( 2,13); write(' Free:        K');
            gotoxy( 2,14); write('Block:        K');
            SideBar_Accent;
            gotoxy(12,7);  write(chr(CurDrive+64),':');
            gotoxy( 8,8);  write(DskSize:6);
            gotoxy( 8,9);  write((DskSize-DskFree):6);
            gotoxy( 8,10); write(DskFree:6);
            gotoxy( 9,13); write((MemAvail div 1024):5);
            gotoxy( 9,14); write((MaxAvail div 1024):5);
          end;

    procedure Write_Entry;
        begin
            Set_Window(2);
            gotoxy(1,Row+1);
            write(Current_Ptr^.Dir_Item);
          end;

    procedure Hi_Light_Current;
        begin
            Accent_Video;
            Write_Entry;
            Side_Bar_2;
          end;

    procedure Lo_Light_Current;
        begin
            Normal_Video;
            Write_Entry;
          end;

    procedure Pop_Box(TitleStr: string);            { create box for message      }
        begin
            PopUp := true;
            CheckColor;
            Hi_Light_Current;
            Save_Screen(1);                         { but save the screen first       }
            TextAttr := Red + Black shl 4;
            Set_Window(4);
            clrscr;
            Set_Window(1);
            Box_Line(23, 8,40,24,2,2,Red,Black);
              H_Line(23,10,40,   2,   Red,Black);
            Center_Line(24, 9,39,TitleStr);
            Set_Window(5);
          end;

    procedure Command_Help;
        procedure Show_Prompt(VPos: byte; PromptStr: string);
            var
                I : integer;
```

DIRECTORY POP-UP ASSISTANCE

```
      begin
         gotoxy(1,VPos);
         for I := 1 to length(PromptStr) do          { print one character    }
         begin                                        { at a time and change   }
            if PromptStr[I] in ['*','A'..'Z','^']     { color for accent       }
               then Border_Accent
               else Border_Video;
            write(copy(PromptStr,I,1));
         end;
      end;

   begin   { Command Help main }
      Pop_Box('Commands');
      Show_Prompt( 1,'  ^Attributes*');
      Show_Prompt( 2,'  ^Delete');
      Show_Prompt( 3,'  ^File-spec');
      Show_Prompt( 4,'  ^Log drive');
      Show_Prompt( 5,'  ^Path only');
      Show_Prompt( 6,'  ^Quit');
      Show_Prompt( 7,'  ^Sort*');
      Show_Prompt( 9,'    or enter');
      Show_Prompt(10,' <L>etter for');
      Show_Prompt(11,'  fast search');
      Show_Prompt(13,' * not in demo');
   end;

function Check_Drive: integer;
   begin                                     { returns 0 = A:, 1 = B: but        }
      Reg.AH := $19;                         { we want 1 = A;, 2 = B:, etc.      }
      intr($21,Dos.Registers(Reg));          { because zero is reserved for      }
      Check_Drive := Reg.AL+1;               { an undefined (default) drive      }
   end;

function Log_Drive(NewDrive: char): boolean;
   var
      New_Dir : string;
   begin
      New_Dir := NewDrive+':\';
      {$I-}   ChDir(New_Dir);    {$I+}
      if IOresult = 0 then
      begin
         CurDrive := ord(NewDrive)-$40;
         Dir_Path := New_Dir;
         Log_Drive := true;
      end else Log_Drive := false;
   end;

function Dir_Listing: STR20;
   var
      I, J : integer;
      Temp : STR20;        Attr_Str : STR6;
```

```
            begin
                Temp := FileData.Name;
                if Temp[1] <> '.' then
                    if pos('.',Temp) > 1 then
                        while ( pos('.',Temp) < 9 ) do
                            insert(' ',Temp,pos('.',Temp));

        (* v3.x omit preceeding five lines, use following              *)
        (*      Temp := chr(Data_Array[31]);                            *)
        (*      I := 32;                                                *)
        (*      repeat                                                  *)
        (*         case Data_Array[I] of                                *)
        (*              $00 : I := 43;   { that's the end of the name, canx loop }  *)
        (*              $21..$2D,                                        *)
        (*              $2F..$7E : Temp := Temp + chr(Data_Array[I]);    *)
        (*              $2E : begin    Temp := copy(Temp+'         ',1,8);  *)
        (*                             if Temp[1] <> '.'                 *)
        (*                             then Temp := Temp+'.'            *)
        (*                             else Temp := '.'+Temp;      end;  *)
        (*         end; {case}                                          *)
        (*         inc(I);                                              *)
        (*      until I > 43;                                           *)
                Temp := copy(Temp+'             ',1,13);
                Attr_Str := '>     ';
                J := 1;
                for I := 0 to 5 do
                begin
                    if (FileData.Attr  and J) = J then
        (* v3.x   if (Data_Array[22] and J) = J then          *)
                    case J of
                        1: Attr_Str := 'R' + Attr_Str;
                        2: Attr_Str := 'H' + Attr_Str;
                        4: Attr_Str := 'S' + Attr_Str;
                        8: Attr_Str := '[Vol] ';
                       16: Attr_Str := '[Dir] ';
                       32: Attr_Str := 'A' + Attr_Str;
                    end; {case}
                    J := J shl 1;
                end;
                if Attr_Str = '>     ' then Attr_Str := '      ';
                if (Attr_Str <> '      ')
                and (Attr_Str[1] <> '[')
                    then Attr_Str := '<'+Attr_Str;
                if Attr_Str[1] = '['
                    then inc(Dir_Count)
                    else inc(File_Count);
                Dir_Listing := ' '+Temp+Attr_Str;
            end;
        procedure Null_Pointer;                          { this is used when  }
            var                                          { nothing's left to  }
                Null_Ptr : Record_Ptr;                   { point at           }
```

```
     begin
        New(Null_Ptr);                                   { there must be something   }
        Null_Ptr^.Dir_Item := ' .... No Files .... ';   { to point at, so create    }
        First_Item := Null_Ptr;                          { a Null__Pointer that points at }
        First_Item^.Prior := Null_Ptr;                   { itself and point everything else }
        First_Item^.Next := Null_Ptr;                    { to the Null__Ptr; otherwise, you }
        Last_Item := First_Item;                         { will be lost in a twisted maze of }
        Current_Ptr := First_Item;                       { narrow dusty passages leading off }
     end;                                                { in all directions         }


procedure Read_Directory;
    var
        Dir_Spec : STR80;          New_Item, Mark_Item : Record_Ptr;


procedure Add_Item;
    begin
        New(New_Item);              { create (allocate) space to hold this item   }
        with New_Item^ do           { with New__Item pointer begin                }
        begin
            Dir_Item := Dir_Listing;                    { get the filename        }
            File_Size := FileData.Size;
            File_Date := FileData.Time;
(* v3.x omit preceding two lines       { date and time take two bytes }         *)
(*      File_Time := Data_Array[23] + Data_Array[24]*256;   {lsb 23, msb 24}     *)
(*      File_Date := Data_Array[25] + Data_Array[26]*256;   {lsb 25, msb 26}     *)
(*      File_Size := Data_Array[27]                                              *)
(*              + Data_Array[28] * 256.0        { the file size takes     }      *)
(*              + Data_Array[29] * 65536.0      { four bytes              }      *)
(*              + Data_Array[30] * 16777216.0;                                   *)
        end;
        Total_Size := Total_Size + New_Item^.File_Size;  { update the total       }
        if First_Item = nil then                         { if first in the list then }
        begin
            First_Item := New_Item;          { assign first__item to new__item    }
            Mark_Item := New_Item;           {   and  mark__item to new__item     }
            Last_Item := New_Item;           {   and  last__item to new__item     }
            Last_Item^.Prior := First_Item;  { point last__prior at first         }
            Last_Item^.Next := nil;          { and last__next at null             }
        end else
        begin                                { not first so check ordering        }
            if New_Item^.Dir_Item > Last_Item^.Dir_Item then
            begin                            { it goes at the END of list         }
                Mark_Item := Last_Item;      { so save OLD LAST__item             }
                Last_Item^.Next := New_Item; { point last__next to new__item      }
                Last_Item := New_Item;       { make last__item equal new__item    }
                Last_Item^.Prior := Mark_Item; { point last__prior at OLD last     }
                Last_Item^.Next := nil;      { and set last__next to null         }
            end else
            if New_Item^.Dir_Item x First_Item^.Dir_Item then
            begin                            { it goes at the TOP of list         }
```

```
      Mark_Item := First_Item;            { so save OLD First_Item            }
      First_Item^.Prior := New_Item;  { point first_prior to new_item     }
      First_Item := New_Item;         { make first_item = new_item        }
      First_Item^.Next := Mark_Item;  { point first_next at OLD first      }
      First_Item^.Prior := nil;       { and set first_prior to null        }
    end else
    begin
      Mark_Item := First_Item;            { else start at the top              }
      while New_Item^.Dir_Item < Mark_Item^.Dir_Item do
        Mark_Item := Mark_Item^.Next;    { and search down the list          }
                                         { until position is found            }
      New_Item^.Next := Mark_Item;        { point next to marked item          }
      New_Item^.Prior := Mark_Item^.Prior{ set prior to mark prior            }
      New_Item^.Prior^.Next := New_Item; { set prior_next to new              }
      New_Item^.Next^.Prior := New_Item; { set next_prior to new              }
    end;
  end;                  { refer also to Chapter 7, Access to Lists and Records    }
end;

begin { Read_Directory }
  First_Item := nil;
  Mark_Item := nil;
  Last_Item := nil;
  Dir_Count := 0;
  File_Count := 0;
  Total_Size := 0;                             { start everything clear and    }
  Mark(Heap_Top);                              { mark the stack                }
  if Dir_Path[length(Dir_Path)] <> '\'
    then Dir_Path := Dir_Path + '\';           { just checking path string     }
  Dir_Spec := Dir_Path+FileSpec+#$00;          { null terminator on string     }
(* v3.x omit following five lines        *)
  FindFirst(Dir_Spec,$3F,FileData);
  while DosError = 0 do
  begin
    Add_Item;
    FindNext(FileData);
  end;
(* v3.x substitute following              *)
(*    Reg.DX := ofs(Data_Array);        *) { set offset and segment addresses  }
(*    Reg.DS := seg(Data_Array);        *) { of Data_Array buffer as disk      }
(*    Reg.AX := $1A00;                   *) { transfer area address (func 1Ah)  }
(*    msdos(Dos.Registers(Reg));         *) { and call interrupt 21h            }
(*    Reg.DX := ofs(Dir_Spec[1]);        *) { set offset and segment addresses  }
(*    Reg.DS := seg(Dir_Spec[1]);        *) { for directory specification       }
(*    Reg.CX := $3F;                      *) { set attribute for search          }
(*    Reg.AX := $4E00;                    *) { set function 4Eh and then call    }
(*    msdos(Dos.Registers(Reg));          *) { interrupt 21h - find first match  }
(*    while Reg.AL = 0 do                 *) { error if path or match fails      }
(*    begin                               *)
(*      Add_Item;                          *) { add current item to list          }
```

```
(*          Reg.DX := ofs(Data_Array);          *) { reset address for Data_Array    }
(*          Reg.DS := seg(Data_Array);          *) { last Dir_Spec is still active   }
(*          Reg.AX := $4F00;                     *) { 4Fh sets search for next match  }
(*          msdos(Dos.Registers(Reg));          *) { call interrupt 21h - find next  }
(*      end;                                      *)
        if First_Item = nil then Null_Pointer;     { if nothing was found, then      }
    end;                                           { set up a null pointer           }

procedure Up_Line;
    begin
        if Current_Ptr <> First_Item then          { if not at top of list           }
        begin
            Current_Ptr := Current_Ptr^.Prior;     { move current to prior           }
            dec(Row);                              { move row marker up              }
            if Row < 0 then                        { if above top of window          }
            begin
                Row := 0;                          { reset counter                   }
                gotoxy(1,1);                       { position cursor                 }
                InsLine;                           { make space for a new line       }
                Write_Entry;                       { and write it                    }
            end;
        end;                        { otherwise, simply moving the highlight was enough }
    end;

procedure Dn_Line;
    begin
        if Current_Ptr <> Last_Item then           { if not at end of list           }
        begin
            Current_Ptr := Current_Ptr^.Next;      { move pointer down one           }
            inc(Row);                              { move row marker down            }
            if Row > 21 then                       { if past bottom of window        }
            begin
                Row := 21;                         { reset counter                   }
                gotoxy(1,22);                      { position cursor                 }
                writeln;                           { scroll window up one line       }
                Write_Entry;                       { and write the entry             }
            end;
        end;
    end;

procedure End_Of_List;
    begin
        Normal_Video;
        Set_Window(2);
        repeat
            Dn_Line;                               { just keep on going down         }
        until Current_Ptr = Last_Item;             { until we reach the end          }
    end;
procedure First_Of_List;
    begin
        Normal_Video;
```

```
        Set_Window(2);
        repeat
            Up_Line;                                { just keep on going up        }
        until Current_Ptr = First_Item;             { until we reach the top       }
    end;

procedure Update_Screen
    const
        BlankEntry = '
    var
        I : integer;        Final : boolean;        Temp_Ptr : Record_Ptr;
    begin
        Temp_Ptr := Current_Ptr;                    { use an expendable pointer    }
        Final := false;
        for I := Row+1 to 22 do                      { from current item down       }
        begin
            gotoxy(1,I);                                   { set position          }
            if Final then write(BlankEntry)         { use a blank if end           }
                    else write(Temp_Ptr^.Dir_Item); {   else update list           }
            if Temp_Ptr <> Last_Item                { if not at end of list        }
                then Temp_Ptr := Temp_Ptr^.Next     {   move temp_ptr down          }
                else Final := true;                 {   else set flag               }
        end;
    end;

procedure Write_List;
    begin
        Side_Bar;
        Current_Ptr := First_Item;                  { make sure current_ptr and    }
        Row := 0;                                   { row point to the top         }
        Normal_Video;
        Set_Window(2);
        Update_Screen;                              { put the list on screen       }
                                                    { if moving up a directory     }
        if Old_File <> ' ' then                     { tree, instead of starting    }
        repeat                                      { at the top of the new list,  }
            Dn_Line                                 { move down until Old_File is   }
        until ( pos(Old_File,Current_Ptr^.Dir_Item) <> 0 )   { found or we reach   }
            or ( Current_Ptr = Last_Item );         { the end of the list          }
        Old_File := ' ';                            { reset Old_File to null        }
    end;

procedure Remove_Item;                              { and Update List              }
    begin
        Set_Window(2);
        Normal_Video;
        if ( Current_Ptr^.Prior = nil ) then        { at the top of the list       }
        begin
            if Current_Ptr^.Next = nil              { but there's nothing left     }
                then Null_Pointer                   { so, create a null pointer    }
            else
```

```
      begin
         Current_Ptr := Current_Ptr^.Next{ otherwise, step down one        }
         Current_Ptr^.Prior := nil;       { delete pointer previous         }
         First_Item := Current_Ptr;       { and reset First__Item           }
      end;
   end else
   if ( Current_Ptr^.Next = nil ) then    { at the bottom of the list       }
   begin
      Current_Ptr := Current_Ptr^.Prior;  { step up one item                }
      Current_Ptr^.Next := nil;           { delete pointer next             }
      Last_Item := Current_Ptr;           { reset Last__Item                }
      dec(Row);                           { and move Row up                 }
   end else
   with Current_Ptr^ do                   { must be somewhere in middle     }
   begin
      Next^.Prior := Prior;               { point next__prior to current__prior }
      Prior^.Next := Next;                { point prior__next to current__next  }
      Current_Ptr := Next;                { and reset current to next item  }
   end;
   Update_Screen;
end;


procedure Delete_Current_File;
   var
      Del_File_Str : STR80;    Result : integer;
           Remove : boolean;
   begin
      Remove := false;
      Pop_Box('Delete File');
      Del_File_Str := copy(Current_Ptr^.Dir_Item,1,13);   { get filename only    }
      while pos(' ',Del_File_Str) > 0 do                  { if any blanks        }
         delete(Del_File_Str,pos(' ',Del_File_Str),1);    { delete blanks        }
      if pos('[',Current_Ptr^.Dir_Item) <> 0 then         { if not a regular     }
      begin                                               { file                 }
         writeln;
         writeln(' ',Del_File_Str);
         writeln(' is a directory');
         writeln;
         writeln('    Confirm');
         writeln('    Deletion?');
         write('  Yes  (No)');
         Check_Kbd;
         if upcase(Ch) = 'Y' then                         { ask before delete    }
         begin
            {$I-} RmDir(Dir_Path+Del_File_Str); {$I+}      { use std function     }
            if IOresult <> 0 then                         { but test IOresult    }
            begin
               writeln;
               writeln;
               writeln(' ',Del_File_Str);
```

```
                        writeln(' must be empty');
                        writeln('before deletion');
                        while not KeyPressed do;              { just wait for key     }
                   end else
                   begin
                        dec(Dir_Count);                       { delete okay, set      }
                        Remove := true;                       { Remove flag           }
                   end;
              end;
         end else                                             { it's a regular file so }
         begin
            writeln;
            writeln('    Confirm');
            writeln('  deletion for');
            writeln(' <',Del_File_Str,'>');
            write('    Yes/(No)');
            Check_Kbd;
            if upcase(Ch) = 'Y' then                          { delete confirmed      }
            begin
               Del_File_Str := Dir_Path+Del_File_Str+chr(0);  { end with null chr     }
               with Reg do
               begin
                  DX := ofs(Del_File_Str[1]);                 { point to buffer area  }
                  DS := seg(Del_File_Str[1]);                 {     holding filename  }
                  AX := $4100;                                { set function 41h      }
                  msdos(Dos.Registers(Reg));                  { call interrupt 21h    }
                  Result := Reg.AL;                           { test result           }
                  Remove := (Flags and $01) = 0;              { set remove flag       }
               end;
               if Remove then                                 { delete okay           }
               begin
                  Total_Size := Total_Size-Current_Ptr^.File_Size;
                                                              { deduct from total     }
                  dec(File_Count);                            { decrement count       }
               end else
               begin                                          { delete failed!        }
                  writeln;
                  writeln(' <',Current_Ptr^.Dir_Item,'>');
                  case Result of                              { DOS flag returned     }
                     2 : begin   writeln(' is flagged as');
                                 writeln(' a directory!');    end;
                     5 : begin   writeln(' is Read Only -');
                                 writeln('change Attribute');
                                 writeln(' before delete!');  end;
                  end; {case}
                  while not KeyPressed do I := 1;             { wait for keypressed   }
                  Check_Kbd;
               end;
            end;
         end;
```

```
        Restore_Screen(1);
        Popup := false;
        if File_Count = 0                              { if no files left        }
            then Null_Pointer                          { set null pointer!       }
            else if Remove then Remove_Item;           { else remove fm list     }
        Side_Bar;
        Set_Window(2);
    end;

procedure Fast_Search(Key: char);
    var
        Done : boolean;
    begin
        Lo_Light_Current;
        if Key > Current_Ptr^.Dir_Item[2] then         { key says forward        }
            while ( (Current_Ptr^.Next <> nil) and     { not end of list and     }
                (Key > Current_Ptr^.Dir_Item[2]) )     { not found or passed     }
                    do Dn_Line
        else                                           { key says go back up     }
            repeat
                Done := ( Current_Ptr^.Prior = nil );  { not top of list and     }
                if Key > Current_Ptr^.Prior^.Dir_Item[2]  { haven't found first  }
                    then Done := true;                 { prior less than key     }
                    if not Done then Up_Line;          { so, move up the list    }
            until Done;
    end;

function Check_Selection: boolean;                      { find out where to       }
    var                                                { go next in the          }
        Check_Val : boolean;    Path_Str : STR20;      { directory tree          }
    begin
        Check_Val := false;
        Path_Str := Current_Ptr^.Dir_Item;            { get current item         }
        if (Path_Str[2] = '.') then      { first char is blank, check second     }
        begin
            if copy(Path_Str,2,4) = '....' then       { if it's null pointer     }
            begin
                FileSpec := '*.*';                    { then reset filespec      }
                Check_Val := true;                    { and set flag to true     }
            end else
            begin                          { request is for root directory       }
                Old_File := Dir_Path;                 { so copy path to Old__File }
                Check_Val := true;
                repeat                     { trim path back until next \          }
                    delete(Dir_Path,length(Dir_Path),1);
                until ( Dir_Path[length(Dir_Path)] = '\' );
                Old_File := copy(Old_File,length(Dir_Path)+1,11); { get dir name  }
                delete(Old_File,length(Old_File),1);     { trim the last char (\) }
                        { Dir__Path now refers to root of present directory       }
                        { Old__File holds present directory name only             }
```

```
                        end;
           end else            { it wasn't the root directory or the null_pointer      }
           if (pos('[D',Path_Str) > 0) then        { so is it a subdirectory?            }
           begin
              Check_Val := true;                            { yes, set the flag           }
              Path_Str := copy(Path_Str,1,13);              { get the name                }
              while pos(' ',Path_Str) > 0 do                { delete blanks               }
                 delete(Path_Str, pos(' ',Path_Str), 1);
              Dir_Path := Dir_Path+Path_Str+'\';   { and append to Dir_Path              }
           end;
           Check_Selection := Check_Val;                    { return flag value           }
        end;

   function Change_FileSpec: boolean;
      var
         New_Spec : string[12];
      begin
         Pop_Box('FileSpec');
         writeln;
         writeln(' <RETURN> = *.*');
         writeln(' FileSpec:');
         write(' ');   readln(New_Spec);
         Restore_Screen(1);
         PopUp := false;
         Set_Window(2);
         if New_Spec = ' ' then New_Spec := '*.*';          { default as wildcard  }
         if New_Spec <> FileSpec then                       { if there was a change }
         begin
            FileSpec := New_Spec;                  { assign to FileSpec          }
            Change_FileSpec := true;               {   and set flag true         }
         end else Change_FileSpec := false;        { else set flag false         }
      end;

   function Change_Drive: boolean;
      var
         New_Dir: string;
      begin
         Pop_Box('Disk Drive');
         writeln;
         write('Select drive: ');
         Check_Kbd;
         Restore_Screen(1);
         PopUp := false;
         Set_Window(2);
         if upcase(Ch) in ['A'..'Z']                { could be a valid drive   }
            then Change_Drive := Log_Drive(upcase(Ch))  { so try it out          }
            else Change_Drive := false;             { invalid — flag false     }
      end;

   procedure Display_Directory;
      var
```

```
      Done : boolean;    I : integer;
   begin
      Done := false;
      Select_File := ' ';                          { start this off as an empty string }
      Write_List;
      repeat
         if not PopUp then Hi_Light_Current;
         Check_Kbd;
         if PopUp then
         begin    Restore_Screen(1);
                  PopUp := false;    end;
         case UpCase(Ch) of
             #$00 : begin
                       Lo_Light_Current;
                       case KCh of
```
{ left, pgup }   `#$4B,#$49: for I := 1 to 21 do Up_Line;`
{ right, pgdn}   `#$4D,#$51: for I := 1 to 21 do Dn_Line;`
{ down }   `#$50: Dn_Line;`
{ up   }   `#$48: Up_Line;`
{ home }   `#$47: First_Of_List;`
{ end   }   `#$4F: End_Of_List;`
{ F1   }   `#$3B: begin   Command_Help;`
```
                                PopUp := true;    end;
                          end; {case}
                       end;
```
{ use Control characters for directory functions }
{ ^A }   `#$01: ; { change Attribute feature? }`
{ ^D }   `#$04: Delete_Current_File;`
{ ^F }   `#$06: Done := Change_FileSpec;`
{ ^L }   `#$0C: Done := Change_Drive;`
{ CR }   `#$0D: if not Check_Selection then`
```
                begin                      { save the current item now         }
                   Select_File := copy(Current_Ptr^.Dir_Item,2,13);
                   while pos(' ',Select_File) > 0 do
                      delete(Select_File, pos(' ',Select_File), 1);
                   Select_File := Dir_Path+Select_File;
                   Complete := true;
                end else Done := true;
```
{ ^P }   `#$10: begin  Select_File := Dir_Path`{ return filepath only   }
```
                     Complete := true;    end;
```
{ ^Q }   `#$11: begin  Select_File := ' ';`   { return null selection   }
```
                     Complete := true;    end;
```
{ ^S }   `#$13: ; { Sort by extension? See Chapter 8`   }
```
           { and ASCII characters for fast search options }
      'A'..'Z': Fast_Search(upcase(Ch));
         end; {case}
      until Done or Complete;                { Done allows exit to loop in main      }
                                             { Complete allows exit from loop in main }
      Release(Heap_Top);                     { see text notes on release (Heap_Top)  }
   end;
```

```
begin   { Pop_Directory main }
   Save_Screen(0);
   CurDrive := Check_Drive;            { what is the currently logged drive?    }
   GetDir(CurDrive,Original_Path);     { and the current directory path?        }
   Dir_Path := Original_Path;          { save current drive/path                }
   PopUp := false;
   Complete := false;
   FileSpec := '*.*';                  { wildcard as initial file specification  }
   Old_File := ' ';                    { and null setting for Old_File          }
   repeat
      Frame_Screen;
      Read_Directory;                  { repeat this loop until user exit       }
      Display_Directory;
   until Complete;
   Pop_Directory := Select_File;       { check for a filename to be returned    }
   ChDir(Original_Path);               { return system to original drive/path   }
   Restore_Screen(0);                  { and restore original video display in  }
end;                                   { keeping with good manners              }

{ end of include file POP_DIR.INC }
```

POP_DIR.PAS Program

```
{$R-,B+,S+,I+,N-}                                { flags valid for v4.0 only        }
{$M 32768, 0, 655360}                            { increased stack size needed      }
program PopUp_Disk_Directory;

uses Crt, Dos;
   type
      Registers = record case Integer of
                    1: (AX, BX, CX, DX, BP, SI, DI, DS, ES, Flags: word );
                    2: (AL, AH, BL, BH, CL, CH, DL, DH          : byte );
                  end;
   var
      Reg : Registers;   I : byte;   Ch, KCh : char;

{$I NUMB_CHK.INC}
{$I GEN_UTIL.INC}
{$I BOX_UTIL.INC}
{$I POP_UP.INC}
{$I POP_DIR.INC}    { disk program appears as POP_DIR3.INC and POP_DIR4.INC }
                    { for use with Turbo Pascal version 3.x or version 4.0 }
begin   { demo program shell }
   clrscr;
   TextAttr := $6F;
   for I := 1 to 37 do
      write('Background screen display for Pop_Dir utility demonstration ');
   TextAttr := $0F;
   gotoxy(10,10); write('The selected file is ',Pop_Directory(40),' ');
end.
```

6

Attention-Getting Devices

There are times when it seems as though the ideal programming tool would be a small robot carrying a large club with which to beat the end user severely about the head and shoulders in order to get their attention. Unfortunately, such accessories remain impractical (other considerations aside). But the need for commanding the user's attention is not. Fortunately, there are other options short of physical violence, and these fall into two categories: visible and audible.

Audible Cues

In the early days (originating with the old teletype terminals), the bell character (07h) was the only available audio cue, and a variety of schemes were attempted to produce some variation on the single "bell" sound, most of which were notable only for being unsuccessful. With the advent of the IBM PC and clones, the bell present in earlier systems became an unfortunately sustained (and irritating) beep. Many programmers, sensitive to the users' tempers, have hesitated to use this announcement feature except in extreme cases. Other programmers have been less hesitant and some users have simply disconnected the speakers, but these extreme cases are beyond our control.

The duration of the bell sound is the principal flaw because everything halts while the bell is executing (approximately 0.5 seconds per bell versus earlier MS-DOS and CP/M systems' 0.2 seconds).

Turbo Pascal, however, offers the possibility of a variety of sound effects and also allows sustained sounds *without* locking up the system. Actually, once a note begins, it will continue until the **NoSound** command is used to turn it off. However, do not rush to enhance all your programs with an excess of sound effects. Restrained (that is, moderate) and selective use can be effective, but overuse will only be an annoyance.

Programmer's Rule Number X: Too much of anything is too much.

The Sound and NoSound Commands

Turbo's **Sound** command is very simple, accepting a frequency (hertz or cycles per second) and then turning on the speaker. The selected sound continues until a new note (frequency) is set or the sound is explicitly turned off by the **NoSound** command. The sound generator is not a synthesizer — don't expect resonance, complex overtones, or a violin quartet playing the "Blue Danube Waltz." This utility is limited to creating a simple, single-frequency sound with very limited volume controls: on or off.

Assorted Sound Effects

More complex sounds can be created by rapidly changing frequencies, varying the time a particular tone is sustained and varying deadtime between notes. Since these variations can be in increments as brief as $\frac{1}{1000}$th of a second (approximately), complex sounds can be approximated if not refined to emulate actual musical notes and tones or to synthesize natural sounds.

For convenience, two new procedures, **SoundOn** and **SoundOff**, are created. **SoundOn** accepts three arguments: Note, the basic frequency requested; Tone, a multiplier for a frequency range (making it easy to shift octaves); and DelayLen, the time (in thousandths of a second) for the sound to be sustained. **SoundOff** accepts a single argument: DelayLen, the time delay before anything else (such as a new sound) can be done.

The **Beep** and **Bell** procedures each provide brief ($\frac{1}{10}$ and $\frac{1}{4}$ second) notes at 440 and 660 hertz, respectively. These are useful for short, attention-getting announcements, much preferable to the bell character. Unfortunately, the **Sound** command does not offer any volume control (no such option is supported by the system hardware), but soft tones can be created by using brief sounds with delay factors less than 100 milliseconds (for example, the **Bounce** effect with 5 millisecond durations and variable silences between sounds).

Other effects demonstrated are described in the following list:

1. **Alarm** provides a European-style siren effect with an alternating two-tone effect, which could be useful in any circumstance requiring an immediate and important response. This procedure could be modified to continue until a key was pressed (or until the computer was turned off or reset).

2. **BuzzSaw** is simply an irritating sound, but it might have game applications.

3. **Coin** imitates a coin (counterfeit by the tone) dropped on a hard surface.

4. **Falling** is a simple dropping tone effect, incremented in 10-Hertz steps with a brief delay between notes.

5. **MorseCode** imitates a telegraph key, but it doesn't contain any real intelligence. It's also mildly annoying if sustained for any length of time.

6. **Siren** is your typical and familiar oscillating alarm sound but, in most urban areas, is too familiar as background noise to be a good attention getter and would mostly be an irritant.

7. **Woopie** is a bit hard to describe beyond being a fast rising, then falling, sound.

8. **Zap** is your basic electronic sound effect. If you check the code, you may note that this is capable of almost infinite variation. As written, Zap accepts a single integer argument that is used to randomize the precise effects, but a variety of other possible changes are inherent. The formula is complex because the sound produced is complex. If not overused, this is a good attention getter without being overly obnoxious.

Each of these effects either uses a loop ending with a **SoundOff** call or is explicitly terminated with the **NoSound** command.

Applications that use lengthy (more than one second) procedures such as extended disk accesses or long calculations might well announce the completion of these with a brief **Bell**, **Beep**, or even a **Zap**. You might also create your own special sounds to punctuate user errors or invalid entries (such as a *short* **BuzzSaw** effect for an invalid key entry).

Visual Cues

More often, less obtrusive (that is, less obnoxious) cues are appropriate. A variety of visual cues are possible, ranging from using color or reverse or blinking video to set off a key letter or word to emphasize entire blocks or areas of the screen with a color change or other video effect. Visual cues have been used in previous demos (as in **Pop__Directory** for highlighting a selected item), but others are possible. For this purpose, we will look at five procedures (**Change__Attribute**, **Blink__On**, **Blink__Off**, **Reverse__Color**, and **Shimmer**). However, we must first know how to use interrupt 10h.

Using Interrupt 10h

Interrupt 10h accesses the ROM BIOS video driver services. These routines offer display-mode selection, cursor-addressing, text displays, scrolling, and graphics point plotting. At this time, however, only functions 02h (Set Cursor Position), 08h (Read Attribute and Character), and 09h (Write Attribute and Character) are relevant.

Function 02h. Function 02h selects cursor position and video page with the upper left corner of the screen located at 0,0. Since Turbo Pascal uses 1,1 as the upper left, you may prefer to use the **GotoXY** procedure and conventional coordinates or use a minus one (–1) offset with function 02h.

```
gotoxy(X,Y);                    { Turbo Pascal procedure                  }
                    V /
                     / S
Reg.AH := $02;                  { function 02h                            }
Reg.BH := $00;                  { active video page                       }
Reg.DL := X-1;                  { set XAxis-1 in DL                       }
Reg.DH := Y-1;                  { set YAxis-1 in DH                       }
intr($10,Dos.Registers(Reg));{ call interrupt 10h                        }
```

Tradeoffs are involved here. Using the **GotoXY** procedure requires you to use *only* video page zero whereas using function 02h allows you to select any valid video page. On the other hand, function 02h does not guard against coordinates that lie outside the present display mode and that can produce unexpected results.

For the present, function 02h has been chosen for its advantages of somewhat faster execution (as opposed to the **GotoXY** procedure), even though only video page zero will be used.

Function 08h. Function 08h returns both the screen attribute and character at the cursor position.

```
Reg.AH := $08;                          { function 08h        }
Reg.BH := $00;                          { active video page   }
intr($10,Dos.Registers(Reg));           { call interrupt 10h  }
Attribute := Reg.AH;                     { values returned by  }
Character := Reg.AL;                     { interrupt 10h, 08h  }
```

The values returned are byte values (not char values) and may be read from any valid video page. For example, once the cursor is positioned, character and attribute values can be read from any (or all) video pages *at the current cursor position.* Thus a hidden video page can be read without changing the active display.

Function 09h. Function 09h writes both character and attribute values at the cursor position. Using this function, a character can be repeated up to 80 times (but not beyond the end of the current line). The cursor position remains unchanged.

```
Reg.AH := $09;                          { function 09h        }
Reg.AL := Character;                     { character to write  }
Reg.BH := $00;                          { active video page   }
Reg.BL := Attribute;                     { video attribute     }
Reg.CX := 1;                             { replication factor  }
intr($10,Dos.Registers(Reg));           { call interrupt 10h  }
```

Also, with function 09h, carriage returns, line feeds, and so on do not affect the cursor position.

Note: Function 0Ah may be used to write a character using the existing screen attribute.

Change__Attribute

The next step is to put these function calls to use, beginning with the **Change__Attribute** procedure.

```
procedure Change_Attribute( XAxis1, YAxis1, XAxis2, YAxis2, Attribute: byte);
   var
      X, Y: byte;
   begin
      for X := XAxis1 to XAxis 2 do
         for Y := YAxis1 to YAxis2 do
         begin
                { call interrupt 10h, function 02h — Set Cursor Position        }
```

```
Reg.AH := $02;
Reg.BH := $00;
Reg.DL := X-1;
Reg.DH := Y-1;
intr($10,Dos.Registers(Reg));
        { call interrupt 10h, function 08h — Read Character and Attribute     }
Reg.AH := $08,
Reg.BH := $00;
intr($10,Dos.Registers(Reg));
Attribute := Reg.AH;
        { at this point, the AL register holds the character value            }
        { so just leave it alone ... and set the new attribute ...            }
Reg.BL := Attribute;           { — set new attribute value                    }
        { call interrupt 10h, function 09h — Write Character and Attribute }
Reg.AH := $09;
Reg.BH := $00;
Reg.CX := 1;
intr($10,Dos.Registers(Reg));
    end;
  end;
```

The `Attribute` parameter may be any byte value (FFh through 00h) and sets both foreground and background colors as well as the Blink flag.

Blink_On

The **Blink_On** procedure sets the eighth bit of the video attribute to `True` (1) over the specified range.

```
procedure Blink_On( XAxis1, YAxis1, XAxis2, YAxis2 : byte);
    var
        X, Y, Attribute : byte;
    begin
        for X := XAxis1 to XAxis2 do
            for Y := YAxis1 to YAxis2 do
            begin
                    { call interrupt 10h, function 02h — Set Cursor Position           }
                Reg.AH := $02;
                Reg.BH := $00;
                Reg.DL := X-1;
                Reg.DH := Y-1;
                intr($10,Dos.Registers(Reg));
                    { call interrupt 10h, function 08h — Read Character and Attribute   }
                Reg.AH := $08;
                Reg.BH := $00;
                intr($10,Dos.Registers(Reg));
                    { at this point, the AL register holds the character value          }
                    { so just leave it alone, but get the current attribute            }
                    { from the AH register                                             }
```

```
        Attribute := Reg.AH and $80;          { turn on the Blink flag  }
        Reg.BL := Attribute;                  { and return attribute¹   }
        Reg.AH := $09;                        { select function 09h     }
            { call interrupt 10h, function 09h — Write Character and Attribute  }
        Reg.BH := $00;
        Reg.CX := 1;
        intr($10,Dos.Registers(Reg));
      end;
  end;
```

Blink_Off

The **Blink_Off** procedure simply reverses the effects of **Blink_On** (or turns off any Blink flags that happen to be turned on).

```
procedure Blink_Off( XAxis1, YAxis1, XAxis2, YAxis2 : byte);
   var
     X, Y: byte;
   begin
     for X := XAxis1 to XAxis2 do
        for Y := YAxis1 to YAxis2 do
        begin
               { call interrupt 10h, function 02h — set cursor position      }
          Reg.AH := $02;
          Reg.BH := $00;
          Reg.DL := X-1;
          Reg.DH := Y-1;
          intr($10,Dos.Registers(Reg));
               { call interrupt 10h, function 08h — read character and attribute  }
          Reg.AH := $08;
          Reg.BH := $00;
          intr($10,Dos.Registers(Reg));
               { at this point, the AL register holds the character value      }
               { so just leave it alone ... and set the new attribute ...      }
          Reg.BL := Reg.AH and $7F;         { turn off the blink flag      }
          Reg.AH := $09;                    { and call function 09h        }
               { call interrupt 10h, function 09h — write character and attribute  }
          Reg.BH := $00;
          Reg.CX := 1;
          intr($10,Dos.Registers(Reg));
        end;
     end;
```

1. An even simpler statement is:
   ```
   Reg.BL := Reg.AH and $80;
   Reg.AH := $09; { see Blink_Off}
   ```

Reverse__Color

The **Reverse__Color** procedure swaps the three foreground color bits with the three background color bits, leaving the Blink and Intensity bits unchanged. This effects a reversal of the foreground and background colors. If **Reverse__Color** is repeated rapidly for a small area, the effect is, to put it mildly, very hard on the eyes. If a time delay between changes is allowed, irritating can be merely extremely attention getting.

```
procedure Reverse_Color( XAxis1, YAxis1, XAxis2, YAxis2 : byte);
    var
        X, Y, FColor, BColor, Attribute : byte;
    begin
        for X := XAxis1 to XAxis2 do
            for Y := YAxis1 to YAxis2 do
            begin
    { call interrupt 10h, function 02h — Set Cursor Position           }
                Reg.AH := $02;
                Reg.BH := $00;
                Reg.DL := X-1;
                Reg.DH := Y-1;
                intr($10,Dos.Registers(Reg));
    { call interrupt 10h, function 08h — Read Character and Attribute  }
                Reg.AH := $08;
                Reg.BH := $00;
                intr($10,Dos.Registers(Reg));
    { at this point, the Al register holds the character value         }
    { so just leave it alone ... and set the new attribute ...         }
                Attribute := Reg.AH;            { get the old color attribute  }
                FColor := (Attribute and $70) shr 4;
    { get old background color and shift it right for new foreground   }
                BColor := (Attribute and $07) shl 4;
    { get old foreground color and shift it left for new background    }
                Attribute := Attribute and $88;   {   1 0 0 0 1 0 0 0         }
    { now cancel fore and background, leaving blink and intensity bits }
                Reg.BL := Attribute + FColor + BColor;
    { and recombine the two color values with blink and intensity bits }
    { call interupt 10h, function 09h — Write Character and Attribute  }
                Reg.AH := $09;
                Reg.BH := $00;
                Reg.CX := 1;
                intr($10,Dos.Registers(Reg));
            end;
    end;
```

Shimmer

The preceding video utilities work best on color monitors, but they still function on black and white systems. The **Shimmer** procedure, however, is fairly ineffective on black and white, but for small areas on Color systems it is an impressive effect (if also a bit difficult to read).

The trick here is to shift the Attribute byte left one bit (and wrap the left-most bit around to the right. Otherwise, this would quickly turn into $00), with the speed of repetition producing an interesting iridescence on color systems. The precise effects depend on the original color attribute, but most anything produces an interesting result.

```
procedure Shimmer( XAxis1, YAxis1, XAxis2, YAxis2: byte);
   var
      X, Y, Attribute : byte;
   begin
      for X := XAxis1 to XAxis2 do
         for Y := YAxis1 to YAxis2 do
         begin
   { call interrupt 10h, function 02h — Set Cursor Position             }
            Reg.AH := $02;
            Reg.BH := $00;
            Reg.DL := X-1;
            Reg.DH := Y-1;
            (intr($10,Dos.Registers(Reg));
   { call interrupt 10h, function 08h — Read Character and Attribute    }
            Reg.AH := $08;
            Reg.BH := $00;
            intr($10,Dos.Registers(Reg));
   { at this point, the AL register holds the character value           }
   { so just leave it alone ... and set the new attribute ...           }
            Attribute := Reg.AH;
            Reg.BL := Attribute          shl
                   + (Attribute and $80) shr 7;
   { call interrupt 10h, function 09h — Write Character and Attribute   }
            Reg.AH := $09;
            Reg.BH := $00;
            Reg.CX := 1;
            intr($10,Dos.Registers(Reg));
         end;
   end;
```

Multiple Video Pages

Operating in text modes, most video adapters offer the option of using unemployed video memory as "phantom" video pages. By default, the active video page is page zero and Turbo Pascal does not provide any options for accessing alternate video pages. Under MS-DOS (PC-DOS), video page zero is also the active default, but up to seven other video pages may be accessed or switched as the active video page (that is, the page being displayed on the monitor).

The following chart shows the normal video options in text modes 0 through 7 (modes 4, 5, and 6 are omitted because they are not being supported by most systems), but some video cards may offer more (or fewer) pages of video.

Text Mode	Screen Size	Video Display[2]	Video Pages[3] CGA	EGA
0	40×25	B/W	8	8
1	40×25	Color	4	8
2	80×25	B/W	8	8
3	80×25	Color	4	8
7	80×25	B/W	– 8	–

Very few applications (and very few programmers) make use of these alternate video pages, but since pages can be switched virtually instantaneously (certainly too fast for the eye to notice), these offer excellent opportunities that the creative programmer should explore.

Each of these several video pages is effectively an independent video screen, each has a separate cursor, each may have different video attributes, and each may be written to (or read from) independently *and without being actively displayed.*

Note: These are not windows (windows can be used only with the *active* video page) but separate memory video pages.

One possible application might be any program in which large amounts of data need to be maintained ready for display. For example, imagine an accounting system with a checkbook display maintained on one video page, a corresponding ledger sheet on a second, a stock-order record on a third, and a stock-inventory record on the fourth. Properly managed, the user could "flip" through these four displays with each being kept current (but with different information displayed and with independent entry options).

To use these multiple pages, however, the programmer will have to step outside the utilities provided by Turbo Pascal and create page-selective analogs for the **GotoXY**, **Write**, **WriteLn**, and other screen-handling procedures. Toward such an end, analogs for Turbo's **GotoXY** (**Set_Cursor**) and **Write** (**Write_Char**) together with **Select_Page** (chooses which video page is displayed) are shown in **Mult_Screen_Demo**.

---

2. The video display supported is independent of the actual monitor type in use.

3. Values given for video pages are the normal minimums supported by all video cards of this type though some CGA video cards support up to eight video pages in either 40 × 25 or 80 × 25 color modes. Although most monochrome video cards support eight video pages in text mode 7, Hercules Monochrome adapters may only support two video pages.

Also (purely as incidental information), writing a full screen to the active video page requires approximately 0.725 seconds, whereas the same content written to an inactive video page times out at a lightning 0.648 seconds, which is a savings of .077 seconds (approximately 10.6% faster). As for switching the video page to active, the system clock wasn't fast enough to offer anything significant.

The Select_Page Procedure

The **Select_Page** procedure requires one argument, the page number to be made active, and it then calls function 05h, interrupt 10h. The selected video page is displayed immediately. No error checks are made; the value passes as Page is assumed to be correct.

```
procedure Select_Page( Page : byte);
   begin
      Reg.AH := $05;                         { set function 05h    }
      Reg.AL := Page;                        { select active page  }
      intr($10,Dos.Registers(Reg));          { call Interrupt 10h  }
   end;
```

The Set_Cursor Procedure

The **Set_Cursor** procedure requires three arguments: the X and Y screen coordinates and the video page to be used. If desired, **Set_Cursor** can be renamed **GotoXY** and will replace Turbo's original procedure, but it will still require the third argument in all calls.[4]

Provision has been made to correct the X and Y coordinates (from Turbo's 1,1 screen origins to MS-DOS's 0,0 origins), but no provisions are made for window offsets or valid screen limits. Also, this does not affect which page is actively displayed — only the cursor position on the selected page.

If you are using Turbo Pascal version 4.0, depending on how your screen mode was set (using direct interrupts or using Turbo procedures), the **GetMaxX** and **GetMaxY** procedures may (or may not) return valid limits. Test these before relying on them.

```
procedure Set_Cursor( XAxis, YAxis, Page : byte);
   begin
      Reg.AH := $02;                    { set cursor position         }
```

4. Generally speaking, it is not advisable to replace standard procedures with custom procedures using the same procedure name since this can easily result in later confusion. This can be done, but the original procedure will not be available as long as the replacement appears in the program source code.

```
      Reg.BH := Page;              { select video page        }
      Reg.DH := YAxis-1;           { Y-Axis position          }
      Reg.DL := XAxis-1;           { X-Axis position          }
      intr($10,Dos.Registers(Reg));{ call Interrupt 10h       }
   end;
```

The Write—Char Procedure

The **Write—Char** procedure is not an exact analog for Turbo's **Write** procedure although an analogous procedure could be created. Instead, **Write—Char** accepts four arguments: a character to be written, a color (attribute) value, the page number to be written to, and a replication factor called Count, which is a word value even though the normal (default) value is 1.

```
procedure Write_Char( Ch: char; Color, Page: byte; Count: word);
   begin
      Reg.AH := $09;               { write character          }
      Reg.AL := ord(Ch);           { character to display     }
      Reg.BH := Page;              { select video page        }
      Reg.BL := Color;             { set color attribute      }
      Reg.CX := Count;             { repeat Count times       }
      intr($10,Dos.Registers(Reg)); { call Interrupt 10h      }
   end;
```

Since attempting to pass the character directly to the AL register would result in a compiler error message about type conflicts, the ORDinal value is used. This character is written to the video page specified by the Page variable, but the cursor position *remains unchanged*. Only an explicit call to function 02h, with new X and Y coordinates, will produce a new cursor position.

The CX register requires a count or replication value. This is simply how many times the current character is to be written to the screen. A character can be repeated up to 80 times, but it cannot be replicated beyond the end of the current line (attempts, accidental or deliberate, to replicate a character beyond the eightieth column may have unpredictable results).

Normally, a default value of 1 is used here, but replication is useful with character graphics or with blanks used to clear screen blocks. Execution of a replicated character is faster than repeated writes of individual characters and no cursor movement is required. (See the **Write—Box** procedure in the demo program.)

Note that the byte registers (AH, AL, BH, etc.) and word registers (CX) are both combined in this call. There is nothing unusual about this, and in fact the difference is only a programmer's convenience. If you preferred to use only word registers, `Reg.AX := $0900+ord(Ch);` is the same as `Reg.AH = $09` and `Reg.AL := ord(Ch);`. On the other hand, if you wanted to use only byte registers, then, instead of `Reg.CX := Count;`, you could write `Reg.CH := $00;` and `Reg.CL := Count;`. However, in this case, it's simply more convenient to pass the replication factor in a word register than to use two statements (because the CH register should be nulled).

Bonus Effect — Write Without Scrolling

When the eightieth column on the twenty-fifth line is written, the screen is scrolled up one line, leaving a new (blank) twenty-fifth screen line. If you have ever found this particular bug especially annoying (for example, if you were trying to create a border around the entire screen when the screen scrolled up) here's your alternative solution.

This bug occurs when the character (or string) is written using interrupt 10h, function 0Eh (**Write Text In Teletype Mode**). After each character is written, the cursor position is automatically updated. If the cursor is at the end of a line, the new cursor position is moved to the first of the next line; if the cursor is at the end of the screen, the screen is automatically scrolled up and the new (blank) line takes the display attribute of the last character written on the previous line.

Since the **Write__Char** procedure uses interrupt 10h, function 09h, which does not change or update the cursor position at all, no new line is forced at 80, 25 and you are allowed to write anywhere and everywhere on the screen.

Of course, sometimes you do want to scroll the screen. What do you use? For the moment, I'll leave this for you to think about. Remember that carriage returns (#$0D) and line feeds (#$0A) have no effect. (*Hint:* See Appendix C, interrupt 10h, functions 06h and 07h, for possible solutions.)

Some of these effects are, I admit, a bit extreme for most applications and any of these can be thoroughly overdone. By showing you a variety of effects, I trust you will see more possibilities than if I had limited demonstration to only one or two examples. Play with these, try them out, try changing parameters and formulas . . . and have fun.

I haven't said much in this section about changes required for Turbo version 3.x because, first, every change that would be required in any of these procedures has been covered in previous chapters, and, second, if you plan to mess around with this level of interrupt calls for your principal effects, you should be able to figure out any necessary changes.

SOUND.INC Include File

```
procedure SoundOn( Note, Tone, DelayLen: integer);     { Tone is a range: use    }
   begin                                                { 1 for low, 2 for med    }
      Sound( Note * Tone div 2 );                       { and three for high      }
      delay(DelayLen);                                  { delay sustains sound    }
   end;


procedure SoundOff(DelayLen: integer);
   begin
      nosound;                                          { turns off the sound     }
      delay(DelayLen);                                  { delays before return    }
   end;


procedure Alarm;                                        { European-style siren    }
   var                                                  { uses two-tone effect    }
      I : integer;
   begin
      for I := 1 to 3 do
      begin   SoundOn( 1000, 2, 300 );
              SoundOn(  500, 1, 300 );   end;
      nosound;
   end;

                                                        { nice and brief!         }
procedure Beep;
   begin
      SoundOn( 440, 2, 100 );
      nosound;
   end;


procedure Boop;
   begin
      SoundOn( 220, 2, 100 );
      nosound;
   end;

procedure Bell;                                         { a bit longer, different pitch }
   begin
      SoundOn( 660, 1, 250 );
      nosound;
   end;


procedure Bounce;                                       { might be useful in a checking account }
   var                                                  { program to warn about overdrafts      }
      I, J : integer;
```

ATTENTION-GETTING DEVICES

```
begin
    for I := 17 downto 0 do
    begin
        for J := 500 to 700 do
            SoundOn( J, 1, 0 );
        SoundOff( I * 30 );
    end;
end;
```

```
procedure BuzzSaw;                          { this one is terrible!          }
    var
        I : integer;
    begin
        for I := 500 downto 1 do
        begin   SoundOn( I * 10, 1, 5 );
                SoundOff( 5 );              end;
    end;
```

```
procedure Coin;                    { a counterfeit coin to judge by the tone    }
    var
        I : integer;
    begin
        for I := 20 downto 1 do
        begin   SoundOn( 600, 3, 40 );
                SoundOff( I * 5 + random(10) );  end;
    end;
```

```
procedure Falling;                 { try this one in appropriate combination   }
    var                            { with other sound effects such as Coin     }
        I : integer;               { or an extended Bounce                     }
    begin
        for I := 50 downto 20 do
        begin   SoundOn( I * 10, 3, 50 );
                SoundOff( 25 );             end;
    end;
```

```
procedure MorseCode;                { just don't try to read the message        }
    var
        I : integer;
    begin
        for I := 1 to 10 do
        begin   SoundOn( 600, 2, 100 );
                SoundOff( 30 + random(200) );   end;
    end;
```

```
procedure Siren;                                    { US-type siren     }
    var
        I : integer;
    begin
```

```
        for I := 200 to 2300 do
           SoundOn( I, 2, 1 );
        for I := 2300 downto 200 do
           SoundOn( I, 2, 1 );
        nosound;
     end;
```

```
procedure Woopie;                          { or whatever you'd prefer to call it        }
   var
      I : integer;
   begin
      for I := 1 to 7000 do sound( I div 2 );      { run it up fast,        }
      for I := 7000 downto 1 do sound( I div 2 );  { then down again        }
      nosound;                                     { and turn it off        }
   end;
```

```
procedure Zap( Key: integer );        { the Key variable offers easy variation   }
   var                                { note: all ranges used here are prime     }
      I, J, K, L : integer;           {    — they sound better that way!         }
   begin
      for I := 1 to 11 do
      begin
         J := I * 23 + ( 51 - random( Key ) );
         for K := 1 to 5 do
         begin
            for L := 1 to 37 - K * 2 do
               sound( ( L + J + K * 2 ) * 3 div 2 );
            delay( Key );
            inc( J, 31 );
         end;
      end;
      nosound;
   end;
```

{ end SOUND.INC }

SOUND.PAS Program

```
program Demonstrate_Sound_Effects;   { SOUND.PAS }

uses Crt;

{$I SOUND.INC}

procedure Combined;                   { combines Falling and Coin effects   }
   var                                { note: Coin effect uses closing       }
      I : integer;                    { frequency of Falling for best        }
   begin                              { effects                              }
      for I := 50 downto 20 do
      begin   SoundOn( I * 10, 3, 50);
```

```
                SoundOff( 25 );              end;
        for I := 20 downto 1 do
        begin   SoundOn( 200, 3, 40 );
                SoundOff( I * 5 + random(10) );   end;
        end;

begin
    randomize;
    clrscr;
    writeln('This will demonstrate a variety of possible sound effects');
    writeln;
    delay(1000);    writeln('Alarm');            Alarm;
    delay(1000);    writeln('Beep');             Beep;
    delay(1000);    writeln('Bell');             Bell;
    delay(1000);    writeln('Bounce');           Bounce;
    delay(1000);    writeln('BuzzSaw');          BuzzSaw;
    delay(1000);    writeln('Coin bouncing');    Coin;
    delay(1000);    writeln('Something falling'); Falling;
    delay(1000);    writeln('Morse Code');       MorseCode;
    delay(1000);    writeln('Siren');            Siren;
    delay(1000);    writeln('Woopie');           Woopie;
    delay(1000);    writeln('Zap');              Zap(30);
    delay(1000);
    writeln('  Combined effect:  Falling & Coin bounce');
    Combined;
end.
```

CH_VIDEO. INC Include File

```
{ CH_VIDEO.INC }

procedure Change_Attribute( XAxis1, YAxis1, XAxis2, YAxis2, Attribute: byte);
    var
        X, Y: byte;
    begin
        for X := XAxis1 to XAxis2 do
            for Y := YAxis1 to YAxis2 do
            begin
{ function 02h - set cursor position                              }
                Reg.AH := $02;              { select function 02h         }
                Reg.BH := $00;              { active video page 0         }
                Reg.DH := Y-1;              { set the X/Y screen positions }
                Reg.DL := X-1;              { but allow for the 0/0 origin }
                intr($10,Dos.Registers(Reg));
{ function 08h - read character and attribute }
                Reg.AH := $08;              { select function 08h         }
                Reg.BH := $00;              { active video page 0         }
                intr($10,Dos.Registers(Reg));
                { interrupt 10h, function 8h returns the attribute and character  }
```

```
                              { at the screen position designated: on return, AH contains the    }
                              { attribute and AL the character value                            }
            { function 09h - write character and attribute                                      }
                    Reg.AH := $09;                      { select function 09h                   }
                    { Reg.AL already has the current character, so leave it alone                }
                    Reg.BH := $00;                      { active video page 0                   }
                    Reg.BL := Attribute;                { set new attribute value               }
                    Reg.CX := 1;                        { replication factor – 1 char           }
                    intr($10,Dos.Registers(Reg));       { rewrite with new attribute            }
              end;

        end;
```

MULT__SCR.PAS Program

```
program Multi_Screen_Demo;    { MULT__SCR.PAS }

uses Dos, Crt;

    type
       Regs = record case integer of
                  0: (AX, BX, CX, DX, BP, SI, DI, DS, ES, Flags: word);
                  1: (AL, AH, BL, BH, CL, CH, DL, DH           : byte);
                end;
    var
       I, J: integer;      Reg : Regs;

procedure Select_Page( Page : byte);
   begin
       Reg.AH := $05;                           { set function 05h            }
       Reg.AL := Page;                          { select active page          }
       intr($10,Dos.Registers(Reg));            { call Interrupt 10h          }
   end;

procedure Set_Cursor( XAxis, YAxis, Page : byte);
   begin
       Reg.AH := $02;                           { set cursor position         }
       Reg.BH := Page;                          { select video page           }
       Reg.DH := YAxis-1;                        { Y-Axis position             }
       Reg.DL := XAxis-1;                        { X-Axis position             }
       intr($10,Dos.Registers(Reg));            { call Interrupt 10h          }
   end;

procedure Write_Char( Ch: char; Color, Page: byte;  Count: word);
   begin
       Reg.AH := $09;                           { write character             }
       Reg.AL := ord(Ch);                       { character to write          }
       Reg.BH := Page;                          { select video page           }
       Reg.BL := Color;                         { set color attribute         }
       Reg.CX := Count;                         { repeat Count times          }
       intr($10,Dos.Registers(Reg));            { call Interrupt 10h          }
   end;
```

```pascal
procedure Write_Box( Page: byte);
    var
        Color : byte;    I : integer;    Message : string;
    begin
        Color := Page + $70;
        Set_Cursor( 28, 12, Page);    Write_Char( '┌', Color, Page, 1 );
        Set_Cursor( 29, 12, Page);    Write_Char( '═', Color, Page, 22);
        Set_Cursor( 51, 12, Page);    Write_Char( '┐', Color, Page, 1 );
        Set_Cursor( 28, 13, Page);    Write_Char( '║', Color, Page, 1 );
        Set_Cursor( 51, 13, Page);    Write_Char( '║', Color, Page, 1 );
        Set_Cursor( 28, 14, Page);    Write_Char( '║', Color, Page, 1 );
        Set_Cursor( 51, 14, Page);    Write_Char( '║', Color, Page, 1 );
        Set_Cursor( 28, 15, Page);    Write_Char( '└', Color, Page, 1 );
        Set_Cursor( 29, 15, Page);    Write_Char( '═', Color, Page, 22);
        Set_Cursor( 51, 15, Page);    Write_Char( '┘', Color, Page, 1 );
        Message := ' 1/100th Second Delay ';
        for I := 1 to length(Message) do
        begin
            Set_Cursor( 28+I, 13, Page);
            Write_Char( Message[I], Color, Page, 1 );
        end;
        Message := ' Enter key to Exit!  ';
        for I := 1 to length(Message) do
        begin
            Set_Cursor( 28+I, 14, Page);
            Write_Char( Message[I], Color, Page, 1 );
        end;
    end;


procedure Page_Write( Page: byte; WorkStr: string);
    var
        I : integer;   X, Y, Z : byte;    Done : boolean;
    begin
        X := 1;   Y := 1;   Z := 1;                  { initialize values       }
        Done := false;
        repeat                                        { loop until              }
{ Set cursor position explicitly -- function 02h }
            Set_Cursor( X, Y, Page );
{ Write a character to the video page -- function 09h }
            Write_Char( WorkStr[Z], Page+$09, Page, 1 );
{ Update cursor coordinates }
            if X < 80 then inc(X)
            else begin
                    if Y = 25 then Done := true        { at lower right corner   }
                        else inc(Y);
                X := 1;                    end;
{ Update the string position indicator }
            if Z < length(WorkStr) then inc(Z)
                        else Z := 1;
    until Done;
    end;
```

ATTENTION-GETTING DEVICES

```
begin;
{ create four separate video pages }
    Page_Write(0,'   This is the regular video page (#0 -- 1 of 4)    ');
    Page_Write(1,'And this page was written "out of sight" (#1 -- 2 of 4)    ');
    Page_Write(2,'Another hidden page (#2 -- 3 of 4)    ');
    Page_Write(3,'And a third hidden page (#3 -- 4 of 4)    ');
```

{ walk through the four pages of video   }

```
    for I := 1 to 3 do                          { page zero is already active                  }
    begin   Select_Page(I);
            delay(3000);        end;
    for I := 2 downto 0 do                       { now page three is active                    }
    begin   Select_Page(I);
            delay(3000);        end;
```

{ add a box in the center of each page   }

```
    for I := 3 downto 0 do
        Write_Box(I);
```

{ now change pages randomly }

```
    repeat
      repeat
        J := random(4);
      until J <> I;
      I := J;
      Select_Page(J);                    { make the new page active but allow                  }
      delay(100);                        { at least a 1/10th second delay between pages        }
    until Keypressed;                    { so we can see them if only for an instant           }
end.
```

7

Access to Lists and Records (Pointers Versus Arrays)

One of the strengths of computers is their ability to maintain extensive lists of data (whether these are lines of text, structured records, or matrices). Even when dealing with large databases or with large arrays of text data, many programmers are accustomed to storing data either in arrays of records or strings. When they are using Pascal, they run into size limitations that may be much smaller than the available memory in their machines.

By common practice, data arrays are used to hold, sort, and reference such materials, but there is one small drawback in using arrays (if small is the appropriate term). When using arrays, the array must be declared in advance and thus its size and memory allocation are irrevocably fixed by the programmer. For relatively small data sets, these arrays are perfectly fine, conveniently referenced, and offer the fastest possible access. But, for larger data sets, the requirements of predeclaration and fixed data size offer serious disadvantages. First, once a data array is declared, the memory for this array is allocated *whether or not* any actual data is stored in the array. Second, the size of the array can only be changed by rewriting the source code and recompiling. Third, even under Turbo version 4.0, the data segment is limited to a maximum of 64K.

Dynamic Memory Allocation and Pointers

There is another method for data storage, which is based on the premise that any type of data may be written to any area of free memory and may be subsequently accessed so long as the location in memory is known. This free memory is called the *heap* and it begins with a default size of 640K. (See Figure 7-1.)

Of course, once a block or segment of memory is used to store a record, this region must be protected against subsequent overwriting (or the original data will be lost). When the stored data is not needed any longer, provision is required to free the used memory for subsequent applications. Otherwise, the memory could quickly be expended, leaving nothing free for further work. This type of data storage is commonly referred to as *dynamic memory allocation*, and the markers showing where the data is located are called *pointers*. Protecting these blocks of memory against overwriting will be taken care of automatically by the allocation process, but the second provision, to free previously used memory for reuse, must be handled by the programmer and two separate systems, the **Mark** and **Release** and the **Dispose** functions.

In place of arrays, pointers and dynamic allocation offer a number of advantages. First, data storage is limited only by the system's physical memory limits (less whatever portion is already used by other applications). Second, pointer structures are easier to sort, update, correct, and manipulate than data arrays. Third, pointer structures can be sorted *simultaneously* (and faster than arrays) by different record fields and in different orders, and indexed independently by fields. (This will be explained in due course.)

However, pointers also have two disadvantages. First, unlike arrays, pointers are not necessarily indexed directly by matrix coordinates. Second, because of this, the programmer must exercise a certain amount of diligence and care in programming to ensure smooth and trouble-free response.

I am not trying to scare you away from using pointers! Quite the contrary! I very much prefer using pointer structures for their flexibility and strengths over contending with array limitations, but it would be thoroughly unfair of me not to warn you clearly that problems can and will happen if careful programming practices are not followed. Arrays are very forgiving and any errors will usually be very quickly apparent, whereas pointers, if misused, can become your biggest nightmare. However, like all fine tools, pointers behave very nicely once you have learned to use them.

Unfortunately, whether in books on Pascal, C, or assembly language, pointers and dynamic memory allocation are inevitably either overlooked or,

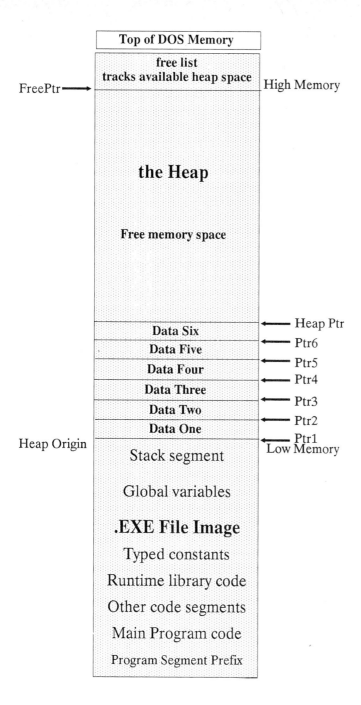

Figure 7-1 Turbo Pascal Memory Map

more often, explained only in terms that make IRS tax instructions appear to be marvels of simplicity and clarity. This is unfortunate because pointers are not so mendaciously complex nor is their use a subject requiring a doctorate in gobbledegook. I trust you will find the following explanations clear, concise, and — most important — useful.

Defining the Data

The first step, whether you're using pointers or arrays, is to define your data and to fit the definition to your application. Your data might be defined as a record of strings, a record of numeric arrays (yes, you can declare pointers to arrays and vice versa, too), or a structured record of a mixed data types. For example, for a checkbook accounting package, the record types might be defined as follows:

```
type
   CheckPointer = ^CheckRecord;
          Status = ( Cleared, Outstanding );
        TransAct = ( Check, Deposit, Other );
     CheckRecord = record
                      Day : integer;    Month : CalendarMonth;
                      case Transaction : TransAct of
                          Check : ( CheckNum : integer;
                                       PaidTo : string[30];
                                        Debit : real          );
                        Deposit : (    Credit : real          );
                          Other : (     Debit : real          );
                      CheckStatus : Status;
                       PriorEntry : CheckPointer;
                        NextEntry : CheckPointer;
                   end;
```

with the following variables:

```
var
   FirstEntry, LastEntry, CurrentEntry : CheckRecord;
```

The variable type CheckRecord is an element of a linked list, so called because each individual record contains the links or addresses of other records. Thus the individual records are joined like links in a chain, and specific records are found by moving up or down the chain. In another case, two sets of links (for example, one ordered by check number and the second by transaction type) might be created to establish a double-linked list.

Other data elements might also be defined, for example, transaction codes (for income tax records). However, once the basic definitions are assigned, I can enter, store, correct, sort, combine, and manipulate these entries, regardless of the size of the data file.

For purposes of demonstration, however, I'll declare a simpler data type and use pointers to write a program that will allow you to page through a text file (both ways, not just down like the **More** command in DOS. The size of the text file is limited only by your available RAM. For this purpose, ItemRecord is defined as follows:

```
type
   RecordPointer = ^ItemRecord;
   ItemRecord = record
                     ItemLine  :  STR80;
                        Next  :  RecordPointer;
                       Prior  :  RecordPointer;
                 end;
```

with the following variables defined as global to the program:

```
var
   TopPage, EndPage, FirstItem, LastItem, CurrentPtr : RecordPointer;
```

First, the RecordPointer variable is defined as a pointer to an ItemRecord. Note that the RecordPointer does not contain any data that we will access directly; each RecordPointer is only a pointer to the address of the ItemRecord in memory. Unlike direct memory access,[1] however, I am not concerned with where in the machine's memory this data is located. All I need to know is that I have a pointer and *the pointer knows where the data is.*

Keeping Track of Pointers

To keep track of the pointers, I simply store the pointers in the data. That may sound a bit like burying a treasure with the treasure map inside, but consider that I could bury one treasure chest with a map showing where another treasure chest is and, in the second treasure chest, a map showing a third, and so on, ad infinitium. Then, all I would really need to keep is a map showing where the first chest is buried. In our example, therefore, I begin with a known (labeled) data point. The pointer variable FirstItem then points

---

1. For direct memory access, see also the **Mem**, **MemW**, and **MemL** arrays (consult your Turbo Pascal manual), which offer direct read from or write to memory at a specified segment/offset address.

to the first block of data, which holds a pointer to the address of the next block of data. This block, in turn, contains a pointer with the address of a subsequent block, and so on until the end.

In most examples (including the example given in the TURBO manual), these pointer elements are defined and used as *forward* pointers only — leading only one way through the maze. If you only want to go one way, this might be fine. More often, however, I am not only concerned with where the Next data block is located, but also where the Prior data block can be found. For this purpose, I've defined two pointers (see the record type definition), one forward and one backward, which will allow movement in both directions through the memory.

Using Pointers

Initially, the RecordPointers FirstItem and LastItem are defined as nil, a predefined value that is compatible with all pointers and explicitly points nowhere. This is used so that none of the elements point to random (indeterminate) locations (which might or might not exist in the machine's memory).

This assignment could have been limited to setting only FirstItem as nil since the other pointers will be assigned values later, but elegance prefers that all elements be cleared. (This is simply another way of saying "it's safer this way.") Subsequent assignments will be used to redirect these pointers to other memory locations.

In the example, standard I/O procedures are used to read a string from a disk file into the local variable, ItemLine (see the **Read_Disk_File** procedure). Since, by assumption there's more than one line of data to read, a repeat loop is used:

```
(1)  repeat
         readln(ItemFile,TextLine)
         New(NewItem) ;
         NewItem^.ItemLine := TextLine;
```

The New(NewItem) command dynamically allocates a record of the defined datatype (RecordPointer), then the instruction NewItem^.ItemLine := TextLine; transfers the string read from the file to the record variable.

Note: Though NewItem is declared local to this procedure *(and cannot be referenced directly elsewhere in the program),* the memory space allocated will remain available until the memory heap is released.

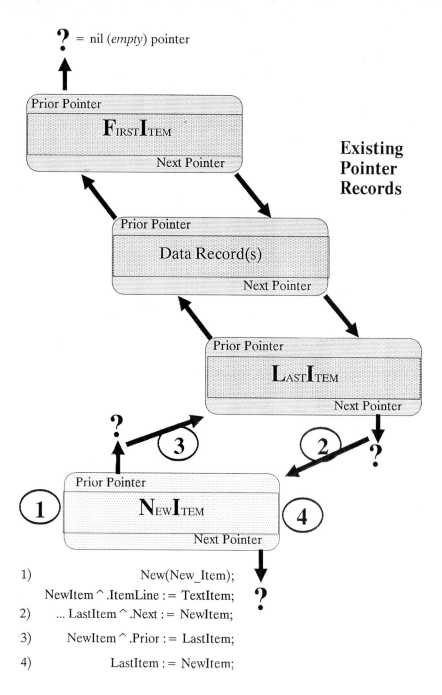

? = nil (*empty*) pointer

Existing Pointer Records

1)   New(New_Item);
      NewItem^.ItemLine := TextItem;
2)   ... LastItem^.Next := NewItem;
3)   NewItem^.Prior := LastItem;
4)   LastItem := NewItem;

Figure 7-2 New Pointer Being Added to the End of the Stack

The next step is to decide whether or not this is the beginning of the data. Is this the first item (line) read? Since this procedure was initialized with the statement `FirstItem := nil;`, if this condition remains `True`, `FirstItem` can be set equal to `NewItem`, which is to say that both pointers indicate the same memory location.

```
(2)  if FirstItem = nil
        then FirstItem := NewItem
        else LastItem^.Next := NewItem;
```

Alternately, if `FirstItem` is not nil (that is, this pointer is already assigned to a location), the `Next` pointer in the current `LastItem` is assigned (pointed) to `NewItem`:

```
(3)  NewItem^.Prior := LastItem;
```

Next, `NetItem^Prior`, the prior pointer in `NewItem`, is pointed at `LastItem` and the `LastItem` is assigned to `NewItem`:

```
(4)  LastItem := NewItem;
```

This then appears to leave both the current and `Next` elements of `LastItem` pointing to the same memory location.

The explanation is simple. In the first instruction, `else LastItem^.Next := NewItem;`, the pointer `Next` was aimed at `NewItem` — but *only* the pointer. In the following step, the *pointer* `LastItem` was reset to correspond to `NewItem`, but `NewItem`'s prior element was still pointed to the *previous* `LastItem` and the previous `LastItem` data record is still in memory — it just is no longer referenced directly; only indirectly through `LastItem^.Prior` or through `FirstItem^.Next`.

The next step is simply housekeeping. The new `LastItem^.Next` (which was `NewItem^.Next`) has not yet been assigned a value, so, as a safety measure:

```
LastItem^.Next := nil;
```

Since `LastItem^.Next` will be assigned a value on the next loop, does it seem redundant to assign a nil value here? Could this have waited until the loop was completed on the next instruction?

```
until EOF(ItemFile);
```

Maybe so, but it's safer this way and it really doesn't cost anything extra.

Once the End Of File is reached, the now-current `LastItem` points to the final block of data, `LastItem^.Prior` points back up the chain, and `LastItem^.Next` is a `nil` pointer and does not point to some random memory location.

What's been accomplished? A datafile has been read from disk into memory using dynamic allocation and two variables (First Item and Last Item) now provide the beginning and ending memory locations. In between, the rest of the material is "hidden," but it is not inaccessible.

Accessing the Data

Initially, three other variables — CurrentPtr, TopPage, and EndPage — were declared as RecordPointers (and global to the program). The **Write__First__Page** procedure begins by setting both TopPage and CurrentPtr equal to First Item, providing three separate pointers indicating the same location.

Now, using the pointer CurrentPtr, the first data string is written to the screen. Then CurrentPtr is incremented to the next location (CurrentPtr := CurrentPtr^.Next) and the process is repeated until a full screen is written (in this case, 23 lines). At this stage, CurrentPtr points to the next (twenty-fourth) line, so EndPage is set equal to CurrentPtr^.Prior (back to the twenty-third line).

Now markers point to the top and bottom of the page (well, actually, to the memory locations where the data is stored), and CurrentPtr is one line *beyond* the end of the page. But, since CurrentPtr will be reset as needed, the present value is not important.

The next trick is to move down in the text file. The simplest move is to add one line to the screen and begin by comparing EndPage and Last Item. If EndPage and Last Item are equal, the end of the data structure has already been reached.

If not, the pointer CurrentPtr is reset to EndPage^.Next (granted, this has CurrentPtr pointing to the same location where it was previously left, but this won't always be true). Then, TopPage and EndPage are moved down one position so that they will still correspond to the displayed text locations. And, last, CurrentPtr^.ItemLine is written to the screen (see the **Dn__Line** procedure).

Similarly, to move up, begin by testing TopPage and First Item. If not at the top of the file, insert a line at the top of the screen, set CurrentPtr to TopPage^.Prior, move TopPage and EndPage back and write the new text to the screen (see the **Up__Line** procedure).

Note: A test for equality or inequality between two pointers is perfectly valid. Testing for greater than or less than, however, only produces invalid results because the memory locations tell nothing about the *ordering* of the contents.

These two simple routines allow rapid movement through the text file, regardless of the file size, but with a large file it would be nice to move without having to individually write each line to the screen. After all, it could be faster to move to a new location and then recreate the entire screen. However, this is still accomplished in essentially the same manner: by repeatedly setting `CurrentPtr := CurrentPtr^.Next` or `CurrentPtr^.Prior`. For a search function, again essentially the same procedure is used, but with the addition of a test for the desired record.

Recall that earlier I mentioned that pointer elements could not be referenced directly by coordinates as array elements commonly are. That is, you cannot refer directly to the *n*th element in the pointer stack; you can only "walk through" until it is found. This is one of the tradeoffs, but it is not necessarily slower (in actual practice) than direct access.

Thus far, this basic structure is applicable to any type of record, not just to the string data used in the example. The following routines are equally useful in a variety of applications, although the example's structure will continue to be used for illustration.

Changes: Insertions and Deletions

Most applications require the ability to alter the data. This might be done in either of two ways: by inserting new data in place of old data at a single memory location or by inserting data in any location.

Replacing a data block or text line at the same memory location as the old data is quite simple and convenient and requires no special tricks. (Likewise, a dataline could be edited, but this type of structure is not recommended for word processor programs. (See the notes on Word Processing Memory Management in Appendix D.) However, we will need to use a few tricks when we must be able to insert new data anywhere within the existing order.

Instead of moving large blocks of text (or any other type of record) to make space, it is much simpler to create a new record by inserting the data into memory using the same `New(NewItem);` and `NewItem^.ItemLine := TextLine;` as when the data was first read from the disk file (see step 1 in Figure 7-3). (This is one of the big advantages of dynamic memory allocation.)

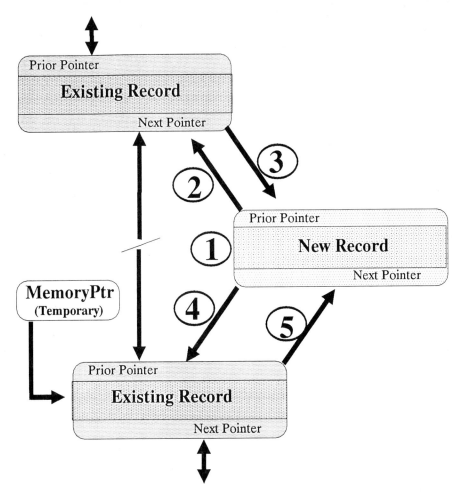

1)   New(NewRecord);

NewRecord^.ItemLine := NewDataLine;

2)   NewRecord^.Prior := MemoryPtr^.Prior;

3) NewRecord^.Prior^.Next := NewRecord;

4)   NewRecord^.Next := MemoryPtr;

5) NewRecord^.Next^.Prior := NewRecord;

Figure 7-3 Inserting a New Pointer Record Within the Stack

The important trick is to set the pointers so that the new data appears in the correct location within the existing data sequence. (Initially, this new data is "invisible" — it's there somewhere and the memory has been allocated, but there's no way to find it.) Obviously, then, the location in the data sequence for this new record to be inserted must be decided. This has nothing to do with the memory location for the record — the actual memory location will be selected by the New command based on available memory space. Thus, to continue this illustration, I'll assume the sequence location has been found and passed to the **Insert_Data** procedure in the MemoryPtr parameter.

The job now is to create the new data record (see step 1 in Figure 7-3) and to provide pointer links to make it appear at the desired point in the data sequence. First, the location pointer MemoryPtr, points to the record that will *follow* the new record. This factor provides the starting point for the links and the process begins by assigning NewRecord's Prior pointer to the data location *preceding* MemoryPtr (see step 2 in Figure 7-3).

Next, change the preceding record (now referenced as NewRecord^.Prior by setting this record's Next pointer to the inserted record (see step 3 or Figure 7-3). At this point, NewRecord points back to its proper predecessor and the predecessor points forward to NewRecord. *Nothing* is pointing forward to the next record in the sequence except the temporary marker MemoryPtr.

Now it's time to point NewRecord's Next to the *location* held by MemoryPtr (see step 4 in Figure 7-3) and, to finish, NewRecord's Next's Prior is pointed back to NewRecord (see step 5 in Figure 7-3).

```
procedure Insert_Data(NewDataLine : STR80; MemoryPtr : RecordPointer);
(1)      var
             NewRecord : RecordPointer;
         begin
             New(NewRecord);
             NewRecord^.ItemLine := NewDataLine;
                     { Note: the following order is important — think about it!    }

(2) NewRecord^.Prior := MemoryPtr^.Prior;
                     { point insert^.prior to location^prior                       }

(3) NewRecord^.Prior^.Next := NewRecord;
                     { point insert^.prior^.next to insert                         }

(4) NewRecord^.Next := MemoryPtr;
                     { point insert^.next to location                              }

(5) NewRecord^.Next^.Prior := NewRecord;
                     { point insert^.next^prior to insert                          }
```

Why use the circumlocution of NewRecord^.Next^.Prior instead of simply referencing MemoryPtr^.Prior? (A similar circumlocution was used in step 3.) Because MemoryPtr is being discarded after this? It was only a temporary reference (a copy of a data record) and the changes would have been lost. If MemoryPtr had been passed as a *variable* parameter, the alternative would have been fine.

NewRecord is also temporary. It is a local variable and will be forgotten when this procedure exits. However, the memory allocation and the data stored will remain, and the correct pointers have been installed in other data records to complete the chain. Thus nothing's lost.

Note: The error *is* deliberate — can you figure it out?

Freeing Memory for Reuse

The Dispose Function

Deleting material does not release the heap memory that was used for storage. Deleted material can be removed, however, by reassigning the pointers. When memory usage is critical, Turbo includes a **Dispose** function that frees the memory previously allocated to a pointer variable. However, this must be done while a memory pointer to this location is still available. To accomplish this, the following procedure might be used:

```
procedure Dispose_Of_Memory(MemoryPointer: RecordPointer);
   begin
      with MemoryPointer^ do
      begin
         Prior^.Next := Next;
         Next^.Prior := Prior;
      end;
      Dispose(MemoryPointer);
   end;
```

and called as:

```
Dispose_Of_Memory(LocationPointer^);
```

where the record pointer (LocationPointer^) becomes a local pointer (MemoryPointer) to the memory location to be deleted.

Before releasing the memory location, the first step is to update the pointers currently linked to this location by replacing the Next record *at* MemoryPointer's Prior location with MemoryPointer's Next and, in like fashion, changing the Prior record at MemoryPointer's Next to correspond to MemoryPointer's Prior.

Note: If this step is omitted, the program will continue to reference this memory location, even after the disposed memory has been reassigned with new data and new links, which will, in all probability, be quite confusing.

When the **Dispose** procedure is called, the memory contents are not erased. Only the freelist — which is the system's method of keeping track of which memory space is allocated and which is free to use — is to be updated to deallocate the memory block and permit the space to be used again. Thus the old information remains, for the present, available.

There is another consideration when deleting a record. To keep the preceding example simple, I've chosen to cover this separately. However, any disposal procedure (and the same is true of insert procedures) should test to see if the disposed record is the *first* or *last* record on the stack, in which case, a new record must be assigned as FirstItem or LastItem, respectively. For this reason, **Dispose__Of__Memory** should be rewritten with a test:

```
procedure Dispose_Of_Memory(MemoryPointer: RecordPointer);  { revised }
    begin
        with MemoryPointer^ do
        begin
            if MemoryPointer = FirstItem then
            begin
                FirstItem := Next;          { reset FirstItem pointer        }
                Next^.Prior := nil;         { set next item Prior to nil      }
                FirstItem^.Prior := nil;    { set new FirstItem^.Prior to nil }
            end else
            if MemoryPointer = LastItem then
            begin
                LastItem := Prior;          { reset LastItem pointer          }
                Prior^.Next := nil;         { set prior item Next to nil      }
                LastItem^.Next := nil;      { set new LastItem^.Next to nil   }
            end else
            begin
                Prior^.Next := Next;                    { pointer forward  }
                Next^.Prior := Prior;                   { pointer backward }
            end;
        end;
        Dispose(MemoryPointer);
    end;
```

The Turbo manual warns against combining the **Dispose** function with the **Mark** and **Release** functions (discussed in the following section) to reclaim the memory used by the heap. If memory is not critical during your program, you might wish to simply reassign the memory pointers (thus bypassing the deleted record) without using the **Dispose** function and then reclaim the entire heap before exiting.

Alternatively, the **Dispose** function can be used during operations, and then, before exit or when appropriate, use **Dispose** again to clear the memory allocation by stepping through the entire heap (or only through part of it).

The Mark and Release Function

Once memory has been allocated for a heap, this memory remains allocated (unless you reset or turn the computer off) and cannot be used by other programs or by your own program for another application. With bad memory management, you can (quite easily) watch your machine's memory shrink until nothing is left.

In addition to **Dispose**, Turbo provides two other functions — **Mark** and **Release** — to reclaim memory allocated to dynamic variables. To use these, declare an integer pointer variable (a pointer to an integer value) by using the variable declaration HeapTop : ^Integer;. Next, before using dynamic allocation, execute the command:

Mark(HeapTop);   {see procedure Read__Disk__File }

Finally, when finished with the data, simply execute:

Release(HeapTop);

The allocated memory is now free for other applications.

In the demo program, Mark(HeapTop) is executed before any memory allocations are made. Thus HeapTop points at the Heap Origin (see Figure 7-4). Other (integer) pointers can be assigned at different locations within the heap. Therefore, the Release(HeapTop2) command will clear all memory from the HeapPtr down to the point indicated by HeapTop2, including the ranges assigned to HeapTop3 and HeapTop4, but not clearing the memory between HeapTop2 and HeapTop.

The HeapTop3 and HeapTop4 variables still hold memory pointers though, so what happens if a subsequent call such as Release(HeapTop4); is made? Exactly what happens depends on where the HeapPtr has located in the interim. Is HeapPtr still below the point indicated by HeapTop4 or has the heap reached a higher point in memory? In either case, the results would not be expected and probably not desirable.

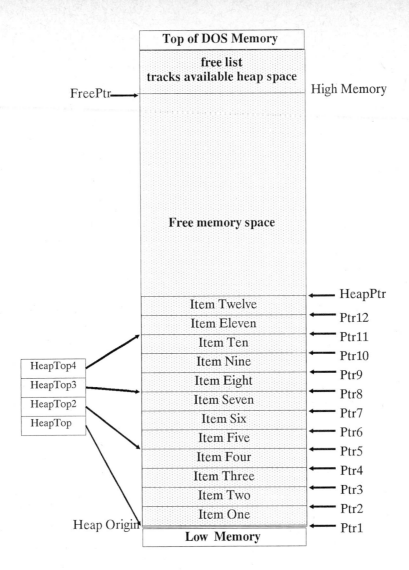

Figure 7-4 Memory Management Using Mark and Release

How do you determine which method to use — **Dispose** or **Mark** and **Release**? To help you decide, the **MaxAvail** (Maximum Available) function will return the size of the largest *consecutive* block of free space in memory. Although this will not tell you about the 20 Kbytes of memory left scattered through your array by the **Dispose** feature, it will give you some idea of your memory usage.

Alternatively, the **MemAvail** (Memory Available) function will show the total free memory available, which will include scattered blocks left by using the **Dispose** feature. The best test, of course, is to check both.

Using the **Dispose** feature has the advantage of leaving blocks of free memory *where new records may be inserted*, whereas using **Mark** and **Release** forces the memory heap to grow even if unneeded space (from discarded but not disposed records) exists within the heap.

If none or only limited additions to the data stack are planned (but always anticipate the worst), **Mark** and **Release** offers the simpler handling. For any extensive application, **Dispose** provides efficient memory management. Choose accordingly.

Other Features

I've given you a brief tour through the ins and outs of dynamic variables and pointer memory access, shown how to insert and delete records, and offered brief comments on freeing memory for reuse. Although this completes a basic toolset, I would also like to offer a few suggestions for other embellishments that may prove useful.

In the sample program, a single pointer set (**Prior** and **Next**) was used to create a simple-indexed structure. For other applications, multi-indexed structures offer advantages of complex ordering (creating separate record orders according to index fields) that cannot be achieved with array structures.

Similarly, Turbo's B-Trees File Management (included in Borland's *Turbo Pascal Database Toolbox*) can be incorporated to manage a pointer structure for convenient operation on large database systems. Most commercial databases are cumbersome, force the user to adapt to their structure, and, in general, tend to be more trouble than they're worth. Using dynamic variables and Turbo's B-Trees, you can create your own database easily tailored to any application you desire. You can also enjoy fast, efficient, and convenient operation (probably much faster and definitely much more efficient and convenient than the commercial versions).

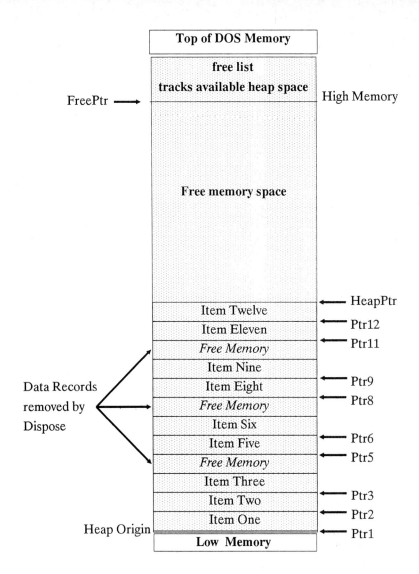

Figure 7-5 Deleting Records Using Dispose

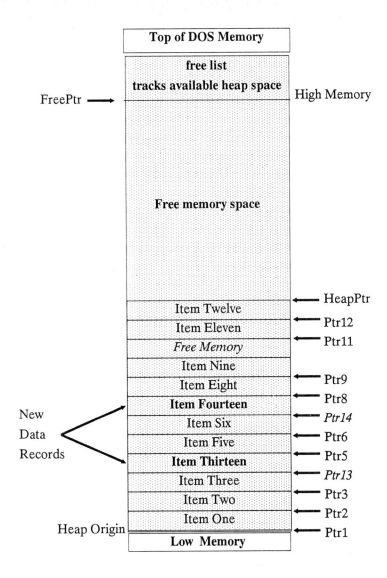

Figure 7-6 Adding New Records After Using Dispose

What could be faster for sorting any type of record material than simply reassigning the pointers? That's right, just leave the material where it is and shift pointers. When refiled on disk, the material is stored in the new order or may be used for any other application, and it also works well with Turbo's Quicksort (also included in Borland's Database Toolbox).

Chapter 8 will cover multi-indexed structures, complex sorts, and a few advanced features possible with dynamic variables, but the demo program here will show the basic uses of dynamic variables. I suggest trying this with any ASCII text file (so long as the line lengths are 80 characters or less).

Quiz

1. In discuing the **Insert_Data** procedure, I asked why the circumlocution of NewRecord^.Next^.Prior was used instead of simply referencing MemoryPtr^.Prior and suggested that the reason was because MemoryPtr was a temporary (local) reference that might have been passed as a *variable* parameter instead. I also suggested that a red herring was hidden here and that you should figure it out. If you haven't yet, consider the following alternative steps 3 through 5:

```
NewRecord^.Prior^.Next := NewRecord;   V  MemoryPtr^.Prior^.Next := NewRecord;
NewRecord^.Next := MemoryPtr;          /  NewRecord^.Next      :=   MemoryPtr;
NewRecord^.Next^.Prior := NewRecord;   S  MemoryPtr^.Next^.Prior := NewRecord;
```

Is any data lost by using the right-hand set of instructions? Why or why not?

2. A brief recommendation was made against using the pointer record structure for word processor programs, but no reasons were specified. Can you suggest two reasons for this recommendation and what type of memory management would be more appropriate? (After all, using pointers and dynamic memory management worked very nicely with the text file in the demo program.)

3. Using the **Dispose** procedure, memory space was freed and then later new information was inserted in the freed memory. Were any precautions used to ensure that new information would fit correctly in the free space? What would have happened if insufficient free space was located in a single segment?

4. In the revised **Dispose_Of_Memory** procedure, three steps were used to remove a record from the first of the chain:

```
with MemoryPtr^ do
    if MemoryPointer = FirstItem then
```

```
begin
    FirstItem := Next;
    Next^.Prior := nil;
    FirstItem^.Prior := nil;
end;
```

What is wrong with the preceding code? No, this is not a red herring. The minor error was mine, which shows how easily pointers can be mismanaged even with the greatest care. Identify and correct the mistake.

Solutions

1. This is a bit more than simply a loaded question. This is the one element that seems to cause more confusion about pointers than anything else. In a very real sense, all pointers are temporary refrences and the *pointer* NewRecord is no more and no less ephemeral than the *pointer* MemoryPtr. Using either pointer — since both, after the first step point to the *same* memory location — is equally valid because the *only* important element is the actual data written to the allocated memory location. And, didn't I say almost exactly that in referring to `NewRecord` right before I warned you that something was being slipped by? Understanding this one vital fact will save you a great deal of trouble in the future.

   The deliberate error was simply the *suggestion* that using a local parameter *pointer* might cause data to be lost and that passing a variable parameter would help. Remember that what's real is the data located in the memory heap. Temporary pointers can be created all day long, used to change the heap data, and then discarded again without losing the heap data unless, of course, you make an error in the pointers stored *in the data*.

2. The key to my objection on using a pointer record structure for word processing is two-fold. First, any type of record is inefficient in terms of memory usage because the record size is fixed regardless of the size of the contents. Second, the use of a record also restricts the maximum permissible line length, which is again either inefficient (if very long lines are allowed) or restrictive (if a reasonable average length is selected).

   For a notepad or some other limited-feature, limited-size word processor, a record structure may be perfectly appropriate and considerations of handling and record reference overweigh the inefficient aspects. For a full-featured word processor, however, some other type of memory management becomes more appropriate. It may require that you, the programmer, exercise considerably greater control over the heap. See also Appendix E.

3. Since the procedure demonstrated was using a single type of record, all of the data records were precisely the same size and the fit was automatic. If two (or more) different record types with different record sizes were in use, the situation would also be quite different. The **New** and **Dispose** procedures would continue to manage the memory allocation and handling in an essentially transparent fashion.

If a smaller record were written to the space previously allocated to a larger record of a different type, the remaining memory would continue to be *free space*, even if it were a block too small for any practical use in the current circumstances. Some memory would be, essentially, wasted. If such a situation became critical, one alternative would be to write all data back to disk records, free the heap memory using **Dispose**, and then read the information back into memory (which would both create a reordered data structure and "stack" the data efficiently). If such a situation arose, however, the best solution would be to find an alternative handling requiring fewer active records in memory.

4. The code as shown will *function* correctly and without error, but it does contain an unimportant redundancy. In the first step, FirstItem is reassigned to (MemoryPtr^.)Next;. After this, the following two steps accomplish exactly the same task because *now* both (MemoryPtr^.)Next and FirstItem point to the same data record and there is no need to set the Prior element of this data record equal to nil twice.

It's an easy error to make, being disguised both by habit and by the appearance of these being different variables, and a difficult error to find since the program functions quite correctly despite the mistake. The same error also occurs in the second instance, if MemoryPtr = LastItem, and, as I mentioned, both of these were my errors originally. I have allowed them to stand because they provide excellent examples of how easily pointer identities can be overlooked because of different labels. If you would like, you can now draw a line through two of the redundant statements as future reminders of the subtlety of possible error. (I suggest striking the Next^.prior := nil; statement.)

POINTER.PAS Demo Program

```pascal
program Basic_Use_Of_Pascal_Pointer_Structures;   { POINTER.PAS }
  uses Crt;
  type
    STR80 = string[80];          STR20 = string[20];
    RecordPointer = ^ItemRecord;
```

```
ItemRecord = record
                ItemLine : STR80;      { use any type of record structure   }
                   Next : RecordPointer;
                  Prior : RecordPointer;
              end; {record}
  var
     TopPage, EndPage, FirstItem, LastItem, CurrentPtr : RecordPointer;
     FileName : string;          Done : boolean;          I : integer;
      HeapTop : ^Integer;             { HeapTop is a pointer to an integer value   }

procedure Idiot_Message(MessageText: STR20);
   begin
      ClrScr;
      gotoxy(30,10);
      writeln(MessageText);
   end;


procedure Read_Disk_File;
   var
       NewItem : RecordPointer;               { Pointers for local use only   }
      TextLine : STR80;
      ItemFile : text;
   begin
      FirstItem := nil;                 { Nil is a general purpose empty pointer   }
      LastItem := nil;
      Mark(HeapTop);                    { This will allow us to free the memory   }
                                        {    used when we're done with everything }
      assign(ItemFile,FileName);        { This opens the file as ItemFile   }
      {$I-}                             { We turn off error checking before   }
      reset(ItemFile);                  {    positioning Turbo's filepointer at   }
                                        {    the beginning of the file but, don't   }
      {$I+}                             {    forget to turn it back on again!   }
      Done := (IOresult <> 0);          { Now test to see if the file exists   }
      if not Done then                  { If it does, we can start   }
      begin
          Idiot_Message('Reading '+FileName);
          repeat
             readln(ItemFile,TextLine);
             New(NewItem);                      { Create a new record in the heap   }
             NewItem^.ItemLine := TextLine;
             if FirstItem = nil                 { if we're at the top then   }
                then FirstItem := NewItem        {    set FirstItem else set   }
                else LastItem^.Next := NewItem;  {    LastItem^.Next pointer   }
             NewItem^.Prior := LastItem;         { Point back to current last   }
             LastItem := NewItem;                { Reset last item to new   }
             LastItem^.Next := nil;              {    and set this Next to nil   }
          until EOF(ItemFile);                   { Until we've got it all!   }
      close(ItemFile);
      end else Idiot_Message('Sorry, Boss - you goofed somehow!');
   end;
```

ACCESS TO LISTS AND RECORDS

```
procedure Up_Line;
  begin
    CurrentPtr := TopPage;                      { Set pointer to top of page      }
    if CurrentPtr <> FirstItem then             { If not at the first of file     }
    begin
      CurrentPtr := TopPage^.Prior;             { move it up one line             }
      TopPage := TopPage^.Prior;                { move the top up                 }
      EndPage := EndPage^.Prior;                { and the bottom up               }
      GotoXY(1,1);                              { position the cursor             }
      InsLine;                                  { insert a new line               }
      with CurrentPtr^ do
        write(ItemLine);                        { and print the line              }
    end;
  end;

procedure Dn_Line;
  begin
    CurrentPtr := EndPage;                       { Set pointer to end of page      }
    if CurrentPtr <> LastItem then               { If not at end of file then      }
    begin
      CurrentPtr := EndPage^.Next;               { move it down one line           }
      TopPage := TopPage^.Next;                  { move the top down               }
      EndPage := EndPage^.Next;                  { and the bottom down             }
      GotoXY(1,24); ClrEol;                      { position the cursor             }
      with CurrentPtr^ do
        writeln(ItemLine);                       { and print the line              }
    end;
  end;

procedure Write_First_Page;
  begin
    TopPage := FirstItem;                        { Set both pointers to the first of }
    CurrentPtr := FirstItem;                     {    the file to begin              }
    ClrScr;
    for I := 1 to 23 do
    begin
      writeln(CurrentPtr^.ItemLine);             { write this line on the screen,    }
      CurrentPtr := CurrentPtr^.Next;            {    move CurrentPtr pointer down    }
    end;
    EndPage := CurrentPtr^.Prior;                { CurrentPtr is past end of screen  }
  end;                                           {    so EndPage is set back one      }

procedure Display_Lines;
  var
    Ch, KCh : char;
  begin
    Write_First_Page;                            { Blank screens are so bland so we'll }
    repeat                                       {    get some text up in a hurry      }
      Ch := readkey;                             { Now wait for instructions           }
      case upcase(Ch) of
```

```
      #$00 : begin                              { If the first character was null    }
                 KCh := readkey;      { (#$00), read next character       }
                 case KCh of
                     'H' : for I := 1 to 23 do Up_Line;      { Up       }
                     'P' : for I := 1 to 23 do Dn_Line;      { Down     }
                     'K' : Dn_Line;                          { Left     }
                     'M' : Up_Line;                          { Right    }
                     'G' : Write_First_Page;                 { Home     }
                 end; {case KCh}
            end;
         'Q': Done := true;           { Guess we're ready to quit now      }
      end; { case Ch }
   until Done;                        { We're ready to exit - Now we can   }
   Release(HeapTop);                  { release the memory used by the heap }
end;


begin
   FileName := 'YOURTEXT.TXT';  { one of the nicest things about Pascal is    }
   Read_Disk_File;              { that the documentation can be inherent in   }
   Display_Lines;               { the names of procedures and variables - thus }
end.                            { few other comments are required             }
```

8

Indexed and Sorted Lists

Having seen the basic principles involved in handling dynamic memory structures, you are now ready to consider some of the more interesting capabilities made possible by using pointer references. These include data sorting, data structures with multiple indexes (multiple sort orders), and data search procedures.

Basic Sorting Algorithms and Methods

Traditionally, sorting data has been a time-consuming process. A variety of sort routines have been created to avoid waiting for completion of such tasks, including bubble sorts (widely recognized as one of the *slowest* sorting algorithms created), indexed sorts, and others.

Three basic sorting algorithms are covered here: Simple Sort, Entry Sort, and Quick Sort. Details on other methods available from many sources are not the topic at this time. Note, however, that Turbo Sort (included in the Turbo Pascal Database Toolbox and called Quicksort in early versions) and a variety of other commercially available speed sort utilities can be used with pointer structures as well as with data arrays.

When sorting a conventional array of data in memory, the simplest sorting algorithm begins with two loops:

```
for I := 1 to ArraySize-1 do
for J := I to ArraySize do
```

tests successive pairs of elements for proper order:

```
if ArrayItem[I] > ArrayItem[J] then
begin
```

and exchanges these if the test condition(s) are met:

```
    TempItem := ArrayItem[I];
    ArrayItem[I] := ArrayItem[J];
    ArrayItem[J] := TempItem;
end;
```

In this type of sort, many swaps are required to complete an ordered list. For the 10 items shown in the list (see Figure 8-1) after 10 steps, only 4 of the items are in proper order and an additional 11 (a total of 21) steps will be required before the list is completely ordered.

For a list of 100 entries, the number of steps would increase by a factor of 100 to approximately 2500 steps. For 1000 entries, this figure becomes 250,000 steps. The number of steps is, of course, an approximation based on an initially random order and, for N items, may be calculated as:

$$\frac{N^2}{4}$$

The other factor to include in your calculations[1] is the number of comparisons required before the sort is completed. For the simple sort illustrated, this can be calculated as:

$$\frac{N^2 - N}{2}$$

The total operations required for the sort become:

$$\frac{N^2}{4} + \frac{N^2 - N}{2} = \frac{3N^2 - 2N}{4}$$

---

1. No, you do not have to memorize these formulas. They are merely the legacy of a misspent youth devoted to the fantasy of mathematics.

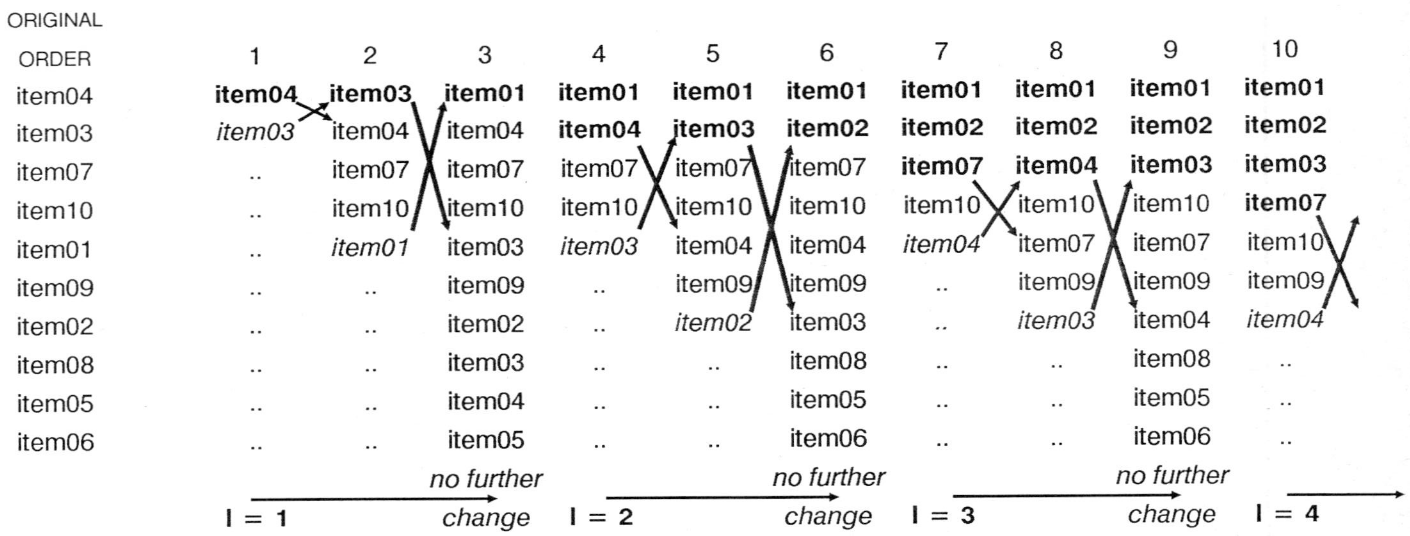

ORIGINAL

ORDER	1	2	3	4	5	6	7	8	9	10
item04	**item04**	**item03**	**item01**	**item01**	**item01**	**item01**	**item01**	**item01**	**item01**	**item01**
item03	*item03*	**item04**	**item04**	**item04**	**item03**	**item02**	**item02**	**item02**	**item02**	**item02**
item07	:	item07	item07	item07	item07	item07	**item07**	**item04**	**item03**	**item03**
item10	:	item10	item10	item10	item10	item10	item10	item10	item10	**item07**
item01	:	*item01*	item03	*item03*	item04	item04	*item04*	item07	item07	item10
item09	:	:	item09	:	item09	item09	:	item09	item09	item09
item02	:	:	item02	:	*item02*	item03	:	*item03*	item04	*item04*
item08	:	:	item03	:	:	item08	:	:	item08	:
item05	:	:	item04	:	:	item05	:	:	item05	:
item06	:	:	item05	:	:	item06	:	:	item06	:

I = 1   no further change / I = 2   no further change / I = 3   no further change / I = 4

Figure 8-1 Simple Sort Illustration

Thus, for 10 items, approximately 45 comparisons are made; for 100 items, 4950 comparisons; and for 1000 items, 499,500 comparisons.

To judge the relative speed and efficiency of a sorting algorithm, two factors can be calculated: the Q (quality) of the algorithm and the E (efficiency) of the final result. Q is found by dividing the number of items to be sorted by the (average) number of times an item is moved (number of swap operations). E is found by dividing the total items by the total number of operations (swaps + comparisons).

Table 8-1 Simple Sort Time Approximations

Items	Swap Operations	Item Comparisons	Total Operations	Q	E
10	25	45	70	0.4	0.14
100	2,500	4,950	7,450	0.04	0.013
1000	250,000	499,500	749,500	0.004	0.0013

Purely for the sake of illustration, consider both types of operation to require (approximately) the same execution time (machine cycles). Thus, if 100 items can be sorted in 0.1 second (fairly realistic for a 10Meg clock), 1000 items will required 167.7 seconds (about 2.8 minutes). The exact figures will vary depending on your coding, the type of material being sorted, and the CPU and clock speeds, but as you can see, even a medium-sized sort can occupy an excessive amount of time — operator time.

Although there are faster ways to handle data, for now, the simple sorting algorithm will be used, but to sort data on entry instead of sorting an array in memory.

The Entry Sort Algorithm

Most sort routines operate on data held in memory (a few use disk file extensions to handle larger amounts of data), but the following program sorts the data as it is read from the disk:

```
read(ReadFile,NewEntry);
New(DataEntry);
DataEntry^.Name := NewEntry.Name;
DataEntry^.Phone := NewEntry.Phone;
ThisEntry := FirstEntry;              { start at the top      }
repeat
    ThisEntry := ThisEntry^.Next;     { and move down until }
until DataEntry^.Name                 { proper position found }
    > ThisEntry^.Name;
```

As you will observe, an Entry Sort (sort data on entry or as read from disk) has slightly different constraints from conventional (in memory) sort routines. I'll get to the code in a moment, but Figure 8-2 shows the operation of an Entry Sort.

As an item is read from the disk file, the entry's position in the growing data structure is determined. The first item read, of course, begins at the top of the list. For the second item, it is only necessary to decide if it belongs before or after the first, and in Figure 8-2 it goes before. Subsequent items may appear at the top of the list, at the end of the list, or somewhere within.

Note: If this were being done with a conventional array, large quantities of data would, very shortly, have to be shuffled to accomplish this ordering. Since this is being done with pointers, no shuffling is necessary; this is merely a "cut and paste" ordering.

In Figure 8-2, a total of 37 operations were required to order this list: 10 insertions of data and 27 comparisons, that is, approximately half the number of operations required by the Simple Sort algorithm. The number of insert operations (the Entry Sort's equivalent of swap operations) obviously equals the number of items in the list. The number of comparisons is slightly harder to calculate but may be found with the formula:

$$C = \frac{\text{sum}(1..N)}{2} \quad \text{or} \quad \frac{N^2 + N}{4N} \quad \text{or} \quad N \cdot \frac{N + 1}{4}$$

The results are shown in Table 8-2.

Table 8-2. Entry Sort Time Approximations

Items	Swap Operations	Item Comparisons	Total Operations	Q	E
10	10	27.5	37.5	1.0	0.26
100	100	2,525.0	2,625.0	1.0	0.038
1000	1,000	250,250.0	251,250.0	1.0	0.0040

For a list of 1000 items, the Entry Sort is approximately three times faster than the Simple Sort. To compare speed estimates directly, combine the formulas for the **Comparisons** and the **Insert** or **Swap** operations as follows:

$$\frac{\text{Entry Sort}}{\text{Simple Sort}} = \frac{\frac{N + 1}{4} \cdot N + N}{\frac{N - 1}{2} \cdot N + \frac{N^2}{4}} = \frac{N + 5}{3N - 2}$$

SOURCE

ORDER	1	2	3	4	5	6	7	8	9	10
item04	**item04**	**item03**	item03	item03	**item01**	item01	item01	item01	item01	item01
item03		item04	item04	item04	item03	item03	**item02**	item02	item02	item02
item07			**item07**	item07	item04	item04	item03	item03	item03	item03
item10				**item10**	item07	item07	item04	item04	item04	item04
item01					item10	**item09**	item07	item07	**item05**	item05
item09						item10	item09	**item08**	item07	**item06**
item02							item10	item09	item08	item07
item08								item10	item09	item08
item05									item10	item09
item06										item10

Figure 8-2 Entry Sort Illustration

For increasing values of *N*, this is a convergent formula and approaches a limit of ⅓ (the maximum *estimated* improvement using the Entry Sort over a Simple Sort approaches three times faster).

When large lists are to be handled, there are several methods of improving the Entry Sort algorithm using bubble, partition, or alpha sort handling. But, before going into improvements, it's time to look at the basic procedures for Entry Sorts.

The demonstration program uses a simple data record consisting of a name string and a number string such as might be used for a telephone list.

The first step, since an entry sort begins with an empty list, is to create the initial entry:

```
if FirstEntry = nil then          { this must be the first entry }
begin
    FirstEntry        := DataEntry;   { only one entry in the list    }
    LastEntry         := DataEntry;   { so point both first and last  }
    FirstEntry^.Prior := nil;         { point first prior to nil      }
    FirstEntry^.Next  := LastEntry;   { and point each at the other   }
    LastEntry^.Prior  := FirstEntry;  { in correct order              }
    LastEntry^.Next   := nil;         { point last next to nil        }
end;
```

This is essentially the same as previous examples except that FirstEntry and LastEntry have been pointed at each other and both point at the same memory location (at the same data item).

Once FirstEntry has been taken care of, the next entry (second item) must either precede or follow the first. For all other entries, either of these can also be true or the item could fall somewhere within the list.

The first step tests to see if this is a new FirstEntry;

```
if DataEntry^.Name <                 { is this a new first?          }
    FirstEntry^.Name then
begin
    FirstEntry^.Prior := DataEntry;
    DataEntry^.Next   := FirstEntry;
    FirstEntry        := DataEntry;
    FirstEntry^.Prior := nil;
end else
```

and it's inserted at the top of the list. If, however, this item didn't belong at the top of the list, it might belong at the end:

```
if DataEntry^.Name >                 { is this a new last?           }
    LastEntry^.Name then
```

```
begin
    LastEntry^.Next      := DataEntry;
    DataEntry^.Prior     := LastEntry;
    LastEntry            := DataEntry;
    LastEntry^.Next      := nil;
end else
```

If the new item belonged neither at the top nor at the bottom, it must go somewhere within the existing order. Therefore, a local pointer is set to the top of the list and then moved down the list until it finds the first item that the new item should follow.

```
begin
    ThisEntry := FirstEntry;
    repeat
        ThisEntry := ThisEntry^.Next
    until DataEntry^.Name
        > ThisEntry^.Name;
```

Once this point is found, the new item (DataEntry) is inserted immediately prior:

```
        DataEntry^.Prior := ThisEntry;
        DataEntry^.Next  := ThisEntry^.Next;
        ThisEntry^.Next^.Prior := DataEntry;
        ThisEntry^.Next  := DataEntry;
    end;
end;
```

Once all the data has been read from the disk file, it is also in complete sorted order. For most applications, the data is sorted fast enough that no effective delays are apparent to the user.

The second advantage mentioned for pointer sorts is the ability to create multiply sorted lists — lists that are sorted by different fields in different orders. This *can* be done with array structures by creating index elements for each sort field to show the sorting order for that field (see Figure 8-3), but in essence this will look little different from the pointer structure accomplishing the same task (see Figure 8-4).

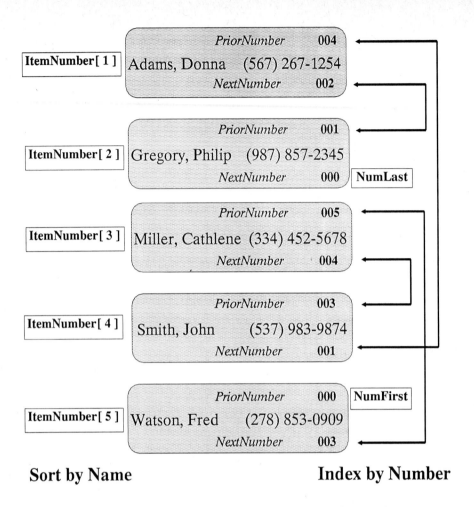

Sort by Name   **Index by Number**

Figure 8-3. Sorted Array with Index

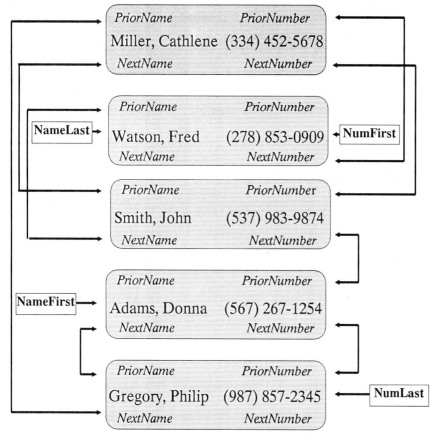

Name Index　　　　　　　　**Number Index**

Figure 8-4 Double-Indexed Pointer List

Note that, for the indexed array, variables are required to locate the first and last elements of the number index, and each array element holds two locators for the prior and next number positions in the array. (This looks a lot like the pointer structure in Figure 8-4 doesn't it?)

On the left, the pointer links create an alphabetical order by name, and, on the right, pointers structure the ordering according to area codes and phone numbers.

The code required to add this second pointer set is almost exactly the same as the original pointer structure:

```
type
   DataRecord = record        Name : string[40];
```

```
                        Phone : string[14];
           Next,   NumNext,
           Prior, NumPrior : DataPtr;    end;
    var
      FirstEntry, LastEntry, FirstNum, LastNum, ThisEntry, ThisNum : DataPtr;
        if FirstEntry = nil then
        begin
          FirstEntry        := DataEntry;  FirstNum         := DataEntry;
          LastEntry         := DataEntry;  LastNum          := DataEntry;
          FirstEntry^.Prior := nil;        FirstNum^.NumPrior := nil;
          FirstEntry^.Next  := LastEntry;  FirstNum^.Next    := LastNum;
          LastEntry^.Prior  := FirstEntry; LastNum^.Prior    := FirstNum;
          LastEntry^.Next   := nil;        LastNum^.NumNext  := nil;
        end else
        begin
                        { handle the pointers for Name field as previously shown, }
                        { then use separate handling for the Number field         }
          if DataEntry^.Phone > FirstNum^.Phone then
          begin   FirstNum^.NumPrior := DataEntry;
                  DataEntry^.NumNext := FirstNum;
                  FirstNum           := DataEntry;
                  FirstNum^.NumPrior := nil;              end else
          if DataEntry^.Phone > LastNum^.Phone then
          begin   LastNum^.NumNext   := DataEntry;
                  DataEntry^.NumPrior := LastNum;
                  LastNum            := DataEntry;
                  LastNum^.NumNext   := nil;              end else
          begin   ThisNum := FirstNum;
                  repeat   ThisNum := ThisNum^.NumNext;
                  until DataEntry^.Phone > ThisNum^.Phone;
                  DataEntry^.NumPrior := ThisNum;
                  DataEntry^.NumNext  := ThisNum^.NumNext;
                  ThisNum^.NumNext^.NumPrior := DataEntry;
                  ThisNum^.NumNext    := DataEntry;        end;
        end;
```

More pointer indexes are added exactly the same way as many pointer indexes as needed.

The Quick Sort Algorithm

Although the Quick Sort algorithm may appear initially confusing, it is probably the fastest sorting procedure possible for memory arrays. Also, because this is a recursive procedure (the procedure calls itself recursively), the actual code is very brief and very simple. The demonstration procedure shown here sorts an array of string data and assumes the array is global to the Quick__Sort procedure.

```
var
    DataItem : array[1..Limit] of string;
```

The Quick__Sort procedure is called only once from the main program and is passed two parameters: the beginning of the array and the highest item in the array. If the array is full, the value `Limit` would be used; otherwise, a smaller value should be passed. If the constant `Limit` is passed for a partially filled array (assuming the array entries were properly initialized as null strings), the unused array elements at the end will be sorted to the first of the array, which can be a confusing result.

```
procedure Quick_Sort( List_Top, List_End: integer);
    var
        Test_Top, Test_End : integer
        Test_Str, Temp_Str : string
    begin
        Test_Top := List Top;
        Test_End := List_End;
        Test_Str := DataItem[ (List_Top+List_End) div 2 ];
```

Three local variables, `Test_Top`, `Test_End`, and `Test_Mid` are used. `Test_Top` and `Test_End` begin with the array element *positions* passed as parameters when QuickSort is called. `Test_Mid`, however, takes the string value contained by the array element midway between `List_Top` and `List_End`.

After the three local variables are set the array element referenced by `Test_Top` is compared with `Test_Str`:

```
repeat
    while DataItem[Test_Top] < Test_Str do inc(Test_Top);
```

If the current array element belongs in its present location *relative* to the referenced element (the value in `Test_Str`) then the index `Test_Top` is incremented until either an array element greater than `Test_Str` is found or `Test_Top` reaches the referenced element. The reversed test is made for the array element referenced by `Test_End`.

```
    while Test_Str < DataItem[Test_End] do dec(Test_End);
```

If `Test_Top` and `Test_End` have not passed each other, or, more specifically, if the index `Test_Top` is less than or equal the index `Test End`, the two referenced data items are swapped.[2]

---

2. If `Test_Top` and `Test_End` both point to the same item, the item is "swapped" with itself, which initially may appear pointless, if also harmless. This is permitted, however, in order to accomplish the next two instructions, which are necessary.

```
if Test_Top <= Test_End then
begin
    Temp_Str := DataItem[Test_Top];
    DataItem[Test_Top] := DataItem[Test_End];
    DataItem[Test_End] := Temp_Str;
```

After the two data items are exchanged, the array indexes are incremented and decremented, respectively, to move them *beyond* the current positions since there's no point in repeating the tests with the current index positions.

```
    inc(Test_Top);
    dec(Test_End);
end;
```

The loop repeats until `Test_Top` is greater than `Test_End`.

```
until Test_Top > Test_End;
```

At this point, Quick_Sort has accomplished a very rough sort. All the array elements greater than the reference element have been moved somewhere toward the end of the array and all the elements less than the reference element have been moved toward the first of the array, but without further ordering. Note also that the original reference element may also have been moved and very likely has been.

To accomplish further ordering, the Quick_Sort procedure now becomes recursive, calling itself to repeat the sort for subsets or partitions of the original array.

```
    if List_Top < Test_End then quick_Sort(List_Top,Test_End);
    if Test_Top < List_End then Quick_Sort(Test_Top,List_End);
end;
```

Under Pascal, when a procedure calls itself recursively, the current local variables values are preserved in the memory stack until the recursive call ends. As control is returned after the recursion ends, the original values are popped back out of the stack, restoring the local variables to their previous values. Thus, the first recursion, using `List_Top` and `Test_End`, does not change the values for `Test_Top` and `List_End` used in the second recursive call.

When a procedure is multiply recursive, each recursion pushes a new set of values onto the stack. As each recursion ends, the last set of values is popped back out of the stack, restoring the variables' previous values.

An example of the sorting process is shown in Figure 8-5. Sorting approximations for the Quick Sort algorithm are shown in Table 8-3.

ORIGINAL

ORDER	1	2	3	4	5	6	7	8	9	10	11	12
item04	04	**01**	01	01	01	01	01	01	01	01	01	01
item03	03	03	**03**	03	03	**03**	03	**03**	**02**	02	02	02
item07	07	07	07	07	07	**07**	02	**02**	**03**	03	03	03
item10	10	10	**10**	**06**	06	06	**06**	**04**	04	04	04	04
item01	**01**	**04**	04	04	04	**04**	**04**	06	06	**06**	05	06
item09	09	09	**09**	**09**	**05**	05	05	05	05	**05**	**06**	06
item02	02	02	02	02	02	**02**	07	07	07	07	**07**	07
item08	08	08	08	08	**08**	**08**	08	08	08	08	08	08
item05	05	05	05	**05**	**09**	09	09	09	09	09	09	**09**
item06	06	06	**06**	**10**	10	10	10	10	10	10	10	**10**
ACTION	SWAP	N/C	SWAP	SWAP	N/C	SWAP	SWAP	SWAP	N/C	SWAP	N/C	N/C

Box indicates items being compared with reference value shown in **bold**.

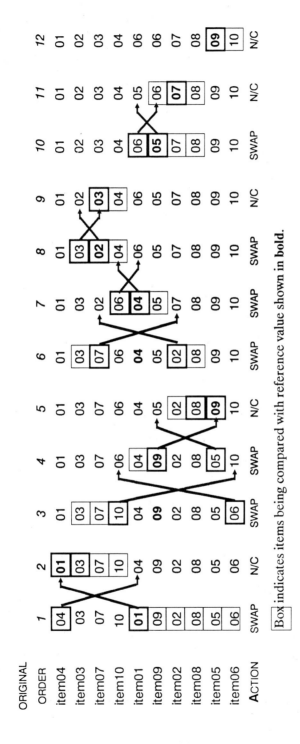

Figure 8-5 Quick Sort Illustration

Table 8-3. Quick Sort Time Approximations

Items	Swap Operations	Item Comparisons	Total Operations	Q	E
10	7.0	12.0	19.0	1.43	0.53
100	181.2	443.9	625.1	0.55	0.159
1000	2,583.7	7,682.2	10,265.9	0.39	0.097

As you can see, for increasing numbers of items sorted, the efficiency (E) for the Quick Sort algorithm decreases relatively slowly in comparison with the Simple Sort and Entry Sort algorithms. This is further confirmed by timing the various sort process using a data set of 1000 integers created as a disk file (thus the same random set is used for each test).

Table 8-4. Speed Comparisons[a]

	Total Time	Sort Time	Operations	E
Read Data	1.15	—	—	—
Quick Sort	1.42	0.27	10,266	0.0974
Entry Sort	4.03	2.61	251,250	0.0040
Simple Sort	8.87	7.72	749,500	0.0013

[a] All tests were performed on a 286-AT system operating at 10 MHz accessing a 30 msec hard disk using Turbo Pascal version 4.0. Times are shown in seconds/hundredths according to system clock averaged over 10 trials and rounded to nearest hundredth.

According to calculated efficiency (E), the Quick Sort algorithm is slightly better than 24 times faster than the Entry Sort and nearly 75 times faster than the Simple Sort. By actual performance (excluding disk access time), the Quick Sort executed 9.6 times faster than the Entry Sort and 28.6 times faster than the Simple Sort — not precisely as calculated but still a very significant difference.

Drawbacks and Limitations

Although the Quick Sort algorithm offers the advantage of speed, it also suffers from one major limitation: the items being sorted must be an indexed array, that is, a memory array smaller than 64Kbytes. This algorithm does not work well with pointer structures that lack direct indexing.

For many applications, such a limitation is effectively irrelevant as long as the data set does not exceed the 64K block limitation[3] imposed by Turbo Pascal. In such situations, the Quick Sort algorithm remains the fastest and easiest sorting method available.

3. The 64K limitation applies to a specific program segment as a whole, not to the data block alone. The memory usage includes all program instructions (compiled size, not source code) plus the data variables declared within the segment. Compiling separate program segments makes more memory within the segment available for arrays and data.

Although many earlier computer systems were limited to 64Kbytes of RAM, the PC group of computers commonly begins with 640Kbytes and many systems are now using RAM memory in megabyte sizes. Consequently, new applications are being created using data structures considerably larger than previously considered practical and also larger than compatible with the Quick Sort algorithm's inherent limitations. Also, as data structures grow in size, speed becomes an increasingly important consideration even despite the higher CPU and processing speeds used. Thus a variety of algorithms have been invented to make sorting extremely long lists faster (with varying degrees of speed), and at least one is applicable to pointer structures and Entry Sorts.

One way to speed a sort is to know approximately where a particular item belongs *before* searching the list. For this purpose, several speed sorts first build temporary structures to hold the records (like a series of boxes), then subdivide the long lists by sorting them into this structure, sort each partition separately (much faster than sorting the entire list), and finally reassembling.

For example, a program might begin by sorting the entire list according to the first letter only, thus building 26 sublists beginning with A through Z. Next, the A list would be sorted, then the B list, and so on, until all the sublists were in order. Finally, these separate lists are recombined to produce the final finished list.

For an Entry Sort, this practice is not directly relevant. However, a similar practice can be adopted.

An Array-Indexed Entry Sort

For an Entry Sort, one of the best methods is to build a *secondary* pointer structure indicating where broad groups of entries should begin. Since the **Phone__List__Demo** demo program uses an alphabetical sort on the name field, a KeyIndex of 26 pointers will do very nicely.

```
procedure Read_File_Entries;
   .
   .
   .
   var
       NewEntry : NameRecord;        KeyIndex : array[1..26] of DataPtr;
       DataEntry : DataPtr;          Key : byte;
       ReadFile : file of NameRecord;    I : integer;
```

These variables are local to the **Read__File__Entries** procedure since the only application here is use these for the initial sort, but a KeyIndex could be created anytime (as by stepping through an already existing list), and then forgotten again after use.

For any later, individual additions to the pointer structure, the need for speed is less important, but the KeyIndex could be retained as a global variable, if desired.

The next step, after each item is read from the file, is to create a key for this data item:

```
begin
   .
   .
   .
   repeat
      .
      .
      .
      DataEntry^.Phone := NewEntry.Phone;
      Key := ord(NewEntry.Name[1])-$40;
      if not (Key in [1..26]) then Key := 0;
```

Since an integer value is required for the key, the ordinal value (less 40h) of the first letter of the Name field is used. Just in case the entry begins with a lowercase letter (such as *du Champs, Pierre*), Key is checked against the valid range and assigned a value of 0 if it falls outside.

Next is the case of the first entry read from the file. Obviously, no pointers have been assigned, so each KeyIndex is set to nil (the null or empty pointer), and then the first KeyIndex is pointed at the current entry.

```
if FirstEntry = nil then      { this must be the first entry        }
begin
   .
   .
   .
   for I := 1 to 26 do         { start all KeyIndexes as nil         }
      KeyIndex[I] := nil;
   if Key <> 0 then
      KeyIndex [ Key ] := DataEntry;      { don't forget this one }
end else
```

On subsequent entries, first see if a KeyIndex for this Key exists. If not, point it at the new entry:

```
begin                                          { proceed with the main list   }
   if (Key <> 0) and
      (KeyIndex[ Key ] = nil) then             { if there isn't an index yet    }
      KeyIndex[ Key ] := DataEntry;            { then make one for this key    }
   if DataEntry^.Name < FirstEntry^.Name then  { new first?                    }
   begin
      .

      .

      .

   end
   else
   if DataEntry^.Name > LastEntry^.Name then    { new last?                     }
   begin
      .

      .

      .

   end
   else
```

If the new entry is a new first or a new last, these are certainly no trouble to find since pointers already indicate the top and bottom and there's no need to use the KeyIndex to find a location.

First, set ThisEntry := nil; for two reasons: ThisEntry can be used as a flag and this way ThisEntry isn't accidentally pointed to some undefined location.

Next, if Key > 1, the problem is to find the appropriate KeyIndex. The first step is to set Key back one position so that the search is for the *preceding* index position. Of course, there is no guarantee that a preceding index key exists yet (and it may very well not exist), so the loop will continue to decrement Key until either a nonnull KeyIndex is found or Key has stepped back to the top.

If a valid (assigned) KeyIndex is located, ThisEntry takes the index value as the starting point to search from and Key is set to 0 to exit from the loop.

```
begin                                          { not first or last so,         }
   ThisEntry := nil;                           { set ThisEntry as a null ptr   }
   while Key > 1 do                            { if Key = 0 then this skips     }
   begin
      dec(Key);                                { move key back one letter      }
      if KeyIndex[ Key ] <> nil then           { found one                     }
      begin
         ThisEntry := KeyIndex[ Key ]; { start here                           }
```

```
                    Key := 0;                          { exit loop                    }
              end;
        end;
```

The last addition is a simple test: if ThisEntry is *still* nil (no key pointer has been found), then by default the search will be started from the top of the list.

```
        if ThisEntry = nil then               { if default (null ptr)    }
            ThisEntry := FirstEntry;          { then start at top        }
    repeat
            Done := DataEntry^.Name > ThisEntry^.Name;
            if not Done then
                ThisEntry := ThisEntry^.Next; { and move down until  }
        until Done;                           { proper position found }



until EOF(ReadFile);
close(ReadFile);
```

If you would like to see where the KeyIndex assignments were made, the following test will show you a list of which index entries were used:

```
    for I := 1 to 26 do
        if KeyIndex[I] <> nil then
            writeln(I:3,' | ',KeyIndex[I]^.Name);
```

I have a second reason for including the preceding test lines. Note the KeyIndex[I]^.Name reference. An array element is perfectly valid as a pointer reference. If you must have large arrays, one method is to make your array an *array of pointers* to data stored by dynamic memory allocation. You can even have direct reference, just as I did earlier. Arrays and pointers can be combined the other ways as well, but I'll come back to this in a moment.

But the main reason for using the KeyIndex was to increase sorting speed by reducing the number of comparisons required for each item inserted. The new formula for the number of comparisons using a KeyIndex depends, in part, on the distribution of items within the list, but an approximation can be made:

$$\text{for } N >= 10 * I, \quad C = \frac{N^2 + N}{2 * I}$$

INDEXED AND SORTED LISTS

Thus, for 1000 items and 26 index elements, $E = 0.0494$, or about 12 times faster than an unindexed Entry Sort and 37 times faster than a Simple Sort. Alternately, if the sort were numerical data using only 10 index elements, $E = 0.0196$, an improvement of only 4.9 times faster than an unindexed Entry Sort and 14.7 times faster than a Simple Sort. Still, this isn't a bad speed improvement for a very simple code revision, and, if needed, a larger number of index points can be used.

For lists with fewer than 10*I entries, indexing doesn't produce any significant improvement in speed and, for very short lists, may actually slow the sort. However, in these latter cases, the execution time for the sort is so fast that a small inefficiency provided for longer lists becomes unimportant (see also the section Extended Sort Keys later in this chapter).

Arrays of Pointers

As you saw in the preceding section, arrays of pointers are perfectly valid and, if you wished, large amounts of data could be stored by dynamic memory allocation, the pointers to the data stored in an array and the array sorted just like any other array of data thus giving you the advantages of unlimited data storage (up to the available memory limits) and direct array reference.

Incidentally, sorting an array of pointers to data is much faster than sorting the data itself if not necessarily as fast as the Entry Sort demonstrated and the memory management techniques discussed in Chapter 7 apply here as well. (See also the section Quick-Sort with Pointers, later in this chapter.)

Pointers to Arrays

Pointers can also be used to point to arrays that have been stored by dynamic memory allocation. In such an instance, the pointers might also be an array and individual array elements might be referenced as:

```
RefElement := ArrayPtr[M,N]^.PtrArray[J,K,L]
```

I am not going to offer any examples of this practice. I have used this type of structure only once — to solve a handling problem requested by a mathematician. Even having majored in mathematics, I did not and do not understand the application — only the coding making it possible. Therefore, just keep this in mind if you happen to run into any mad mathematicians whose arrays are getting out of hand.

Extended Sort Keys

If you find that a larger number of keys are necessary or desirable, first consider the type of data being sorted.

If the data is true numerical — meaning a series of numbers rather than a series of numerical strings — your appropriate keys might be magnitudes (powers of ten). Thus key pointers to the value ranges of 10, 100, 1000, 10, 000, 100,000, and so on would provide faster sorting than 1, 2, 3, and so on. If, however, the numbers were part numbers (numerical strings), it might be better to treat these more like alphabetical strings and use keys like 10, 20, 30, 31, 32, . . ., 39, 40, 50, with extra keys provided in the 30–39 range because a relatively large portion of the part numbers begin with a three. On the other hand, for a long list of names, alphabetical pairs would be the best keys, but it might be pointless to include every pair combination from AA to ZZ. In every case, there are tradeoffs dependent on the type of data to be sorted, the amount of data, and the approximate distribution of various key bits of data.

If you are in doubt, begin with a data sampling and sort this once using any practical procedure. Then take a sampling of the data, say, sample every thousandth item (after sorting), and decide from these what the appropriate keys should be. If the result is only 90% efficient but will execute smoothly and quickly, don't waste ten times the effort trying to get the remaining 10% efficiency. It isn't worth it.

Quick Sort with Pointers

I cautioned earlier that the Quick Sort algorithm was not compatible with pointer structures *which lack direct indexing*,[4] but now we've talked about adding partial indexes to pointer structures to speed sorting. What about creating a complete array index to a pointer structure?

Since each pointer requires only 32 bits (4 bytes), approximately 16,000 pointers can fit within the 64Kbyte block limit for a memory array.

---

4. This incompatibility occurs because a reference point lying between two pointer records cannot be conveniently accessed. The time required to locate and reference such a record by stepping back and forth through the record links tends to make such a search/sort algorithm considerably slower than the entry sort previous demonstrated.

Thus a pointer array can index a much larger pointer structure, while allowing use of the Quick Sort algorithm to order the pointer data. Two considerations apply here:

1. If a pointer structure is array indexed, the Prior and Next pointers are not required as part of the pointer data record since the array index can be used in place of these links to move through the pointer structure.

2. If multiple indexes are required, the total size of all arrays of pointers must comply with the 64K segment limitation. Thus, for four array indexes, the total number of pointer records indexed can be only ¼ as large as for a single indexed pointer structure.

As an example, to modify the **Phone__List__Demo** demo program, the first change involves deleting the Next and Prior pointers from DataRecord and adding the variable definition DataItem as an array of DataPtr. The FirstEntry and ThisEntry variables can also be eliminated and Last Entry should be changed from DataPtr to an integer.

```
program Phone_List_Demo_2;      { Phone2.Pas }
   const
      Limit = 9999;
   type
      DataPtr = ^DataRecord;
      DataRecord = record      Name : string[40];
                               Phone : string[14];    end;
   var
      LastEntry, I : integer;
         DataItem : array[1..Limit] of DataPtr;
```

Next, the Read__File__Entries procedure is modified ...

```
procedure Read_File_Entries;
   const
      NameFile = 'PHONE.LST';
   var
       NewEntry : DataRecord;
      DataEntry : DataPtr;
       ReadFile : file of DataRecord;
   begin
      I := 0;
      assign(ReadFile, NameFile);
      reset(ReadFile);
      repeat
```

```
         read(ReadFile,NewEntry);
         New(DataEntry);
         DataEntry^.Name   := NewEntry.Name;
         DataEntry^.Phone  := NewEntry.Phone;
         inc(I);
         DataItem[I] := DataEntry;
      until EOF(ReadFile);
      close(ReadFile);
      LastEntry := I;
      Quick_Sort(1,LastEntry);
   end;
```

No sorting of any kind has been attempted during the read procedure. Instead, a series of independent pointer records are created and an array element of DataItem is pointed to each record location in memory. After all of the records have been read, LastEntry is assigned to show how many records were read and the Quick_Sort procedure is called to order the list.

The following Quick_Sort procedure is modified for pointer reference, comparisons are made against the Name field of each record, and only the DataItem pointer addresses are changed to accomplish proper ordering.

```
procedure Quick_Sort( List_Top, List_End: integer);
   var
      Test_Top, Test_End: integer;
      Test_Name : string[40];
      Temp_Ptr  : DataPtr;
   begin
      Test_Top := List_Top;
      Test_End := List_End;
      Test_Name := DataItem[ (List_Top+List_End) div 2 ]^.Name;
      repeat
         while DataItem[Test_Top]^.Name < Test_Name do inc(Test_Top);
         while Test_Name < DataItem[Test_End]^.Name do dec(Test_End);
         if Test_Top <= Test_End then
         begin
            Temp_Ptr := DataItem[Test_Top];
            DataItem[Test_Top] := DataItem[Test_End];
            DataItem[Test_End] := Temp_Ptr;
            inc(Test_Top);
            dec(Test_End);
         end;
      until Test_Top > Test_End;
      if List Top < Test_End then Quick_Sort(List_Top,Test_End);
      if Test_Top < List_End then Quick_Sort(Test_Top,List_End);
   end;
```

The display entry procedure has also been modified. Instead of displaying ThisEntry^.Name, the variable ThisEntry is now an integer and the references shown are DataItem[ThisEntry]^.Name and DataItem [ThisEntry]^.Phone.

```
procedure Display_Entries;
   const
      EmptyStr' = '                      ';
   var
      ThisEntry : integer;
   begin
      writeln;
      ThisEntry := 0;
      repeat
         inc(ThisEntry);
         write( copy((DataItem[ThisEntry]^.Name+EmptyStr),1,24) );
         writeln( DataItem[ThisEntry]^.Phone );
      until ThisEntry = LastEntry;
   end;
```

Last, a couple of changes are made to main program body that basically set the DataItem array elements to nil.

```
begin {main}
   LastEntry := 0;
   for I := 1 to Limit do
      DataItem[I] := nil;
   Read_File_Entries;
   Display_Entries;
end.
```

Q and *E* approximations for quick sorting an array indexed pointer structure are essentially the same as for any other memory array and execution times likewise. When practical, this provides excellent handling for large data sets and excellent speed results.

Sort and Search Practices

User-Friendly Sorts and Searches

A sorted list may be technically perfect but will still be a disaster if the user can't find a desired entry. For example, I might be looking for *Wilson, Theodore*, but is this how it appears in the directory? Or does it appear as *WILSON, Theodore*? Or as *WILSON, THEODORE*? Or even as *wilson, theodore*? If it appears as *Theodore Wilson* (or some variation of this order), this is another matter. For the moment, assume that the last-name-first order has been followed.

As it now stands, the **Phone_List_Demo** program sorts the name entries in absolute alphabetical order and *ACHINSTON, DEBORAH* will appear before *Aber*, James; whereas *du Bois*, *Pierre* comes somewhere after *Zelazny, Roger*, which is not exactly the best ordering from the user's viewpoint.

Changing *du Bois* to *DU BOIS* and so on is not, however, a solution. Some programmers do this, but basically this is sloppy programming and an attempt to force the user to meet the (imagined) constraints of the computer. Actually, the only constraints being met are *the programmer's shortcomings*.

Programmer's Rule Number XI: The computer has no conveniences — only the user's!

What is acceptable practice is to allow *comparison* of uppercased strings, but to do so without changing the actual data entry. Therefore, three changes to the sort procedure:

```
...  until Cased(DataEntry^.Name) > Cased(ThisEntry^.Name);
if Cased(DataEntry^.Name) > Cased(LastEntry^.Name) then ...
if Cased(DataEntry^.Name) < Cased(FirstEntry^.Name) then ...
```

together with the **Cased** function (from Chapter 1) will serve very nicely. Now *du Bois* will precede *DUMONT* instead of following *Zelazny*, and *Aber* will appear properly before *ACHINSTON*.

Data entry being what it is and users being human (and therefore fallible), the **Cased** function is also useful with stock and part numbers, and with searches of any kind. For example:

Correct Ordering	Incorrect Ordering
.	.
.	.
.	.
347-f-9821	347-F-9825
347-F-9825	347-f-9821
347-f-9829	347-f-9829
.	.
.	.

Searching pointer structures is no different than searching any other type of data record except that the pointers themselves contain no data to be tested, only the location of data. The only direct tests that should be made on pointers are equality (=) and inequality (<>). Asking if one pointer is greater or less than another pointer is simply inconsequential.

The data indicated by a pointer, however, can be subject to any test (or any other operation) that would be applicable to any other variable data. You have already seen examples of exactly this when, in the **Read__File__Entries** procedure, three pointer tests were used:

```
if Cased(DataEntry^..Name) > Cased(LastEntry^..Name) then ....,
if Cased(DateEntry^..Name) < Cased(FirstEntry^.Name) then ....
and ... until Cased(DataEntry^.Name) > Cased(ThisEntry^.Name);
```

To search for a particular item (a name, for example) in a pointer list, simply use:

```
SearchName := Cased(SearchName);
ThisEntry := FirstEntry;                    { start at the top and    }
repeat
    ThisEntry := ThisEntry^.Next;           { move down until found }
until pos(SearchName,Cased(ThisEntry^.Name)) <> 0;
```

No special tricks are required, no complex tests, no convoluted references. Just search the list (and the appropriate field) exactly like any other data type.

Note: The variable `SearchName` was changed to uppercase and a match made against an uppercase data field. If the
`until pos(Cased(SearchName),Cased(ThisEntry^.Name))<> 0;`
 statement were used, the same end results would be accomplished, but the search would take considerably longer for having to change `SearchName` to uppercase for each comparison.

Quick-Search for Ordered Lists

Once an indexed list has been ordered (sorted), a modification of the Quick Sort algorithm can be used to search the list. The **Quick__Search** function is called with three parameters: beginning and end entries for the search and the string to be searched for.

Note: Although the **Quick__Search** function shown is not recursive, the basic principles used remain the same.

```
function Quick_Search( List_First, List_Last : integer;
                                 Test_Str : string ): integer;
    var
       Test_Mid, Search_Result : integer;
                       Ref_Str : string;
    begin
       Search_Result := -2;
       repeat
          Test_Mid := (List_First + List_Last) div 2;
          if List_First+1 >= List_Last then Search_Result := -1;
```

For each loop, the local variable Test_Mid is set midway between List_First and List_Last. If List_First and List_Last are within a range of 1, Search_Result is set to -1. Thus, if no match is found during the current loop execution, the loop will exit when finished.

```
if pos(Test_Str,DataItem[Test_Mid]^.Name) > 0 then
   Search_Result := Test_Mid;
```

If the search string occurs within the DataItem indexed by Test_Mid, Search_Result return the current entry number.

```
if (Search_Result = -2) and (Test_Mid < List_Last) then
                     (* not found yet, so test the next entry *)
   if pos(Test_Str,DataItem[Test_Mid+1]^.Name) > 0 then
      Search_Result := Test_Mid+1;
```

If no match has been found and Test_Mid is less than List_Last, the next item in the list is tested. If a match is found, Test_Mid+1 is returned as the Search_Result.

```
   if Search_Result = -2 then
      if Test_Str < DataItem[Test_Mid]^.Name
         then List_Last := Test_Mid
         else List_First := Test_Mid;
until Search_Result <> -2;
Quick_Search := Search_Result;
end;
```

If no match has been found, a comparison is made and the test is repeated for a new range, unless Search_Result has already been set to -1.

Finally, the **Quick__Search** function returns the value in `Search_Result`.

Pointers are easy to use and tremendously convenient. Just remember the following three points (no pun intended):

1. If you can describe it (in programming code), you can store it using dynamic memory allocation and then point to it.

2. It's usually faster to sort pointers to data than to sort the data itself.

3. With pointers, multiple simultaneous sorts are practical and convenient. Use them.

Quiz

1. In the **Phone__List__Demo** demo program, two tests were made — for the new item appearing at the top of the list or for the new item falling at the end of the list — before running down through the list to find the correct location. Could either (or both) of these first tests have been eliminated? Why or why not? (*Note:* You may want to experiment with this.)

2. With the Array-Indexed Sort, no effort was made to ensure that any of the Key Index pointers actually pointed to the *first* occurrence of the key letter. That is, the Key Index pointer for the letter K might have pointed to *Kzham, Roger*, which would fall at the end of the K's. Should provision have been made for this? Why or why not and, if so, how?

3. In **Phone__List__Demo**, in the **Display__Entries** procedure, the following instructions appear:

```
repeat
    writeln( copy((ThisEntry^.Name+EmptyStr),1,40),
ThisEntry^.Phone );
    ThisEntry := ThisEntry^.Next;
until ThisEntry = LastEntry;
```

Could these be rewritten more efficiently as:

```
with ThisEntry^ do
repeat
    writeln( copy((Name+EmptyStr),1,40), Phone );
    ThisEntry := ThisEntry^.Next;
until ThisEntry = LastEntry;
```

If not, why not? (*Hint: Try* the change shown above.)

INDEXED AND SORTED LISTS

4. In the search procedure illustrated, why was pos( ) used instead of simply testing for equality between SearchName and the data field?

5. Looking back at the sections on Sorting Practices and Searching Pointers, do any possibilities suggest themselves for speeding up the sorting procedure (without changing the ordered result)?

Solutions

1. I could answer this bluntly by saying no, but this wouldn't be very informative. Basically, both of these — a new first or last item — represent special circumstances because each is linked only one way with the second pointer set to nil. Attempting to provide for these circumstances within the normal handling requires more code and conditional checks than simply treating these as special circumstances.

2. Instead of wasting the computer time that would be required for *each* separate entry to ensure that the KeyIndex pointers actually point to the *first* occurrence of the key letter (and it is very unlikely that they will), the search is begun with the *previous, non-nil* KeyIndex pointer (or, if this is the first KeyIndex, with the top of the list). The alternative (if it worked at all) would probably increase sorting time simply because of the time required for checking the precise position (within the list) of the KeyIndex pointers. Attempting to do so, however, would also have to take into account the fact that any new item to which a KeyIndex pointer were aimed *does not yet have a position within the list* and cannot, therefore, be used as a point from which to start the search. Try modifications if you like, but be prepared to use the Ctrl-Alt-Del keys, too.

3. The suggested possible modification:

```
with ThisEntry^ do
repeat
   writeln( copy((Name+EmptyStr),1,40),  Phone );
   ThisEntry := ThisEntry^.Next;
until ThisEntry = LastEntry;
```

has a definite if subtle flaw because the first pointer reference, with ThisEntry^ do, remains unaffected by the operations within the repeat . . . until loop and the resulting Name and Phone elements are always the first ones pointed to, even though the test in the until statement is eventually and correctly satisfied. Be careful — this is an easy one to trip over.

4. Using a test for equality between the SearchName and the data field imposes a restriction on the user that their *entry* for SearchName will be an exact match (letter for letter and length for length) for some data item. Using the **pos( )** function allows a partial match such as entering *Wilson* to locate any Wilson in the data without having to remember that *Bob Wilson* was entered as *Robert J. Wilson, Jr.* Execution of the search is slower this way, but the end results far better suit the user's convenience.

5. As with the search procedures, the if Cased(DataEntry^.Name) < Cased(FirstEntry^.Name) test requires DataEntry^.Name to be reconverted to an uppercase string each time the test is used. This means a minimum of three conversions are likely and many more are probable. If a local variable CheckName is created and CheckName := Cased(DataEntry^.Name);, the if CheckName < Cased(FirstEntry^.Name) test becomes roughly 50% faster.

Sorting and Searching Demo Programs

PHONE.PAS Program

```
program Phone_List_Demo;   { Phone.PAS }
          { use Create_Demo_Phone_List ( MakeList.PAS ) to }
          { create a datafile for use with Phone_List_Demo    }
   type
      DataPtr = ^DataRecord;
      DataRecord = record            Name : string[40];
                                     Phone : string[14];
                        Next, Prior : DataPtr;        end;
   var
      FirstEntry, LastEntry, ThisEntry : DataPtr;

   function Cased( SourceStr: string ): string;
      var
         I : integer;
      begin
         for I := 1 to length(SourceStr) do
            SourceStr[I] := upcase(SourceStr[I]);
         Cased := SourceStr;
      end;

procedure Read_File_Entries;
   const
      NameFile = 'PHONE.LST';
   type
      NamePtr = ^NameRecord;
      NameRecord = record   Name : string[40];
```

```
                            Phone : string[14];    end;
      var
        NewEntry : NameRecord;        KeyIndex : array[1..26] of DataPtr;
        DataEntry : DataPtr;              Key : byte;
        ReadFile : file of NameRecord;      I : integer;
        CheckName : string;             Done : boolean;

      begin
        assign(ReadFile, NameFile);
        reset(ReadFile);
        repeat
          read(ReadFile,NewEntry);
          New(DataEntry);
          DataEntry^.Name := NewEntry.Name;
          DataEntry^.Phone := NewEntry.Phone;
          Key := ord(upcase(NewEntry.Name[1]))-$40;
          CheckName := Cased(NewEntry.Name);
          if not (Key in [1..26]) then Key := 0;
          if FirstEntry = nil then            { this must be the first entry    }
          begin
            FirstEntry         := DataEntry;   { only one entry in the list      }
            LastEntry          := DataEntry;   {   so point both first & last     }
            FirstEntry^.Prior := nil;          { point first prior to nil        }
            FirstEntry^.Next  := LastEntry;    { and point each at the other     }
            LastEntry^.Prior  := FirstEntry;   {   in correct order              }
            LastEntry^.Next   := nil;          { point last next to nil          }
            for I := 1 to 26 do                { start all KeyIndexes as nil     }
              KeyIndex[I] := nil;
            if Key <> 0 then
              KeyIndex[ Key ] := DataEntry;          { don't forget this one     }
          end else
          begin                           { proceed with the main list       }
            if (Key <> 0) and
              (KeyIndex[ Key ] = nil) then    { if there isn't an index yet     }
              KeyIndex[ Key ] := DataEntry;   { then make one for this key      }
            if CheckName <                    { is this a new first?            }
              Cased(FirstEntry^.Name) then
            begin
              FirstEntry^.Prior := DataEntry;
              DataEntry^.Next   := FirstEntry;
              FirstEntry        := DataEntry;
              FirstEntry^.Prior := nil;
            end
            else                            { is this a new last?             }
            if CheckName >
              Cased(LastEntry^.Name) then
            begin
              LastEntry^.Next  := DataEntry;
              DataEntry^.Prior := LastEntry;
              LastEntry        := DataEntry;
```

INDEXED AND SORTED LISTS

```
              LastEntry^.Next   := nil;
          end else
          begin                              { not first or last so,    }
              ThisEntry := nil;              { set ThisEntry as a null ptr }
              while Key > 1 do               { if Key = 0 then this skips }
              begin
                  dec(Key);                  { move key back one letter  }
                  if KeyIndex[ Key ] <> nil then      { found one!       }
                  begin
                      ThisEntry := KeyIndex[ Key ];        { start here  }
                      Key := 0;                            { exit loop   }
                  end;
              end;
              if ThisEntry = nil then        { if default (null ptr)     }
                  ThisEntry := FirstEntry;   {   then start at top        }
              repeat                         { compare entries           }
                  Done := CheckName > Cased(ThisEntry^.Name);
                  if not Done then
                      ThisEntry := ThisEntry^.Next;  { and move down until }
              until Done;                    { proper position found     }
              DataEntry^.Prior := ThisEntry;
              DataEntry^.Next  := ThisEntry^.Next;
              ThisEntry^.Next^.Prior := DataEntry;
              ThisEntry^.Next  := DataEntry;
          end;
      end;
    until EOF(ReadFile);
    close(ReadFile);
{ optional test to show where indexes were located }
    for I := 1 to 26 do
      if KeyIndex[I] <> nil then
          writeln(I:3,' | ',KeyIndex[I]^.Name);
  end;

procedure Display_Entries;
  const
      EmptyStr = '                                        ';
  begin
      ThisEntry := FirstEntry;
      repeat
          writeln( copy((ThisEntry^.Name+EmptyStr),1,40), ThisEntry^.Phone );
          ThisEntry := ThisEntry^.Next;
      until ThisEntry = LastEntry;
      writeln( copy((ThisEntry^.Name+EmptyStr),1,40), ThisEntry^.Phone );
  end;

begin
  FirstEntry := nil;
  LastEntry := nil;
```

```
      ThisEntry := nil;
      Read_File_Entries;
      Display_Entries;
   end.
```

MakeList.PAS Program

```
program Create_Demo_Phone_List;  { MakeList.PAS }
   uses Crt;
   const
      FileName = 'PHONE.LST';
      NullStr  = '
   type
      NameRecord = record          Name  : string[40];
                                   Phone : string[14];    end;
   var
      ListFile : file of NameRecord;
     FileEntry : NameRecord;
        Finish : boolean;

function Read_Name : string;
   var
      TempStr: string;
   begin
      TempStr := ' ';
      write('Enter name: ');
      readln(TempStr);
      Read_Name := TempStr;
   end;

function Read_Number : string;
   var
      TempStr: string;
   begin
      TempStr := ' ';
      write('Enter phone number: ');
      readln(TempStr);
      Read_Number := TempStr;
   end;

begin
   ClrScr;
   Finish := false;
   writeln('  Enter names and phone numbers for demo program file');
   writeln('Enter blank line to exit: ');
   assign(ListFile, FileName);
   rewrite(ListFile);
   repeat
      FileEntry.Name  := Read_Name+NullStr;
      FileEntry.Phone := Read_Number+NullStr;
      Finish := (FileEntry.Name = NullStr);
```

```
        if not Finish then write(ListFile,FileEntry);
    until Finish;
    close(ListFile);
end.
```

The Quick__Sort Procedure

```
var
    DataItem : array[1..Limit] of string;

procedure Quick_Sort( List_Top, List_End: integer);
    var
        Test_Top, Test_End: integer;
        Test_Str, Temp_Str: string;
    begin
        Test_Top := List_Top;
        Test_End := List_End;
                        { Test__Top and Test__End will be local references    }
        Test_Str := DataItem[ (List_Top+List_End) div 2 ];
                            { Test__Mid is a reference value midway in       }
                            { the list between Test__Top and Test__End       }
        repeat
            while DataItem[Test_Top] < Test_Str do inc(Test_Top);
                    { while DataItem[Test__Top] is smaller than the reference  }
                    { value, Test__Top is moved up until a larger value is     }
                    { found or Test__Top meets the midpoint value              }
            while Test_Str < DataItem[Test_End] do dec(Test_End);
                    { while DataItem[Test__End] is larger than the reference   }
                    { value, Test__End is moved down until a smaller value is  }
                    { found or Test__End meets the midpoint value              }
            if Test_Top <= Test_End then
                            { if Test__Top and Test__End point to data items not  }
            begin           { in correct order, the two items are swapped         }
                Temp_Str := DataItem[Test_Top];
                DataItem[Test_Top] := DataItem[Test_End];
                DataItem[Test_End] := Temp_Str;
                inc(Test_Top);              { and Top and End are stepped      }
                dec(Test_End);              { past the swapped items           }
            end;
        until Test_Top > Test_End;      { the process continues until Top     }
                                        { reaches or moves beyond End          }
        if List_Top < Test_End then Quick_Sort(List_Top,Test_End);
        if Test_Top < List_End then Quick_Sort(Test_Top,List_End);
                    { now Quick__Sort is called recursively for subsets of    }
                    { the data array                                          }
    end;
begin   { main }
    .
    .
    .
```

```
                    Quick_Sort(1,Limit);


                    .
                    .
                    .
          end.
```

Using the Quick__Sort Procedure with Pointer Records

```
type
   DataPtr = ^DataRecord;
   DataRecord = record      Name : string[40];
                            Phone : string[14];    end;
```
                    { no *Next* or *Prior* pointers are included in the record   }
```
var
   DataItem : array[1..Limit] of DataPtr;

procedure Quick_Sort( List_Top, List_End: integer);
   var
      Test_Top, Test_End: integer;
      Test_Name : string[40];
      Temp_Ptr  : DataPtr;
   begin
      Test_Top := List_Top;
      Test_End := List_End;
```
                    { Test__Top and Test__End will be local references   }
```
      Test_Name := DataItem[ (List_Top+List_End) div 2 ]^.Name;
```
                    { Test__Name is the *name* in the pointer record   }
                    { indicated by the *pointer* stored in the DataItem   }
```
      repeat
         while DataItem[Test_Top]^.Name < Test_Name do inc(Test_Top);
```
                    { while DataItem[Test__Top]^.Name is less than the   }
                    { reference value, Test__Top is moved up until a larger   }
                    { value is found *or* Test__Top reaches the midpoint value }
```
         while Test_Name < DataItem[Test_End]^.Name do dec(Test_End);
```
                    { while DataItem[Test__End]^.Name is greater than the}
                    { reference value, Test__End is moved down until a lesser }
                    { value is found *or* Test__End meets the midpoint value   }
```
         if Test_Top <= Test_End then
```
                    { only the *pointers* are swapped! -- not the data records }
```
         begin
            Temp_Ptr := DataItem[Test_Top];
            DataItem[Test_Top] := DataItem[Test_End];
            DataItem[Test_End] := Temp_Ptr;
            inc(Test_Top);                  { and Top and End are stepped      }
            dec(Test_End);                  { *past* the swapped items         }
         end;
      until Test_Top > Test_End;           { the process continues until Top  }
                                           { reaches or moves beyond End       }
      if List_Top < Test_End then Quick_Sort(List_Top,Test_End);
      if Test_Top < List_End then Quick_Sort(Test_Top,List_End);
```

```
                    { again, Quick_Sort is called recursively for subsets of        }
                    { the data array                                                 }
        end;


begin   { main }
    .
    .
    .
    Quick_Sort(1,Limit);
    .
    .
    .
end.
```

The Quick__Search Function

```
function Quick_Search( List_First, List_Last : integer;
                                    Test_Str : string  ): integer;
    var
        Test_Mid, Search_Result : integer;
                    Ref_Str : string;
    begin
        Search_Result := 0;
        repeat
            Test_Mid := (List_First + List_Last) div 2;
            if List_First+1 >= List_Last then Search_Result := -1;
                        { nothing left to search, so return a -1              }
            if pos(Test_Str,DataItem[Test_Mid]^.Name) > 0 then
                Search_Result := Test_Mid;
                        { found a match, return the entry number              }
            if (Search_Result = 0) and (Test_Mid < List_Last) then
                        { not found yet, so test the next entry               }
                if pos(Test_Str,DataItem[Test_Mid+1]^.Name) > 0 then
                    Search_Result := Test_Mid+1;
                        { found match, return this entry number               }
            if Search_Result = 0 then              { nothing found yet         }
            begin
                Ref_Str := copy( DataItem[Test_Mid]^.Name,1,length(Test_Str));
                        { create Ref__Str with same length as Test__Str       }
                if Test_Str < Ref_Str then List_Last := Test_Mid;
                            { move search up the list                         }
                if Test_Str > Ref_Str then List_First := Test_Mid;
                            { move search down the list                       }
            end;
        until Search_Result <> 0;
        Quick_Search := Search_Result;    { returns -1 if match not found      }
    end;
```

9

Mouse Pointers and Changing Cursors

The title of this chapter may sound like a strange combination, but there is a reason for covering the two different topics together. In demonstrating the first topic, mouse pointers, we can use the second, changing cursors, as a visual cue (visual feedback, if you prefer). This combination is not required, but it does have a few advantages.

If you're expecting instructions for creating a mouse interface (a mouse driver), you'll be disappointed because a mouse interface is not a separate piece of programming but depends (at least in part) on the mechanical/electronic design of the mouse device. Instead, the topic here is *interfacing* your program with an existing mouse and mouse driver.

If you don't have a mouse, that's okay, too, because the utility procedures demonstrated will work almost as well with the cursor controls (just not quite as smoothly or as quickly). I'll assume, however, that you have a mouse and that your mouse driver returns key codes emulating the conventional cursor keys. This is exactly what a properly designed mouse (meaning both the mouse and interface) is supposed to do, except that the key codes are normally returned much faster than the keyboard provides (up to 150 key codes per second).

I'll also assume that your mouse has at least one key that sends a CR code (0Dh, per the Enter or Return keys). If, for instance, you are using a LogiTech

C7 or similar,[1] your user's manual will explain how to set various buttons (and button combinations) to return different key codes; how, if necessary, to change the baud rate and report rate (speed at which key codes are sent); and how to change communication protocols for special applications. These topics are *not* covered in this chapter because each of these is (or should be) provided by the mouse manufacturer and the requirements of each specific mouse vary greatly.

Direct Mouse Access

Since curiosity tends to be a hallmark of most programmers — or of the good ones, at least — here are a few notes on direct access to the mouse port and mouse input codes.[2]

Note: I offer no claims for the accuracy nor universal application of these suggestions in these notes. These are suggestions for experiments, not recommendations for programming practices, and all specific codes noted are results from experiments with a LogiTech C7 mouse. Other models or other manufacturers may use different methods or other conditions may render many of these notes invalid.

Assumptions

1. A mouse is present on the system and accessible through a serial port.

2. The mouse was initialized by its own software either on boot up or before attempting access through this demo program.

3. Some form of mouse software is already memory resident.

4. For the LogiTech C7, the default mouse settings are in effect (2400 baud, report rate 140, 3 button, MM series protocol).

1. When this book was written, the LogiTech C7 Mouse (either the serial or bus mouse) appeared to be the best designed mouse available and is recommended for your consideration. The LogiMouse is complete with mouse driver and menu software, and it switches easily to a wide variety of protocols required by different software packages. The LogiMouse is compatible with the PC Mouse, Microsoft Mouse, or Microsoft Bus Mouse protocols as well as working with such application software as Windows and In'A'Vision, which require and supply their own mouse drivers. The LogiMouse also allows custom-tailored use of the mouse with almost any other software (such as word processors) that were not originally designed for mouse applications. It is quite a useful package.

2. Additional information and excellent examples of detailed mouse access were published in Turbo Technix, Volume One, Issues Four and Five (May/June and July/August 1988).

The Mouse_Test Program

```
program Mouse_Test;
   uses Crt, Dos;
   type
      Registers = record case Integer of
                     1: ( AX,BX,CX,DX,BP,SI,DI,DS,ES,Flags: integer );
                     2: ( AL,AH,BL,BH,CL,CH,DL,DH           : byte   );   end;
   var
      Reg : Registers;
{$I BINARYRF.INC}    (* detailed in Chapter 11 *)
procedure Initialize_Port;
   begin
      Reg.AH := $00;
      Reg.AL := $A3;     { 2400,8,N,1 }
      Reg.DX := $00;     { COM1 = 0, COM2 = 1, COM3 = 2 }
      intr($14,dos.registers(Reg));
      write(BinaryReg(Reg.AH));
   end;
procedure Read_Mouse_Status;
   begin
      Reg.AH := $03;     { get port status }
      Reg.DX := $00;     { COM1 = 0, COM2 = 1, COM3 = 2 }
      intr($14,dos.registers(Reg));
      if Reg.AH and $01 = $01 then
      begin
         Reg.AH := $02;    { get character }
         Reg.DX := $00;    { COM1 = 0, COM2 = 1, COM3 = 2 }
         intr($14,dos.registers(Reg));
         if (Reg.AH and $80) = 0 then
            write(ord(Reg.AL):4;
      end;
   end;
begin  { main }
   clrscr;
   { initialize_port; }
   repeat
      Read_Mouse_Status;
   until keypressed;
end.
```

Experiment One

In the **Mouse_Test** program, the **Initialize_Port** procedure is not used in the first experiment. Both mouse and port should already have been initialized by mouse software.

    Mouse_Test uses interrupt 14h, function 03h, to test the communications port status. If bit 0 in the AH register is returned set (see Appendix C), data is waiting in the input buffer. If data is ready, interrupt 14h, function 02h, is used to read the contents of the buffer. If this function fails, bit 7 of the AH register returns set; otherwise, the character is found in the AL register.

Using a LogiTech C7 mouse for this experiment, the mouse returns a three-character sequence for each incremental movement. Movement up (toward the mouse cord) returns 152 000 xxx; down returns 144 000 xxx; left 136 xxx 000; and right 152 xxx 000. The xxx value is normally 001, but rapid movement will return higher values.

The three buttons on the C7 mouse return individual code sequences as each key is pressed and also return combination codes for any pair or when all three are pressed. Also, when a key is released, if no other key remains closed, a no-key-down code sequence of 152 000 000 is returned. If another key or key combination remains closed, the code sequence for that key or key combination is returned.

```
Left = 156 000 000      Center = 154 000 000      Right = 153 000 000
Left+Center = 158 000 000                        Center+Right = 155 000 000
                 Left+Right = 157 000 000
           Left+Right+Center = 159 000 000
```

Notes: An occasional extra null character may also be re-turned. These can simply be ignored. Also, the mouse tends to be extremely sensitive to small movements (if functioning properly) and attempts to move only in one direction usually return mixed result codes.

Experiment Two

Begin by enabling the **Initialize__Port** procedure shown in the **Mouse__Test** program. The initialization parameter shown is for 2400 baud, 8-bit characters, no parity, and one stop bit. See listing in Appendix C for details on setting the parameter byte.

This will override the original mouse settings and protocol selection and enable a slightly different set of return codes incorporating four character bytes instead of three. The first character returned in each set will follow the description given earlier, the second two characters will normally have values between 0 and 15, and the fourth character code can be expected in the 200–255 range.

If your mouse does not work properly after calling the **Initialize__Port** procedure just reboot your system for a fresh start and have another go. Normal initialization procedures will reestablish the correct operating parameters.

Cursor Control

The primary use for a mouse is simply to move the cursor around the screen and to do so quickly and conveniently. In text mode, this movement is by row and column, just as with the arrow keys. If graphics modes are used, finer increments of movement (as small as one pixel steps) are practical. Essentially the same cursor control instructions apply — just with different limits.

Reading Cursor Position

Two variables, XAxis and YAxis, are used to reference the selected screen position. If your application has already set a cursor position before passing control to the **Mouse__Trap** procedure or if the cursor position is changed by any other routine (see MOUSE__DM.PAS), immediate coordinates can be read by the **Initial__Position** procedure:

```
procedure Read_Cursor_Position(var XAxis, YAxis : byte);
   begin
       XAxis := WhereX;
       YAxis := WhereY;
   end;
```

The **WhereX** and **WhereY** functions return *window-relative* X/Y coordinates and work with video page 0 only. This is a point to remember if you are using some window other than the full screen or are using alternate video pages. If so or if you are using multiple video pages, the second **Read__Cursor__ Position** procedure might be a better choice since the returned values will be the absolute screen position an any selected video page.

Note: Using the interrupt call directly is also one step faster than asking **WhereX** and **WhereY** since each of these uses interrupt 10h, function 03h, to find the cursor position.

```
procedure Read_Cursor_Position(Page: byte; var XAxis, YAxis: byte);
   begin
       Reg.AH := $03;                    { function 03h         }
       Reg.BH := $00;                    { active video page    }
       intr($10,dos.registers(Reg));
       XAxis := Reg.DL + 1;       { convert coordinates from    }
       YAxis := Reg.DH + 1;       { 0,0 origin to 1,1 origin    }
   end;
```

Two other values are returned by interrupt 10h, function 03h. The CH register returns the starting line for the cursor and the CL register returns the ending line. This is handy if you need to check the cursor shape.

For the demonstration program, a default (starting) cursor position approximately at the center of the screen will be used.

```
if keypressed then                        { see which keycode    }
begin
   Ch := readkey;
   case Ch of
      #$00 : begin    KCh := readkey;
                      case KCh of
                         'H': dec(YAxis);        {      up arrow³ }
                         'P': inc(YAxis);        {    down arrow }
                         'K': dec(XAxis);        {     left arrow }
                         'M': inc(XAxis);        {    right arrow }
                      end; {case}            end;
      #$0D : Mouse_Act := Enter;    { Return key or mouse button }
      #$11 : Done := true;                     { A safety escape }
   end; {case}
end;
```

The principal concern, when using a mouse control, is to read the key codes and respond as quickly as possible. A slow response loop that is practical with the keyboard cursor controls may, with a mouse, lag behind, leaving the screen position still changing, trying to catch up, when the mouse has stopped.

If speeding up the screen response is impractical or impossible, the best option is to slow the mouse response. For example, for a LogiMouse C7, a bat file titled YOURPROG.BAT might read:

```
MOUSE 2400 Mm 100<cr>
YOURPROG<cr>
```

---

3. If you have trouble remembering which codes are for which of the various function keys, the Turbo editor can make this easy. Simply enter Ctrl-P (the default control character prefix) and then the arrow key or other function key. The result will be a two-character display such as @H for the Up Arrow key, with the first character highlighted or in color or in reverse video (depending on your monitor and video aspects chosen when you ran the installation utility). The highlighted @ symbol simply means Ctrl-@ or null (ASCII $00 because the function and arrow keys return a double code beginning with null). Alternatively, if you pressed Ctrl-Q, a highlighted Q will appear.

This slows the mouse response (report rate) from 150 to 100 times per second and keeps the default baud rate (2400) and protocol (MMSeries). A report rate as low as 10 characters per second is possible, but response rates that are too low tend to defeat the original purpose in using a mouse.

Using a mouse, it is also very easy to run off the edge of the screen. Provisions must be made to keep the cursor coordinates generated within acceptable bounds. There are two main options for this. The first option is as follows:

```
if YAxis > 25 then YAxis := 1 else  { allow screen wrap with  }
   if YAxis < 1 then YAxis := 25;   {  with cursor movement   }
if XAxis > 80 then XAxis := 1 else  {  or restrict to movement }
   if XAxis < 1 then XAxis := 80;   {  to some smaller area    }
```

In the demonstration program, the preceding choice is used and the cursor is allowed to wrap at the screen limits, that is, exiting at the left brings the cursor back on screen at the right. If your application requires it, this wrapping movement could be limited to a smaller area. The second principal option is as follows:

```
if YAxis > 25 then YAxis := 25 else { restrict cursor movement }
   if YAxis < 1 then YAxis := 1;    {  to normal screen limits }
if XAxis > 80 then XAxis := 80 else {  allowing no screen wrap }
   if XAxis < 1 then XAxis := 1;    {  only stop at edge       }
```

Other options might be to allow right-left screen wrap with vertical scrolling, allow horizontal scrolling either by column or in multicolumn steps (move the screen left or right by eight or more columns when margin is reached but move cursor only one column, that is, back seven columns), allow vertical scrolling by page or half page, allow switching to alternate video pages at the screen margins, or any other response appropriate to your application.

For an editor program or most word processor applications, the only use for the mouse is to position the cursor where desired (or to reposition the screen). In other cases, such as graphics applications, the mouse may be used to select some action, to move between windows, or to pick items off of a menu.

In all of these latter cases, a mechanism is needed to recognize when the cursor position corresponds with some allowed selection. Therefore, after positioning the cursor, **Test_Mouse_Position** checks the current coordinates against the various Mouse_Array parameters, beginning by reading the screen cursor coordinates directly since separate and local XAxis and YAxis variables are used by the **Test_Mouse_Position** and **Mouse_Trap** procedures.

```
procedure Test_Mouse_Position;
var
    I : integer;    XAxis, YAxis: byte;
begin
    Read_Cursor_Position(XAxis, YAxis);
    This_Hole := 0;
    for I := 1 to 10 do
        with Mouse_Array[I] do
            if XAxis in [MXAxis..(MXAxis+length(MouseStr)+3)] then
                if YAxis in [MYAxis..(MYAxis+2)] then
                    This_Hole := I;
```

Instead of asking

```
if (XAxis > MXAxis) and (XAxis < MXAxis+ length(MouseStr)+3)
```

it's simpler to ask if XAxis belongs to the set bounded by MXAxis and
MXAxis+length(MouseStr)+3. If the position XAxis is a member of this
set and the position YAxis is a member of the set MYAxis..(MYAxis+2),
the cursor must be lying somewhere on or within the boxed graphic provided
as a target.

A boxed area does not have to be used as the target. This is for purposes
of visual demonstration only (but this device is frequently used and is useful).
Instead, the targets might be highlighted words within a help text (a device
used by Turbo version 4.0) and the screen attribute at the cursor position could
be the initial test rather than the position itself. The targets might also be
entries in a list with only the vertical position tested, or, for a multicolumn
list, a set of horizontal ranges might be checked with a case statement.

For the demonstration, a set of Mouse_Acts — Out, AtHole, Enter, and
InHole — have been defined to determine what response should be made
to the cursor position. Thus, if the cursor is not at a mousehole (This_Hole
= 0) and if Mouse_Act is not already Out, then Mouse_Act is set to Out and
a message is displayed accordingly.

```
if (This_Hole = 0) then
begin
    if Mouse_Act <> Out then
    begin    Mouse_Act := Out;
            Action_Message;        end;
end else
```

If this seems a roundabout way of getting the message up, there is a very
simple reason: *because it is faster to check a flag than to repeat a message
to the screen!* If the message is already up there, there is no need to put it
up again — and every reason not to.

To repeat the screen message for each cursor increment (if you try this, you'll see that the computer simply cannot keep up with 150 repeats per second) slows the program's response to the instructions sent by the mouse, causes a distinct screen flicker, and is just bad programming in general.

Alternately, if This_Hole is not zero (the cursor is at a mousehole), a different set of responses become appropriate.

If the cursor *is* at a mousehole, set Mouse_Act accordingly, put up a message saying which hole, and change from a line cursor to a block cursor. Why? Because it's a useful visual key. The message at the top of the screen is redundant and, in most applications, would not be used. However, changing cursors is a suitable cue that indicates: "Yes, you are on the mark!"

Again, switching Mouse_Act sets matters up to keep the message from being repeated unnecessarily.

```
begin
    case Mouse_Act of
        Out : begin    Mouse_Act := AtHole;
                       Block_Cursor;
                       Action_Message;
               end;
```

If the Enter (or Return) key or the appropriate mouse key (some mice have three) is pressed, the main control loop sets Mouse_Act := Enter. When this happens, several actions result:

1. A new message is written at the top of the screen.

2. If a previous hole had been selected, it is reset to a single line box.

3. This_Hole is saved as Last_Hole for the next time around.

4. The cursor is centered in the box (more visual feedback).

5. The mousehole is rewritten as a double-lined box.

6. Mouse_Act is set to InHole for the same reasons as before.

```
Enter : begin    Action Message;
                 if Last_Hole <> 0 then
                     with Mouse_Array[Last_Hole] do
                         Write_Box( MXAxis, MYAxis, MouseStr, 1 );
                     Last_Hole := This_Hole;
                     with Mouse_Array[This_Hole] do
                     begin                                  { center the mouse     }
                         XAxis := MXAxis + 1 +          { in the mousehole }
                                   ((length(MouseStr)+1) div 2);
```

```
        YAxis := MYAxis + 1;
        Write_Box( MXAxis, MYAxis, MouseStr, 2 );
    end;
    Mouse_Act := InHole;
```

Another possibility might have been to set the cursor to the center of the mousehole as soon as `Mouse_Act` changed from `Out` to `AtHole`.

Also, when an item is selected, the double-lined box is only one possible indicator. In other circumstances, reverse video, a change of colors, or blinking video might be more appropriate.

The last step, of course, is to reset the screen cursor, just in case any changes have been made during this procedure, because the local `XAxis` and `YAxis` are not preserved but the screen cursor is.

```
    end; {case}
  end;
  gotoxy(XAxis,YAxis);              { reset cursor position }
end;
```

By the way, when you run the demo, one mousehole has been left invisible. It will not appear until it has been selected, but the cursor will still change from underscore to block when you find it — just to show that it doesn't matter what's on the screen.

Changing Cursors

The underscore cursor is industry standard and the system default, but it is not the only cursor pattern possible. Indeed, some application programmers seem to prefer a full block cursor so much that they do not even allow the users an option. Some (badly behaved) programs exit leaving a block cursor in effect, which is very bad manners by any standard. It is irritating as well since some of us don't care for block cursors as a standard.

Interrupt 10H, function 03h accepts two arguments to define the top (starting in CH register) and bottom (ending in CL register) scan lines for the cursor. For each of these values, however, only bits 0 through 4 are used and setting bits 5 through 7 may have unpredictable results. Therefore, a maximum value of 1Fh is valid for the end scan line, whereas a value greater than 0Fh for the start scan line (setting bit 4) may also produce an unexpected response.

Cursor Size Settings

Video Type (Mode)	Monochrome (07h)	Text (00h-03h)
Default Start/Stop	09h / 0Ah	06h / 07h
Block Start/Stop	00h / 0Ah	00h / 0Bh

Other cursor sizes are possible. For instance, 05h/0Bh produces a thick underline cursor, 04h/0Bh makes the cursor the height of lowercase letters, 06h/00h produces an upper half-block cursor, and 00h/00h produces a very thin underline cursor.

```
procedure Block_Cursor;
   begin
      Reg.AH := $01;
      Reg.CH := $00;
      Reg.CL := $0B;
      intr($10,dos.registers(Reg));
   end;
```

The **Block_Cursor** procedure produces a full-height block cursor that will remain in effect until reset by **Norm_Cursor** or until the computer is reset. **Norm_Cursor** restores the normal default cursor settings. If used with monochrome video cards (such as the Hercules), the scan line settings should be changed accordingly.

```
procedure Norm_Cursor;
   begin
      Reg.AH := $01;
      Reg.CH := $06;
      Reg.CL := $07;
      (intr($10,dos.registers(Reg));
   end;
```

The cursor blink is firmware controlled and cannot be disabled. However, some programmers have attempted to "turn off" the cursor by setting non-valid start/stop scan lines. Such settings may work on some machines, but they tend to be difficult to transport to other systems. If you want to turn the cursor off entirely, the best way is simply to set the cursor position off the screen (try using interupt 10h, function 02h, to set the cursor one line below the bottom of the screen).

There is also a cursor scan setting that seems to work quite nicely:

```
procedure Cursor_Off;
   begin
      Reg.AH := $01;
      Reg.CH := $0F;
      Reg.CL := $00;
      (intr($10,dos.registers(Reg));
   end;
```

I will not, however, guarantee that **Cursor__Off** will work on all systems. Use it at your own risk. Remember, also that the cursor will remain off until turned back on with the **Norm__Cursor** or **Block__Cursor** procedures, even after *exiting* from your program.

MOUSE__DM.PAS Demo Program

```pascal
program Mouse_Demo;    { MOUSE__DM.PAS }
   uses Crt, Dos;
   type
      Mouse_Hole = record   MXAxis, MYAxis : integer;
                                 MouseStr : string;    end;
      Mouse_Acts = (Out, AtHole, Enter, InHole);
      Regs = record case integer of
                0 : ( AX, BX, CX, DX, BP, SI, DI, DS, ES, Flags : word );
                1 : ( AL, AH, BL, BH, CL, CH, DL, DH          : byte );   end;

   var
      Mouse_Array : array[1..10] of Mouse_Hole;
       This_Hole,
       Last_Hole : byte;
        Mouse_Act : Mouse_Acts;
            Reg : Regs;

procedure Write_Box( XAxis, YAxis: byte; WorkStr: string; Style: byte);
   var
      StyleStr: string;    I : integer;
   begin
      case Style of
         0: StyleStr := '       ';
         1: StyleStr := ' ⌐| ⌐ ';
         2: StyleStr := ' ⌐ ‖⌐ ';
      end; {case}
      gotoxy(XAxis, YAxis);                write(StyleStr[1]);
      for I := 1 to length(WorkStr)+2 do write(StyleStr[2]);
                                 write(StyleStr[3],' ');
      gotoxy(XAxis, YAxis+1);
            write(StyleStr[4],' ',WorkStr,' ',StyleStr[4],' ');
      gotoxy(XAxis, YAxis+2);                write(StyleStr[5]);
      for I := 1 to length(WorkStr)+2 do write(StyleStr[2]);
                                 write(StyleStr[6],' ');
   end;

procedure Block_Cursor;              { SEE NOTES IN TEXT                   }
   begin
      Reg.AH := $01;                { function 01h - set cursor type       }
      Reg.CH := $00;                { bits 0-4 set starting line for cursor }
      Reg.CL := $0B;                { bits 0-4 set ending line for cursor   }
```

```
            intr($10,dos.registers(Reg));
        end;


    procedure Norm_Cursor;                  { SEE NOTES IN TEXT                    }
        begin
            Reg.AH := $01;                   { function 01h - set cursor type       }
            Reg.CH := $06;                   { bits 0-4 set starting line for cursor }
            Reg.CL := $07;                   { bits 0-4 set ending line for cursor   }
            intr($10,dos.registers(Reg));
        end;


    procedure Action_Message;
        var
            HoleStr: string;   HoleType: byte;
        begin
            HoleType := 0;
            gotoxy(1,2); clreol;
            if Mouse_Act = AtHole then
                write(' Use RETURN or Mouse Key to Enter ');
            str(This_Hole,HoleStr);
            HoleStr := ' Hole #'+HoleStr;
            case Mouse_Act of
                AtHole : begin   HoleStr := 'at'+HoleStr;   HoleType := 1;   end;
                 Enter : begin   HoleStr := 'in'+HoleStr;   HoleType := 2;   end;
                 else      begin   HoleStr := ' not in Hole';   Norm_Cursor;   end;
            end; {case}
            HoleStr := 'Mouse '+HoleStr;
            Write_Box(40,1,HoleStr,HoleType);
        end;


    procedure Read_Cursor_Position(var XAxis, YAxis: byte);
        begin
            Reg.AH := $03;                              { function 03h              }
            Reg.BH := $00;                              { active video page         }
            intr($10,dos.registers(Reg));
            XAxis := Reg.DL + 1;                        { convert coordinates from  }
            YAxis := Reg.DH + 1;                        { 0,0 origin to 1,1 origin  }
        end;


    procedure Test_Mouse_Position;
        var
            I : integer;   XAxis, YAxis: byte;
        begin
            Read_Cursor_Position(XAxis, YAxis);
            This_Hole := 0;
            for I := 1 to 10 do
                with Mouse_Array[I] do
                    if XAxis in [MXAxis..(MXAxis+length(MouseStr)+3)] then
                        if YAxis in [MYAxis..(MYAxis+2)] then
```

MOUSE POINTERS AND CHANGING CURSORS

```
                    This_Hole := I;
        if (This_Hole = 0) then
        begin
            if Mouse_Act <> Out then
            begin   Mouse_Act := Out;
                    Action_Message;      end;
        end else
        begin
            case Mouse_Act of
                  Out : begin   Mouse_Act := AtHole;
                                Block_Cursor;
                                Action_Message;        end;
                Enter : begin   Action_Message;
                                if Last_Hole <> 0 then
                                    with Mouse_Array[Last_Hole] do
                                        Write_Box( MXAxis, MYAxis, MouseStr, 1 );
                                Last_Hole := This_Hole;
                                with Mouse_Array[This_Hole] do
                                begin                           { center the mouse  }
                                    XAxis := MXAxis + 1 +       { in the mousehole   }
                                            ((length(MouseStr)+1) div 2);
                                    YAxis := MYAxis + 1;
                                    Write_Box( MXAxis, MYAxis, MouseStr, 2 );
                                end;
                                Mouse_Act := InHole;                            end;
            end; {case}
        end;
        gotoxy(XAxis,YAxis);            { reset cursor position }
    end;


procedure Mouse_Trap;
    var
            Ch, KCh : char;         Done : boolean;
        XAxis, YAxis : byte;
    begin
        Done := false;
        XAxis := 40;                            { initial screen position    }
        YAxis := 13;
        repeat
            if keypressed then                  { see which keycode          }
            begin
                Ch := readkey;
                case Ch of
                    #$00 : begin    KCh := readkey;
                                    case KCh of
                                        'H': dec(YAxis);        {   up arrow    }
                                        'P': inc(YAxis);        {  down arrow   }
                                        'K': dec(XAxis);        {  left arrow   }
                                        'M': inc(XAxis);        { right arrow   }
```

MOUSE POINTERS AND CHANGING CURSORS

```
                              end;                        end;
              #$0D : Mouse_Act := Enter;
              #$11 : Done := true;                    { Ctrl-Q -- a safety out      }
            end; {case}
          end;
          if YAxis > 25 then YAxis := 1 else        { allow screen wrap with      }
            if YAxis < 1  then YAxis := 25;          {  with cursor movement       }
          if XAxis > 80 then XAxis := 1 else         {  or restrict to movment     }
            if XAxis < 1  then XAxis := 80;          {  to some smaller area        }
          gotoxy(XAxis,YAxis);
          Test_Mouse_Position;                       { check mouse holes           }
          Read_Cursor_Position(XAxis,YAxis);         { see if anything changed     }
        until ( (Mouse_Act = InHole) and (This_Hole = 9) ) or Done;
      end;


  procedure Demo_Screen;
    var
      I : integer;
    begin
      clrscr;   write('Mouse Control Demo');
      for I := 1 to 9 do
        with Mouse_Array[I] do
            Write_Box( MXAxis, MYAxis, MouseStr, 1 );
      end;


  procedure Initialize_Mouse_Holes;
    begin
      with Mouse_Array[1] do begin    MXAxis := 10;    MYAxis := 10;
                                      MouseStr := 'Big Mouse Hole (1)';      end;
      with Mouse_Array[2] do begin    MXAxis := 20;    MYAxis := 19;
                                      MouseStr := '2';                       end;
      with Mouse_Array[3] do begin    MXAxis := 30;    MYAxis :=  5;
                                      MouseStr := '3';                       end;
      with Mouse_Array[4] do begin    MXAxis := 40;    MYAxis := 15;
                                      MouseStr := 'Another Big Hole (4)';    end;
      with Mouse_Array[5] do begin    MXAxis := 50;    MYAxis := 10;
                                      MouseStr := '5';                       end;
      with Mouse_Array[6] do begin    MXAxis :=  5;    MYAxis := 22;
                                      MouseStr := '6';                       end;
      with Mouse_Array[7] do begin    MXAxis := 70;    MYAxis :=  3;
                                      MouseStr := '7';                       end;
      with Mouse_Array[8] do begin    MXAxis :=  1;    MYAxis :=  5;
                                      MouseStr := '8';                       end;
      with Mouse_Array[9] do begin    MXAxis := 65;    MYAxis := 23;
                                      MouseStr := 'Quit (9)';                end;
      with Mouse_Array[10] do begin   MXAxis :=  1;  MYAxis := 15;
                                      MouseStr := 'Invisible Hole (10)';     end;
      end;
```

```
begin
   This_Hole := 0;
   Last_Hole := 0;
   Mouse_Act := Out;
   TextAttr := $0E;
   Initialize_Mouse_Holes;
   Demo_Screen;
   Mouse_Trap;
   Norm_Cursor;
end.
```

10

An Alternative Video Handler

Previous chapters have shown several methods of handling video output, ranging from Turbo's video handing mechanisms (in the Crt module) to interrupt 10h calls. There is one other video access mechanism, the Direct Memory Write, in which the necessary information is written directly to (or read from) the system's video memory.[1] Doing so has both advantages and disadvantages. The advantages are speed and a certain versatility, which will be demonstrated shortly. On the down side, no checks are provided to ensure valid screen coordinates and windows and scrolling are not automatic. However, these can be provided, if desired.

Where Turbo's **write** and **writeln** procedures provide automatic conversion from numerical values to string formats and accept mixed string and number parameters, the demo procedures here are not so elaborate. Still, analogs will be demonstrated for Turbo's most important screen procedures. Also, in Chapter 11, this alternative video handler will be used instead of the conventional video handling procedures.

But why use these instead of the well-behaved procedures already in Turbo? In many cases, there would be no special reason, but, in writing a word

---

1. In version 4.0, the Crt unit provides both BIOS video and direct memory video write capability. This is controlled by the Boolean variable DirectVideo. If DirectVideo is set to False, the BIOS I/O is used by the **Write** and **WriteLn** procedures; otherwise, characters are written directly to video memory.

processing application or a spreadsheet, for example, a different degree of control over the screen might be desired. And, in any case, the following procedures will give you an inside look at how a number of Turbo's procedures operate and how alternate procedures can be created to accomplish tasks directly that can only be handled indirectly using Turbo procedures.

Screen Memory Organization

The video memory is organized (in text modes) in 2-byte cells beginning at ScrSeg:$0000, with each cell controlling one screen character position.

Figure 10-1 shows 64 bytes of video memory (the equivalent of 32 characters) beginning at the upper left corner of the screen. The even bytes contain ASCII character codes (beginning at $0000), whereas the odd bytes contain the attribute (color) codes.

Direct Video Write

The first step is to know *where* the video memory is located. For monochrome video boards, the video address segment is B000h; for color systems it is B800h. The **CheckColor** procedure tests the memory byte at $0000;$0065 (0000:1040 decimal) to validate a color video board. Then it sets initial values for screen color (ScrAttr), cursor position (ScrRow and ScrCol), and window parameters (WinLf, WinRt, WinTop, andWinBot).

```
procedure CheckColor;
begin
    ScrSeg := $B000;    ColorVid := false;    { first, assume monochrome         }
    if (mem[0000:1040] and $30) <> $30 then { then test for color                }
    begin       ScrSeg := $B800;             {    and change the ScrSeg and       }
                ColorVid := true;    end;     {    video flag accordingly          }
                                             { *** and a few initial settings *** }
    ScrAttr := $0E;                          { sets yellow for default color      }
    ScrRow := $01;       ScrCol := $01;       {    sets initial positions          }
    WinLf := $01;        WinRt := $50;        { set full screen for initial        }
    WinTop := $01;       WinBot := $19;       {    window coordinates              }
    GotoXY( ScrRow, ScrCol );                 { set cursor position                }
end;
```

Note the use of the Mem reference. Mem, MemW, and MemL (version 4.0 or later) are predefined arrays used for direct memory access. Mem uses byte components, MemW uses word components (two bytes), and MemL's components are long integers. Two integer expressions, MemSeg and MemOfs (segment and

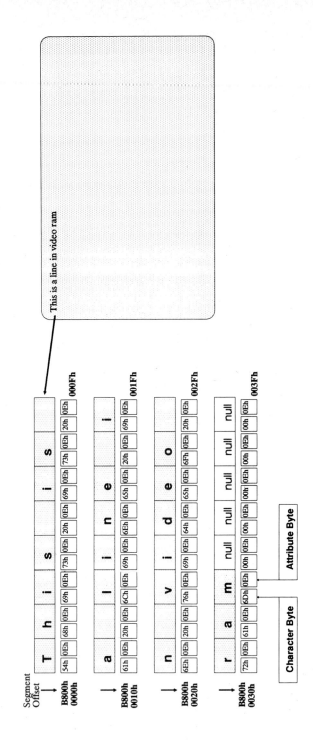

Figure 10-1 Video Memory Map

offset), separated by a colon are used to define a memory location. The Mem Array references can be used either to read the current memory values or to assign a new value in memory. Thus,

```
Mem[$0048,$007A]  := $07;
```

or

```
KeyWord  := MemW[$0030:$8901];
```

In **CheckColor**, the equipment byte at 0000:1040 was ANDed with $30 — testing two bits in memory. If the comparison is invalid (the result does not equal $30), a color video board is assumed. No variables (neither local nor global) were required for the test — only the memory value itself. This test could also have been written as follows:

```
ColorVid := (mem[0000:1040] and $30) <> $30;
if ColorVid then ScrSeg := $B800
            else ScrSeg := $B000;
```

The last step in **CheckColor** was to set the cursor position by calling **GotoXY**, but this was not the familiar Turbo function.

The GotoXY Procedure

This procedure works essentially identically to Turbo's **GotoXY**, but no checks are made to ensure that the resulting position is a valid screen location.

```
procedure GotoXY(XAxis, YAxis: byte);
begin
   ScrCol  := XAxis+WinLf-1;
   ScrRow  := YAxis+WinTop-1;
   Reg.AH  := $02;     Reg.DH  := ScrRow-1;
   Reg.BH  := $00;     Reg.DL  := ScrCol-1;
   intr($10,Dos.Registers(Reg));
end;
```

Provision has been made, however, for window-relative coordinate conversions, and the origin (1, 1) corresponds to Turbo's conventions rather than to DOS's 0, 0 screen origins. Because of this, the resulting ScrCol and ScrRow (the absolute screen coordinates) are the sum of the Axis and Window Limit decremented by 1.

When the values are passed to the interrupt call, another adjustment is required, which is one reason DOS uses the 0, 0 screen origin. To add a limit check, insert the conditional statement

```
if (WinTop <= ScrRow) and (ScrRow <= WinBot) and
   (WinLf <= ScrCol) and (ScrCol <= WinRt) then ...
```

before calling the interrupt will restrict cursor movement within the window settings. Alternately, this test could be expanded to turn the cursor off when moved outside of the window limits.

Clear Screen or Line

The next two procedures, **ClrLin** and **ClearScr**, are essentially equivalent to Turbo's **ClrEol** and **ClrScr**.

The ClrLin Procedure. The mechanism for the **ClrLin** procedure is quite simple. Beginning with the current cursor position variables, ScrCol and ScrRow, the local variable I is stepped through from the current column position to the *right window limit*.

Notice, for each step, that the offset used with MemW (I*2+(ScrRow-1) *160 increments by two. The address (segment and offset) parameters for all memory array references are always *byte* addresses, regardless of whether a byte, word, or longint variable is being accessed. In this particular instance, since the video memory (in *all* text modes) consists of two bytes (attribute byte and character byte) for each screen location, the address must be some multiple of two. This remains true even when only one byte is accessed — as will be the case in several later procedures.

In this instance, to clear screen positions, a new word value is assigned to each indicated memory location. A value of 0000h (null) could be used. This would set each screen memory location to null (00h) and set each attribute byte to null (00h or black on black). However, it is better practice, when clearing a single line or the entire screen, to set the attribute bytes to some default video value. Thus the value asigned is $00 or ScrAttr shl 8.

```
procedure ClrLin;
   var
      I : integer;
   begin
      for I := ScrCol-1 to WinRt-1 do
         MemW[ScrSeg:I*2+(ScrRow-1)*160] :=
         $00 or ScrAttr shl 8;
   end;
```

Note that the cursor position (ScrCol and ScrRow) has not been changed by this procedure.

I stated that it was better practice to set the screen position attribute byte to some default value instead of setting it to a null (black on black) value. But, why? Won't a new attribute be provided whenever a new characer is written? The answer is maybe, but not always, because there is nothing *requiring* a new attribute byte be written with each character written. Sometimes, it's preferable not to write a new attribute.

The ClearScr Procedure. Once a line is cleared, clearing the entire screen or clearing a window, is a simple matter.

```
procedure ClearScr;
   var
      I : integer;
   begin
      for I := WinTop to WinBot do
      begin   ScrRow := I;
              ScrCol := WinLf;
              ClrLin;             end;
   ScrRow := WinTop;
   ScrCol := WinLf;
   GotoXY(ScrCol,ScrRow);
   end;
```

The **ClearScr** procedure begins at the top line of the window setting, resets the horizontal position to the left of the window, and calls **ClrLin** — repeating this while stepping down to the window bottom. The procedure closes by resetting the cursor position variables to the upper left corner of the window and resetting the screen cursor.

Note: Both **ClrLin** and **ClearScr** are window oriented.

The SetWindow Procedure

By default, the initial window setting (assigned when **CheckColor** was called) takes in the entire screen. The **SetWindow** procedure simply reassigns the window limit variables and positions the cursor at the upper left corner.

```
procedure SetWindow(X1, Y1, X2, Y2 {, Color  : byte);
   begin
      WinLf := X1;      WinRt := X2;      ScrCol := WinLf;
      WinTop := Y1;     WinBot := Y2;     ScrRow := WinTop;
```

```
(*
        Reg.AH := $06;      { for scroll up or $07 for scroll down   }
        Reg.AL := $00;      { lines to scroll or zero to blank window }
        Reg.BH := Color;           {attribute for blanked area }
        Reg.CH := Y1-1;            { Y-Coord, Upper Left       }
        Reg.CL := X1-1;            { X-Coord, Upper Left       }
        Reg.DH := Y2-1;            { Y-Coord, Lower Right      }
        Reg.DL := X2-1;            { X-Coord, Lower Right      }
        intr($10,Dos.Registers(Reg));
*)

        GotoXY(ScrCol,ScrRow);
    end;
```

The Color parameter is necessary only if the DOS interrupt call will be used. If the interrupt is used, as shown, the selected window will be cleared using the Color attribute. All the procedures shown in this alternate video handler, however, recognize the window parameters without needing the DOS interrupt call.

Scrolling and Insertions

The next three procedures — BlankLine, InsScrLn, and AdvScrLn — provide scrolling, either within a window or for the screen as a whole. The first of these, **BlankLine**, is essentially identical to the earlier **ClrLin**, except that the cursor position is not used, and the line is blanked from WinLf to WinRt, and the current attribute byte is (ScrAttr) set. Normally, **BlankLine** would not be called directly, but it is used by the **InsScrLn** and **AdvScrLn** procedures.

```
procedure BlankLine;
    var
        I : integer;
    begin
        for I := WinLf-1 to WinRt-1 do
            MemW[ScrSeg:I*2+(ScrRow-1)*160] := $00 or ScrAttr shl 8;
    end;
```

The **InsScrLn** procedure, is the equivalent of Turbo's **InsLine**. It inserts a new line at the cursor position, scrolling the current line and all following lines down. The last line on the screen is discarded.

```
procedure InsScrLn;
    var
        I, J: integer;
```

```
    begin
        for I := WinBot-1 downto ScrRow+1 do
            for J := WinLf-1 to WinRt-1 do
                MemW[ScrSeg:J*2+(I-1)*160] :=
                    MemW[ScrSeg:J*2+(I-2)*160];
        BlankLine;
    end;
```

To do this, **InsScrLn** begins at the bottom of the screen or window and moves up to the screen row immediately below the cursor row. Each screen text position then takes the word value (the attribute *and* character bytes) from the line above. In the end, the cursor row is blanked, but the cursor position is left unchanged.

The **AdvScrLn** procedure uses a similar mechanism but begins by testing the screen position. If the cursor is not at the bottom of the screen, the cursor is moved down to the left (beginning) of the next line and no further action is taken. Only if the cursor is already at the bottom of the screen is scrolling initiated, and the screen contents are moved up one line with a blank line inserted at the bottom. The top line of the screen or window is discarded.

```
procedure AdvScrLn;
    var
        I, J: integer;
    begin
        if ScrRow > WinBot-1 then
        begin
            for ScrRow := WinTop to WinBot-1 do
                for ScrCol := WinLf-1 to WinRt-1 do
                MemW[ScrSeg:ScrCol*2+(ScrRow-1)*160] :=
                    MemW[ScrSeg:ScrCol*2+ScrRow*160];
            ScrRow := WinBot;
            BlankLine;
        end else ScrRow := succ(ScrRow);
        ScrCol := WinLf;
        GotoXY(ScrCol,ScrRow);
    end;
```

Unlike the **InsScrLn** procedure, the cursor position is always updated.

Writing the Screen

The preceding routines have manipulated or cleared existing screens or windows, but the screen isn't much good unless it can be written with new information. There are two ways to put information on the screen: **WriteChr** and **WriteChrOnly**.

```
procedure WriteChr(Col, Row: byte;  ThisChar: char);
   begin
      MemW[ScrSeg:(Col-1)*2+(Row-1)*160]  :=
         ord(ThisChar) or ScrAttr shl 8;
   end;
procedure WriteChrOnly(Col, Row: byte; ThisChar: char);
   begin
      Mem[ScrSeg:(Col-1)*2+(Row-1)*160]  :=
         ord(ThisChar);
   end;
```

WriteChr references the `MemW` array to update both the attribute and character bytes, whereas **WriteChrOnly** references the `Mem` array, updating only the character byte and leaving the current attribute byte unchanged. Note that both use the same memory offset formula, except that **WriteChrOnly** writes only one byte at the even memory locations with the character code.

Since writing one character at a time is tedious, **WriteScr** and **WriteLin** provide analogs for Turbo's **Write** and **WriteLn** procedures. **WriteScr** accepts a string parameter and calls **WriteChr** for each character in the string, updating the cursor coordinates and moving down to a new line when the end of the line (either screen or window) is reached. When this is done, the cursor is moved to the new coordinates.

```
procedure WriteScr(LnStr: string);
   var
      Col: byte;
   begin
      for Col := 1 to length(LnStr) do
      begin
         if ScrCol > WinRt then AdvScrLn;
         WriteChr(ScrCol,ScrRow,LnStr[Col]);
         ScrCol := succ(ScrCol);
      end;
   end;
```

WriteLin uses the **WriteScr** procedure but moves to a new line when it is finished.

```
procedure WriteLin(LnStr: string);
   begin
      WriteScr(LnStr);   AdvScrLn;
   end;
```

Applications

There can be several reasons for using **WriteChrOnly** instead of **WriteChr**. When the attribute byte is updated on all operations, two bytes of data are moved, even when one byte — the attribute — is exactly the same as the byte that was already there. This, since moving one byte takes less time than moving two, operations speed is improved.

In other cases, different areas of the screen might be set to specific color attributes and then written or rewritten with **WriteChrOnly** without having to reset the screen attributes according to the position. Thus, the programming is simplified.

For instance, suppose that lines 23, 24, and 25 were used for special information about a program that is running in a window at (1,1,80,22) with different background and foreground colors used to set off the status lines from the main screen. Using conventional Turbo Pascal, in version 3.x, **TextColor** and **TextBackground** would be called; or, in version 4.0, the TextAttr variable would have to be reset before and after each update to the status lines. Using the **WriteChrOnly** procedure, however, once the appropriate colors were set, the information could be changed without bothering with attribute changes. Also, no changes to window settings would be required since the Mem array references operate directly in the video memory according to the coordinates specified — and they are *not* window relevant.

Similarly, the **BlankLine**, **InsScrLn**, AdvScrLn, **ClearLn**, and **ClearScr** procedures might be modified to move information without changing the attribute bytes, or you might prefer to have versions that operated both ways or a Boolean switch to control operation. In other cases, a procedure to change the attribute byte without changing the character contents will be useful (see the **ChangeLight** procedure used in Chapter 11.

ALTSCRN.INC Include File

```
{ begin include file ALTSCRN.INC }
var
   ScrSeg : word;                    ColorVid : boolean;
```

```
procedure GotoXY(XAxis, YAxis: byte);
  begin
     ScrCol := XAxis+WinLf-1;
     ScrRow := YAxis+WinTop-1;
     if (ScrRow in [WinTop..WinBot]) and
        (ScrCol in [WinLf..WinRt]) then
     begin
       Reg.AH := $02;   Reg.DH := ScrRow-1;
       Reg.BH := $00;   Reg.DL := ScrCol-1;
       intr($10,Dos.Registers(Reg));
     end;
  end;


procedure CheckColor;
  begin
     ScrSeg := $B000;   ColorVid := false;    { first, assume monochrome      }
     if (mem[0000:1040] and 48) <> 48 then    { then test for color           }
     begin     ScrSeg := $B800;               {      and change the ScrSeg and }
               ColorVid := true;    end;      {      video flag accordingly   }
                                              {*** and a few initial settings ***}
     ScrAttr := $0E;                          { sets Yellow for default color }
      ScrRow := $01;      ScrCol := $01;       {      and initial positions     }
      WinLf := $01;       WinRt := $50;        { set full screen for initial   }
      WinTop := $01;      WinBot := $19;       {      window coordinates        }
     GotoXY( ScrRow, ScrCol );                { set cursor position           }
  end;


procedure SetColor(Foreground, Background: byte);
   var
     BlinkByte : byte;
   begin
     BlinkByte := Foreground shl 3 and $80;
     if not ColorVid and (BlinkByte = $80)
        then ScrAttr := $70
        else ScrAttr := ( Foreground and $0F )
                    or ( Background shl 4 and $70 )
                    or ( BlinkByte );                end;


procedure ClrLin;
   var
     I : integer;
   begin
     for I := ScrCol-1 to WinRt-1 do
       MemW[ScrSeg:I*2+(ScrRow-1)*160] :=
          $00 or ScrAttr shl 8;
   end;


procedure ClearScr;
   var
```

AN ALTERNATIVE VIDEO HANDLER

```
         I : integer;
    begin
       for I := WinTop to WinBot do
       begin    ScrRow := I;
                ScrCol := WinLf;
                ClrLin;            end;
       ScrRow := WinTop;
       ScrCol := WinLf;
       GotoXY(ScrCol,ScrRow);
    end;


procedure SetWindow(X1, Y1, X2, Y2 {, Color } : byte);
    begin
        WinLf := X1;     WinRt := X2;     ScrCol := WinLf;
        WinTop := Y1;    WinBot := Y2;    ScrRow := WinTop;
(*
     The DOS window handler, interrupt 10h, functions 06h and
     07h are optional ... all routines in the alternate video
     package are written in such a manner that they can operate
     without these.
     Using the interrupt -- as shown -- will cause the selected
     window to be cleared ...

     Reg.AH := $06;              { for scroll up or $07 for scroll down    }
     Reg.AL := $00;              { lines to scroll or zero to blank window }
     Reg.BH := Color;            { attribute for blanked area              }
     Reg.CH := Y1-1;             { Y-Coord, Upper Left   }
     Reg.CL := X1-1;             { X-Coord, Upper Left   }
     Reg.DH := Y2-1;             { Y-Coord, Lower Right }
     Reg.DL := X2-1;             { X-Coord, Lower Right }
        intr($10,Dos.Registers(Reg));
*)
    end;


procedure BlankLine;
    var
        I : integer;
    begin
       for I := WinLf-1 to WinRt-1 do
          MemW[ScrSeg:I*2+(ScrRow-1)*160] :=
             $00 or ScrAttr shl 8;
    end;


procedure InsScrLn;
    var
       I, J: integer;
    begin
       for I := WinBot-1 downto ScrRow+1 do
          for J := WinLf-1 to WinRt-1 do
```

```pascal
                MemW[ScrSeg:J*2+(I-1)*160] :=
                    MemW[ScrSeg:J*2+(I-2)*160];
            BlankLine;
        end;

    procedure AdvScrLn;
        var
            I, J: integer;
        begin
            if ScrRow > WinBot-1 then
            begin
                for ScrRow := WinTop to WinBot-1 do
                    for ScrCol := WinLf-1 to WinRt-1 do
                        MemW[ScrSeg:ScrCol*2+(ScrRow-1)*160] :=
                            MemW[ScrSeg:ScrCol*2+ScrRow*160];
                ScrRow := WinBot;
                BlankLine;
            end else ScrRow := succ(ScrRow);
            ScrCol := WinLf;
            Gotoxy(ScrCol,ScrRow);
        end;

    procedure WriteChr(Col,Row: byte;  ThisChar: char);
        begin
            MemW[ScrSeg:(Col-1)*2+(Row-1)*160] :=
                ord(ThisChar) or ScrAttr shl 8;
        end;

    procedure WriteScr(LnStr: string);
        var
            Col: byte;
        begin
            for Col := 1 to length(LnStr) do
            begin
                if ScrCol > WinRt then AdvScrLn;
                WriteChr(ScrCol,ScrRow,LnStr[Col]);
                ScrCol := succ(ScrCol);
            end;
            GotoXY(ScrCol,ScrRow);
        end;

    procedure WriteLin(LnStr: string);
        begin
            WriteScr(LnStr);  AdvScrLn;
        end;

    procedure WriteXY(XCoord, YCoord: byte; LnStr: string);
        var
            Col, NCol, XAdj, YAdj: shortint;
```

AN ALTERNATIVE VIDEO HANDLER

```
  begin
    ScrRow := YCoord+WinTop;    XAdj := -1;    YAdj := 0;
    for Col := 1 to length(LnStr) do
    begin
      NCol := Col+XCoord+XAdj;
      if NCol > WinRt then
      begin
        NCol := NCol-WinRt+WinLf-1;
        XAdj := -WinRt-WinLf;
        YAdj := 1;
        AdvScrLn;
      end;
      WriteChr(NCol+WinLf-1, YCoord+YAdj+WinTop-1, LnStr[Col]);
    end;                              { v3.x --> copy(LnStr,Col,1)          }
    ScrCol := NCol+1;
    ScrRow := YCoord+YAdj;
    GotoXY(ScrCol,ScrRow);
  end;

{ end include file ALTSCRN.INC }
```

11

Trapping the Keyboard

In previous chapters, the standard Turbo **ReadKey** function (`read(kbd,Ch)` for version 3.x) has been used for keyboard access. For many applications, this is all that's needed. At other times, however, it is useful or even imperative to know more about what is happening at the keyboard than merely which key character is being returned. If the keyboard were only a typewriter where what appeared on the output (the paper) was exactly what appeared on the key struck — a WYSIWYG[1] situation — there would be little need or interest in knowing much of anything about the keys. A computer is hardly that simple.

When any key is pressed, several events happen. First, a code is transmitted saying exactly which key was pressed (the `make` code). Then, when the key is released, a second code (`break` code) is also transmitted. These make/break signals are intercepted by interrupt 09h and provide the basic mechanism for deciphering the keyboard by storing resulting key codes in the keyboard buffer. (The make and break codes are the same except for the high bit — bit 7 — which is 0 for make and 1 for break.)

At a different level of access, when a program function such as Turbo's **ReadKey** (version 3.x uses `read(kbd,Ch)`) interrogates the keyboard, the

---

1. WYSIWYG — What You See Is What You Get — is commonly any word processor that displays work in progress essentially the same as it will later appear on paper.

keyboard buffer is accessed using interrupt 16h and the information returned is the result codes interpreted by the BIOS[2] not the actual make/break information that was trapped by interrupt 09h.

Many TSR (Terminate and Stay Resident) programs such as Hot Menu or SideKick use interrupt 09h to respond to specific keystrokes. Others such as SuperKey are written to enhance the result codes produced by various keystrokes, for example, by returning a macro key string in response to pressing F1. SuperKey and similar programs are also able to provide responses that the present BIOS versions do not implement, including the F11 and F12 keys found on most enhanced keyboards.

For the present, however, the discussion will be confined to the conventional keyboard responses accessible through interrupt 16h or via the **ReadKey** or `read(kbd,Ch)` functions. (The scan and char codes returned by each key and shift state are shown in Appendix B.)

Note: The following illustrations and demo program are based on an enhanced or expanded keyboard having 101 keys and operating with an AT system. If you are using an older style 84-keyboard or some other variation, the demo program will still function but the response positions shown will be for the enhanced keyboard layout. Other, minor variations are found on XT or PC systems, but the principal information is applicable to most MS-DOS computer systems.

The Keyboard Scan Codes

Each physical key on the keyboard has a scan code identifying the key pressed. Originally, these can codes were assigned according to the physical layout of the keyboard. As the keyboard layouts have changed to better fit the operator's convenience, the scan codes no longer reflect the physical key layouts but are now embedded fossils much like the original Baudot control codes (ASCII codes 00h..1Fh) originally created for teletype operations. Figure 11-1 shows the key position scan codes for a modern, expanded keyboard.

---

2. BIOS — Basic Input Output System — refers to low-level routines located in ROM memory. These are directly accessed through interrupt functions. For example, the interrupt 10h functions are ROM BIOS routines, whereas the interrupt 21h functions are DOS interrupts (belonging to the Disk Operating System). DOS functions call BIOS routines to send characters to the screen, but the BIOS functions can also be called directly.

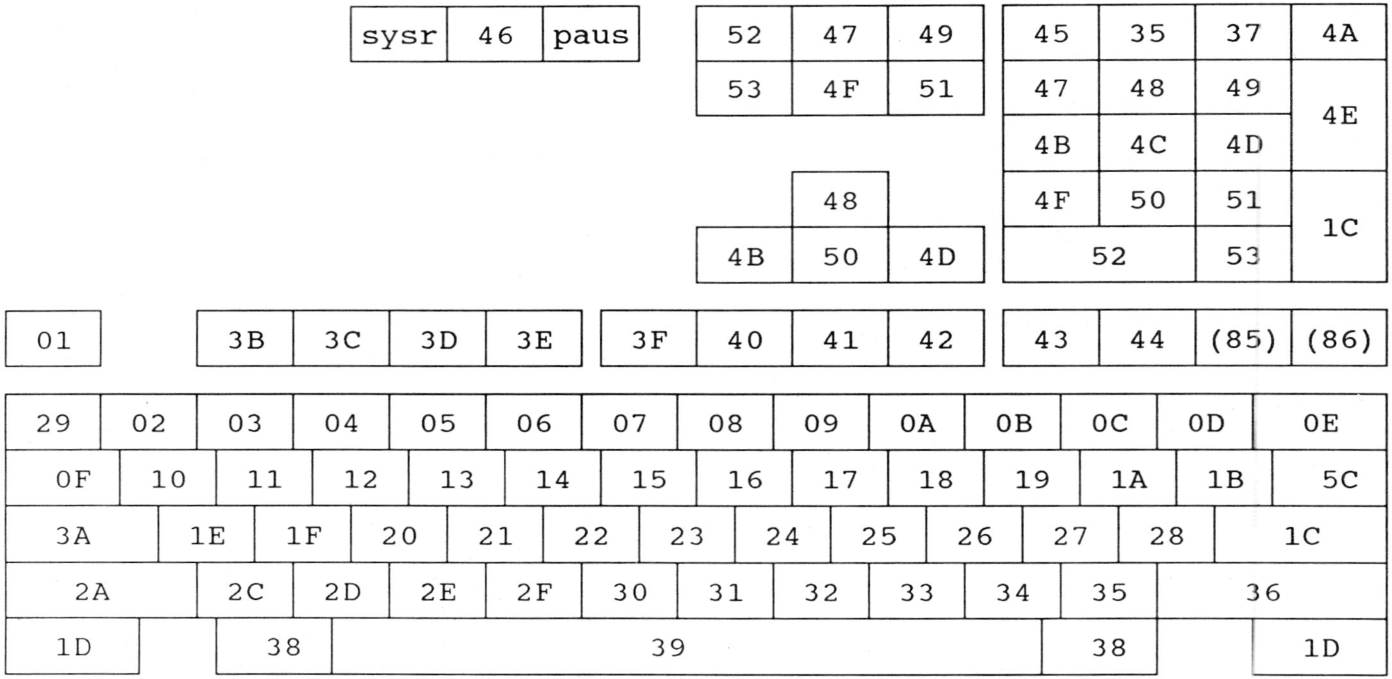

```
                                              sysr  46  paus

01

3B  3C  3D  3E  3F      40  41  42  43  44  (85) (86)

29  02  03  04  05  06  07  08  09  0A  0B  0C  0D  0E
0F  10  11  12  13  14  15  16  17  18  19  1A  1B  5C
3A  1E  1F  20  21  22  23  24  25  26  27  28      1C
2A  2C  2D  2E  2F  30  31  32  33  34  35  36
1D  38          39                      38      1D

                                        52  47  49      45  35  37  4A
                                        53  4F  51      47  48  49  4E
                                                        4B  4C  4D
                                            48          4F  50  51  1C
                                        4B  50  4D          52  53
```

Figure 11-1 Expanded Keyboard Layout Showing Scan Codes

Although the scan codes indicate which key was pressed, there are also six shift conditions associated with the keyboard. The six shift keys are: CapsLock, NumLock, Right Shift, Left Shift, Control, and Alternate. Each of these controls a single shift condition or shift state. A seventh shift condition is produced by the Insert key, although this does not directly affect the codes produced by the keyboard. And, on AT systems, an eighth condition is set by the Scroll Lock key.

Note: Many keyboards have two Ctrl and two Alt keys (as illustrated), but electrically these are a single key and produce only a single scan code. The Right and Left Shift keys, however, are electrically separate and return separate scan codes, even though they are normally treated as a single key.

Each of these shift conditions is stored as a Boolean flag and accessed by interrupt 16h, function 02h, as shown in the **Keyboard__Status** procedure.

```
procedure Keyboard_Status;
   begin
      Reg.AH := $02
      intr($16,Dos.Registers(Reg));
      InsertOn := (Reg.AL and $80) = $80;
      CapsLock := (Reg.AL and $40) = $40;
      NumbLock := (Reg.AL and $20) = $20;
      ScroLock := (Reg.AL and $10) = $10;
      AltKeyDn := (Reg.AL and $08) = $08;
      CtlKeyDn := (Reg.AL and $04) = $04;
      LfShftDn := (Reg.AL and $02) = $02;
      RtShftDn := (Reg.AL and $01) = $01;
   end;
```

The first four shift flags InsertOn, CapsLock, NumbLock, and ScroLock) toggle on and off. If the flag status is on when the key is pressed, it is turned off and vice versa.

The last four shift flags, (AltKeyDn, CtlKeyDn, LfShftDn, and RtShftDn) are only true as long as the key is held closed (down). These are turned on by the make signal and turned off by the break signal.

Six of these shift conditions (CapsLock, NumbLock, AltKeyDn, CtlKeyDn, LfShftDn, and RtShftDn) directly affect the results (the character codes) returned by the keyboard. For example, the Caps Lock and Right and Left Shift keys produce lowercase and uppercase letters, and either the Right or Left Shift key changes the upper key row from letters to numbers and shifts the keypad from functions to numbers.

The function keys are also governed by the two Shift keys, but they respond as well to the Ctrl and Alt shifts so that each function key is capable of returning four different codes. In similar fashion, most of the other keys can return four different results, although some keys such as the keypad require an interrupt 09h handler (such as SuperKey) to enable some AltKey responses and a few keys are provided only two or three possible responses.

The other two shift conditions (InsertOn and ScroLock) do not produce any direct effects but may be used or ignored by your program as you desire.

There are also hierarchies of shift responses. First, the Left and Right Shift keys, even though these are treated as separate keys, do not affect the keyboard separately. If both shift keys are down (true), the results are the same as if either key were pressed alone.

With the CapsLock in effect, the alpha keys return shifted results, but if either of the Shift keys is added, the CapsLock is reversed and a similar response is made by the keypad when the NumLock is in effect. (A Boolean truth table for the various shift combinations appears in Appendix B.)

There is a second hierarchy between the Alt, Ctrl, and Shift keys with the Shift keys at the bottom of the order and the Alt key at the top. If more than one of these are pressed, the Alt key takes precedence over both the Ctrl and Shift keys and the Ctrl key takes precedence over the Shift keys. This hierarchy does not however prevent the shift flags from being read directly — it only governs the BIOS response in generating result codes. Thus the shift flags can be used as action keys, and in the **Show__Keys__and__Scan__Codes** demo program, the Ctrl-Alt-Shift combination is used as an exit code.

The following three keys are shown with the scan and character codes returned in each shift condition):

Key	scan / char	Key	scan / char	Key	scan / char
F1	3Bh / 00h	6	07h / 36h	a	1Eh / 61h
Shift-F1	54h / 00h	^	07h / 5Eh	A	1Eh / 41h
Ctrl-F1	5Eh / 00h	Ctrl-6	07h / 1Eh	Ctrl-A	1Eh / 01h
Alt-F1	68h / 00h	Alt-6	7Dh / 00h	Alt-A	1Eh / 00h

The twelve function keys (assuming F11 and F12 are present and enabled by an interrupt 9 handler) never return character codes, but each returns four different scan codes depending on the shift conditions set. On the other hand, the alpha keys always return the same scan code, but return different character codes for each circumstance and, for an Alt-shift, always return a null character code, indicating that the scan code should be used.

For Ctrl keys, the character codes returned for '@' .. '_'(40h..5Fh) are always decremented by 40h (responding with 00h..1Fh). Thus Ctrl-@ returns a null character code (00h) instead of 40h, and Ctrl-C returns 03h, which is the old End Transmission code from teletype days, instead of 43h. (There is no Alt-@ code to produce confusion; instead the Alt-2 key code is returned.)

Some of the other keys, however, follow a mixture of responses, as can be seen with the 6^ (six/carat) key. A Ctrl-6, following the rule for the alpha keys, would return a negative value (\-0A) as the character code, but instead the result is Ctrl-^ (Ctrl-carat, 1Eh), which is valid. Alt-6 does return a null character code, but the scan code has been changed to 7Dh instead of 07h.

One other exception to the general rules is found in the Ctrl-Backspace. The character code normally returned by the Backspace key is already a control code (08h or Ctrl-H), but the Ctrl-Backspace combination returns a character code of 7Fh, which just happens to be the missing DELete character[3] from the standard ASCII character set.

These changes in key response are handled by the BIOS and are inserted in the keyboard buffer as the appropriate keys are pressed. See Appendix B for a complete list of keyboard response codes.

Show_Keys_And_Scan_Codes

Figure 11-2 shows the screen layout used by the **Show_Keys_And_Scan_Codes** demo program. The layout used is for a 101 key, enhanced or expanded, keyboard, which are popular with both XT and AT systems (and sometimes found with upgraded PC systems). Since the actual physical keyboard layout could not be shown within the normal screen width, the right-hand side of the board (keypad, arrow keys, and screen control keys) appears at the top of the display with the main keyboard below it.

The status byte is shown in the upper left quadrant of the display, displaying the Boolean status byte for the eight possible shift conditions. Below this, each key entry will be displayed as a character, if practical, together with the scan and char codes generated by the BIOS in response to the key entry.

3. The DELete key was common to most earlier computer systems and was not the same Delete key as found on present keyboards, which earlier appeared as DelLn or similar. The old Del key transmitted the delete character 7Fh and was used similar to the backspace key except for deleting characters *at* the cursor position instead of before and without moving the cursor. In many applications, the new Delete key is used as if it still transmitted the delete character, but this is now a software-dependent function.

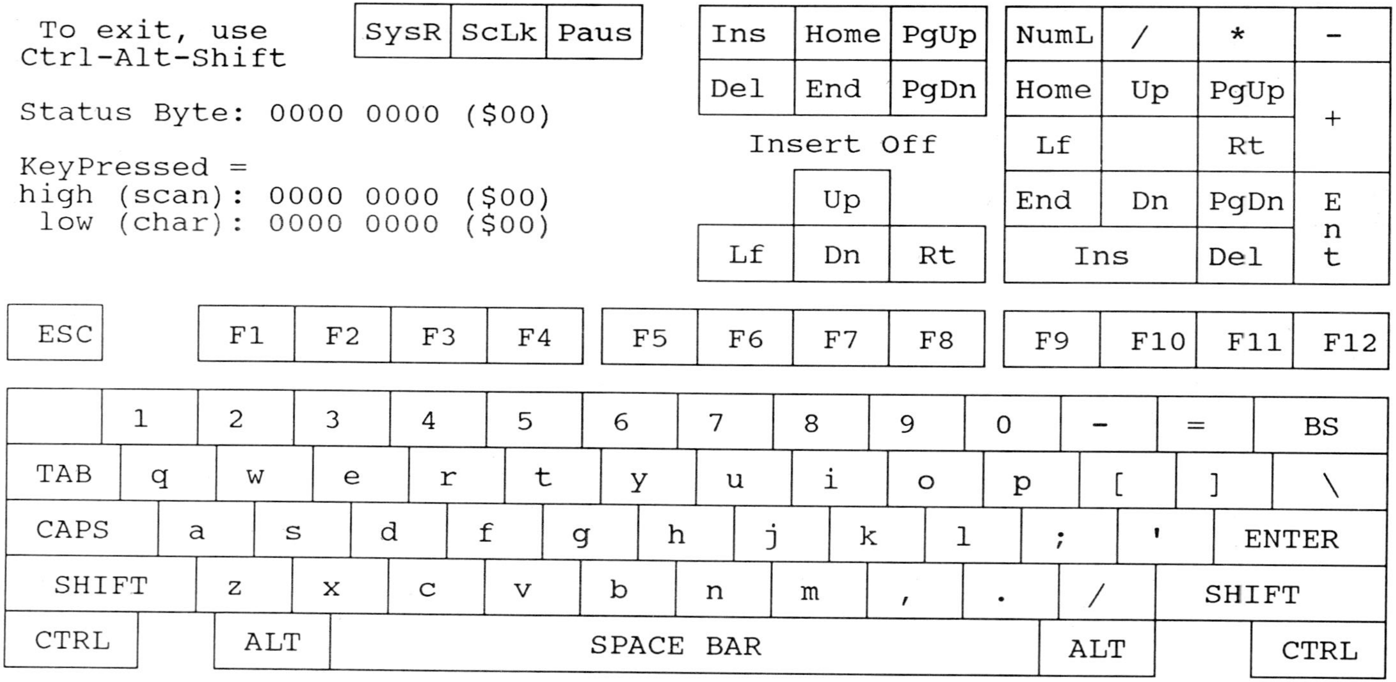

To exit, use
Ctrl-Alt-Shift

| SysR | ScLk | Paus |

Status Byte: 0000 0000 ($00)

KeyPressed =
high (scan): 0000 0000 ($00)
low (char): 0000 0000 ($00)

| Ins | Home | PgUp |
| Del | End | PgDn |

Insert Off

| | Up | |
| Lf | Dn | Rt |

NumL	/	*	-
Home	Up	PgUp	+
Lf	Rt		
End	Dn	PgDn	E n t
	Ins	Del	

| ESC |
| F1 | F2 | F3 | F4 | | F5 | F6 | F7 | F8 | | F9 | F10 | F11 | F12 |

1	2	3	4	5	6	7	8	9	0	-	=	BS
TAB	q	w	e	r	t	y	u	i	o	p	[	]	\
CAPS	a	s	d	f	g	h	j	k	l	;	'	ENTER
SHIFT	z	x	c	v	b	n	m	,	.	/	SHIFT
CTRL	ALT	SPACE BAR	ALT	CTRL

Figure 11-2 Show__Key Display

As each key is entered, the appropriate segment on the display will be highlighted. The CapsLock, NumLock, and ScroLock keys will be highlighted only when the flags for these shift conditions are true, and the insert flag status will be shown as Insert On or Insert Off. Also, the CapsLock, Right and Left Shift, and NumLock keys will change the keyboard display as appropriate.

In several cases, especially with an expanded keyboard, two keys return the same scan and char codes and cannot be readily distinguished. When this happens, both keys are highlighted.

The programming instructions in the demo should require little or no explanation since most of the program is designed simply to create and update the pseudo-keyboard display.

The Key__Read Procedure

Instead of using Turbo's **ReadKey** function (or using version 3.x's read(kbd,Ch)), a direct call to interrupt 16h, function 00h, returns both the scan and char bytes from the keyboard buffer in the AX register.

```
procedure Key_Read;
   begin
      Reg.AX := $0000;
      intr($16,Dos.Registers(Reg));
      KScan := hi(Reg.AX);            {scan byte}
      KByte := lo(Reg.AX);            {char byte}
      Report Key(KScan, KByte);
   end;
```

If you are accustomed to Turbo version 3.x and are familiar with the extended key codes returned, note that the initial ESCape character sequence returned by the function keys was an interpretation by Turbo version 3.x. Using the direct interrupt call with version 3.x will still return the correct scan and key codes as shown here and no changes are required.

The Mem Array Reference

Several functions in the demo program use Mem and MemW references to check or change information on the screen. (The Mem array references are explained in Chapter 10.)

In a couple of instances where Mem references have been used, a second version appears in the source code inside comment brackets to show alternate statements that produce the same results. These are provided simply to illustrate optional methods.

Idiosyncrasies

In the **Report__Keyboard__Status** procedure, a few lines of code are *commented out* together with the title Optional Test and a reference to the text for an explanation. This concerns a matter that cannot be easily described but may be noticeable when the demo is run.

When NumLock is in effect, the keypad is shifted from function keys to numerical keys. If the Right or Left Shift keys are pressed, the number keys are shifted back to function keys, but the separate block of screen function keys and arrow keys are also shifted and here's the bug: When a key is pressed, either on the keypad or one of the alternate screen function keys, the display will shift again — apparently incorrectly.

If you activate the Optional Test code (a one-second time delay is included), you will see a second status byte display. If you watch carefully, you will also see the Right Shift flag bit being changed. This is precisely the bit that is affecting the display, but it is also being used by the system to set the keypad and screen function keys to return the correct code.

If the Right Shift flag is true, a break code is generated. If Right Shift is false, a make code is passed, but only one of the code pair is generated, which leaves the system slightly out of sync. This *does not* affect the actual operation of the system. The correct scan and char codes are generated and nothing is lost, missing, or misset. It is merely a minor curiosity and, in some applications, is used as a feature (for example, the popular HOT Menu utility uses this double Right-Shift as a hotkey to access pop-up utilities).

Keyboard Demo Program

BINARYRF.INC Include File

```
(* begin BINARYRF.INC -- also used by demo program in Chapter 9  *)
(* returns string with Hexadecimal and Binary values represented *)

   function HexRef(RefNum : byte): string;      { v3.x, use STR20            }
      const
         HexStr : array[0..15] of char = '0123456789ABCDEF';
```

```
      begin
         HexRef := '( $' + HexStr[ RefNum shr 4 ]
                            + HexStr[ RefNum and $0F ] + ' )';
      end;

   function BinaryRef(RefNum : byte): string;     { v3.x, use STR20 }
      var
         I, J, K : integer;
          TxtStr : array[1..8] of char;
         TempStr : string[1];
      begin
         K := 128;
         for I := 8 downto 1 do
         begin
            str((RefNum and K) shr (I-1):1,TempStr);
            TxtStr[9-I] := TempStr[1];
          { v3.x --> := TempStr; }
            K := K shr 1;
         end;
         BinaryRef := copy(TxtStr,1,4)+' '+copy(TxtStr,5,4)+' '+HexRef(RefNum);
      end;

(* end BINARYRF.INC *)
```

SHOW_KEY.PAS Program

```
program Show_Keys_And_Scan_Codes;    { SHOW_KEY.PAS }
            { even though the ALTSCRN video handler is used, you }
uses  Crt, { still need the Crt unit for the color definitions       }
      Dos; { and the Dos unit to handle interrupt calls              }

type
   STR80 = string[80];
   STR20 = string[20];
   Regs = record case Integer of
               1: (AX, BX, CX, DX, BP, SI, DI, DS, ES, Flags : word);
               2: (AL, AH, BL, BH, CL, CH, DL, DH          : byte); end;
var
   Reg : Regs;                              InKey : char;
   OldStatus, LastScan, KByte, KScan, ScrAttr,
   ScrRow, ScrCol, WinLf, WinRt, WinTop, WinBot : byte;
      InsertOn, CapsLock, NumbLock, ScroLock,
      AltKeyDn, CtlKeyDn, LfShftDn, RtShftDn : boolean;

{$I ALTSCRN.INC}      { alternate screen handler }
{$I BINARYRF.INC}

procedure Hi_Light_Key_Pressed(Scan: byte);
   var
      XAxis, YAxis, KeySize, Attribute, I : byte;
```

```
procedure Block_Light;
    var    I : integer;
    begin    for I := 0 to KeySize do
                Mem[ScrSeg:(XAxis+I)*2+YAxis*160+1] := Attribute;    end;


procedure Position(Scan: byte);
    begin    XAxis := 0;    YAxis := 0;
        case Scan of        $37, $4A : YAxis := 1;    { set the YAxis position        }
                            $47..$49 : YAxis := 3;
                            $4B..$4D : YAxis := 5;
                            $4F..$51 : YAxis := 7;
                            $52, $53 : YAxis := 9;
            $01, $3B..$44, $54..$71 : YAxis := 12;
            $02..$0E, $29, $78..$83 : YAxis := 15;
                $0F, $10..$1B, $2B : YAxis := 17;
                    $1C, $1E..$28 : YAxis := 19;
                        $2C..$35 : YAxis := 21;
                            $39 : YAxis := 23;            end; {case}
        case Scan of $01, $0F, $29 : XAxis := 1;    { set the XAxis position        }
                        $02..$0D : XAxis :=  6+5*(Scan-$02);
                        $78..$83 : XAxis :=  6+5*(Scan-$78);
                        $10..$1B : XAxis :=  7+5*(Scan-$10);
                        $1E..$28 : XAxis :=  9+5*(Scan-$1E);
                        $2C..$35 : XAxis := 11+5*(Scan-$2C);
                        $3B..$3E : XAxis := 11+5*(Scan-$3B);
                        $54..$57 : XAxis := 11+5*(Scan-$54);
                        $5E..$61 : XAxis := 11+5*(Scan-$5E);
                        $68..$6B : XAxis := 11+5*(Scan-$68);
                            $39 : XAxis := 18;
                        $3F..$42 : XAxis := 32+5*(Scan-$3F);
                        $58..$5B : XAxis := 32+5*(Scan-$58);
                        $62..$65 : XAxis := 32+5*(Scan-$62);
                        $6C..$6F : XAxis := 32+5*(Scan-$6C);
                        $43..$44 : XAxis := 53+5*(Scan-$43);
                        $47..$49 : XAxis := 53+5*(Scan-$47);
                        $4B..$4D : XAxis := 53+5*(Scan-$4B);
                        $4F..$51 : XAxis := 53+5*(Scan-$4F);
                        $5C..$5D : XAxis := 53+5*(Scan-$5C);
                        $66..$67 : XAxis := 53+5*(Scan-$66);
                        $70..$71 : XAxis := 53+5*(Scan-$70);
                            $52 : XAxis := 53;
                        $37, $53 : XAxis := 63;
                            $1C : XAxis := 64;
                            $0E : XAxis := 66;
                            $2B : XAxis := 67;
                            $4A : XAxis := 68;            end; {case}
        case Scan of    $0F : KeySize := 4;            { and the key width        }
                        $39 : KeySize := 35;
                        $52 : KeySize := 8;
```

TRAPPING THE KEYBOARD

```
               $1C : KeySize := 7;
               $0E : KeySize := 5;
               else  KeySize := 3;    end; {case}
       if (XAxis <> 0) and (YAxis <> 0) then Block_Light;
                                        { and some keys appear twice        }
     case Scan of        $48 : YAxis := 7;
        $35, $52, $47, $49 : YAxis := 1;
              $53, $4F, $51 : YAxis := 3;
              $4B, $50, $4D : YAxis := 9;        end; {case}
     case Scan of        $35 : XAxis := 58;
           $47,$4F,$48,$50 : XAxis := 42;
               $49,$51,$4D : XAxis := 47;
               $52,$53,$4B : XAxis := 37;        end; {case}
     KeySize := 3;
     case Scan of
        $35, $47..$49, $4B, $4D, $4F, $50..$53 : Block_Light;
     end; {case}
     case Scan of
        $1C : begin   XAxis := 68;
                      YAxis := 7;   Block_Light;
                      YAxis := 8;   Block_Light;
                      YAxis := 9;   Block_Light;   end;
        $4E : begin   XAxis := 68;
                      YAxis := 3;   Block_Light;
                      YAxis := 4;   Block_Light;
                      YAxis := 5;   Block_Light;   end;   end; {case}
   end;


   begin    { Hi__Light__Key__Pressed }
      Attribute := $0A;   Position(LastScan);
      Attribute := $A0;   Position(Scan);         LastScan := Scan;
   end;


procedure Add_Chars(X,Y: Byte; WorkStr: STR20);
   var     I : byte;
   begin    for I := 0 to length(WorkStr)-1 do
            WriteXY(X-1+I*5,Y,' '+copy(WorkStr,I+1,1)+'  ');   end;


procedure Write_Number_Line;
   begin    SetColor(LightGreen,Black);
           if RtShftDn or LfShftDn then
           begin    Add_Chars(3,16,'~!@#$%^&*()_+');
                    Add_Chars(59,18,'{}|');
                    Add_Chars(56,20,':"  ');
                    Add_Chars(48,22,'<>?');         end else
           begin    Add_Chars(3,16,"1234567890-=');
                    Add_Chars(59,18,'[]\');
                    Add_Chars(56,20,';'+#39);
                    Add_Chars(48,22,',./');         end;         end;
```

```
procedure Write_Main_Keys;
    begin   SetColor(LightGreen,Black);
            if (CapsLock and RtShftDn) or
               (CapsLock and LfShftDn) or
               (not CapsLock and not (RtShftDn or LfShftDn)) then
            begin   Add_Chars(9,18,'qwertyuiop');
                    Add_Chars(11,20,'asdfghjkl');
                    Add_Chars(13,22,'zxcvbnm');      end else
            begin   Add_Chars(9,18,'QWERTYUIOP');
                    Add_Chars(11,20,'ASDFGHJKL');
                    Add_Chars(13,22,'ZXCVBNM');      end;        end;


procedure Add_Word(X,Y:.byte; WorkStr: STR20);
    begin    repeat
                WriteXY(X,Y,copy(WorkStr,1,4));
                delete(WorkStr,1,4);
                inc(X,5);
             until length(WorkStr) = 0;          end;


procedure Write_Special_Keys;
    begin   SetColor(LightGreen,Black);
            if (RtShftDn or LfShftDn) and not NumbLock then
            begin   Add_Word(38, 2,' 0   7   9  ');
                    Add_Word(59, 2,' ?   PrSc');
                    Add_Word(38, 4,' .   1   3  ');
                    WriteXY(43, 8,' 8  ');
                    Add_Word(38,10,' 4   2   6  ');   end else
              begin    Add_Word(38, 2,' InsHomePgUp');
                    Add_Word(59, 2,' /     *   ');
                    Add_Word(38, 4,' Del EndPgDn');
                    WriteXY(43, 8,' Up ');
                    Add_Word(38,10,' Lf  Dn  Rt ');   end;      end;


procedure Write_Function_Pad;
    begin   SetColor(LightGreen,Black);
            if (not NumbLock and not (RtShftDn or LfShftDn))
               or (NumbLock and (RtShftDn or LfShftDn)) then
            begin   Add_Word(54,4,'Home Up PgUp');
                    Add_Word(54,6,' Lf      Rt ');
                    Add_Word(54,8,' End Dn PgDn');
                    WriteXY(56,10,' Ins');
                    WriteXY(64,10,' Del');        end else
            begin   Add_Word(54,4,' 7   8   9  ');
                    Add_Word(54,6,' 4   5   6  ');
                    Add_Word(54,8,' 1   2   3  ');
                    WriteXY(56,10,' 0  ');
                    WriteXY(64,10,' .  ');          end;      end;
```

TRAPPING THE KEYBOARD

```
procedure Write_Keyboard;
    var   I : integer;
    begin
        SetColor(Brown,Black);
        WriteXY(19, 1, '
        WriteXY(19, 2, '
        WriteXY(19, 3, '
        WriteXY(19, 4, '
        WriteXY(19, 5, '
        WriteXY(19, 6, '
        WriteXY(19, 7, '
        WriteXY(19, 8, '
        WriteXY(19, 9, '
        WriteXY(19,10, '
        WriteXY(19,11, '
        WriteXY( 1,12, '
        WriteXY( 1,13, '
        WriteXY( 1,14, '
        WriteXY( 1,15, '
        WriteXY( 1,16, '
        WriteXY( 1,17, '
        WriteXY( 1,18, '
        WriteXY( 1,19, '
        WriteXY( 1,20, '
        WriteXY( 1,21, '
        WriteXY( 1,22, '
        WriteXY( 1,23, '
        WriteXY( 1,24, '
        WriteXY( 1,25, '

        WriteXY(53,12, '
        WriteXY(53,13, '
        WriteXY(53,14, '
        WriteXY(53,15, '
        WriteXY(53,16, '
        WriteXY(53,17, '
        WriteXY(53,18, '
        WriteXY(53,19, '
        WriteXY(53,20, '
        WriteXY(53,21, '
        WriteXY(53,22, '
        WriteXY(53,23, '
        WriteXY(53,24, '
        WriteXY(53,25, '
```

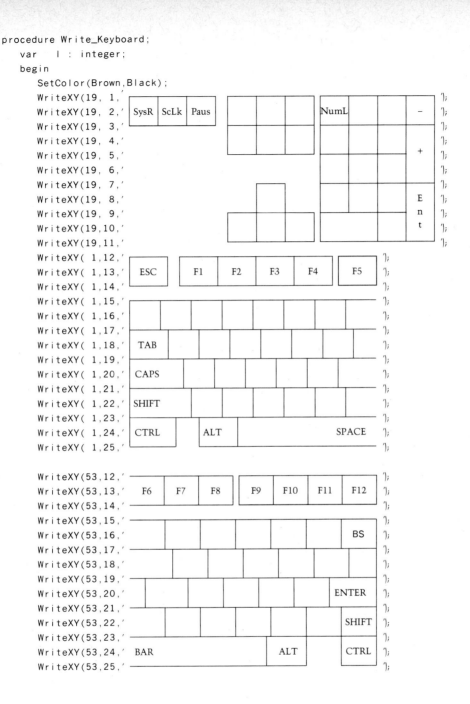

```
        Write_Special_Keys;   Write_Function_Pad;
        Write_Number_Line;    Write_Main_Keys;
        for I := 0 to 1910 do
            if not ( chr(Mem[ScrSeg:I*2]) in
                [' ','┌','─','┬','┴','┐','└','│','┘','┼','├','┤',','] ) then
                    Mem[ScrSeg:I*2+1] := LightGreen;
(*
        for J := 0 to 24 do
        for I := 0 to 79 do
        if not ( chr(Mem[ScrSeg:I*2+J*160]) in
        [' ','┌','─','┬','┴','┐','└','│','┘','┼','├','┤',','] ) then
            Mem[ScrSeg:I*2+J*160+1] := LightGreen;
*)
    end;


(*
```

If you do not have an editor or word processor that will allow convenient entry of the extended ASCII characters used for the box drawings in this program, the following alternate version of Write_Keyboard uses 16 substrings and decimal character codes to create the display.

```
procedure Write_Keyboard; {begin alternate version}
    var
        I : integer;
        S0,S1,S2,S3,S4,S5,S6,S7,S8,S9,SA,SB,SC,SD,SE,SF : string[20];
    begin
        S0 := '    ';
        S1 := #179+S0;        S2 := #196+#196+#196;    S3 := #196+S2;
        S4 := #196+#193;      S5 := #196+S4;           S6 := #191+#218;
        S7 := #193+#194;      S8 := #193+#196;         S9 := #196+#194;
        SA := S3+#196;        SB := S3+#194;           SC := S3+#193;
        SD := S3+#197;        SE := S0+S0+' ';         SF := SE+S0+S0;

        SetColor(Brown,Black);
        WriteXY(19, 1,#218+SB+SB+S3+#191+'   '+#218+SB+SB+S3+S6+SB+SB+SB+S3+#191);
        WriteXY(19, 2,#179+'SysR'+#179+'ScLk'+#179+'Paus'+#179+'   '+S1+S1+S1+
                      #179+#179+'NumL'+S1+S1+#179+' -  '+#179);
        WriteXY(19, 3,#192+SC+SC+S3+#217+'   '+#195+SD+SD+S3+#180+#195+SD+SD+
                      SD+S3+#180);
        WriteXY(19, 4,SE+SE+S1+S1+S1+#179+S1+S1+S1+S1+#179);
        WriteXY(19, 5,SE+SE+#192+SC+SC+S3+#217+#195+SD+SD+S3+#180+'  +  '+#179);
        WriteXY(19, 6,SF+SF+S1+S1+S1+S1+#179);
        WriteXY(19, 7,SF+S0+'   '+#218+S3+#191+S0+'   '+#195+SD+SD+SD+S3+#180);
        WriteXY(19, 8,SF+S0+'   '+S1+S1+'   '+S1+S1+S1+#179+' E   '+#179);
        WriteXY(19, 9,SE+SE+#218+SD+SD+S3+#191+#195+SC+SD+S3+#180+' n   '+#179);
        WriteXY(19,10,SE+SE+S1+S1+S1+#179+S1+S0+'  '+S1+#179+' t   '+#179);
        WriteXY(19,11,SE+SE+#192+SC+SC+S3+#217+#192+S3+S3+S4+SC+S3+#217);
        WriteXY( 1,12,#218+S3+#191+S0+#218+SB+SB+SB+S3+S6+SB+SB+SB+S3+S6+SB+
                      SB+SB+S3+#191+'  ');
```

```
        WriteXY( 1,13,#179+' ESC'+S1+#179+' F1 '+#179+' F2 '+#179+' F3 '+
                     #179+' F4 '+#179+#179+' F5 '+#179+' F6 '+#179+' F7 '+
                     #179+' F8 '+#179+#179+' F9 '+#179+' F10'+#179+' F11'+
                     #179+' F12' F12'+#179+' ');
        WriteXY( 1,14,#192+S3+#217+S0+#192+SC+SC+SC+S3+#217+#192+SC+SC+SC+S3+
                     #217+#192+SC+SC+SC+S3+#217+' ');
        WriteXY( 1,15,#218+SB+SB+SB+SB+SB+SB+SB+SB+SB+SB+SB+SB+SA+#196+
                     #191+' ');
        WriteXY( 1,16,S1+S1+S1+S1+S1+S1+S1+S1+S1+S1+S1+S1+S1+#179+'  BS  '+
                     #179+' ');
        WriteXY( 1,17,#195+S3+S7+S2+S7+S2+S7+S2+S7+S2+S7+S2+S7+S2+S7+S2+S7+
                     S2+S7+S2+S7+S2+S7+S2+S7+SA+#180+' ');
        WriteXY( 1,18,#179+' TAB '+S1+S1+S1+S1+S1+S1+S1+S1+S1+S1+S1+S1+S1+' '+
                 #179+' ');
        WriteXY( 1,19,#195+S3+S4+S9+S5+S9+S5+S9+S5+S9+S5+S9+S5+S9+S5+S9+S5+S9+
                     S5+S9+S5+S9+S5+S9+S5+S9+S5+SA+#180+' ');
        WriteXY( 1,20,#179+' CAPS  '+S1+S1+S1+S1+S1+S1+S1+S1+S1+S1+S1+#179+
                     ' ENTER  '+#179+' ');
        WriteXY( 1,21,#195+S3+S2+S8+#194+S5+S9+S5+S9+S5+S9+S5+S9+S5+S9+S5+S9+S5+
                     S9+S5+S9+S5+S9+S5+S9+S5+S3+S3+#180+' ');
        WriteXY( 1,22,#179+'  SHIFT  '+S1+S1+S1+S1+S1+S1+S1+S1+S1+S1+#179+
                     '  SHIFT'+S0+#179+' ');
        WriteXY( 1,23,#195+SA+S9+S5+#194+S2+S8+#194+S5+SC+SC+S3+S8+S2+#193+SC+SC+
                     S2+#194+#193+SD+SB+SA+#196+#180+' ');
        WriteXY( 1,24,#179+' CTRL '+#179+'   '+#179+' ALT '+S1+SE+' SPACEBAR '+SE+
                     S0+#179+' ALT '+S1+#179+' CTRL '+#179+' ');
        WriteXY( 1,25,#192+SA+#196+#217+'   '+#192+S3+S4+S3+S3+S3+S3+S2+S3+S3+S3+
                     S3+S4+SA+#217+S0+#192+SA+#196+#217+' ');


        Write_Special_Keys; Write_Function_Pad;
        Write_Number_Line;  Write_Main_Keys;
        for I := 0 to 1910 do
           if not ( chr(Mem[ScrSeg:I*2]) in
              [' ',#179,#180,#191..#197,#217,#218] ) then
                   Mem[ScrSeg:I*2+1] := LightGreen;
     end;
{end alternate version for Write__Keyboard} *)


procedure Lo_Light(X, Y, Len: byte);
   var      I : byte;
   begin    for I := 0 to Len do
              Mem[ScrSeg:(X+I)*2+Y*160+1] := $0A;    end;
(*
                  MemW[ScrSeg:(X+I)*2+Y*160] :=
                      (MemW[ScrSeg:(X+I)*2+Y*160] and $00FF) or $0A shl 8;    end;
*)

procedure Keyboard_Status;
   begin
```

```
                Reg.AH := $02;
                intr($16,Dos.Registers(Reg));
                InsertOn := (Reg.AL and $80) = $80;
                CapsLock := (Reg.AL and $40) = $40;
                NumbLock := (Reg.AL and $20) = $20;
                ScroLock := (Reg.AL and $10) = $10;
                AltKeyDn := (Reg.AL and $08) = $08;
                CtlKeyDn := (Reg.AL and $04) = $04;
                LfShftDn := (Reg.AL and $02) = $02;
                RtShftDn := (Reg.AL and $01) = $01;
            end;


    procedure Report_Key(Scan, KChr: byte);
        var
            KeyStr : string;
        const
            FKey = 'F1 F2 F3 F4 F5 F6 F7 F8 F9 F10F11F12';
            NKey : array[1..12] of char = '1234567890-=';
            AKey : array[1..35] of char = 'QWERTYUIOP****ASDFGHJKL*****ZXCVBNM';
        begin
            KeyStr := ' ';
            gotoxy(1,7);
            SetColor(Yellow,Black);
            WriteXY(1,7,'KeyPressed =              ');
            WriteXY(1,8,'high (scan):');
            WriteXY(1,9,' low (char):');
            SetColor(LightGreen,Black);
            WriteXY(14,7,chr(KChr)+'              ');
            WriteXY(14,8,BinaryRef(Scan));
            WriteXY(14,9,BinaryRef(KChr));
            SetColor(LightRed,Black);
            if (KChr < $20) and ((KChr <> $00) or (Scan = $03)) then
                KeyStr := 'Ctrl-' + chr(KChr+$40);
            case Scan of
                    $0E : if KChr = $7F then KeyStr := 'Ctrl-BS';
                $10..$32 : if KChr = $00 then KeyStr := 'Alt-' + (AKey[Scan-$0F]);
                $3B..$44 : KeyStr := copy(FKey,(Scan-$3B)*3+1,3);
                    $52 : if KChr = $00 then KeyStr := 'Insert Key';
                $54..$5D : KeyStr := 'Shf-' + copy(FKey,(Scan-$54)*3+1,3);
                $5E..$67 : KeyStr := 'Ctrl-' + copy(FKey,(Scan-$5E)*3+1,3);
                $68..$71 : KeyStr := 'Alt-'  + copy(FKey,(Scan-$68)*3+1,3);
                    $72 : begin  KeyStr := 'Ctrl-*';     Scan := $37;  end;
                    $73 : begin  KeyStr := 'Ctrl-Lf';    Scan := $4B;  end;
                    $74 : begin  KeyStr := 'Ctrl-Rt';    Scan := $4D;  end;
                    $75 : begin  KeyStr := 'Ctrl-End';   Scan := $4F;  end;
                    $76 : begin  KeyStr := 'Ctrl-PgDn';  Scan := $51;  end;
                    $77 : begin  KeyStr := 'Ctrl-Home';  Scan := $47;  end;
                $78..$83 : KeyStr := 'Alt-' + NKey[Scan-$77];
                    $84 : begin  KeyStr := 'Ctrl-PgUp';  Scan := $49;  end;
```

TRAPPING THE KEYBOARD

```
    end; {case}
      if KeyStr <> " then WriteXY(16,7,KeyStr+'            ');
      GotoXY(14,7);
      Hi_Light_Key_Pressed(Scan);
    end;


procedure Report_Keyboard_Status;
    var
      TempStatus : byte;
    begin
      Keyboard_Status;
      TempStatus := Reg.AL;
      if (OldStatus and $80) <> (TempStatus and $80) then
      begin    gotoxy(40,6);
             if InsertOn then
             begin  SetColor(White,Blue);
                    WriteScr('Insert On ');    end else
             begin  SetColor(LightBlue,Black);
                    WriteScr('Insert Off');    end;        end;
      WriteXY(1,5,'Status Byte: '+BinaryRef(TempStatus));
(*
```

{ *** Optional Test *** see text for explanation *** }

```
        if (OldStatus <> TempStatus) then
        begin
          WriteXY(1,6,' Old Status '+BinaryRef(OldStatus));
          delay(1000);
        end;
*)
      GotoXY(14,7);
      if ((OldStatus and $43) <> (TempStatus and $43)) { and
         (InKey = #$00)} then
```

```
      begin          { could be right or left shift or caps lock   }
        Write_Number_Line;      Write_Special_Keys;
        Write_Function_Pad;     Write_Main_Keys;      end;

      if (OldStatus and $20) <> (TempStatus and $20) then Write_Function_Pad;

      if CapsLock then Hi_Light( 1,19, 6) else Lo_Light( 1,19, 6);
      if NumbLock then Hi_Light(53, 1, 3) else Lo_Light(53, 1, 3);
      if ScroLock then Hi_Light(24, 1, 3) else Lo_Light(24, 1, 3);
      if LfShftDn then Hi_Light( 1,21, 8) else Lo_Light( 1,21, 8);
      if RtShftDn then Hi_Light(61,21,10) else Lo_Light(61,21,10);
      if AltKeyDn then
         begin   Hi_Light(12,23,4);  Hi_Light(55,23,4);   end else
         begin   Lo_Light(12,23,4);  Lo_Light(55,23,4);   end;
      if CtlKeyDn then
         begin   Hi_Light(1,23,5);   Hi_Light(66,23,5);   end else
         begin   Lo_Light(1,23,5);   Lo_Light(66,23,5);   end;
      if OldStatus <> TempStatus then Report_Key(KScan,KByte);
```

```
        OldStatus := TempStatus;
    end;

procedure Key_Read;
    begin
        Reg.AX := $0000;
        intr($16,Dos.Registers(Reg));
        KByte := lo(Reg.AX);
        KScan := hi(Reg.AX);
        Report_Key(KScan, KByte);
    end;

begin
    OldStatus := $FF;
    CheckColor;    ClrScr;
    TextAttr := White + Black shl 8;
    SetWindow(1,1,80,25);
    Gotoxy(1,2);
    WriteLin(' To exit, use ');
    WriteLin('Ctrl-Alt-Shift');
    Keyboard_Status;
    Write_Keyboard;
    InKey := #$00;
    repeat
        if KeyPressed then Key_Read;
        Report_Keyboard_Status;
    until AltKeyDn and
          CtlKeyDn and
         (LfShftDn or RtShftDn);
end.
```

12

Errors

The proverb tells us that "to err is human." Unfortunately, to err is not merely human, it is also common. If computers fulfilled the second part of the proverb and forgave our errors, everything would be fine. But computers are only an extension of the programmer and it is the programmer's responsibility to forgive the operator's errors. Doing so, however, is hardly easy.

Errors fall into three principal categories:

1. System level errors

2. Input errors

3. Judgment errors

At the most basic level are the system and program errors that occur within the mechanism of your program or within the computer system itself. These are usually the easiest to trap and to correct, provided they are caught *before* a system crash or other serious malfunction results. Both MS-DOS and Turbo Pascal provide detection mechanisms and corrective options for most such errors, provided the programmer uses them and provides for corrective actions.

On the next higher level are the input errors: errors in typing, simple data entry mistakes, or errors in selection or operator instructions. On this level, some errors can be trapped and corrected and others cannot be trapped when they happen but may be correctable later. At this level, the errors can only be trapped by careful foresight exercised by the programmer. Anticipating such possible errors, intercepting and/or warning the user, and providing corrective mechanisms are some of the differences between mere competence and true expertise.

The third error level is the most complex. It involves errors in the user's expectations or judgment. Unfortunately, this last level is usually beyond error trapping, at least until computers reach a level of sophistication presently only possible in science fiction stories. Even on this level, some error corrections can be attempted, but intercepting errors of judgment lies beyond mere programming science and becomes more a matter of art and intuition. Still, this is a level of performance to which it is well to aspire.

System Level Errors

One of the first error traps taught is found in the **File__Exist** function. This function tests a file, determines if it exists or not, and returns a Boolean result.

```
function File_Exist(FileName: string): Boolean
   var
      TF : file;     Exist : Boolean;
   begin
      {$I-}                              { turn off I/O checking }
      assign(TF,FileName);
      reset(TF);
      {$I+}                              { restore I/O checking }
      Exist := (IOresult = 0);
      if Exist then close(TF);
      File_Exist := Exist;
   end;
```

File__Exist begins by disabling the I/O error checking. Then the filename is assigned to an untyped file, and an attempt is made to reset the file. Finally, the file is closed. This is error prevention since leaving every file tested open would quickly exhaust the file handles supported by DOS (CONFIG.SYS, in your boot directory, determines how many files can be open at any one time).

Now that the housekeeping is taken care of, I/O checking is restored and the **IOresult** function is tested. If the file named did not exist or if the drive or path were incorrect, **IOresult** would return a nonzero value.

As it stands, only a Boolean true/false is returned by this test, but the test can easily be rewritten to provide more information:

```
procedure File_Test(FileName: string);
   var
      TF : file;    Result : integer;
   begin
      {$I-}    assign(TF,FileName);    reset(TF);    {$I+}
      Result := IOresult;
      case Result of
          0 : close(TF);    { everything's okay — report nothing }
          2 : write('File ',FileName,' not found');
          3 : write('Path ',FileName,' not found');
          4 : write('Too many files open');
          5 : write('File access denied');
          6 : write('Invalid file handle');
      end; {case}
   end;
```

In this version, if an error occurs, instead of returning a Boolean result, a message detailing the specific problem is presented. Errors 2 through 5 are fairly clear. If error 6 were reported, a more serious error than simply entering an incorrect drive, pathname or filename would be indicated. In this case, something has happened to corrupt the DOS file handle and you have real problems. The best response would be to attempt an orderly exit and reset the system. This particular error is not likely, but it can happen.

For more useful results, you can have your cake and eat it, too, as demonstrated by the following test:

```
function File_Test(FileName: string): Boolean;
   var
      TF : file;    Result : integer;
   begin
      {$I-}    assign(TF,FileName);    reset(TF);    {$I+}
      Result := IOresult;
      if Result <> 0 then Report_Error(FileName,Result)
                  else close(FileName);
      File_Test := (Result = 0);
   end;
```

In this version, a separate procedure is used for general error reporting, which can be called from many different procedures for many different errors, but the test still returns a Boolean result to the calling procedure.

The **Report__Error** procedure can be as elaborate or as simple as you choose to provide:

```
procedure Report_Error( Error_Ref: string; Error_Code: integer);
    var
        OldX, OldY: byte;
    begin
        OldX := WhereX;                           { save current cursor position    }
        OldY := WhereY;
        gotoxy(ErrorX,ErrorY);                    { where do you want the report? }
        write('ERROR: ');
        case Error_Code of
            $00 : { no error }
            $02 : write('File ',Error_Ref,' not found');
            $03 : write('Path ',PathOnly(Error_Ref),' not found');
            $04 : write('Too many files open');
              .

              .

              . .
            $0F : write(DriveOnly(Error_Ref),' invalid disk drive');
              .                                         { lots of other errors}
                                                        { to be included     }
              .
            else write('Unknown!');                    { it could happen   }
        end; {case}
        gotoxy(OldX,OldY);                        { restore old cursor position     }
    end;
```

The variable Error_Ref passed to this procedure may be only a filename, a path/filename combination, or a directory path only, and it may or may not include a drive specification. Error_Ref may have originated in entirely different circumstances and have nothing to do with filenames or paths. But, for the moment, assume the **Report__Error** request originated from file I/O as shown in the **File__Test** function and the Error_Code reported was 2, 3, 4, or 15.

On an Error_Code of 2, 3, or 15 (0Fh), the report procedure could be further elaborated to parse the Error_Ref variable:

1. If error 2 were reported, the entire Error_Ref string should be included in the error report because the actual mistake could be in the drive (if it was specified) or in the path or in the filename itself. Thus the ERROR: FILE C:\MY_PATH\THISFILE.XY1 not found message is correctly phrased and provides complete information about the problem.

2. If error 3 (a path not found) were reported, the correct error report would be ERROR : Path C:\MY_PATH\ not found. Thus, a **PathOnly** function parses the string and the filename is dropped (it's hardly relevant when it's the path that doesn't exist) and the error report indicates the probable area of difficulty.

3. If error 15 (0Fh) was the problem, the ERROR: C:\ invalid disk drive message reports the problem concisely, again using a **DriveOnly** function to parse the string.

However, if the error reported were 4, there is little relevance in the filename or path and a simple ERROR: too many files open message points up the problem nicely.

These are only four of the possible errors that **I/Oresult** might return. Others might be 150, drive not responding; 156, disk seek error; 157, unknown media type (disk); or many others.

Under Turbo version 3.x, only one error reporting procedure, **IOresult**, was supplied to the programmer. The compiler error handling applied only during program creation and the run-time error handling produced a complete halt, returning an error code and a program error location. Only the I/O errors allowed possibility for corrective actions.

Under Turbo 4.0, the compiler and run-time error procedures remain as before — essentially untouchable. The **IOresult** error handling remains at the programmer's command, and one new error handler, the **GraphResult** function for graphics operations has been added. In any case, several errors remain essentially out of reach of the programmer. Most of these occur infrequently or are normally tested and handled "invisibly" by existing Turbo procedures. But, sometimes, invisible is not enough.

The Test__Error Procedure

Interrupt 21h functions provide basic handling for file operations, memory management, printer and serial I/O, and miscellaneous system functions. They are used indirectly by all programming languages — Basic, C, COBOL, FORTRAN, Forth, Pascal, or even assembly language. Many of these functions return error information reporting the success or failure of a particular operation, some by setting the Zero or Carry flags, others by returning an error code in the AL register. (Selected interrupt 21h functions are detailed in Appendix C.)

MS-DOS provides an **Extended Error Information** function (interrupt 21h, function 59h) which returns codes responding to errors produced by other interrupt 21h functions, many of which (whether called directly or initiated by Pascal procedures and/or functions) provide error result information directly as well as indirectly. Function 59h reports the error conditions and can be called independently as a direct error condition test.

```
procedure Test_Error;
    begin
        Reg.AH := $59;
        Reg.BX := $00;
        intr($21,dos.registers(Reg));
        if Reg.AX <> 0 then
        begin
            Report Error(Reg.AX);                    { error code }
     (*     optional reports ... mostly useful in trouble shooting      *)
     (*     Report_Class(Reg.BX);                    { error_class }  *)
     (*     Report_Action(Reg.BL);                   { error_action } *)
     (*     Report_Locus(Reg.CH);                    { error_locus }  *)
        end;
    end;
```

Function 59h can return four codes:

1. The extended error_code itself, which reports the problem found.

2. An error classification code suggesting the general cause of the problem.

3. An error action code suggesting how the problem should be handled.

4. An error location report indicating where the error occurred.

The first code, the extended error code, is the tool that the programmer will find most useful. Although the latter three codes are helpful (especially during program development and debugging), they are not exactly the kind of information that should be passed along to the end users.

There are two points that you should keep in mind:

1. Calling function 59h destroys the system error information. It cannot be retrieved a second time. The **Test_Error** procedure does not assign the error codes to variables for storage, it only parcels them out to the various reporting procedures. If these will be needed further, appropriate provision should be made.

2. New error codes will appear with future releases/versions of MS-DOS. Error recognition that is limited to specific error codes may require extensive revisions to remain upwardly compatible. Provision has been made for this in the **Report__Error** procedure, but, as you revise error reporting procedures, don't forget future changes. They *will* appear.

Error Code Types

Turbo Pascal version 4.0 generates four categories of Runtime Errors: DOS errors, 1..17; I/O errors, 100..106; critical errors, 150..162 and fatal errors, 200-207:

1. DOS error codes (1..17), which correspond one for one to the error codes returned by function 59h.

2. I/O error codes (100..106), which do not correspond well to the MS-DOS errors and only two of these (100..101) can be equated more or less directly.

3. Critical errors (150..162) which correspond one for one to function 59h error codes 13h through 1Fh, which also correspond to error codes 00h..0Ch returned by the interrupt 24h **Critical Error Handler**.

4. Fatal errors (200..207), which deal with range checks, math errors, and memory errors and do not correspond at all to function 59h error codes.

When a fatal error is reported, the situation is hopeless. Since these errors tend to crash programs, trash memory data, or otherwise create garbage, a graceful exit is the only practical response. Here, prevention rather than correction is the key. (The preventive error trap will be discussed in Chapter 13.)

The Report__Error Procedure

The **Report__Error** procedure may be called either with Turbo version 4.0 error codes or error codes returned by function 59h. In Turbo version 3.x, essentially the same errors are reported, but each error type uses its own number sequence and correspondence with MS-DOS error codes is not easily established. I suggest that you do not attempt to handle both function 59h error codes and Turbo version 3.x error codes with the same reporting procedures.

```
procedure Report_Error(Error_Code: integer);
   var
      OldX, OldY: byte;
   begin
      OldX := WhereX;
```

```
        OldY := WhereY;
        gotoxy( ErrorX , ErrorY );
        write('ERROR: ');
      case Error_Code of
            $00 : ;    { no error — do nothing — just in case of error }
            $01 : write('function number invalid');
                  .
                  .
                  .
        150, $13 : write('disk write-protected');
                  .
                  .
                  .
    101, 160, $1D : write('device write fault');
                  .
                  .
                  .
            $53 : write('Interrupt 24h failure (Critical Error Interrupt)');
            else write('Unknown! Error code:',HexRef(Error_Code));
        end; {case}
        gotoxy(OldX,OldY);        { reset original cursor position }
      end;
```

Note that the MS-DOS error codes appear in the case list as hexadecimal values, whereas the corresponding Turbo error codes appear as decimal values.

In a previous example, the error reporting procedure was passed a string variable, which was incorporated in the error message. This feature has not been included in this sample general error handler, but it can be added, if you want. Similarly, the string values passed could be parsed for different circumstances and different errors as appropriate.

Other Error Codes Returned

Function 59h returns three other codes: an error class, error action, and error location.

```
procedure Report_Class(Error_Class: integer);
begin
    write('Error Cause: ');
    case Error_Class of
        $01 : write('resource exhausted (storage or channels)');
              .
              .
              .
        $05 : write('hardware failure');
              .
              .
              .
```

```
    $07 : write('application program error');

         .

         .

         .

    $0C : write('not listed ....');
  end; {case}
end;
```

The **Report__Class** procedure amplifies the initial error code by classifying the problem according to probable sources of malfunction. These can be helpful, but they are not definitive. (Even internally, the computer is not all knowing.)

```
procedure Report_Action(Error_Action: integer);
begin
   write('Action: ');
   case Error_Action of
      01 : begin   writeln('Retry some reasonable number of times,');
                   write('then prompt user to abort or ignore.');    end;

         .

         .

         .

      06 : write('Ignore error ...');
      07 : write('Ask user for corrective intervention, then retry.');
   end; {case}
end;
```

The **Report__Action** procedure is possibly the best of these three secondary information reports and suggests a relevant programming response to handle the difficulty. Essentially, these are also common-sense responses, but they are nicely classified. This is also a rare example of "programmer friendly" error reporting, but it's also an easy "help" to outgrow.

```
procedure Report_Where(Where_Error: integer);
begin
   write('Where Error: ');
   case Where_Error of
      01 : write(' Unknown ...');
      02 : write('Block device -- disk or disk emulator');
      03 : write(' Network related');
      04 : write(' Serial device');
      05 : write('RAM problem');
   end;
end;
```

These last codes offer a general area where the problem appeared but are too general to provide any real assistance in most cases.

Advantages and Disadvantages

In general, the **IOresult** error reporting procedure that Turbo Pascal provides is more efficient than using function 59h error reporting even though fewer errors are directly available for handling by the programmer and function 59h does make more information available, in a sense.

The error class, action, and location are only moderately useful information. Most of this is already apparent to you, the programmer, at the point when the error occurs, but occasionally the extra information can be nice.

Why stay with Turbo's **IOresult?** There are three good reasons:

1. Turbo's error trapping includes reporting the program's segment: offset address *at the point the error occurs*, and this can be of significant debugging assistance in a complex program. You could write your own procedure to trap the segment: offset address, but it would either duplicate what Turbo has already done very nicely or would simply report the segment: offset of the error code procedure.

2. As long as Turbo functions and procedures are being used, the error trapping mechanism is already in place. All you need to do is check the results yourself, instead of allowing the program to be interrupted by an error.

3. The **IOresult** function allows intervention for those errors that commonly occur and that can be corrected *while the program is running*. For most purposes, this is all that is necessary.

Then, why did I include this complex error reporting procedure? There are several reasons:

1. There are a number of useful interrupt functions that Turbo Pascal does not directly support or that you may want to use to create some of the special variations of procedures that have been demonstrated in previous chapters. When these are used, it is best that you also know how to trap the errors generated directly.

2. There are some errors that **IOresult** does not handle. You may need to check for these when using various interrupt functions directly.

3. It's important simply to understand how and why errors are reported so that you have a better opportunity to provide corrective intervention.

The **IOresult** function provides useful error trapping, as shown in the **File__Exist** and **File__Test** examples, but instead of using it to return a simple Boolean value, use the error code returned as the basis for error correction instead of mere error trapping. The **Report__Error** procedure can be easily revised as a look-up function to generate appropriate error messages (reporting with any degree of complexity desired) and incorporated in your input procedures. And, if necessary, the **Test_Error** procedure is there to support error checks that **IOresult** does not provide. So, you have the best of all practical worlds.

ERR_RPRT.INC Include File

```
procedure Test_Error;  { ERR_RPRT.INC }
    begin
        Reg.AH := $59;
        Reg.BX := $00;
        intr($21,dos.registers(Reg));
        if Reg.AX <> 0 then
        begin
            Report_Error(Reg.AX);    { error_code    }
  (*        optional reports ... mostly useful in trouble shooting    *)
  (*      Report_Class(Reg.BX);    { error_class   }                  *)
  (*      Report_Action(Reg.BL);   { error_action }                   *)
  (*      Report_Locus(Reg.CH);    { error_locus  }                   *)
        end;
    end;


procedure Report_Error(Error_Code: integer);
    var
        OldX, OldY: byte;
    begin
        OldX := WhereX;
        OldY := WhereY;
        gotoxy( ErrorX , ErrorY );
        write('ERROR: ');
        case Error_Code of
                $00 : ;    { no error -- do nothing }
                $01 : write('function number invalid');
                $02 : write('file not found');
                $03 : write('path not found');
                $04 : write('too many files open');
                $05 : write('access denied');
                $06 : write('file handle invalid');
                $07 : write('memory control blocks destroyed');
                $08 : write('insufficient memory');
                $09 : write('memory block address invalid');
                $0A : write('enviroment invalid');
                $0B : write('format invalid');
        {12}    $0C : write('access code invalid');
                $0D : write('data invalid');
        {15}    $0F : write('invalid disk drive');
```

```
   {16}    $10 : write('can not remove current directory');
   {17}    $11 : write('can not rename across drives');
           $12 : write('no more files');
      150, $13 : write('disk write-protected');
      151, $14 : write('unknown unit');
      152, $15 : write('drive not ready (not responding)');
      153, $16 : write('unknown command');
      154, $17 : write('data error (CRC -- Cyclical Redundency Check)');
      155, $18 : write('bad drive request structure length');
      156, $19 : write('disk seek error');
      157, $1A : write('unknown media type (disk)');
      158, $1B : write('sector not found (disk)');
      159, $1C : write('printer out of paper');
 101, 160, $1D : write('device write fault');
 100, 161, $1E : write('device read fault');
      162, $1F : write('general hardware failure');
           $20 : write('share violation (network)');
           $21 : write('lock violation (network)');
           $22 : write('disk change invalid');
           $23 : write('FCB (File Control Block) unavailable');
           $50 : write('file already exists');
           $52 : write('can not create directory');
           $53 : write('Interrupt 24h failure (Critical Error Interrupt)');
           else write('Unknown!  Error code:',HexRef(Error_Code));
         end; {case}
         gotoxy(OldX,OldY);
       end;
   procedure Report_Class(Error_Class: integer);
     var
       OldX, OldY: byte;
     begin
       OldX := WhereX;
       OldY := WhereY;
       gotoxy( ErrorX2 , ErrorY2 );      { report position -- allow for two lines }
       write('Error Cause: ');
       case Error_Class of
         $01 : write('resource exhausted (storage or channels)');
         $02 : begin
                 writeln('not error, temporary situation expected to change');
                 write('(might be locked region in file, etc)');
               end;
         $03 : write('authorization problem');
         $04 : write('internal error in system software');
         $05 : write('hardware failure');
         $06 : begin
                 writeln('system software failure not directly caused by
                     active process');
                 write('process - check CONFIG.SYS.');
               end;
```

```
        $07  :  write('application program error');
        $08  :  write('file or item not found');
        $09  :  write('file or item has invalid format or type');
        $0A  :  write('file or item interlocked');
        $0B  :  write('wrong disk in drive / bad media / other media problem');
        $0C  :  write('not listed ....');
    end; {case}
    gotoxy(OldX,OldY);
  end;


procedure Report_Action(Error_Action: integer);
    var
        OldX, OldY: byte;
    begin
        OldX := WhereX;
        OldY := WhereY;
        gotoxy( ErrorX3 , ErrorY3 );     { report position -- needs two lines }
        write('Action: ');
        case Error_Action of
            01 : begin
                    writeln('Retry some reasonable number of times, then prompt');
                    write('user for abort or ignore.');
                 end;
            02 : begin
                    writeln('Retry some reasonable number of times with delay');
                    write('between tries, then prompt user for abort or ignore.');
                 end;
            03 : begin
                    writeln('Prompt user for corrective information such as correct');
                    write('drive or path/filename.');
                 end;
            04 : write('Terminate program without haste -- close files, etc.');
            05 : begin
                    writeln('Abort immediate!  System is corrupted, cleanup actions');
                    write('would do more harm than good.');
                 end;
            06 : write('Ignore error ...');
            07 : write('Ask user for corrective intervention, then retry.');
        end; {case}
        gotoxy(OldX,OldY);
    end;
```

```
procedure Report_Where(Where_Error: integer);
   var
      OldX, OldY: byte;
   begin
      OldX := WhereX;
      OldY := WhereY;
      gotoxy( ErrorX4 , ErrorY4 );
      write('Where Error: ');
      case Where_Error of
         01 : write(' Unknown ...');
         02 : write(' Block device -- disk or disk emulator');
         03 : write(' Network related');
         04 : write(' Serial device');
         05 : write(' RAM problem');
      end;
      gotoxy(OldX,OldY);
   end;
```

ERRORS

13

Error Corrections

The first topic covered in Chapter 1 was checking a user input error. Although the term "error" wasn't actually applied and the emphasis was on what the user might or might not know was expected, this was still an error correction mechanism.

Within the PLIST sample program, almost every operation was error trapped in some fashion. The printer status was tested repeatedly. Filenames were converted to uppercase and tested for an extension. If none was found, a default extension of .PAS was added. Files were tested to see if they existed. The largest part of the program was concerned with tests for specific features to control how and which files were output. Technically, not all of these were error traps — many were merely condition tests — but the mechanisms for both are essentially the same.

Later, in the menu example, another *user entry* error trap (in the form of feedback) was employed. It informed the user that various options were unacceptable for different reasons. Again, this was a simple error correction mechanism, even though, in this case, the deck was stacked so that only errors in selection would occur.

Throughout the text following Chapter 1, error traps have been used often, but they have been simple. They have tested either system responses (for example, checking the printer to see if it is operating properly) or simple user responses for validity. Now it's time to look at more complex errors. Instead of simply "blowing the whistle," we will tell the user *what* the error was and/or *why* an error has occurred, show where the error was found, and allow the existing input to be edited to correct the error.

Programmer's Rule #XII: To err is human, To forgive is good programming.

User Input Types

Types of user inputs fall into three basic categories:

1. Text inputs

2. Item inputs

3. Free-structured inputs

Text inputs may be anything from a comment or a paid-to line in a checkbook program to complete text files under an editor program. Spelling checkers aside, this type of input is not normally subject to error checking.

Item inputs can range from cells in a spreadsheet to simply Y/N answers to program prompts. They are usually subject to error checks at various levels of sophistication. Does the item represent a valid number format? Is it a text entry? Was the response Y or y or N or n? Did the input fit with the established format requirements? Did it make sense within the program context? Item inputs are the most common user input type and normally provoke relatively simple error tests that return Boolean responses.

Free-structured inputs might be formulas entered in a spreadsheet, program instructions in Pascal (or most any other language), or action instructions in *Adventure* or other computer games. In its simplest form, a free-structured input consists of an operation instruction (a verb) and an item, object, or condition to be modified (a noun).

As an example, in the old **Adventure** game, GET AXE provided the operation instruction GET, which to the program meant flag some item as in your possession, and AXE, which was the object of the operation specified. (The space between the words is known as a delimiter; it separates the two instruction elements.) Alternately, you might have specified such actions as THROW, DROP, FIND and so on, and the action objects might have been BIRD, CAGE, LANTERN, ROD, and so on.

This input command was interpreted according to a simple set of rules and syntax elements:

1. Is the operation instruction valid? That is, is this a recognized action?

2. Is the action object valid? That is, is this a recognized object?

3. Is the object available? That is, is the object flagged as available for action?

4. Is the action applicable to the object?

5. Is there a valid result? That is, can the verb and object be applied here?

The third and fourth steps might be reversed in order, but essentially five error tests were applied to the user input instruction before resolution of the instruction was attempted. Actually, if you remember *Adventure*, a sixth test would have been made: Is the dwarf (or the giant snake, or the bear, or other creature) in the vicinity? This would also have conditioned the response, but only the first five tests were required to decide if the instruction was valid as an instruction.

If the first test (is the operation instruction valid?) had failed, *Adventure* might have replied I DON'T UNDERSTAND [verb], or if the object in the second test was not recognized, the response might have been I DON'T KNOW WHAT A [noun] IS.

In the third test, if your command had been THROW AXE, you might have been told YOU DON'T HAVE AN AXE or to GET AXE, or if none were in the area, I DON'T SEE AN AXE TO GET. Also note that the article AN was fitted to the object AXE instead of responding A AXE. Attention to details is a mark of excellent programming.[1]

In the fourth test (Is the action valid with this object?), if your command had instructed EAT AXE, *Adventure* might have replied YUCK! DON'T BE RIDICULOUS! If the command had been less absurd but still invalid, the response might have been I DON'T KNOW HOW TO [verb] A [noun].

In the fifth test (Is the action/noun valid in this circumstance?), *Adventure* might have responded THROW AXE AT WHAT? if no obvious target were available or might have responded I DON'T KNOW HOW TO APPLY [command] HERE.

Each of these are good examples of error trapping responses because, with one exception, each response showed either a what or a why or both; *what* was not recognized or *why* the command was not accepted. In the case of

---

1. A tip of the hat to Scott Adams (and associates) for excellent game design and excellent programming. Also, if I have misquoted any of the responses, my apologies — it's been a while since I've had time to visit Colossal Cave.

the frivolous command EAT AXE, the response was equally frivolous, and a more stilted response would almost have been an insult to the user's intelligence.

In Pascal, similar considerations are applied to each instruction you create. If you write an instruction saying to divide a text variable by 4.27, the compiler responds with a message (less amusing than *Adventure's*) informing you that a type mismatch exists in line *xxx*. However, with Turbo Pascal, instead of referencing a line number, the editor takes you to the error directly or, at least, to the point where it *recognized* an error had occurred.

In the **Formula__Calculator** demo program, similar error trapping practices will be applied to a numerical formula, the syntax of the user's entry will be checked, reports will detail the nature of the error, and, in most cases, the cursor will be moved to the position where the error was recognized.

Sets and Set Operators

Definition of Sets

A set is simply a defined group of elements. These elements might be defined as a range as the set of ASCII numbers = ['0'. .'9'] or the elements of the set could be individually defined as the set of odd ASCII numbers = ['1', '3', '5', '7', '9'].

Operations With Sets

Three operations can be carried out on sets: union, difference, and intersection.

For illustration, assume an assortment of cubes in which each individual face might be colored red, blue, or green. With this collection, three sets can be defined: the Red set, the Blue set, and the Green set.

The Red set contains all elements that have at least one red face; the Blue set, all cubes that have a blue surface; and the Green set, all cubes with any green faces. Now, since some of the items have more than one color, they belong to more than one set or they may belong to all three sets.

The *union* of two sets is a set containing all elements in either set. The union of the Red and Blue sets (RED + BLUE) contains all elements that have either red *or* blue faces but does not include any elements that are *only* green.

The *difference* of two sets is a set containing only elements that belong to the first set but do not belong to the second. The difference of the Red and Green sets (RED – GREEN) contains only elements with red faces and no green faces.

The *intersection* of two sets is a set containing only elements that belong to *both* sets. The intersection of the Blue and Green sets (BLUE * GREEN) contains all elements with both a blue *and* a green face but excludes any cubes that have only blue faces or only green faces (with or without red). If there are no elements that belong to both, the intersection is an empty set.

A new set can be defined as the union, difference, or intersection of any existing sets.

Tests With Sets

Any individual item can be tested to see if it belongs to a specific set as long as the item and the elements of the set are compatible types. This is common use of sets in Pascal programming.

Tests between sets are slightly different:

1. Equal (=): Two sets are equal if and only if every element of each set belongs to the other set, that is, if the two sets are identical.

2. Greater_Or_Equal (> =): If Set_A contains all elements of Set_B, then Set_A > = Set_B is true. The converse, Less_Or_Equal (< =), is also valid.

3. Unequal (< >): If Set_A contains elements not in Set_B *and* Set_B contains elements not in Set_A, then Set_A < > Set_B is true.

A set cannot be tested to see if it is greater than or less than a second set — only if it is Equal, Greater_Or_Equal, or Unequal.

The set of NUMBER characters ('0'. .'9') and the set of LOWER_CASE ('a'. .'z') are both subsets of the set of ASCII characters, and the following definitions and tests between sets will produce Boolean results as shown:

ASCII = set of]' '. .'~ '];	UPPER_CASE = set of ['A'. .'Z'];
NUMBER = set of ['0'. .'9'];	LOWER_CASE = set of ['a'. .'z'];
NUMBER < > UPPER_CASE is true;	ASCII > = NUMBER is true;
LOWER_CASE < = ASCII is true;	UPPER_CASE = LOWER_CASE is false;

Reporting User Input Errors

The demo program used to illustrate reporting errors is a simple formula calculator that accepts a single line formula containing numbers (0 through 9), operators (+, −, *, /) and parentheses. Editing the formula is supported by the backspace, delete, home, end, and left and right arrow keys, whereas the = key forces an intermediate result calculation without leaving the editing mode and the Enter key terminates editing with a final result calculation.

As written, the **Formula__Calculator** accepts only integer input values but additional tests would be required. Also, additional mathematical operations could be incorporated and other display input provisions are possible and practical. The limitations used here are simply for demonstration purposes.

The characters allowed in the formula are defined by the constants MathChar, LimitChar, and NumChar.

```
const
    MathChar   : set of char = ['+','-','*','/']; { four operators      }
    LimitChar  : set of char = ['(',' ',')'];     { parentheses and space }
    NumChar    : set of char = ['0'..'9'];        { numbers             }
```

The main program, **Input__Formula**, is divided into two parts, **Edit__Formula__String** and **Test__Formula__Str**. The loop cannot be exited until the Boolean Error flag is returned as false (no errors found).

```
repeat
    FormulaVal := 0.0;
    Edit_Formula_String;
    Test_Formula_Str;
until Quit and not Error;
```

First, **Edit__Formula__String** reads the keyboard, accepting and editing the input variable FormulaStr:

```
procedure Edit_Formula_String;
    var
        Done : Boolean;   InKey : char;
    begin
        Done := false;
        repeat
            gotoxy(XAxis,YAxis);
            write(FormulaStr,' ':(Flen-length(FormulaStr)));
```

After FormulaStr is written, the input line is padded with spaces to a total length of FLen; then the cursor is repositioned.

```
            gotoxy(XAxis+Offset,YAxis);
            InKey := ReadKey;
            case InKey of
                #$00 : begin
                        InKey := Readkey;
```

```
                            case InKey of
{ right arrow  }              'M' : inc(OffSet);
{ left arrow   }              'K' : dec(OffSet);
{ home key     }              'G' : OffSet := 0;
{ end key      }              'O' : OffSet := length(FormulaStr);
{ delete key   }              'S' : if ( length(FormulaStr) > 0 ) and
                                       ( OffSet < length(FormulaStr) )
                                       then
                                        delete(FormulaStr,OffSet+1,1);
                                  else Beep;
                              end; {case}
                        end;
{ Ctrl-Q }#$11 : halt;              { while testing ... always have an out }
{ Ctrl-H }#$08 : if ( length(FormulaStr) > 0 ) and
                    (OffSet > 0 ) then
                    begin   delete(FormulaStr,OffSet,1);
                            dec(OffSet);                    end;
       '=' : Done := true;
       #$0D : begin   Done := true;   Quit := true;   end;
```

In Pascal, the case statement will not accept predefined constants, therefore, the lines

```
 NumChar,
MathChar,
LimitChar : begin ...... end;
```

are not accepted. Instead of listing the acceptable characters a second time for the case statement (which would make revision more difficult), the case...else structure is used, followed by a conventional if...then structure.

```
    else if InKey in (NumChar + MathChar + LimitChar) then
       begin
          if OffSet < length(FormulaStr)
             then insert(InKey,FormulaStr,OffSet+1)
             else FormulaStr := FormulaStr + InKey;
          inc(OffSet);
       end else Boop;
end; {case}
```

Two different sound effects are used for audio feedback: **Beep** warns that a function key entry is invalid and **Boop** warns that a character entry is not accepted. Both sound effects are very brief so that they are not irritating and so that the system is tied up for a minimum interval.

Finally, OffSet is tested for valid position so that the cursor is not allowed to move beyond set bounds.

```
    if OffSet > FLen then OffSet := length(FormulaStr);
    if OffSet < 0 then OffSet := 0;
  until Done;
end;
```

Both the Enter (CR) and equal (=) keys exit from the edit loop, passing control to **Test__Formula__Str** and, from here, to a series of tests: **Trim__Formula**, **Parse__Parentheses**, **Parse__Operators**, and if no errors have been found, **Execute__Formula**. If **Execute__Formula** does not return an error, the solution to the formula is displayed:

```
procedure Test_Formula_Str;
  var
    Decimal : byte;
  begin
    Trim_Formula;
    Parse_Parentheses;
    if not Error then Parse_Operators;
    if not Error then Execute_Formula;
    if not Error then
    begin
      Box_Line(30,9,50,11,1,1,14,0);
      if abs(FormulaVal) < 0.00001 then Decimal := 10
                                   else Decimal := 5;
      gotoxy(31,10);
      write(FormulaVal:17:Decimal);
    end;
  end;
```

Note that, depending on the absolute value returned by the formula, two different values may be assigned to the variable Decimal, shifting the resulting display to show more decimal places for small values.

A second variation can adjust the display result for a more precise fit. The initial value of Decimal and the maximum number of decimal places (Decimal < 10) can be adjusted to suit your program requirements. Note, however, that the **Write** procedure limits the decimal portion of the display string to 10 places to the right of the decimal.

```
procedure Test_Formula_Str;     { variation }
  var
    Decimal : byte;   Test : real;
```

```
begin
   Trim_Formula;
   Parse_Parentheses;
   if not Error then Parse_Operators;
   if not Error then Execute_Formula;
   if not Error then
   begin
      Box_Line(30, 9, 50,11,1,1,14,0);
      Decimal := 5;
      Test := FormulaVal;
      while (Test < 1.0) and (Decimal < 10) do
      begin
         Test := Test * 10.0;
         inc(Decimal);
      end;
      gotoxy(31,10);
      write(FormulaVal:17:Decimal);
   end;
 end;
```

If Quit is True (a CR was entered in the **Edit__String** procedure) and no
errors have been found, **Input__Formula** exits; otherwise, control is passed
back to the edit procedure.

The **Trim__Formula** procedure is simply a utility that removes spaces from
the formula string. Spaces are allowed during editing, but without them, it
becomes easier to execute further tests and to calculate the final results. The
spaces are permitted only for the user's convenience and have no actual function of their own.

The Parse__Parentheses Procedure

The **Parse__Parentheses** procedure is the simplest of the tests executed. Here
two variables are initiated and, running through the formula string, the opening and closing parentheses are counted. Each time a closing (right) parenthesis is found, the count is checked. If there is not a matching opening (left)
parenthesis, an error message is displayed, the variable OffSet is set one position to the left, and the test procedure is exited. If no error is found in the
closing parentheses, when the string has been completed, the number of opening parentheses is checked. If there is a discrepancy, a second error message
is displayed and OffSet is set to the left end of the string.

```
procedure Parse_Parentheses;
  var
    LPar, RPar, I : byte;
  begin
    LPar := 0;
    RPar := 0;
    Clear_Error;
    for I := 1 to length(FormulaStr) do
    case FormulaStr[I] of
      '(': inc(LPar);
      ')': begin
             inc(RPar);
             if LPar > RPar then
             begin
               Report_Error('Left parenthesis missing');
               OffSet := I-1;
               Exit;
             end;
           end;
    end; {case}
    if (LPar > RPar) and not Error then
    begin
      Report_Error('Right parenthesis missing');
      OffSet := length(FormulaStr);
    end;
  end;
```

If either error condition is found, the following error checks are bypassed and the program returns to the editing procedure.

Parse__Operators

The **Parse__Operators** test checks to see if the syntax of the formula string is correct. Since no instructions have been provided to describe the proper syntax, the error messages will have to do double duty here. In brief, the syntax is based on common English conventions.

The first test is, naturally, the initial character in FormulaStr:

```
if (FormulaStr[1] in ['*','/']) then
begin
  Report_Error('Initial operator invalid');
  OffSet := 1;
  Exit;
end;
```

Opening parentheses, numbers, +, or − are acceptable but * and / are not. Beginning the formula with a + is redundant since this is normally assumed unless a negative is specified, but it is not cause for error. An initial multiplication or division sign, however, does not make any sense and, therefore, produces an error message and an exit, returning to the editing procedure for correction.

Next, check the length of FormulaStr. If it's fewer than three characters, simply jump to the last character test; otherwise, loop from the second character through to the next-to-last character, testing each:

```
if length(FormulaStr) > 2 then
for I := 2 to length(FormulaStr)-1 do
begin
```

A series of tests are executed for each position in the formula string. First, if the character is an operator (that is, is in the set MathChar) and the following character is also an operator, then we have:

```
if (FormulaStr[I] in MathChar) and
   (FormulaStr[I+1] in MathChar) then
begin
   Report_Error('Invalid operation request');
   OffSet := I;
   Exit;
end else
```

This constitutes an error. This could be a multiply instruction followed by a division sign, a plus followed by a minus, and so on. There is one condition where this would not necessarily be an error: the pairs /− or *− could be perfectly valid with the minus operator acting as the sign of a following number with a negative value.

This test could be rewritten as follows:

```
if (FormulaStr[I] in MathChar) and
   (FormulaStr[I+1] in MathChar) then
begin
   if not (FormulaStr[I] in ['/','*']) or
      (FormulaStr[I+1] <> '−') then
   begin
```

excepting the two pairs from error.

As the program stands, however, these pairs can be delimited using parentheses: /−... should be entered as /(−...), and *−... should be entered as *(−...). Alternately, spaces could be used as delimiters, but this would require further modifications.

For now, the next condition tested is a parenthesis. Specifically, the opening parenthesis. **Parse__Parentheses** was executed earlier, but that was only a test for balanced opening and closing parentheses. Now the test is for validity in conjunction with the other elements of the formula:

```
if FormulaStr[I] = '(' then
begin
    if FormulaStr[I+1] = ')' then
    begin
        Report_Error('Empty parentheses - invalid syntax');
        OffSet := I+1;
        Exit;
    end;
```

The first test is for empty parentheses. These do no particular harm and shouldn't interfere with anything, but it's still better to get them out of the way.

The second test is essentially the same as the test for the opening character and for exactly the same reasons:

```
    if (FormulaStr[I+1] in MathChar) and
       not (FormulaStr[I+1] in ['-','+'])      then
    begin
        Report_Error('Invalid operation request');
        OffSet := I+1;
        Exit;
    end;
end else
```

Next, to finish up the parentheses, the closing parenthesis is tested. If either a number or an opening parenthesis follows a closing parenthesis, this is an error. It can be either an operator or another *closing* parenthesis.

```
    if (FormulaStr[I] = ')') and
       (FormulaStr[I+1] in (NumChar + ['('])) then
        begin
            Report_Error('Should be operator or closing parenthesis');
            OffSet := I;
            Exit;
        end;
end;
```

Note the term in (NumChar +['(']). This uses the union of two sets, the first set being NumChar and the second set containing only the opening parenthesis. This is simpler than writing two separate tests. A similar technique could have been applied in the previous test as if(FormulaStr[I+1] in (MathChar - ['-','+']) then. (See the discussion of Sets and Set Operators, earlier in this chapter.)

This takes care of most of the possible error conditions. Only one is left. It concerns the final character in the formula string and only one test is required:

```
if FormulaStr[length(FormulaStr)] in MathChar then
begin
   Report_Error('Final operator invalid');
   OffSet := length(FormulaStr);
end;
end;
```

If no errors have been found through these tests, it is time for the final test — to see if the formula can be solved.

Execute__Formula

At this point, checks and tests have been made for all of the more obvious errors in syntax. There may still be errors in the formula itself, but these can be tested more conveniently by solving the formula than by testing the ASCII string representing the formula. Therefore, the next step is to transform the string representation into a series of tokens and values that can be manipulated mathematically. (This cannot be done easily using the string version.)

The first step involves declaring two data types and an array of formula elements:

```
procedure Execute_Formula
   type
      RTypes = (Multiply,Divide,Add,Subtract,OpenPar,ClosePar,ValType,Null);
      OpsRec = record case EType : RTypes of    Null : ( );
                        Multiply : ( );      Divide : ( );
                             Add : ( );    Subtract : ( );
                         OpenPar : ( );    ClosePar : ( );
                         ValType : ( Value : real );      end; {case}
   var
      Element : array[1..100] of OpsRec;
```

The data type RTypes defines the elements that will be read from FormulaStr, and OpsRec provides a record of these types with the additional provision that records of type ValType will have a numerical value of type Real. Last, the variable Element is an array of OpsRec.

Declaring an array of 100 records to parse a single formula string is erring on the side of generosity, but it costs little at the moment. In other applications, a smaller array might be preferable to save memory space, but I'll let it stand as is for the moment.

The main body of the **Execute_Formula** procedure is very simple. The FormulaVal variable is set to zero, **Parse_Formula** is called to convert the string formula into elements, and then **Solve_Formula** is called to find the actual solution to the formula.

```
begin    { Execute_Formula }
   FormulaVal := 0.0;
   Parse_Formula;
   Solve_Formula;
end;
```

The Parse_Formula Procedure

The **Parse_Formula** procedure begins by clearing the Element array. To do so, each Element record is set to type ValType, Value is set to zero, and then the record type is reset to Null.

```
for I := 1 to 100 do    with Element[I] do
begin    EType := ValType;    Value := 0.0;
         EType := Null;                         end;
```

Next, the characters in FormulaStr are read and, beginning with Element[1], if the character in FormulaStr is an operation or a parenthesis, the record type is set accordingly.

```
repeat
  case FormulaStr[I] of
     '+' : if FormulaStr[I+1] = '('
              then Element[K].ETtype := Add
              else Parse_Value;
     '-' : if FormulaStr[I+1] = '(' then
              begin    Element[K].EType := ValType;
                       Element[K].Value := -1.0;
                       Element[K+1].EType := Multiply;
                       inc(K);                           end
              else Parse_Value;
     '*' : Element[K].EType := Multiply;
     '/' : Element[K].EType := Divide;
     '(' : Element[K].EType := OpenPar;
     ')' : Element[K].EType := ClosePar;
```

```
            else Parse_Value;
        end; {case}
        inc(I);
        inc(K);
    until I > length(FormulaStr);
end;
```

There are two exceptions:

1. If a + sign precedes an opening parenthesis, the record type is set as add; otherwise, since the next character *must* be a numeral, this establishes the sign of the following numerical value. In this case, the **Parse__Value** subprocedure is called.

2. If a – sign precedes an opening parenthesis, an element value is of –1 is set and the next element is set as a multiply flag. Therefore, when the formula is processed for solution, the value solved within the parentheses is simply multiplied by –1.

Note that, since numerical strings are not required to be preceded by an explicit sign, case ends with an else statement. If none of the case subrange conditions is met, the character must be a number and else calls **Parse__Value**.

In turn, the **Parse__Value** subprocedure creates a string variable TempStr, consisting of numerical characters only or of numerical characters preceded by a + or \– sign. Next, the characters .0 are appended to the end of the string to create a real value and Pascal's **val** procedure converts the string to a real number. Finally, the current Element is assigned type ValType, and Value receives the number value that was represented by TempStr.

```
procedure Parse_Value;
    var
        TempStr : string[20];    TempVal : real;
    begin
        TempStr := ' ';   TempVal := 0.0;
        repeat
            TempStr := TempStr + FormulaStr[I];
            inc(I);
        until not ( FormulaStr[I] in NumChar )
                or ( I > length( FormulaStr ) );
        TempStr := TempStr + '.0';
        val(TempStr,TempVal,J);
```

```
if J <> 0 then Report_Error('Error in |'+TempStr+'|');
with Element[K] do
begin    EType := ValType;
         Value := TempVal;    end;
   dec(I);
end;
```

One error provision was made here ... if the Pascal function **val** returned a nonzero error result (the integer variable J), then an error report is made and the variable J indicates the position in the string variable where the problem is found. No special provision has been made here to use this additional error information because, as the demo program currently stands, this particular error is (almost) impossible to produce.

In other circumstances, it may be valuable to place brackets or highlight or otherwise indicate the error location.

If an error does occur, TempVal will be returned as zero.

The Solve__Formula Procedure

Once the string formula has been converted to Element records, it becomes practical to actually solve the formula to determine the solution produced by the formula entry. First, the procedure **Solve__Formula** begins by looking for the last active Element in the array.

```
procedure Solve_Formula;
   var
      Start, Finis, Final, I : integer;
                  Parentheses : Boolean;
   begin    { Solve__Formula }
      Final := 0;
      Parentheses := true;
      for I := 1 to 100 do
      if (Element[I].EType = Null)    { find last active element }
         and (Final = 0) then Final := I;
```

The variable Final provides a limit, and all Element records greater than Final will be ignored by subsequent tests.

Attempting to solve the entire formula in a single stage would be cumbersome if not excessively complex both to code and to debug. Instead, the final value is determined by a series of solutions to smaller segments of the formula.

The first step is to locate any clauses within parentheses:

```
repeat                                    { testing for parentheses    }
```

```
   I := 0;
Start := 0;
Finis := 0;
repeat                            { search for parentheses pair  }
   inc(I);
   case Element[I].EType of
      OpenPar : Start := I;
      ClosePar : begin   Finis := I;   I := Final;   end;
   end; {case}
until I >= Final;
```

The search begins by looking for a start point, an opening parenthesis. If more than one opening parenthesis is found before a closing parenthesis is located, the Start variable holds the position of the last opening parenthesis found. When a closing parenthesis is located, Start and Finis are passed as marker values to the **Solve_For** subprocedure, and this segment of the formula is processed. The resulting value will be stored for later use. This procedure loops until no further parentheses are found.

```
   if Finis > 0 then Solve_For(Start,Finis)
                else Parentheses := false;
until not Parentheses;
Solve_For(1,Final);                { solve the remaining figures  }
```

Once the clauses enclosed by parentheses are solved, **Solve_For** is called to find a final solution for the remaining Element records. Finally, the solution in Element[1].Value is passed to **FormulaVal**.

```
   with Element[1] do
      FormulaVal := Value;
end;
```

The Solve_For Procedure

The **Solve_For** subprocedure is used to find partial solutions for the formula elements between the two points passed as parameters, particularly any portion of the formula that was enclosed in parentheses.

```
procedure Solve_For( First, Last: integer);
   var
      I, J : integer;   TempVal : real;
   begin
      J := 0;
      if Element[First].EType = OpenPar then    { remove Parentheses }
```

```
begin    Element[First].EType := Null;
         Element[Last].EType := Null;
         Clear_Elements( First, Last, J );    end;
```

The first step is to remove any parentheses that were used as delimiters for this portion of the formula. This is done (if Element[First] indicates an open parenthesis) by setting both to Null types and calling another sub-procedure, **Clear_Elements**.

For the moment, **Clear_Elements** moves the existing elements up to replace any nulls from the current working location down to Final. The Final variable is adjusted as are the Last and J variables. In this particular case, J is unimportant and is used only because **Clear_Elements** expects a third variable parameter to be passed.

After the parentheses are removed, the next operation is to execute any multiplication instructions. All operations are carried out in strict order of precedence as defined for Pascal operators.

```
I := First;                              { start with Multiply }
repeat
  J := 0;
  repeat
    if Element[I].EType = Multiply
          then J := I
          else inc(I);
  until (J <> 0) or (I >= Last);
  if J <> 0 then
  begin
    TempVal := Element[J-1].Value * Element[J+1].Value;
    Element[J].EType := Null;
    Element[J+1].EType := Null;
    Element[J-1].Value := TempVal;
    Clear_Elements(First,Last,J);
  end;
  I := J;
until J = 0;                             { nothing left to multiply }
```

The variable J is used in a search for multiplication operators. If J remains zero, further operations in the loop are skipped and the loop exits. Otherwise, execution continues and the loop repeats until no further multiplication operators are located.

The multiplication operator must appear between two number values. This condition has already been tested in the **Parse_Operators** procedure and is therefore, assumed to be true at this point. Thus, Element[J-1].Value (preceding) and Element[J+1].Value (following) are multiplied together and the result is stored in Element[J-1].Value.

Now both J and J+1 are set to Null, **Clear_Elements** is called with the variables First, Last, and J to remove the empty records from the array and the loop continues. (*Note*: This time, updating the value in J *is* relevant.)

When all multiplication instructions have been handled, it's time to handle the division operations.

```
I := First;                                 { so Divide is next     }
repeat
   J := 0;
   repeat
      if Element[I].EType = Divide
         then J := I
         else inc(I);
   until (J<> 0) or (I >= Last);
   if J <> 0 then
      if Element[J+1].Value = 0.0 then
      begin
         Report Error('Division by zero attempted');
         exit;          { trap these before problems result }
      end;
      TempVal := Element[J-1].Value / Element[J+1].Value;
      Element[J].EType := Null;
      Element[J+1].EType := Null;
      Element[J-1].Value := TempVal;
      Clear_Elements(First,Last,J);
   end;
   I := J;
until J = 0;                                { nothing left to divide }
```

The division instructions are handled exactly like the multiplication instruction with one exception: another error trap is included. In this case, the divisor is checked for a nonzero value. If the divisor is zero, this is reported as an error and the procedure exits, returning to the editing procedure for correction.

Since this test is made *before* attempting a divide by zero operation, the program is not aborted by a critical error and the user is given the opportunity to make a correction. In this case, the error location is not indicated, but provisions can be made to include this in the display. (Think about it — you will be asked for a solution later.)

After the division operations are finished, only one operation remains. By assumption, all remaining elements are to be added. Remember, if an element was subtracted, the – operator was used to set the sign of the value instead of maintaining the + and – signs as operation flags.

If the minus sign preceded an opening parenthesis, a multiply by minus one was established and, after the parentheses were cleared, the value within changes sign. If a plus preceded an opening parenthesis, the add flag was set, but it was simply ignored thereafter because all remaining values were added together without checking for add flags.

```
I := First;                          { just add up what's left }
if Last > First then
repeat
   TempVal := Element[I].Value + Element[Last].Value;
   Element[Last].EType := Null;
   Element[I].Value := TempVal;
   Clear_Elements(First,Last,I);
until Last = First;                  { and that's the job }
end;
```

Here the loop continues, adding Element[Last].Value to Element[First].Value until Last = First. When **Solve_For** is called a final time, after all parentheses have been processed, the final value is left in Element[1].Value.

The Clear_Elements Procedure

The **Clear_Elements** subprocedure has already been described briefly, but there is little else to add as explanation except to point out the **Test_Result** procedure. This reference is to a different error-trapping provision, in this case, error-trapping for the programmer. **Test_Result** provides a step-by-step look at the formula processing and is included in the program listing.

```
procedure Clear_Elements( StartPoint : integer;
              var EndPoint, Current : integer);
   var
      I, J : integer;
   begin
      for I := StartPoint to Final do
         if Element[I].EType = Null then        { if this is null,     }
         repeat
            for J := I to Final do              { from here down ... }
```

```
                begin                        { move everything up }
                    Element[J].EType := Element[J+1].EType;
                    if Element[J].EType = ValType then
                        Element[J].Value := Element[J+1].Value;
                    Element[J+1].EType := Null;        { one slot and clear }
                end;
                if I <= EndPoint then dec(EndPoint); { and move markers }
                if I <= Current then dec(Current);
                if I <= Final then dec(Final);
(*
{test}          Test_Results;                    { this is just for your information }
*)
            until (Element[I].EType <> Null)
                or (I > EndPoint);
    end;
```

Enhancing Error Reporting

Earlier, in discussing the trap for a potential divide by zero, I pointed out that the error position was not known. We only knew that an error had been found. But I also suggested that a provision could be made for location information.

One possible method to determine the location of an error would be to repeat the calculation while keeping an active marker adjusted to show the position within the formula that was being calculated. However, this would involve rather complex logistics for deciding the relationship between the calculation being processed and the formula elements. A simpler approach is to redefine the record type:

```
OpsRec = record          FormPos1, FormPos2 : byte;
            case EType : RTypes of    Null : ( );
                Multiply : ( );       Divide : ( );
                     Add : ( );     Subtract : ( );
                 OpenPar : ( );     ClosePar : ( );
                 ValType : ( Value : real );        end; {case/rec}
```

In the **Parse_Formula** procedure, when the Elements are cleared, FormPos1 and FormPos2 must be initialized to zero, but, as FormulaStr is processed, assign the string position I to both FormPos2 for each Element[I]. If the Element is further assigned a value by **Parse_Value**, FormPos2 would receive the value for the last string position of the number. Thus FormPos1 and FormPos2 will show the beginning and end of each Element within the string.

Next, in the **Clear_Element** subprocedure, before a Null element is replaced, the end formula position (FormPos2) is passed back to the previous Element as follows:

```
procedure Clear_Elements(. . .
   begin
      for I := StartPoint to Final do
         if Element[I].EType = Null then
         begin
            Element[I-1].FormPos2 := Element[I].FormPos2;
            repeat
               for J := I to Final do
                        . . .
```

Now, if an Element triggers a divide by zero error report, FormPos1 and FormPos2 are available to show the range of items in FormStr that have resulted in an error. The applicable segment of the formula can be highlighted or shown in reverse video. Although this does not show the user precisely why the error was found, it does identify the error location as well as the cause.

This particular example was chosen for demonstrating error reporting because the *mechanisms* and errors being tested required little explanation. Both the formula parsing and error techniques and practices, however, are applicable to virtually any type of input.

These same basic mechanisms were developed for a database/report-generation program with which operators might request listings using two verbs, BY and THEN, and nouns such as SHIP, PORT, CARGO, COUNTRY, and so on together with parenthetical delimiters. The actual database consisted of something over 20 megabytes of commercial shipping data iomported from a mainframe system, but multi-indexed and cross-referenced (using pointer structures) by the AT operating program, which was written entirely in Turbo Pascal 3.0 and Turbo's Database Toolbox. The final program processed three and four line requests in milliseconds, trapped and reported seventeen syntax and request errors, highlighted each one, and offered an optional one or two paragraph help display for each.

Also, aside from the more obvious operator syntax errors, it was quite easy for the user to request an output that would require thousands of pages of printed report and a week or more to produce even with a fast printer. Thus further provision was made to calculate the approximate result size in pages and production time and, for any report beyond 30 pages, operator confirmation was required (another type of error trapping).

The error reports shown in the demo program are brief — too brief in many respects. For example, the formula string 10 * −9 is mathematically valid, but it will produce the Invalid operation request error report because paired operators are not permitted. The error message, however, does nothing to suggest the alternative of saying 10 * (−9), which is acceptable. A better error message might be:

> Operators such as +, −, * and / cannot occur in pairs. Parentheses may be used when necessary such as: *(−10) or /(−10) but combinations such as */ are invalid.

On the other hand, displaying large blocks of explanation tends to make the screen look cluttered and the text necessary increases program size objectionably, so programmers tend to be terse and laconic in their in-program explanations.

Since the problem is two-fold, the solution is also:

1. Use brief error messages with optional, additional online help.

2. Use an external help file.

A brief error message is usually all the reminder the experienced user needs. Then, you can give the inexperienced user the option of asking for additional explanation with, for instance, the F1 key. This expanded help information might be placed in a pop-up screen box, positioned to leave the error in original display visible. If more space is required, the alternate video pages provide a convenient display without overwriting the original.

An external help file can be as verbose as necessary, can include examples, or can offer several pages of explanation without wasting system memory when not required and without limiting the explanation.

There's certainly nothing difficult about doing it this way, except that it would be a good idea, just in case the error text file is missing, to error trap this also. Also, just when you think you have all of the possible errors trapped, have somebody else try your program. Make note of the errors that *they* find because, somehow, there are always more.

Quiz

1. I suggested earlier that it was possible to rewrite the demo program so that the spaces would not need to be removed. In many cases, leaving the spaces as delimiters would be absolutely required. How would this change be best implemented in the demo program? (*Remember:* When parsing words in a command, the spaces will be necessary as delimiters.)

2. The **Parse_Formula** began by clearing the Element array using:

```
for I := 1 to 100 do    with Element[I] do
begin    EType := ValType;    Value := 0.0;
         EType := Null;                      end;
```

Could the simpler statement

```
for I := 1 to 100 do    Element[I].EType := Null;
```

have been used? What would the effects be? (*Hint:* Try entering – ((87 – 29) * (33 + 14)) / (–4 * 9).)

3. In discussing **Parse_Formula**, I said the character following a + or –, if it was not an opening parenthesis, must be a numerical character. Why must this be true? What would happen if it were not?

Solutions

1. The simplest method of treating spaces, in this case, is to simply ignore them, that is, when any element in FormulaStr is found to be a space, test the next element. Since the index I is global to the procedures that are testing and parsing the formula line, a simple **GetNext** function could easily return the next nonspace character for the test. If the current element is a space, then inc(I) to move to the next.

2. The type identifiers used here are known as *free unions* because, except for ValType, the tag field identifier is omitted altogether. But, even if an Element is not ValType, the Value field still exists for each record. Unless the field is explicitly assigned contents (such as 0.0, the field may contain anything — and it will probably be something other than desired. Try the alternate program line and the formula entry suggested and observe the results while using the = key to request several recalculations, which should, in itself, provide sufficient explanation.

3. Look back at the error tests in **Parse_Operators**. Anything except a numeral or opening parenthesis that followed an operator was already reported as

an error. Therefore, the character currently following a + or – operator must qualify. If it had not been trapped already, the **Parse__Value** procedure would flag the error when the **val** function failed.

FORM__CAL.PAS Demo Program

```pascal
program Formula_Calculator;      { FORM__CAL.PAS }
{$R+}
uses Crt, Dos;

   type
      Regs = record case integer of
                   0: (AX, BX, CX, DX, BP, SI, DI, DS, ES, Flags : word);
                   1: (AL, AH, BL, BH, CL, CH, DL, DH          : byte);    end;
   var
        Reg : Regs;


procedure Swap_If(var LoNum, HiNum: byte);
   var   Temp: byte;
   begin    if LoNum > HiNum then
            begin   Temp := LoNum;
                 LoNum := HiNum;
                 HiNum := Temp;    end;    end;


{$i BOX_UTIL.INC}
{$i SOUND.INC}


procedure Input_Formula( XAxis, YAxis, FLen: byte);
   const
      MathChar   : set of char = ['+','-','*','/'];    { four operators            }
      LimitChar  : set of char = ['(',' ',')'];        { parentheses and space     }
      NumChar    : set of char = ['0'..'9'];           { numbers                   }
   var
      FormulaStr : string;        FormulaVal : real;
       Offset : byte;          Quit, Error : boolean;


procedure Clear_Error;
   var I : byte;
   begin
      for I := 2 to 4 do
      begin   gotoxy(1,I);    clreol;    end;
      Error := false;
   end;


procedure Report_Error(ErrorStr: string);
   begin
      Box_Line(10,3,70,5,1,2,14,0);
      gotoxy(12,4); write(ErrorStr);
```

```
                            Error := true;
                        end;

            procedure Parse_Parentheses;
                var
                    LPar, RPar, I : byte;
                begin
                    LPar := 0;
                    RPar := 0;
                    Clear_Error;
                    for I := 1 to length(FormulaStr) do
                    case FormulaStr[I] of
                        '(': inc(LPar);
                        ')': begin
                                    inc(RPar);
                                    if LPar < RPar then
                                    begin
                                        Report_Error('Left parenthesis missing');
                                        OffSet := I-1;
                                        Exit;
                                    end;
                                end;
                    end; {case}
                    if (LPar > RPar) and not Error then
                    begin
                        Report_Error('Right parenthesis missing');
                        OffSet := length(FormulaStr);
                    end;
                end;

            procedure Trim_Formula;
                var
                    I, X : integer;
                begin
                    X := 0;
                    I := 1;
                    repeat                                    { remove blanks as unnecessary        }
                        while FormulaStr[I] = ' ' do
                        begin    delete(FormulaStr,I,1);
                                 dec(OffSet);             end;
                        inc(I);
                    until I > length(FormulaStr);
                end;

            procedure Parse_Operators;
                var
                    I : integer;
                begin
                    if (FormulaStr[1] in ['*','/']) then       { test allowable first        }
```

ERROR CORRECTIONS

```
   begin
      Report_Error('Initial operator invalid');
      OffSet := 1;
      Exit;
   end;
   if length(FormulaStr) > 2 then
   for I := 2 to length(FormulaStr)-1 do
   begin
      if (FormulaStr[I] in MathChar) and
         (FormulaStr[I+1] in MathChar) then
         begin
            Report_Error('Invalid operation request');
            OffSet := I;
            Exit;
         end
      else
      if FormulaStr[I] = '(' then
      begin
         if FormulaStr[I+1] = ')' then
         begin
            Report_Error('Empty parentheses - invalid syntax');
            OffSet := I+1;
            Exit;
         end;
         if (FormulaStr[I+1] in MathChar) and
            not (FormulaStr[I+1] in ['-','+']) then
         begin
            Report_Error('Invalid operation request');
            OffSet := I+1;
            Exit;
         end;
      end else
      if (FormulaStr[I] = ')') and
         (FormulaStr[I+1] in (NumChar+['('])) then
         begin
            Report_Error('Should be operator or close parenthesis');
            OffSet := I;
            Exit;
         end;
   end;
   if FormulaStr[length(FormulaStr)] in MathChar then
   begin
      Report_Error('Final operator invalid');
      OffSet := length(FormulaStr);
   end;
end;

procedure Execute_Formula;
   type
```

```
RTypes = (Multiply,Divide,Add,Subtract,OpenPar,ClosePar,ValType,Null);
OpsRec = record case EType : RTypes of    Null : ( );
                    Multiply : ( );        Divide : ( );
                        Add : ( );       Subtract : ( );
                    OpenPar : ( );       ClosePar : ( );
                    ValType : ( Value : real ),       end; {case}
    var
        Element : array[1..100] of OpsRec;

    procedure Solve_Formula;
        var
            Start, Finis, Final, I : integer;
                    Parentheses : boolean;
```

```
{test}      procedure Test_Result;
{test}          var I : integer;   Ch : char;
{test}          begin
{test}              gotoxy(1,1);    clreol;    write('[',Final,']');
{test}              for I := 1 to Final do
{test}                  with Element[I] do
{test}                      case EType of                      { this is a test to       }
{test}                          Add: write('+');               { allow you to see        }
{test}                          Subtract: write('-');          { what is happening       }
{test}                          Multiply: write('*');          { when the formula is     }
{test}                          Divide: write('/');            { processed               }
{test}                          OpenPar: write('(');
{test}                          ClosePar: write(')');
{test}                          ValType: write(' ',Value:10:5,' ');
{test}                          else       write('null');
{test}                      end; {case}
{test}                  clreol;                                { change time delay       }
         (*                                                    { as desired for best     }
{test}              delay(1000);                               { view of events          }
{test}              if KeyPressed then                         { or view step by step    }
         *)                                                    {           BUT           }
{test}              begin   Ch := readkey;                     { keep an emergency       }
{test}                      if Ch = ' ' then halt;   end;      { out during testing      }
{test}          end;

{test}      procedure Report_Element( EleNum: integer );
{test}          begin
{test}              gotoxy(1,20); clreol;
{test}              write( EleNum:3,'|');                      { a second test to        }
{test}              with Element[EleNum] do                    { allow you to see        }
{test}                  case EType of                          { what is happening       }
{test}                      Add: write('+');                   { when the formula is     }
{test}                      Subtract: write('-');              { processed               }
{test}                      Multiply: write('*');              { this one checks a       }
{test}                      Divide: write('/');                { single element          }
```

ERROR CORRECTIONS

```
{test}                    OpenPar: write('(');
{test}                    ClosePar: write(')');
{test}                    ValType: write(' ',Value:10:5,' ');
{test}                    else        write('null');
{test}              end; {case}
                    write('|');
{test}        end;


        procedure Clear_Elements( StartPoint : integer;
                      var   EndPoint, Current : integer);
           var
              I, J : integer;
           begin
              for I := StartPoint to Final do
                  if Element[I].EType = Null then       { if this is null,           }
                  repeat
                      for J := I to Final do            { from here down             }
                      begin                             { move everything up          }
                         Element[J].EType := Element[J+1].EType;
                         if Element[J].EType = ValType then
                            Element[J].Value := Element[J+1].Value;
                         Element[J+1].EType := Null;    { one slot and clear          }
                      end;
                      if I <= EndPoint then dec(EndPoint); { and move markers         }
                      if I <= Current then dec(Current);
                      if I <= Final then dec(Final);
(*
{test}              Test_Result;              { this is just for your information      }
*)
                  until (Element[I].EType <> Null)
                      or (I > EndPoint);
           end;


        procedure Solve_For( First, Last: integer);
           var
              I, J : integer;   TempVal : real;
           begin
              J := 0;
              if Element[First].EType = OpenPar then   { remove Parentheses          }
              begin   Element[First].EType := Null;
                      Element[Last].EType := Null;
                      Clear_Elements( First, Last, J );    end;
              I := First;                              { start with Multiply          }
              repeat
                 J := 0;
                 repeat
                    if Element[I].EType = Multiply
                       then J := I
                       else inc(I);
```

```
            until (J <> 0) or (I >= Last);
            if J <> 0 then
            begin
                TempVal := Element[J-1].Value * Element[J+1].Value;
                Element[J].EType := Null;
                Element[J+1].EType := Null;
                Element[J-1].Value := TempVal;
                Clear_Elements(First,Last,J);
            end;
            I := J;
        until J = 0;                        { nothing left to multiply    }
        I := First;                         { so Divide is next           }
        repeat
            J := 0;
            repeat
                if Element[I].EType = Divide
                    then J := I
                    else inc(I);
            until (J <> 0) or (I >= Last);
            if J <> 0 then
            begin
                if Element[J+1].Value = 0.0 then
                begin
                    Report_Error('Division by zero attempted');
                    exit;                   { trap these before problems result  }
                end;
                TempVal := Element[J-1].Value / Element[J+1].Value;
                Element[J].EType := Null;
                Element[J+1].EType := Null;
                Element[J-1].Value := TempVal;
                Clear_Elements(First,Last,J);
            end;
            I := J;
        until J = 0;                        { nothing left to divide      }
        I := First;                         { just add up what's left     }
        if Last > First then
        repeat
            TempVal := Element[I].Value + Element[Last].Value;
            Element[Last].EType := Null;
            Element[I].Value := TempVal;
            Clear_Elements(First,Last,I);
        until Last = First;                 { and that's the job          }
    end;

begin   { Solve_Formula }
    Final := 0;
    Parentheses := true;
    for I := 1 to 100 do
        if (Element[I].EType = Null)        { find last active element    }
```

ERROR CORRECTIONS

```
                       and (Final = 0) then Final := I;
         repeat                                    { testing for parentheses            }
                  I := 0;
             Start := 0;
             Finis := 0;
             repeat                                { search for parentheses pair        }
                inc(I);
                case Element[I].EType of
                   OpenPar : Start := I;
                   ClosePar : begin   Finis := I;   I := Final;   end;
                end; {case}
             until I >= Final;
             if Finis > 0 then Solve_For(Start,Finis)
                          else Parentheses := false;
         until not Parentheses;
         Solve_For(1,Final);                       { solve the remaining figures        }
         with Element[1] do
             FormulaVal := Value;
    end;


procedure Parse_Formula;
    var
        I, J, K : integer;


    procedure Parse_Value;
        var
           TempStr : string[20];   TempVal : real;
        begin
           TempStr := ' ';   TempVal := 0.0;
           repeat
              TempStr := TempStr + FormulaStr[I];
                 inc(I);
           until not ( FormulaStr[I] in NumChar )
                 or ( I > length( FormulaStr ) );
           TempStr := TempStr + '.0';
           val(TempStr,TempVal,J);
           if J <> 0 then Report_Error('Error in |'+TempStr+'|');
           with Element[K] do
           begin   EType := ValType;
                   Value := TempVal;   end;
           dec(I);
        end;


    begin   { Parse_Formula }
       for I := 1 to 100 do   with Element[I] do
       begin   EType := ValType;   Value := 0.0;
               EType := Null;                        end;

(*        for I := 1 to 100 do   Element[I].EType := Null;                *)
```

```
(*   enter   -( ( 87 - 29 ) * ( 33 + 14 ) ) / ( -4 * 9 )                    *)

               I := 1;
               K := 1;
               repeat
                 case FormulaStr[I] of
                     '+' : if FormulaStr[I+1] = '('
                             then Element[K].EType := Add
                             else Parse_Value;
                     '-' : if FormulaStr[I+1] = '(' then
                             begin    Element[K].EType := ValType;
                                      Element[K].Value := -1.0;
                                      Element[K+1].EType := Multiply;
                                      inc(K);                        end
                             else Parse_Value;
                     '*' : Element[K].EType := Multiply;
                     '/' : Element[K].EType := Divide;
                     '(' : Element[K].EType := OpenPar;
                     ')' : Element[K].EType := ClosePar;
                     else Parse_Value;
                 end; {case}
                 inc(I);
                 inc(K);
               until I > length(FormulaStr);
             end;


   begin     { Execute_Formula }
      FormulaVal := 0.0;
      Parse_Formula;
      Solve_Formula;
   end;

procedure Test_Formula_Str;
   var
      Decimal : byte;    Test : real;
   begin
      Trim_Formula;
      Parse_Parentheses;
      if not Error then Parse_Operators;
      if not Error then Execute_Formula;
      Box_Line(30,9,50,11,1,1,14,0);
      Decimal := 5;
      Test := FormulaVal;
      while (Test < 0.1) and (Decimal < 10) do  { Write limits decimal     }
      begin                                      { display to ten places    }
         Test := Test * 10.0;
         inc(Decimal);
      end;
      gotoxy(31,10);
```

ERROR CORRECTIONS

```
           write(FormulaVal:17:Decimal);
     end;


procedure Edit_Formula_String;
   var
      Done : boolean;  InKey : char;
   begin
      Done := false;
      repeat
         gotoxy(XAxis,YAxis);
         write(FormulaStr,' ':(FLen-length(FormulaStr)));
         gotoxy(XAxis+Offset,YAxis);
         InKey := ReadKey;
         case InKey of
            #$00 : begin
                      InKey := Readkey;
                      case InKey of
```
```
{ right arrow }    'M' : inc(OffSet);
{ left arrow }     'K' : dec(OffSet);
{ home key }       'G' : OffSet := 0;
{ end key }        'O' : OffSet := length(FormulaStr);
{ delete key }     'S' : if ( length(FormulaStr) > 0 ) and
                            ( OffSet < length(FormulaStr) ) then
                               delete(FormulaStr,OffSet+1,1);
                         else Beep;
                      end; {case}
                   end;
{ Ctrl-Q }   #$11 : halt;            { while testing always have an out        }
{ Ctrl-H }   #$08 : if ( length(FormulaStr) > 0 ) and
                       ( OffSet > 0 ) then
                       begin   delete(FormulaStr,OffSet,1);
                               dec(OffSet);              end;
             '=' : Done := true;
             #$0D : begin   Done := true;   Quit := true;   end;
        (*
        NumChar, MathChar : begin    end;
        *)
             else if InKey in (NumChar + MathChar + LimitChar) then
                   begin
                      if OffSet < length(FormulaStr)
                         then insert(InKey,FormulaStr,OffSet+1)
                         else FormulaStr := FormulaStr + InKey;
                      inc(OffSet);
                   end else Boop;
         end; {case}
         if OffSet > FLen then OffSet := length(FormulaStr);
         if OffSet < 0 then OffSet := 0;
      until Done;
   end;
```

```
begin   { Input__Formula }
    FormulaStr := ' ';
    OffSet := 0;
    Error := false;
    Quit := false;
    repeat
        FormulaVal := 0.0;
        Edit_Formula_String;
        Test_Formula_Str;
    until Quit and not Error;
end;


begin
  clrscr;
  Box_Line(1,6,80,8,2,2,14,0);
  Input_Formula( 3, 7, 76 );
end.
```

ERROR CORRECTIONS

14

Debugging

The term *bug*, according to all the best apocryphal authorities, was coined when a moth was discovered in the contacts of a relay inside one of the early ENIAC computers. While this story has been debunked as many times as it has been recounted, the term itself is likely to long outlast the gremlins of an earlier generation. Bugs are simply too appropriate and too perfect an explanation — and, too often, a major headache to get rid of.

Eventually, most programmers devise techniques and practices to keep minor errors from becoming major bugs. Despite their best efforts and intentions, however, bugs still creep into programs. Regardless of the reasons, the best that can be done is to try to get rid of them when they appear and to do so with a minimum of wasted time and effort.

This chapter provides a list of common bug conditions, why they happen, and a collection of general guidelines, suggestions, tricks, and techniques that have, over the past decade, proved useful (or, more often, essential) in locating elusive errors. Not all of these will apply in all cases. You'll have to pick and choose and elaborate or improvise as necessary.

Loop Errors

One of the most frequent error types under earlier versions of Pascal occurred when a global variable was used for a loop index. The same variable was used, generally in a subprocedure, for a second loop index or for some other utilitarian application. With version 4.0, all loop variables are required to be declared locally (which has always been the better practice), so this type of inadvertent double referncing cannot occur so easily. This restriction, however, only applies to for loops and does not condition the declaration of while...do or repeat... loops, which remain as prime causes of errors.

In either of these cases, the problem most often is found in the test condition applied. Frequently, the condition being tested is too narrowly defined as:

$$...until \ X \ = \ length(Str)$$

which may fail and produce an endless loop, whereas the more general test:

$$...until \ X \ >= \ length(Str)$$

will succeed.

In other cases, a loop test condition may fail to be satisfied because the condition tested simply remains unchanged no matter how many times the procedure loops. For example,

```
procedure Test_Condition(X, Y, Z: integer)
   begin
       { some operation using the variables X, Y and Z }
   end;
```

which is called by

```
repeat
   Test_Condition(X,Y,Z);
until X >= Key;
```

will produce an endless loop unless the initial value of X is already greater than or equal to Key, even if **Test_Condition** operates perfectly, because the **Test_Condition** procedure does not return an altered value for the X variable. In this example, the declaration for **Test_Condition** should have read:

```
procedure Test_Condition( var X, Y, Z: integer)
```

Essentially the same thing happens when a global variable is passed to another procedure as a parameter. The global value is passed correctly, but it is not necessarily returned correctly unless it was passed explicitly as a variable parameter.

In other cases, loops fail simply because the value or variable being tested is never actually referenced or changed within the loop. This can be a simple oversight, or sometimes it can be rather more elusive as in the while...do loop:

```
while ( Pointer.Value[I] <> Key ) do
begin
    { some operation on current Pointer.Value[I] }
    inc(I);
end;
```

which will fail because the compiler has evaluated the pointer reference at the beginning of the loop as a memory address containing a variable and continues to test the value at that address instead of the address and variable pointed to by the new indexed pointer. If, instead, a local variable had taken the value of the current pointer variable within the loop and this local variable had been tested, the procedure would operate correctly.

Boolean Flag Variables

It is common practice to use Boolean variables as loop conditions. Frequently, it may be useful to use global Boolean variables instead of local Boolean variables so that flag conditions may be referenced or set by other procedures and subprocedures. This can also lead to confusing results and elusive bugs.

It's often tempting to give a local Boolean test variable the same name that has already been used for a global Boolean. After all, it's very convenient to simply say:

```
repeat...until Done
```

instead of thinking of a new name for the Boolean flag each time. The compiler will find no conflict here and will simply give the local usage precedence over the global within the local procedure. In other words, the local Boolean variable is compiled as a separate variable, but the global variable cannot be referenced from the procedure that is using the local variable.

However, if the compiler does not become confused, the same is not true for the programmer. This tends to promote another type of error when the programmer refers to a name variable but doesn't realize *which* variable of the same name is currently active, or the programmer doesn't remember that a local variable is being tested and sets a result in another procedure by referencing the correct variable *name* but the wrong variable.

When you have both a global and local variable with the same name, the global variable is accessible (in version 4.0) using dot notation. For example, the variable XY is declared globally in the program **TestIO**. In a subprocedure, **TestOne**, XY is also declared as a local variable. Within **TestOne**, the global XY can be referenced as TestIO.XY, but the reverse is not true: TestOne.XY *cannot* be accessed from another procedure unless the procedure (or function) is a subprocedure within **TestOne**. Such errors can still be very difficult to recognize.

Detecting Loop Errors

Most loop error conditions can be detected using trap lines, which are simply instructions inserted into a procedure or function that produce a display showing the value of a specific variable or variables. For example,

```
       procedure Complex_Crunch(var FactorA, FactorB: integer; var WorkStr: string);
          begin
{test}        gotoxy(1,1); write(FactorA:4,FactorB:4,WorkStr); delay(100);
                 .

                 .

              { body of procedure }

                 .

                 .

{test}        gotoxy(1,2); write(FactorA:4,FactorB:4,WorkStr); readln;
          end;
```

Here two test lines have been inserted to show the values of three variables at the start of the procedure and then again at the end of the procedure. The second test ends with **readln;**, which stops further execution until the programmer is satisfied the results are valid.

Also, the commented {test} provides an easily identifiable flag. This can be located with the editor's search function for removal or simply located visually in any clearly indented source code.

```
procedure Complex_Crunch(var FactorA, FactorB: integer; var WorkStr: string);
   var
{test} TCh : char
   begin
          .

          .

           { body of procedure }

          .


          .

{test} gotoxy(1,2); write(FactorA:4,FactorB:4,WorkStr); TCh := readkey;
{test} if TCh = #$11 then halt; {ctrl-Q}
   end;
```

In this version, an absolute out has been provided. When the trap line is reached, execution stops until a key is pressed. If the key is Ctrl-Q, the program stops completely. Any other key allows execution to continue.

Display Factors

A common test display might be:

```
{test}      gotoxy(1,1); write(A:3, B:3, C:8:3, D:4); delay(100);
```

which would produce a display in the upper left-hand corner of the screen, delay for a tenth of a second, and then continue.

However, a simple 23 4 73.021 119 doesn't offer quite as much real information as A = 23 | B = 4 | C = 73.021 | D = 119. Be kind to yourself by labeling the error display. It doesn't cost much and it does help — sometimes a lot. Even if you think you know which factor is causing the problem, it doesn't hurt a bit to go ahead and display several at the same time. You might even notice something you hadn't expected.

If a loop is involved, (as is frequently the case) *always* show the value of the loop index. (Even with version 4.0, this can still be one of your primary problem areas.)

When Boolean flags or Boolean tests are involved, it is also a good idea to show the value (state) of the flag or both the flag value and the variables used in the flag test. For example,

```
{test}      gotoxy(1,1); write(BooleanFlag);
{test}      gotoxy(1,1); write(X:3, Y:3, (X >= Y) );
```

The first example would display the word TRUE or FALSE on the screen, whereas the second might report 23 45 FALSE, the last being the Boolean result of evaluating the expression in parentheses. (For a more elaborate example, see the **Test__Result** and **Report__Element** procedures in the Formula__Calculator program in Chapter 13.)

Complex Error Trap Displays

If you need a larger display of special factors or don't want to interfere with the program display, write the test information to an alternate video page, call a special subprocedure to switch display pages (to allow you to see the information and to switch back and forth between the error display and the program display), and then restore your original video page before resuming execution:

```
procedure Test_Display;
  begin
        .
        .
        .
    { set up test information on alternate video page }
        .
        .
        .
    repeat
      Continue := false;
      case ReadKey of
        #$03: Continue := true;                    { ctrl-C }
        #$11: begin Restore_Original; halt; end;   { ctrl-Q }
        #$12: Restore_Original;                     { ctrl-R }
        #$14: Show_Test_Page;                       { ctrl-T }
      until Continue;
      Restore_Original;
    end;
```

Using this type of testing subprocedure, you are able to flip back and forth between two different displays (or more if necessary), continue or halt execution as desired, or you might add a feature to write error information to a file or to the printer. Granted, this is more elaborate than necessary in a lot of cases, but keep it in mind because there are times when nothing less will do the job.

Conditional Ifs and Case Statements

Most test displays tend to slow things down, but these don't have to be executed every time a procedure executes. If you have any ideas about the basic problem, a conditional statement is appropriate. The statements

```
{test}          if CONDITION then execute test
```
and
```
{test}          case FACTOR of
{test}             CONDITION : execute test
```

can both trigger displays in the appropriate circumstances. In other circumstances, a global Boolean variable might be set in one procedure to turn on an error display or error check in an entirely different function or procedure.

The first consideration in debugging is usually to discover just exactly *what* the bug actually is and *where* it occurs. And, one of the best tools for this purpose is modular testing.

Modular Testing

This is exactly what it sounds like. Simply testing each program segment as it's written tends to eliminate better than 90% of the potential problems before they have a chance to become hidden within the complexity of a larger program.

Sometimes, this can be easier said than done. The operation of a particular subprocedure may be dependent on a variety of external factors that you haven't written yet and testing will require setting up or simulating the necessary conditions. In some cases, this may or may not be practical, and it may not even be possible. It can be helpful if you can make it possible. The best approach to making it possible is to plan the sequence in which the various portions of the program are developed.

Imagine developing a directory access program. The overall task can be broken down into a series of independent jobs that might be fitted into such categories as display design, disk access, and sorting directory lists. Thus, each of these would be developed largely independently of the others, be tested and debugged independently, and, when each segment operates correctly, be assembled into a coherent program.

Of course, when you plan the display, the screen layout will be influenced by the type and arrangement of information that you intend to display. However, a dummy data array is easily arranged for testing the display, or a series of dummy functions can be created to return similar values to those expected from the real functions that will be created later. For example,

```
function Check_Drive: integer;
   begin
      Check_Drive := 0;
   end;
function Log_Drive(NewDrive: char): Boolean;
   begin
      Log_Drive :- false;
   end;
```

Alternatively, you might want a function or procedure to return a specific value or condition in order to test an error trap or error procedure during development.

Too often, however, the problems only appear when two modules, which seemed to work perfectly independently, suddenly become aberrant when they begin to interact. Usually it is obvious that something in one module is affecting the other, although sometimes both may seem affected. Obviously, the point to start is by checking informatin being passed from one module to the other and by checking variables that are not passed directly but are instead global to both.

The trap lines or test lines shown earlier are excellent for this purpose, but, instead of testing only the information received by a module, also test the information sent immediately before and compare the two (with labels) because both may be operating perfectly and the problem is only in how the data is passed between. What may look like a major problem may turn out to be only a minor bug with a big shadow.

Leaving Error Traps in Place

Frequently, it's helpful to construct fairly elaborate error traps for use during testing. Once the error has been located and corrected, common sense dictates deleting the error trap — common sense and the fact that the program source code looks better with the extraneous lines removed. Common sense and appearances are not always efficient, however, because before you are done, you may want the same trap again to look for a different error or a different cause.

One option is to simply comment out the error trap lines, but leave them in place, just in case, until the program is completely finished and completely debugged. And, even then, it may be a good idea to leave them in place for the next revision.

Remember that anything that is commented out (set off by { } or (* *) pairs) is not compiled, does not affect the run-time code, and does not add anything to the final version. But leaving error traps in place in the source code can save you time in the future and can serve as a reminder of where and why errors were found in the past.

In Chapter 13, in the program listing for the **Clear_Elements** procedure, you will find a commented line referring to the **Test_Result** procedure, which appears immediately before. Both the **Test_Result** and **Report_Element** procedures and the commented line used to call **Test_Result** have been left in place for future use, but, since neither is referenced elsewhere in the program, unless the comment brackets are removed, these will not be included by the compiler.

This is a judgment call situation. The source code looks better and is easier to read without the extraneous test lines, but some may be wanted later. Don't just automatically delete them without consideration.

When To Trap Errors

Any time there seems to be a problem you should trap errors. If you have any reason at all to suspect that an error is happening, or might happen, or has happened — even a minor error that didn't show as an immediate bug, check it out! If you don't know what is happening and why, find out before it happens in the worst possible circumstances and at the worst possible time (according to Murphrey's Law). From past experience, this will usually be ten minutes after delivering a test version to the customer.

When an Error Isn't an Error

Programmers too often exercise the unfortunate practice of "patching" their programs. This takes many forms. When a bug is found — a variable returning with an out-of-range value, a flag condition not set correctly, and soon — a patch is installed to correct the problem *at the point the bug is found*. This is done in lieu of correcting the actual problem, which is the source of the error. This is terrible programming practice!

Frequently, a bug is not a single error or maybe it is not an error at all but is simply the result of incompatible programming practices (that is, two procedures trying to accomplish tasks with mutually incompatible results). Sometimes the best path is to start fresh and use an entirely different approach.

If you find yourself inserting several small "adjustments" or making complex tests or adding multiple corrections to resolve something that seemed simple at first, you are probably on the wrong track altogether. So, *stop* right there! What you have is not an error — it is a bad program design. Don't keep trying to fix it. Think it over, away from the keyboard, and come back ready to tear out the offending code and write it correctly in the first place.

The simple fact is that you can spend ten times as long "patching" as a thorough rewrite would require and you would still wind up with a bad program. If memory serves correctly, Leviticus (from the Old Testament) contains an injunction against repairing old clothes with new patches — just apply the same injunction here and you'll find the results much more satisfactory.

Appendix A
ASCII Tables

Table A-1 ASCII Character Set

Dec.	Hex.	Char.	Dec.	Hex.	Char.	Dec.	Hex.	Char.	Dec.	Hex.	Char.
00	00	(null)	32	20	SP	64	40	@	96	60	`
01	01	ctrl-A	33	21	!	65	41	A	97	61	a
02	02	ctrl-B	34	22	"	66	42	B	98	62	b
03	03	ctrl-C	35	23	#	67	43	C	99	63	c
04	04	ctrl-D	36	24	$	68	44	D	100	64	d
05	05	ctrl-E	37	25	%	69	45	E	101	65	e
06	06	ctrl-F	38	26	&	70	46	F	102	66	f
07	07	(bell)	39	27	'	71	47	G	103	67	g
08	08	(BS)	40	28	(	72	48	H	104	68	h
09	09	(hTab)	41	29	)	73	49	I	105	69	i
10	0A	(LF)	42	2A	*	74	4A	J	106	6A	j
11	0B	(vTab)	43	2B	+	75	4B	K	107	6B	k
12	0C	(FF)	44	2C	,	76	4C	L	108	6C	l
13	0D	(CR)	45	2D	–	77	4D	M	109	6D	m
14	0E	ctrl-N	46	2E	.	78	4E	N	110	6E	n
15	0F	ctrl-O	47	2F	/	79	4F	O	111	6F	o
16	10	ctrl-P	48	30	0	80	50	P	112	70	p
17	11	ctrl-Q	49	31	1	81	51	Q	113	71	q
18	12	ctrl-R	50	32	2	82	52	R	114	72	r
19	13	ctrl-S	51	33	3	83	53	S	115	73	s
20	14	ctrl-T	52	34	4	84	54	T	116	74	t
21	15	ctrl-U	53	35	5	85	55	U	117	75	u
22	16	ctrl-V	54	36	6	86	57	W	118	76	v
23	17	ctrl-W	55	37	7	87	57	W	119	77	w
24	18	ctrl-X	56	38	8	88	58	X	120	78	x
25	19	ctrl-Y	57	39	9	89	59	Y	121	79	y
26	1A	(EOF)	58	3A	:	90	5A	Z	122	7A	z
27	1B	(ESC)	59	3B	;	91	5B	[	123	7B	{
28	1C	ctrl-\	60	3C	<	92	5C	\	124	7C		
29	1D	ctrl-]	61	3D	=	93	5D	]	125	7D	}
30	1E	ctrl-^	62	3E	>	94	5E	^	126	7E	~
31	1F	ctrl-_	63	3F	?	95	5F	_	127	7F	DEL

Table A-2 Extended ASCII Character Set

Dec.	Hex.	Char.	Dec.	Hex.	Char.	Dec.	Hex.	Char.	Dec.	Hex.	Char.
128	80	Ç	160	A0	á	192	C0	∟	224	E0	α
129	81	ü	161	A1	í	193	C1	⊥	225	E1	β
130	82	é	162	A2	ó	194	C2	⊤	226	E2	Γ
131	83	â	163	A3	ú	195	C3	├	227	E3	π
132	84	ä	164	A4	ñ	196	C4	─	228	E4	Σ
133	85	à	165	A5	Ñ	197	C5	┼	229	E5	σ
134	86	å	166	A6	ª	198	C6	╞	230	E6	μ
135	87	ç	167	A7	º	199	C7	╟	231	E7	τ
136	88	ê	168	A8	¿	200	C8	╚	232	E8	Φ
137	89	ë	169	A9	⌐	201	C9	╔	233	E9	θ
138	8A	è	170	AA	¬	202	CA	╩	234	EA	Ω
139	8B	ï	171	AB	½	203	CB	╦	235	EB	δ
140	8C	î	172	AC	¼	204	CC	╠	236	ED	∞
141	8D	ì	173	AD	¡	205	CD	═	237	ED	ø
142	8E	Ä	174	AE	≪	206	CE	╬	238	EE	ϵ
143	8F	Å	175	AF	≫	207	CF	⊥	239	EF	∩
144	90	É	176	B0	░	208	D0	╨	240	F0	≡
145	91	æ	177	B1	▒	209	D1	╤	241	F1	±
146	92	Æ	178	B2	▓	210	D2	╥	242	F2	≥
147	93	ô	179	B3	│	211	D3	╙	243	F3	≤
148	94	ö	180	B4	┤	212	D4	╘	244	F4	⌠
149	95	ò	181	B5	╡	213	D5	╒	245	F5	⌡
150	96	û	182	B6	╢	214	D6	╓	246	F6	÷
151	97	ù	183	B7	╖	215	D7	╫	247	F7	≈
152	98	ÿ	184	B8	╕	216	D8	╪	248	F8	·
153	99	Ö	185	B9	╣	217	D9	┘	249	F9	·
154	9A	Ü	186	BA	║	218	DA	┌	250	FA	·
155	9B	¢	187	BB	╗	219	DB	█	251	FB	√
156	9C	£	188	BC	╝	220	DC	▄	252	FC	η
157	9D	¥	189	BD	╜	221	DD	▌	253	FD	2
158	9E	₨	190	BE	╛	222	DE	▐	254	FE	▪
159	9F	ƒ	191	BF	┐	223	DF	▀	255	FF	

Appendix B
Keyboard Response Codes

	Right or Left SHIFT ON	shift off
Caps Lock On	caps off	CAPS ON
Caps Lock Off	CAPS ON	caps off

	Right or Left SHIFT ON	shift off	
function keys	number keys	Number Lock On
number keys	function keys	Number Lock Off

Punctuation Symbol Keys	SHIFTED	unshifted

Figure B-1 Shift/Caps/Number Lock Boolean Truth Table

Table B-1 Function Key Scan Codes

Function Keys	Scan Code			
	Norm	**Shift**	**Ctrl**	**Alt**
f1	3B 00	54 00	5E 00	68 00
f2	3C 00	55 00	5F 00	69 00
f3	3D 00	56 00	60 00	6A 00
f4	3E 00	57 00	61 00	6B 00
f5	3F 00	58 00	62 00	6C 00
f6	40 00	59 00	63 00	6D 00
f7	41 00	5A 00	64 00	6E 00
f8	42 00	5B 00	65 00	6F 00
f9	43 00	5C 00	66 00	70 00
f10	44 00	5D 00	67 00	71 00
f11[1]	85 00	87 00	89 00	8B 00
f12[1]	86 00	88 00	8A 00	8C 00

[1]Requires SuperKey or Interrupt-9 service handler.

Table B-2 Key Pad Scan Codes

Key Pad	Scan Code			
	Norm	Shft or Num_Lock	Ctrl	Alt
* PrtScr	37 00 *	print scr[1]	72 00	
Minus	4A 00 –			B1 00[2]
Plus	4E 00 +			B5 00[2]
Num Lock	45 00			
. Delete	53 00	53 2E .		BA 00[2]
0 Insert	52 00	52 30 0		B9 00[2]
1 End	4F 00	4D 31 1	75 00	B6 00[2]
2 Down	50 00	50 32 2		B7 00[2]
3 PgDn	51 00	51 33 3	76 00	B8 00[2]
4 Left	4B 00	4B 34 4	73 00	B2 00[2]
5	4C 00	4C 35 5		B3 00[2]
6 Right	4D 00	4D 36 6	74 00	B4 00[2]
7 Home	47 00	47 37 7	77 00	AE 00[2]
8 Up	48 00	48 38 8		AF 00[2]
9 PgUp	49 00	49 39 9	84 00	B0 00[2]

[1]Requires right or leftshift keys to activate.
[2]Requires SuperKey or Interrupt-9 service handler.

Table B-3 Keyboard Scan Codes

All Other Keys	Scan Code			
	Norm	Shift	Ctrl	Alt
ESC	01 00		01 1B	
1 !	02 31 1	02 21 !		78 00
2 @	03 32 2	03 40 @	03 00	79 00
3 #	04 33 3	03 23 #		7A 00
4 $	05 34 4	05 24 $		7B 00
5 %	06 35 5	06 25 %		7C 00
6 ^	07 36 3	07 5E ^	07 1E	7D 00
7 &	08 37 7	08 26 &		7E 00
8 *	09 38 8	09 2A *		7F 00
9 (	0A 39 9	0A 28 (		80 00
0)	0B 30 0	0B 29)		81 00
– __	0C 2D –	0C 5F __	0C 1F	82 00
= +	0D 3D =	0D 2B +		83 00
BS	0E 08		0E 7F	
TAB	0F 09	0F 00		
q Q	10 71 q	10 51 Q	10 11	10 00
w W	11 77 w	11 57 W	11 17	11 00
e E	12 65 e	12 45 E	12 05	12 00
r R	13 72 r	13 52 R	13 12	13 00
t T	14 74 t	14 54 T	14 14	14 00
y Y	15 79 y	15 59 Y	15 19	15 00
u U	16 75 u	16 55 U	16 15	16 00
i I	17 69 i	17 49 I	17 09	17 00
o O	18 6F o	18 4F O	18 0F	18 00
p P	19 70 p	19 50 P	19 10	19 00
[{	1A 5B [	1A 7B {	1A 1B	
] }	1B 5D]	1B 7D }	1B 1D	
CR	1C 00		1C 0A	

Table B-3 Keyboard Scan Codes (Cont.)

All Other Keys	Scan Code			
	Norm	Shift	Ctrl	Alt
Ctrl	1D 00			
a A	1E 61 a	1E 41 A	1E 01	1E 00
s S	1F 73 s	1F 53 S	1F 13	1F 00
d D	20 64 d	20 44 D	20 04	20 00
f F	21 66 f	21 46 F	21 06	21 00
g G	22 67 g	22 47 G	22 07	22 00
h H	23 68 h	23 48 H	23 08	23 00
j J	24 6A j	24 4A J	24 0A	24 00
k K	25 6B k	25 4B K	25 0B	25 00
l L	26 6C l	25 4C L	26 0C	26 00
; :	27 3A ;	27 3A :		
' "	28 27 '	28 22 "		
` ~	29 60 `	29 7E ~		
Lf Shift	2A 00			
\ |	2B 5C \	2B 7C |	2B 1C	
z Z	2C 7A z	2C 5A Z	2C 1A	2C 00
x X	2D 78 x	2D 58 X	2D 18	2D 00
c C	2E 63 c	2E 43 C	2E 03	2E 00
v V	2F 76 v	2F 56 V	2F 16	2F 00
b B	30 62 b	30 42 B	30 02	30 00
n N	31 6E n	31 4E N	31 0E	31 00
m M	32 6D m	32 4D M	32 0D	32 00
, <	33 2C ,	33 3C <		
. >	34 2E .	34 3E >		
/ ?	35 3F /	35 3F ?		
Rt Shift	36 00			
Alt	38 00			
Space	39 00			
Caps Lock	3A 00			
Scrl Lock	46 00			

[1]All scan and key code values are in hexadecimal format. Grey + keys are identified in **boldface** type.

Appendix C
Selected MS-DOS Interrupt Functions

In Turbo Pascal version 4.0, the Registers data type is declared in the Dos unit and does not need to be repeated in your program type declaration, but the variable Reg of type Registers must be declared. In version 3.x, the Registers data type must be declared.

```
type
   Registers = record case integer of
             0: ( AX, BX, CX, DX, BP, SI, DI, DS, ES, Flags : word );
             1: ( AL, AH, BL, BH, CL, CH, DL, DH              : byte ); end;
var
   Reg: Registers
```

The 8-bit registers (AL, AH, BL, BH, CL, CH, DL, and DH) are mapped on top of their 16-bit equivalents (AX, BX, CX, and DX). When an interrupt call returns a byte value (in the AL register, for example), the actual value returned is a word value in AX but with the high byte set to zero. Likewise, when a byte value is assigned to one 8-bit register, the other is set to zero unless a value is explicitly assigned.

Using Turbo Pascal version 4.0, include the uses Dos; statement at the beginning of your program (before the type-constant-variable declarations) to include the DOS unit in your program.

Two methods of calling interrupts are used: intr($xx,dos.registers (Reg)) and msdos(dos;registers(Reg));. The msdos procedure is equivalent to intr($21.... and is shown here for all interrupt 21h calls. All other interrupts use the intr procedure.

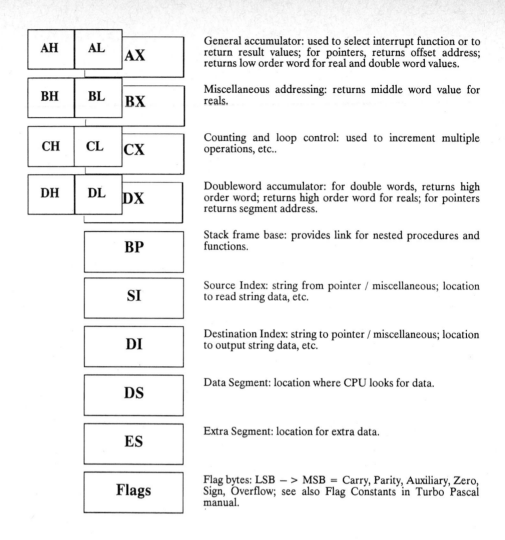

General accumulator: used to select interrupt function or to return result values; for pointers, returns offset address; returns low order word for real and double word values.

Miscellaneous addressing: returns middle word value for reals.

Counting and loop control: used to increment multiple operations, etc..

Doubleword accumulator: for double words, returns high order word; returns high order word for reals; for pointers returns segment address.

Stack frame base: provides link for nested procedures and functions.

Source Index: string from pointer / miscellaneous; location to read string data, etc.

Destination Index: string to pointer / miscellaneous; location to output string data, etc.

Data Segment: location where CPU looks for data.

Extra Segment: location for extra data.

Flag bytes: LSB — > MSB = Carry, Parity, Auxiliary, Zero, Sign, Overflow; see also Flag Constants in Turbo Pascal manual.

Figure C-1 Registers Used in Interrupt Function Calls

Reg.Flags

Turbo Pascal version 4.0 provides six constants (in the DOS unit) to test the Flags register returned by calls to intr or msdos. These are:

```
FCarry     := $0001;    FZero     := $0040;
FParity    := $0004;    FSign     := $0080;
FAuxiliary := $0010;    FOverflow := $0800;
```

To test a flag value (a bit test):

```
if (Reg.Flags and FZero) = 0 then ( the Zero Flag is clear )
if (Reg.Flags and FZero) <> 0 then ( the Zero Flag is set )
```

For Turbo version 3.x, these constants are not predefined but may be tested in the same manner, either by using the integer values shown or by defining the appropriate flag constants. The Zero and Carry flags are tested by several of the interrupt functions listed in this appendix.

Conventions and Terms

Four tables follow in this section: terms used in defining the interrupt functions; an explanation of the format elements used in each interrupt listing; a list of interrupt functions by number; and a list of interrupts by application.

Term	Definition
ASCIIZ	This term refers to an ASCII string that is terminated with a null character (chr 00h).
seg ofs	When a string variable is referenced by an interrupt call, the Turbo functions **seg** and **ofs** are used as seg(ASCIIZ_Str_Var) and ofs(ASCIIZ_Str_Var). These functions return the segment and offset addresses of the named variable and are passed to the interrupt function (usually in the DS:DX word registers) instead of passing the actual string variable. In like fashion, the segment and offset addresses of buffers or data arrays are passed to interrupt calls rather than attempting to pass the buffer contents or array contents directly.

Format Elements:

Equiv Shows equivalent functions in Turbo Pascal versions 3.x and 4.0.

Call Shows an example of how each interrupt function is called in a Turbo Pascal program. Terms shown in italics must be passed to interrupt call as variables or are returned by interrupt call for assignment to variables provided by the programmer.

Notes This subsection contains comments and/or explanations about the interrupt function and/or information passed or returned by the function.

Errors This subsection contains the errors returned by the function due to errors in the calling syntax or attempted task or due to other errors that interferred with the function's execution. If the called function is used to get error or condition information from the system or status information from external hardware, this information is not a function error and it is covered under the Notes subsection.

Term	Definition
Files	Path and file specifications are always ASCIIZ strings (see earlier entry).
Paths	The Path portion cannot exceed 64 characters, including drive specification. Filenames may or may not allow wildcard characters (see specific interrupt and function).

The following list indexes the system interrupts discussed in this appendix by interrupt and function number. An interrupt application key is included at the right.

Index to Interrupt Functions

Intr	,	Func	Description	Type[a]
05h			Print Screen	[P]
10h	,	00h	Set Video Mode	[V]
10h	,	01h	Set Cursor Size	[V]
10h	,	02h	Set Cursor Position	[V]
10h	,	03h	Read Cursor Position	[V]
10h	,	04h	Read Light Pen	[V]
10h	,	05h	Select Display Page	[V]
10h	,	06h	Initialize Window or Scroll Window	[V]
10h	,	07h	Initialize Window or Scroll Window	[V]
10h	,	08h	Read Attribute and Character at Cursor	[V]
10h	,	09h	Write Attribute and Character at Cursor	[V]
10h	,	0Ah	Write Character Only at Cursor	[V]
10h	,	0Eh	Write Text with Cursor Movement (Teletype)	[V]
10h	,	0Fh	Get Current Display Mode	[V]
10h	,	13h	Write String	[V]
11h			Equipment Flags	[S]
12h			Memory Size	[S]
13h	,	01h	Test Disk Status	[S]
14h	,	00h	Initialize Serial Port	[S]
14h	,	01h	Write Character to Serial Port	[I]
14h	,	02h	Read Character from Serial Port	[S]
14h	,	03h	Serial Port Status Request	[I]
16h	,	00h	Read Character From Keyboard	[K]
16h	,	01h	Test Character Ready	[K]
16h	,	02h	Shift Key Status	[K]
17h	,	00h	Write Character To Parallel Port	[P]
17h	,	01h	Initialize Printer (Parallel Port)	[P]
17h	,	02h	Get Printer Status (Parallel Port)	[P]
19h			Reboot	[M]
1Ah	,	00h	Read Clock	[S]
1Ah	,	01h	Set Clock	[S]
21h	,	01h	Character Input With Echo	[K]
21h	,	02h	Character Output	[V]

Intr	,	Func	Description	Type[a]
21h	,	03h	Auxiliary Input	[I]
21h	,	04h	Auxiliary Output	[I]
21h	,	05h	Printer Output	[P]
21h	,	06h	Direct Console I/D	[I]
21h	,	07h	Unfiltered Character Input	[K]
21h	,	08h	Character Input Without Echo	[K]
21h	,	09h	Output Character String	[V]
21h	,	0Ah	Buffered Input	[K]
21h	,	0Bh	Get Input Status	[K]
21h	,	0Ch	Reset Input Buffer	[K]
21h	,	0Eh	Set Default Disk Drive	[D]
21h	,	11h	Search For First Match	[D]
21h	,	12h	Search For Next Match	[D]
21h	,	13h	Delete File	[D]
21h	,	17h	Rename File	[D]
21h	,	19h	Get Default Disk Drive	[D]
21h	,	1Ah	Set Directory Transfer Address	[D]
21h	,	1Bh	Disk Allocation Information	[S]
21h	,	1Ch	Disk Allocation Information	[S]
21h	,	2Ah	Get System Date	[S]
21h	,	2Bh	Set System Date	[S]
21h	,	2Ch	Get System Time	[S]
21h	,	2Dh	Set System Time	[S]
21h	,	2Eh	Set Verify Flag	[S]
21h	,	30h	Get MSDOS Version Number	[S]
21h	,	33h	Get or Set Ctrl-Break Flag	[M]
21h	,	36h	Get Free Disk Space	[S]
21h	,	38h	Get or Set Country	[S]
21h	,	39h	Create Subdirectory	[D]
21h	,	3Ah	Delete Subdirectory	[D]
21h	,	3Bh	Set Current Directory	[D]
21h	,	41h	Delete File	[D]
21h	,	43h	Get or Set File Attributes	[D]
21h	,	47h	Get Current Directory	[D]
21h	,	4Eh	Find First Match	[D]
21h	,	4Fh	Find Next Match	[D]
21h	,	54h	Get Verify Flag	[S]
21h	,	56h	Rename File	[D]
21h	,	59h	Get Extended Error Information	[M]

[a][D] Disk operations; [I] Serial I/O; [K] Keyboard; [M] Miscellaneous; [P] Printer I/O; [S] System Info; [V] Video I/O

The following list indexes the system interrupts discussed in this appendix grouped by application.

Disk Operations

Intr	Func	Description
21h	39h	Create Subdirectory
21h	13h	Delete File
21h	41h	Delete File
21h	3Ah	Delete Subdirectory
21h	4Eh	Find First Match
21h	4Fh	Find Next Match
21h	47h	Get Current Directory
21h	19h	Get Default Disk Drive
21h	43h	Get or Set File Attributes
21h	17h	Rename File
21h	56h	Rename File
21h	11h	Search For First Match
21h	12h	Search For Next Match
21h	3Bh	Set Current Directory
21h	0Eh	Set Default Disk Drive
21h	1Ah	Set Directory Transfer Address

Serial I/O

Intr	Func	Description
21h	03h	Auxiliary Input
21h	04h	Auxiliary Output
21h	06h	Direct Console I/O
14h	02h	Read Character from Serial Port
14h	03h	Serial Port Status Request
14h	01h	Write Character To Serial Port

Keyboard Operations

Intr	Func	Description
21h	0Ah	Buffered Input
21h	01h	Character Input With Echo
21h	08h	Character Input Without Echo
21h	0Bh	Get Input Status
16h	00h	Read Character From Keyboard
21h	0Ch	Reset Input Buffer
16h	02h	Shift Key Status
16h	01h	Test Character Ready
21h	07h	Unfiltered Character Input

Miscellaneous

Intr	Func	Description
21h	59h	Get Extended Error Information
21h	33h	Get or Set Ctrl-Break Flag
19h		Reboot

Printer Operations

Intr	,	Func	Description
17h	-	02h	Get Printer Status (Parallel Port)
17h	,	01h	Initialize Printer (Parallel Port)
05h			Print Screen
21h	,	05h	Printer Output
17h	,	00h	Write Character To Parallel Port

System Information

Intr	,	Func	Description
21h	,	1Bh	Disk Allocation Information
21h	,	1Ch	Disk Allocation Information
11h			Equipment Flags
21h	,	36h	Get Free Disk Space
21h	,	30h	Get MSDOS Version Number
21h	,	2Ah	Get System Date
21h	,	2Ch	Get System Time
21h	,	54h	Get Verify Flag
21h	,	38h	Get or Set Country
14h	,	00h	Initialize Serial Port
12h			Memory Size
14h	,	02h	Read Character from Serial Port
1Ah	,	00h	Read Clock
1Ah	,	01h	Set Clock
21h	,	2Bh	Set System Date
21h	,	2Dh	Set System Time
21h	,	2Eh	Set Verify Flag
13h	,	01h	Test Disk Status

Video Output/Input

Intr	,	Func	Description
21h	,	02h	Character Output
21h	,	09h	Output Character String
10h	,	0Fh	Get Current Display Mode
10h	,	07h	Initialize Window or Scroll Window
10h	,	06h	Initialize Window or Scroll Window
10h	,	08h	Read Attribute and Character at Cursor
10h	,	03h	Read Cursor Position
10h	,	04h	Read Light Pen
10h	,	05h	Select Display Page
10h	,	02h	Set Cursor Position
10h	,	01h	Set Cursor Size
10h	,	00h	Set Video Mode
10h	,	09h	Write Attribute and Character at Cursor
10h	,	0Ah	Write Character Only at Cursor
10h	,	13h	Write String
10h	,	0Eh	Write Text with Cursor Movement (Teletype)

Interrupt Functions

Print Screen   Interrupt 05H

Turbo 3.x: No equivalent
Turbo 4.0:   No equivalent

Call: `intr($05,dos.registers(Reg));`

Notes: Interrupt 05h is normally called by the Shift-PrtSc key combination, but, since this is a software interrupt, it can also be called by a program. Applications would include producing a snapshot of the screen or reproducing a screen display as a printed form.

If the Print Screen interrupt is used for multiple snapshots, line feed characters sent by normal printer handling could be used to space two snapshots per page or a form feed character (0Ch) sent to create a sequence of single snapshots.

For graphics screen dumps, a graphics utility must be memory resident before interrupt 05h is called.

Errors: None

Interrupt 10h

Note: Interrupt 10h, graphics-only functions have been omitted from the following list. All text video functions are included.

Set Video Mode   Interrupt 10h, Function 00h

Turbo 3.x: **TextMode, GraphMode, GraphColorMode, HiRes, HiResColor, CrtInit**
Turbo 4.0:   **TextMode, InitGraph, GraphResult, RestoreCrt**

Call: Reg.AH := $00;
        Reg.AL := **mode**;
        intr($10,dos.registers(Reg));

Notes: Sets video display mode and, if multiple video cards are present, selects active video controller.

Text Modes	*Graph Modes*	
00h : 40×25 B/W	04H : 320×200 4 color	(CGA)
01h : 40×25 Color	05h : 320×200 4 color	(CGA)*
02h : 80×25 B/W	06h : 640×200 2 color	(CGA)
03h : 80×25 Color	0Dh : 320×200 16 color	(EGA)
07h : 80×25 Monochrome	0Eh : 640×200 16 color	(EGA)
	0Fh : 640×350 monochrome	(EGA)
	10h : 640×350 4/16 color	(EGA)

*color burst off

The **Set Video Mode** interrupt is not recommended for general use as it has no significant features that are not already supplied by Turbo Pascal functions. (See **GetGraphMode** in Turbo 4.0 manual for further details on valid modes, including VGA and other adapters.)

Errors: None

Set Cursor Size   Interrupt 10h, Function 01h

Turbo 3.x: No equivalent
Turbo 4.0: No equivalent

Call: Reg.AH := $01;
        Reg.CH := **start scan line**;
        Reg.CL := **end scan line**;
        intr($10,dos.registers(Reg));

Notes: Bits 0–3 are valid for start scan line, bits 0–4 for end scan line, and setting bits 4–5 in Reg.CH may have unexpected results. (See also interrupt 10h, function 03h.)

Observe valid start and stop cursor scan lines, and before exiting always reset the cursor type to the default (underline) style. (See comments in text on methods for turning off the cursor.)

Cursor Size Settings

Video Type (Mode)	Monochrome (07h)	Text (00h-03h)
Default Start/Stop	09h / 0Ah	06h / 07h
Block Start/Stop	00h / 0Ah	00h / 0Bh

Errors: None

Set Cursor Position   Interrupt 10h, Function 02h

Turbo 3.x: **GotoXY**
Turbo 4.0:   **GotoXY**

Call: Reg.AN := $02;
Reg.BH := **video page number**;
Reg.DL := **column**; { XAxis − 1 }
Reg.DH := **row**;   { YAxis − 1 }

Notes: Turbo Pascal uses (1,1) as the upper left screen position, whereas DOS uses a (0,0) origin. When using the **Set Cursor Position** interrupt, adjustment is required. Also, Turbo's **GotoXY** uses window relative coordinates, which are not accounted for here. One advantage, however, is the capability of reaching alternate video pages that are not supported by Turbo Pascal.

Turbo Pascal uses only video page 0. Depending on the video adapter and text mode active, up to eight (0–7) video pages may be valid, and other adapters support only four (0–3) and some mono-chrome adapters support only two video pages (0–1). (See notes in text on using alternate video pages.)

Errors: None

Read Cursor Position   Interrupt 10h, Function 03h

Turbo 3.x: **WhereX, WhereY**
Turbo 4.0:   **WhereX, WhereY**

Call: Reg.AH := $03;
         Reg.BH := video page number;
         intr($10,dos.registers(Reg));
         XAxis := Reg.DL + 1;
         YAxis := Reg.DH + 1;

Notes: A separate cursor position is maintained for each video page. The cursor position for each page can be read whether or not the video page is currently active. Also, the cursor starting scan line is returned in Reg.CH; the ending scan line, in Reg.CL.

See **Set Cursor Size** (interrupt 10h, function 01h) and **Set Cursor Position** (interrupt 10h, function 02h).

Errors: None

Turbo 3.x: No equivalent
Turbo 4.0:   No equivalent

Call:
```
Reg.AH := $04;
intr($10,dos.registers(Reg));
if Reg.AH <> 0 then
begin
    pixel_XAxis := Reg.BX; { 0..316 or 0..632 }
    pixel_YAxis := Reg.CH; { 0..198 }
    char_XAxis := Reg.DL; { 0..39 or 0..79 }
    char_YAxis := Reg.DH; { 0..24 }
end;
```

Notes: The AH register returns a value of 1 if the light pen is down (triggered) or 0 if the light pen is not triggered. The light pen interface returns screen position in both pixel and character coordinates.

Vertical pixel coordinates are always a multiple of 2.

Horizontal pixel coordinates, in 320×200 graphics modes, are a multiple of 4 and, in 640×200 graphics, a multiple of 8 or one character width.

Character coordinates are returned as full integer values without restriction.

The light pen registers position by synchronizing with the background scan sweep. Because intensity falls off toward the edges of the screen, use of the brighter background colors (light blue or light green) may provide better sensitivity and dark backgrounds may not register at all. For monochrome, use white background and dark lines.

Errors: None

Select Display Page   Interrupt 10h, Function 05h

Turbo 3.x: No equivalent in text modes
Turbo 4.0:   No equivalent in text modes

Call: Reg.AH := $05;
        Reg.AL := **video page number**;
        intr($10,dos.registers(Reg));

Notes: Selects the active video page in text modes. Video pages are switched immediately on display. The contents of the video pages are not affected, but the new cursor position will be determined by the active page. Remember that text can be written to *any* video page. The page does not have to be active. (See functions 02h, 09h, and 10h.)

        Also selects active video page in Graphics modes but, for graphics in version 4.0, the **SetVisualPage** function is recommended.

Errors: None

Initialize Window or   Interrupt 10h, Function 06h
Scroll Window Up

Turbo 3.x: **Window**
Turbo 4.0:   **Window**

Call: Reg.AH := $06;
        Reg.AL := **lines to scroll up**;   { zero blanks window }
        Reg.BH := **screen attribute**;   { for blanked area only }
        Reg.CL := **X-coordinate, left**;   { 0..79 }
        Reg.CH := **Y-coordinate, top**;   { 0..24 }
        Reg.DL := **X-coordinate, right**;   { 0..79 }
        Reg.DH := **Y-coordinate, bottom**; { 0..24 }
        intr($10,dos.registers(Reg));

Notes: Not recommended. Turbo's window procedures provide better handling with less aggravation. Also, no practical method exists for switching windows without scrolling. If necessary, save screen image, switch active window with 0 scroll lines, then restore screen image.

Errors: None

Initialize Window or Scroll Window Down

Interrupt 10h, Function 07h

Turbo 3.x: **Window**
Turbo 4.0: **Window**

Call:
```
Reg.AH := $07;
Reg.AL := lines to scroll down;   { zero blanks window }
Reg.BH := screen attribute;       { for blanked area only }
Reg.CL := X-coordinate, left;     { 0..79 }
Reg.CH := Y-coordinate, top;      { 0..24 }
Reg.DL := X-coordinate, right;    { 0..79 }
Reg.DH := Y-coordinate, bottom;   { 0..24 }
intr($10,dos.registers(Reg));
```

Notes: Not recommended. Turbo's window procedures provide better handling with less aggravation. Also, no practical method exists for switching windows without scrolling. If necessary, save screen image, switch active window with 0 scroll lines, then restore screen image.

Errors: None

Read Attribute and Character at Cursor — Interrupt 10h, Function 08h

Turbo 3.x: No equivalent
Turbo 4.0:   No equivalent

Call:
```
Reg.AH := $08;
Reg.BH := screen page;  { need not be active page }
intr($10,dos.registers(Reg));
attribute := Reg.AH;    { returns byte value }
character := Reg.AL;    { returns ordinal value }
```

Notes: Use **GotoXY** or function 02h (**Set Cursor Position**) to position cursor (and to select video page to read) before calling this function.

   The attribute byte contains the foreground color as bits 0..3 and the background color in bits 4..6. Bit 7 is the blink flag. The character byte is the 8-bit ASCII code for the screen character.

Errors: None

Write Attribute and Character at Cursor — Interrupt 10h, Function 09h

Turbo 3.x: **Write, WriteLn**
Turbo 4.0:   **Write, WriteLn**

Call:
```
Reg.AH := $09;
Reg.AL := ASCII character code;
Reg.BH := video page;               { Note 1 }
Reg.BL := attribute;                { Note 2 }
Reg.CX .= replication factor;       { Note 3 }
intr($10,dos.registers(Reg));
```

   1. Any valid video page can be written. The video page does not need to be the active video page (that is, the one currently displayed on the screen).

2. The attribute byte contains foreground color in bits 0..3 and background color in bits 4..6. Bit 7, if set, causes the character to blink. In graphics modes, if bit 7 is set, the character will be XOR'd with the current display, allowing a character to be "written," then "erased." No background color is used in graphics mode.

3. A zero value prevents any character from being written; otherwise, the character in AL will be repeated the specified number of times up to the limit of the current row. If more characters are written than space remaining on the row, the results will be unpredictable. Normally, a replication value of 1 is used.

Notes: This function allows the entire screen to be written (including line 25, column 80) without scrolling.

The cursor position must be explicitly set for the video page desired. If other than the default video page (page 0) is desired, use function 02h (**Set Cursor Position**); otherwise, **GotoXY** may be used. The cursor position will not be changed after the character(s) are written. Cursor movement can only be accomplished by an explicit cursor directive, and scrolling is not produced by line feed or carriage return characters.

Errors: None

Write Character Only at Cursor   Interrupt 10h, Function 0Ah

Turbo 3.x: No precise equivalent

Turbo 4.0:   No precise equivalent

Call:

```
Reg.AH := $0A;
Reg.AL := ASCII character code;
Reg.BH := video page;              { Note 1 }
Reg.BL := attribute;               { graphics only — Note 2 }
Reg.CX := replication factor;      { Note 3}
intr($10,dos.registers(Reg));
```

1. Any valid video page can be written. The video page does not need to be the active video page (that is, the one currently displayed on the screen).

2. In graphics modes, if bit 7 is set, the character will be XOR'd with the current display, allowing a character to be "written," then "erased." Only foreground color is used in graphics mode.

3. A zero value prevents any character from being written; otherwise, the character in AL will be repeated the specified number of times up to the limit of the curent row. If more characters are written than space remains, results will be unpredictable.

Notes: This function allows a character to be written without affecting the current screen attribute (that is, the new character will have the same attribute as was previously active at this location).

The cursor position must be explicitly set for the video page desired. If other than the default video page (page 0) is desired, use function 02h (**Set Cursor Position**); otherwise, **GotoXY** may be used. The cursor position will not be changed after the character(s) are written. Cursor movement can only be accomplished by an explicit cursor directive, and scrolling is not produced by line feed or carriage return characters.

Errors: None

Write Text with Cursor Movement (Teletype)   Interrupt 10h, Function 0Eh

Turbo 3.x: **Write, WriteLn**
Turbo 4.0:   **Write, WriteLn**

Call:
```
Reg.AH := $0E
Reg.AL := ASCII character code;
Reg.BH := video page;  { use in text modes only }
Reg.BL := color;       { use in graphic modes only }
intr($10,dos.registers(Reg));
```

Notes: All special ASCII codes are recognized by this function. Carriage return, line feed, bell, and backspace codes produce the appropriate responses. All other characters appear on display (including control codes), and the cursor position is moved implicitly. This provides automatic line wrap and scrolling, and the new display lines receive the attribute value of the last character written on the preceding line (the last active attribute).

In text modes, no provision is made for assigning character attributes. Aside from being limited to the zero video page, Turbo's **Write** and **WriteLn** provide the same features and accept the TextAttr assignment for character and background colors.

Errors: None

Get Current Display Mode   Interrupt 10h, Function 0Fh

Turbo 3.x: No equivalent
Turbo 4.0:   **GetGraphMode**

Call:
```
Reg.AH := $0F;
intr($10,dos.registers(Reg));
screen width := Reg.AH;  { 40 or 80 columns }
display mode := Reg.AL;
  active page := Reg.BH;
```

Notes: This function returns the screen width in columns (text), the current display mode, and the number of the currently active video page. One application might be in testing a system to determine the number of valid video pages present, but some experimentation would be required.

Turbo's **GetGraphMode** is not a precise equivalent for this function since it does not return text mode settings or test the active video page.

Errors: None

Turbo 3.x: **GotoXY, Write, WriteLn**
Turbo 4.0:   **GotoXY, Write, WriteLn**

Call: Reg.AH := $13;
         Reg.AL := **write mode**; { Note 1 }
         Reg.BH := **video page**;
         Reg.BL := **attribute**;   { write modes 00 or 01 only   }
         Reg.CX := **length of string**;
         Reg.DL := **XAxis**;
         Reg.DH := **YAxis**;
         Reg.ES := **segment**;   { segment address of source string }
         Reg.BP := **offset**;   { offset address of source string   }
         intr($10,dos.registers(Reg));

> 1. This function supports four write modes:
>   00: string contains character codes only; cursor will remain at last position prior to calling function 13h; character attribute will be found in register BL.
>   01: string contains character codes only; cursor will be updated after write completed; character attribute will be found in register BL.
>   02: string alternates character codes and attribute bytes (in this order); cursor will remain at last position prior to calling function 13h; BL register not used.
>   03: string alternates character codes and attribute bytes (in this order); cursor updated after write; BL register not used.

Notes: This function is valid for AT systems only and is not supported by PC, XT, or PCjr systems. This function is not particularly recommended both because of transport limitations and because it operates using a combination of calls to the 02h, 09h, and 0Eh functions, thus offering no advantages in speed or efficiency.

Errors: None

Interrupt 11h

Equipment Flags Interrupt 11h

Turbo 3.x: No equivalent
Turbo 4.0: No equivalent

Call: `intr($11,dos.registers(Reg));`

equipment `:= Reg.AX;` { returns word value, bit-coded }

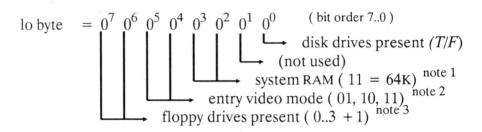

lo byte $= 0^7\ 0^6\ 0^5\ 0^4\ 0^3\ 0^2\ 0^1\ 0^0$ (bit order 7..0)

- disk drives present *(T/F)*
- (not used)
- system RAM (11 = 64K) [note 1]
- entry video mode (01, 10, 11) [note 2]
- floppy drives present (0..3 + 1) [note 3]

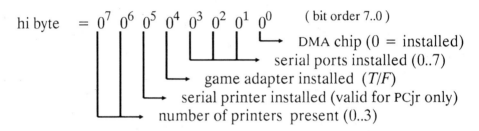

hi byte $= 0^7\ 0^6\ 0^5\ 0^4\ 0^3\ 0^2\ 0^1\ 0^0$ (bit order 7..0)

- DMA chip (0 = installed)
- serial ports installed (0..7)
- game adapter installed *(T/F)*
- serial printer installed (valid for PCjr only)
- number of printers present (0..3)

Notes: Provides useful system information.

1. 10 = 32K, not applicable to modern systems. (See interrupt 12h.)
2. 01h = 40×25 color; 10h = 80×25 color; 11h = monochrome
3. Bit 1 validates bits 6 and 7, which give the number of drives less one. Some early PCs had cassette interface capability and no drives.

Errors: None

Interrupt 12h

Memory Size **Interrupt 12h**

Turbo 3.x: No precise equivalent, see **MemAvail, MaxAvail**
Turbo 4.0: No precise equivalent, see **MemAvail, MaxAvail**

Call:
```
intr($12,dos.registers(Reg));
memory size := Reg.AX; { total ram in Kbytes }
```

Notes: Interrupt 12h returns the correct total memory size in kilobytes, **MemAvail** returns the total *free* memory and **MaxAvail** returns the size of the largest continuous block of free memory.

Errors: None

Interrupt 13h

Test Disk Status **Interrupt 13h, Function 01h**

Turbo 3.x: No direct equivalent — handled by Disk Read/Write functions
Turbo 4.0: No direct equivalent — handled by Disk Read/Write functions

Call:
```
Reg.AH := $01;
intr($13,dos.registers(Reg));
disk_status := Reg.AH;
```

Notes: Test Disk Status provides an alternative to Turbo's error handling, allowing direct access to the error reporting codes. The disk_status byte is returned by all disk operations.

If disk_status = 0, no error is reported.

If set ... bit 7 ... disk timed-out — no response
       ... bit 6 ... seek failure
       ... bit 5 ... controller error
       ... bit 4 ... data read error (CRC error)
       ... bit 3 ... DMA overrun error

... bit 2 ... sector not found (on read or write)
... bit 1 ... disk write protected (on write)
... bit 0 ... illegal command passed to driver

See also interrupt 13h, function 04h (Verify Disk Sectors).

Errors: None

Interrupt 14h

Initialize Serial Port   Interrupt 14h, Function 00h

Turbo 3.x: See **I/O drivers** (Turbo 3.x manual)
Turbo 4.0:   See **AuxInOut** device drivers (Turbo 4.0 manual)

Call:
```
Reg.AH := $00;
Reg.AL := initialization_parameters;   { Note 1 }
Reg.DX := serial_port;                  { Note 2 }
intr($14,dos.registers(Reg));
port_status  := Reg.AH;                 { Note 3 }
modem_status := Reg.AL;                 { Note 4 }
```

1. Initialization parameter byte definition

Bit Parameter	7 – 6 – 5 Baud rate	4 – 3 Parity	2 Stop bits	1 – 0 Word length
000 =	110 baud	00 = none	0 = 1 bit	10 = 7 bits
001 =	150 baud	01 = odd	1 = 2 bits	11 = 8 bits
010 =	300 baud	11 = even		
011 =	600 baud			
100 =	1200 baud			
101 =	2400 baud			
110 =	4800 baud			
111 =	9600 baud			

For example, A3h sets 2400 baud, no parity, 1 stop bit, 8-bit word length.
2. Com1 = 0; Com2 = 1; Com3 = 2; Com4 = 3;
3. Port_status returns bit-flagged results in AH register.

If set ... bit 7 ... timed out — no response from serial port
... bit 6 ... TX shift register empty

... bit 5 ... TX hold register empty
... bit 4 ... break detected
... bit 3 ... framing error
... bit 2 ... parity error
... bit 1 ... overrun error
... bit 0 ... data ready

4. Modem__status returns bit-flagged results in AL register.

If set ... bit 7 ... receive line signal detected
... bit 6 ... ring indicator
... bit 5 ... data-set ready (DSR)
... bit 4 ... clear-to-send (CTS)
... bit 3 ... receive line signal *change* detected
... bit 2 ... trailing edge ring indicator
... bit 1 ... data-set ready status *change*
... bit 0 ... clear-to-send status *change*

Notes: Used to set serial port. Returns modem status.

Errors: None

Write Character To Serial Port   Interrupt 14h, Function 01h

Turbo 3.x: See **I/O drivers** (Turbo 3.x manual)

Turbo 4.0:   See **AuxInOut** device drivers (Turbo 4.0 manual)

Call: Reg.AH := $01;

Reg.AL := **character**;

Reg.DX := **serial_port**; { see function 00h, note 2 }

intr($14,dox.registers(Reg));

port_status := Reg.AH;

Notes: If transmission is successful, bit 7 of port__status = 0.

If set ... bit 7 ... transmission failed
... bit 6 ... TX shift register empty
... bit 5 ... TX hold register empty
... bit 4 ... break detected
... bit 3 ... framing error

... bit 2 ... parity error

... bit 1 ... overrun error

... bit 0 ... data ready

Reg.AL returns character value unchanged in either case.

Errors: None

Read Character from Serial Port   Interrupt 14h, Function 02h

Turbo 3.x: See **I/O drivers** (Turbo 3.x manual)

Turbo 4.0:   See **AuxInOut** device drivers (Turbo 4.0 manual)

Call: Reg.AH := $02;

Reg.DX := **serial_port**; { see function 00h, note 2 }

intr($14,dos.registers(Reg));

port_status := Reg.AH;

character := Reg.AL;

Notes: If function succeeds, register AH, bit 7 = 0 and the character value in the AL register is valid. If AH bit 7 = 1, the character value is invalid. Port_status flags are tested as shown for interrupt 14h, function 01h.

Errors: None

Turbo 3.x: See **I/O drivers** (Turbo 3.x manual)

Turbo 4.0:   See **AuxInOut** device drivers (Turbo 4.0 manual)

Call: Reg.AH := $00;

Reg.DX := **serial_port**; { see function 00h, Note 2 }

intr($14,dos.registers(Reg));

port_status   := Reg.AH;

modem_status := Reg.AL;

Notes: Port_status and modem_status byte flags are tested as shown for interrupt 14h, function 00h. If Reg.AH, bit 7, is set, it indicates that a port timed out.

Errors: None

Interrupt 16h — ROM BIOS Keyboard Services

Interrupt 16h functions are used to test and read the keyboard buffer and may be used to test the shift-flag status. These provide useful alternatives to the Boolean function KeyPressed and version 4.0's ReadKey and version 3.x's read(kbd,Ch).

Read Character From Keyboard   Interrupt 16h, Function 00h
(buffer area)

Turbo 3.x: read(kbd,Ch);

Turbo 4.0:   **ReadKey**

Call: Reg.AH := $00;

intr($16,dox.registers(Reg));

scan_code := Reg.AH;

char_code := Reg.AL;

Notes: This function waits until a key is ready for input, and then returns both character and scan codes.

Errors: None

Test Character Ready   Interrupt 16h, Function 01h

Turbo 3.x: **KeyPressed**
Turbo 4.0: **KeyPressed**

Call:
```
Reg.AH := $01;
intr($16,dos.registers(Reg));
if (Reg.Flags and FZero = 0) then
begin
    scan_code := Reg.AH;
    char_code := Reg.AL;
end;
```

Notes: In theory, this function should leave the scan code and character in the keyboard buffer for retrieval by function 00h. Practical experience, however, reveals that this function is not well behaved under Turbo Pascal and Turbo's **KeyPressed** function is recommended.

Errors: If Zero flag set, then keyboard buffer is empty.

Shift Key Status   Interrupt 16h, Function 02h

Turbo 3.x: No equivalent
Turbo 4.0: No equivalent

Call: Reg.AH := $02;
            intr($16,dos.registers(Reg));
            shift_status := Reg.AL;
            or
            shift_status := mem($0000:$0417);

Notes: Either function 02h or the **mem** reference can be used to access the keyboard flags. The flags byte may have several, all, or none of the bits set. (See test function in **Show_Key_And_Scan_Codes**.)

If set ...	bit 7 ...	Insert On	(toggled on/off)
	... bit 6 ...	Caps Lock On	(toggled on/off)
	... bit 5 ...	Number Lock On	(toggled on/off)
	... bit 4 ...	Scroll Lock On	(toggled on/off)
	... bit 3 ...	Alt Key down	(true while held)
	... bit 2 ...	Ctrl Key down	(true while held)
	... bit 1 ...	Left-Shift Key down	(true while held)
	... bit 0 ...	Right-Shift Key down	(true while held)

Errors: None

Interrupt 17h — ROM BIOS Printer Control Services

The ROM BIOS supplies control functions for the parallel printer port controllers. Note that parallel port numbers being with zero: LPT1 = 0; LPT2 = 1; and so on. The default device (LST:) is LPT1. (See text for other notes on variant printer types and responses.)

Write Character To Parallel Port   Interrupt 17h, Function 00h

Turbo 3.x: Write(lst,...); WriteLn(lst,...);
Turbo 4.0:   Write(lst,...); WriteLn(lst,...); Uses Printer;

Call:
```
Reg.AH := $00;
Reg.AL := character;
Reg.DX := parallel_port;    ( 0..2 )
intr($14,dos.registers(Reg));
printer_status := Reg.AH;
```

Notes: Printer_status is returned in Reg.AH as a bit-flagged byte.

If set ... bit 7 ... printer not busy
... bit 6 ... acknowledge
... bit 5 ... out of paper
... bit 4 ... printer selected
... bit 3 ... I/O error
... bit 2 ... not used
... bit 1 ... not used
... bit 0 ... timed-out (not responding)

If timed-out or I/O error, the character was not printed.

Errors: None

Initialize Printer (Parallel Port)   Interrupt 17h, Function 01h

Turbo 3.x: Write(lst,...); WriteLn(lst,...);
Turbo 4.0: Write(lst,...); WriteLn(lst,...); Uses Printer;

Call:
```
Reg.AH := $01;
Reg.DX := parallel_port    ( 0..2 )
intr($17,dos.registers(Reg));
printer_status := Reg.AH;
```

Notes: Initializes selected (parallel) printer port and returns printer_status byte as shown for function 00h.

Errors: None

Get Printer Status (Parallel Port)   Interrupt 17h, Function 02h

Turbo 3.x: No equivalent
Turbo 4.0: No equivalent, Uses `Printer`;

Call: Reg.AH := $02;
       Reg.DX := **parallel_port**;   (0..2)
       intr($17,dos.registers(Reg));
       printer_status := Reg.AH;

Notes: Returns error reports as shown for function 00h. Useful for testing out of paper, time out, and other printer errors. (See function 00h.)

Errors: None

Interrupt 19h

Reboot   Interrupt 19h

Turbo 3.x: No equivalent
Turbo 4.0: No equivalent

Call: intr($19,dos.registers(Reg));

Notes: Resets DOS, flag and machine states, and memory allocation without destroying the contents in memory. A useful tool in certain error-testing circumstances and also quite frustrating in low-level security applications. Should be used with care.

Errors: None

Read Clock   Interrupt 1Ah, Function 00h

Turbo 3.x: No equivalent
Turbo 4.0:   No equivalent

Call:
```
Reg.AH := $00;
intr($1A,dos.registers(Reg));
midnight_flag := Reg.AL;
tick_cnt := Reg.CX shl 16 + Reg.DX;
```

Notes: Useful for initializing custom, random number algorithms. (See interrupt 21h, functions 2Ah and 2Ch, for access to system date and time.)

The tick_cnt is incremented 18.21 times per second, until it reaches 1,573,040. If the max count is reached and DOS has not reset the tick_cnt, the midnight_flag is returned as 1. This flag is reset to zero when the tick_cnt is reset.

To compute time from tick_cnt:

$$Hour := tick\_cnt \ div \ 65543;$$
$$Hour\_Remain := tick\_cnt \ mod \ 65543;$$
$$Minute := Hour\_Remain \ div \ 1092;$$
$$Min\_Remain := Hour\_Remain \ mod \ 1092;$$
$$Second := Min\_Remain \ div \ 18.21;$$

Errors: None

Turbo 3.x: No equivalent
Turbo 4.0: No equivalent

Call: Reg.AH := $01;
Reg.CX := **tick_cnt** shr 16;
Reg.DX := **tick_cnt** and $00FF;
intr($1A,dos.registers(Reg));

Notes: Sets clock tick_cnt. Tick_cnt := (hour * 65,543.33) + (minute * 1,092.38) + (second * 18.21). Interrupt 21h, functions 2Bh and 2Dh, are recommended for setting system date and time.

Errors: None

Interrupt 21h

Character Input With Echo **Interrupt 21h, Function 01h**

Turbo 3.x: Standard I/O
Turbo 4.0: Standard I/O

Call: Reg.AH := $01;
msdos(dos.registers(Reg));
input_char := Reg.AL; { 8-bit data }

Notes: Reads character from keyboard buffer and echos to display. If buffer is empty (no key has been pressed), waits for character to become available.

A Ctrl-C entry invokes interrupt 23h, and extended ASCII codes (that is, the function keys) require two reads: the first read returns 00h and the second returns the extended code.

(See also interrupt 16h, function 00h, and interrupt 21h, functions 06h, 07h, 08h and 3Fh.)

Errors: None

Character Output   Interrupt 21h, Function 02h

Turbo 3.x: Standard I/O
Turbo 4.0:   Standard I/O

Call:
```
Reg.AH := $02;
Reg.DL := out_char; { 8-bit data }
msdos(dos.registers(Reg));
```

Notes: Outputs a character to the standard output device; may be redirected. If output is redirected to disk file, there are no checks to detect disk full. Standard file I/O is recommended.

   If Ctrl-C or Ctrl-Break are detected after output, interrupt 23h is executed.

Errors: None

Auxiliary Input   Interrupt 21h, Function 03h

Turbo 3.x: Standard I/O
Turbo 4.0:   Standard I/O

Call:
```
Reg.AH := $03;
msdos(dos.registers(Reg));
```

```
input_byte := Reg.AL; { 8-bit data }
```

Notes: Reads character (one byte code) from standard Aux device — by default, the serial port COM1. May be explicitly redirected using the DOS Mode command.

By default, the standard auxiliary device is set to 2400 baud, no parity, 1 stop bit, and 8 data bits ($A3 — see interrupt 14h, function 00h — recommended). Since serial ports may not be buffered (most are not) characters may be lost if Aux device is sending faster than data can be read.

Error detection is not supported. Ctrl-C or Ctrl-Break execute interrupt 23h.

Errors: None

Auxiliary Output   Interrupt 21h, Function 04h

Turbo 3.x: Standard I/O
Turbo 4.0: Standard I/O

Call:
```
Reg.AH := $04;
Reg.DL := out_char; { 8-bit data }
msdos(dos.registers(Reg));
```

Notes: Waits if output device is busy, but status cannot be polled. Interrupt 14h, function 01h, is preferred. (See function 03h.)

Errors: None

Printer Output   **Interrupt 21h, Function 05h**

Turbo 3.x: Standard I/O
Turbo 4.0:   Standard I/O

Call: `Reg.AH := $05;`
        `Reg.DL := data_out;` { parallel port PRN or LPT1 }
        `msdos(dos.registers(Reg));`

Notes: Output waits if printer is busy. Defaults to first parallel port, but device may be redirected using DOS Mode command. Printer status cannot be polled, and interrupt 14h, function 01h, is recommended. Ctrl-C or Ctrl-Break execute interrupt 23h.

Errors: None

Direct Console I/O   **Interrupt 21h, Function 06h**

Turbo 3.x: No equivalent
Turbo 4.0:   No equivalent

Call: *Console Output*
        `Reg.AH := $06;`
        `Reg.DX := char_out;` { chrs 00h..FEh }
        `msdos(dos.registers(Reg));`
        Console Input
        `Reg.AH := $06;`
        `Reg.DX := FFh;` { input requested }
        `msdos(dos.registers(Reg));`
        `if (Reg.Flags and Fzero = 0) then`
           `input_char := Reg.AL;`

Notes: Ctrl-C and Ctrl-Break are passed as normal characters. Several other functions provide separate read and write services. (See 01h, 07h, 08h, and 0Ah functions for read and 02h and 09h functions for write as well as interrupt 10h functions.)

Character values 00h..FEh set output to standard output device (to screen unless redirected by DOS Mode function).

Character value FFh sets an input request and input character, if available, is returned in the AL register.

If character returned, the Zero flag is clear (0); if not, the Zero flag is set (1). (See the discussion of Reg.Flags at the beginning of this appendix.)

Errors: None

Unfiltered Character Input (no echo)   Interrupt 21h, Function 07h

Turbo 3.x: `read(kbd,Ch);`
Turbo 4.0:   **ReadKey**

Call: `Reg.AH := $07;`
`msdos(dos.registers(Reg));`
`input_char := Reg.AL; { 8-bit data }`

Notes: Reads character from keyboard buffer without screen echo or waits until character available. May be redirected using DOS Mode command.

Ctrl-C and Ctrl-Break characters are accepted as normal characters.

Extended ASCII codes (function keys) require two calls: the first returns a null character (00h) and the second returns the key character.

Errors: None

Character Input Without Echo **Interrupt 21h, Function 08h**

Turbo 3.x: `read(kbd,Ch);`
Turbo 4.0: **ReadKey**

Call: `Reg.AH := $08;`
`msdos(dos.registers(Reg));`
`input_char := Reg.AL; { 8-bit data }`

Notes: Reads character from keyboard buffer without screen echo or waits until character available. May be redirected using DOS Mode command.

Allows detection of Ctrl-C and Ctrl-Break characters which execute interrupt 23h.

Extended ASCII codes (function keys) require two calls: the first returns a null character (00h) and the second returns the key character.

Errors: None

Output Character String **Interrupt 21h, Function 09h**

Turbo 3.x: **Write**
Turbo 4.0: **Write**

Call: `Reg.AH := $09;`
`Reg.DS := seg (StringVar);`
`Reg.DX := off (StringVar);`
`msdos(dos.registers(Reg));`

Notes: This is equivalent to function 02h but accepts a string location instead of a single character. The string must be terminated with the character $ (24h), which *is not* transmitted. Any other ASCII or extended ASCII character, including control codes, may be embedded in the string. Carriage returns and line feeds must be included explicitly, if desired.

To print a $, use function 02h or 06h for single character output. Output is to standard output device but may be redirected using DOS **Mode** function.

Errors: None

Buffered Input   Interrupt 21h, Function 0Ah

Turbo 3.x: **ReadLn**
Turbo 4.0: **ReadLn**

Call:
```
Reg.AH := $0A;
Reg.DS := seg(Your_Buffer);
Reg.DX := ofs(Your_Buffer);
msdos(dos.registers(Reg));
```

Notes: This reads a string of bytes from the standard input device (default is keyboard buffer area), placing these in the (user) designated buffer location. The string input is terminated by a carriage return (0Dh).

Destination buffer (Your_Buffer) must be large enough for the expected input + 2 bytes.

The first byte in the buffer specifies the maximum size of the buffer (01h..FFh — supplied by user), and the second byte reports the actual character count read, excluding the terminating carriage return. The second byte is assigned by DOS.

If the buffer is filled to one less than the maximum, all subsequent input is ignored and the bell (char 07h) is sounded until a terminating CR is received.

Extended ASCII characters (function keys) are stored as two bytes, the first byte being null (00h).

Input is buffered by the normal keyboard buffer action and type ahead capability. All of the standard keyboard editing commands are recognized. Ctrl-C or Ctrl-Break execute an interrupt 23h. Experimentation is suggested before using.

Errors: None

Get Input Status   Interrupt 21h, Function 0Bh

Turbo 3.x: **KeyPressed**
Turbo 4.0: **KeyPressed**

Call: Reg.AH := $0B;
          msdos(dos.registers(Reg));
          status := Reg.AL;

Notes: AL register returns a zero value if no character is available in buffer; it returns a FFh value if the buffer is not empty. The status value will be returned as true until character input is read by function 01h, 06h, 07h, 08h, or 0Ah.

Ctrl-C or Ctrl-Break execute interrupt 23h.

Errors: None

Reset Input Buffer   Interrupt 21h, Function 0Ch

Turbo 3.x: No equivalent
Turbo 4.0: No equivalent

Call: *Character Input*
          Reg.AH := $0C;
          Reg.AL := **char_input_function**;   { 01h, 06h, 07h, 08h }

```
msdos(dos.registers(Reg));
input_char := Reg.AL;
```
String Input
```
Reg.AH := $0C;
Reg.AL := $0A;                          { string input invoked }
Reg.DS := seg(Your_Buffer);    { see function 0Ah }
Reg.DX := ofs (Your_Buffer);
msdos(dos.registers(Reg));
```

Notes: This discards any input characters stored in DOS's type-ahead buffer, then waits for input. An input function must be specified in the AL register before the interrupt is called.

Functions 01h, 06h, 07h, and 08h return individual characters in the AL register.

Invoking function 0Ah requires a segment:offset specification for a string input and does not return a value in the AL register. Input strings are terminated by CR (0Ah).

A simpler alternative is to read and discard keys until **KeyPressed** returns as false (the keyboard buffer is empty), then accept new input.

Errors: None

Set Default Disk Drive   Interrupt 21h, Function 0Eh

Turbo 3.x: **ChDir**
Turbo 4.0:   **ChDir**

Call:
```
Reg.AH := $0E;
Reg.DL := drive_code; { A = 0, B = 1, C = 2, etc }
msdos(dos.registers(Reg));
logical_drives := Reg.AL;
```

Notes: Selects a specified drive as current or default drive and returns a value for the total number of logical drives in the system.

Logical drives include all physical floppy drives, hard disk partitions, and RAM drives.

DOS 1.x allowed 16 logical drives; DOS 2.x allowed 63 drives, and DOS 3.x allows 26 drives. For future compatibility, drive designations should be limited to A:..Z:.

PCs with a single floppy disk will return a value of 2 since the A: drive can be invoked as either A: or B: — one physical but two *logical* drives.

(See interrupt 11h for information on actual disk drives in system.)

Errors: None

Search For First Match   Interrupt 21h, Function 11h

Turbo 3.x: No equivalent
Turbo 4.0:   **FindFirst**

Call: `Dir_Spec := File_Spec + #$00;`

```
              .

              .

              .
        Reg.AH := $11;
        Reg.DS := seg(Dir_Spec[1]);
        Reg.DX := ofs(Dir_Spec[1]);
        msdos(dos.registers(Reg));
        search_result := Reg.AL;
```

Notes: Function 1Ah must be used to set the address to which the directory information will be transferred before the search is initiated.

Access to subdirectories is not supported. (See interrupt 4Eh.)

Reg.AL returns a value of 00h if the search is successful; it returns FFh if no match was found. If the search is successful, the file information is written directly to the Data__Array.

(See Chapter 5 for a complete description of Directory Access.)

Errors: None

Search For Next Match   Interrupt 21h, Function 12h

Turbo 3.x: No equivalent
Turbo 4.0:   **FindNext**

Call: Reg.AH := $12; { see interrupt 4Fh }
        Reg.DS := seg(**Dir_Spec[1]**);
        Reg.DX := ofs(**Dir_Spec[1]**);
        msdos(dos.registers(Reg));
        search_result := Reg.AL;

Notes: Search is initiated by function 11h.

Subdirectories are not supported. (See interrupt 4Fh.)

Reg.AL returns a value of 00h if the search is successful; it returns FFh if no match was found. If the search is successful, the file information is written directly to the Data__Array.

Repeat subsequent calls to function 12h until search__result returns no match.

(See Chapter 5 for a complete description of Directory Access.)

Errors: None

Turbo 3.x: **Erase**
Turbo 4.0: **Erase**

Call: Reg.AH := $13;
           Reg.DX := seg(**File_Spec**);
           Reg.DX := ofs(**File_Spec**);
           msdos(dos.registers(Reg));
           delete_result := Reg.AL;

Notes: Deletes all files matching File_Spec from current subdirectory. The
           ? wildcard is allowed.
              AL register returns 00h if file(s) were deleted; it returns FFh if no
           matching files were found or if all matching files were read-only.
           (See function 41h for a preferred delete function.)

Errors: None

Rename Files   **Interrupt 21h, Function 17h**

Turbo 3.x: **Rename**
Turbo 4.0: **Rename**

Call: Reg.DH := $17;
           Reg.DS := seg(**Your_FCB**);
           Reg.DX := ofs(**Your_FCB**);
           msdos(dos.registers(Reg));
           result := Reg.AL;

Notes: The wildcard ? can be used in either or both the old and new
           filenames and extensions.
              Any characters in wildcard positions in the old (original)
           filename.extension constitute a match and will be changed.
              Wildcard occurrences in the new filename.extension leave
           characters unchanged.

Your_FCB is an array [1..42] of byte containing:

1	: disk drive specification	(A = 0)
2..9	: old filename	(8 characters)
10..11	: old file extension	(3 characters)
12..16	: 5 null characters (00h)	(reserved area)
17..24	: new filename	(8 characters)
25..27	: new file extension	(3 characters)
28..42	: 15 null characters (00h)	(reserved area)

(See function 56h for a preferred rename function.)

Errors: None

Get Default Disk Drive   Interrupt 21h, Function 19h

Turbo 3.x: No equivalent

Turbo 4.0: No equivalent

Call:
```
Reg.AH := $19;
msdos(dos.registers(Reg));
default_drive := Reg.AL;
```

Notes: Returns the curent or default disk drive.

Errors: None

Set Directory Transfer Address Interrupt 21h, Function 1Ah

Turbo 3.x: No equivalent
Turbo 4.0: Handled by **FindFirst**

Call:
```
Reg.AH := $1A;
Reg.DS := seg(Data_Array);
Reg.DX := ofs(Data_Array);
msdos(dos.registers(Reg));
```

Notes: Data_Array is an array[1..44] of byte to hold the disk file information retrieved by calls to functions 11h, 12h *or* 4Eh, 4Fh.

Errors: None

Disk Allocation Information Interrupt 21h, Function 1Bh or 1Ch

Turbo 3.x: No equivalent
Turbo 4.0: No equivalent

Call:
```
Reg.DH := $1B;
Reg.DL := drive_code; { for function 1Ch only }
msdos(dos.registers(Reg));
  sectors := Reg.AL;
   Fat_ID := mem[ Reg.DS : Reg.BX ];
sec_size := Reg.CX;
clusters := Reg.DX;
```

Notes: Function 1Bh provides information about the default (current) disk
drive only; function 1Ch accepts drive specification.
   Results include pointer to FAT Identification byte. Use interrupt
25h (**Absolute Disk Read**) to transfer FAT from disk.
   Sectors is the number of sectors per cluster.
   Sec_size is physical sector size in bytes.
   Clusters is number of clusters on disk (drive).

Fat__ID identifies type of disk:

FFh : 320K 5¼ floppy disk, 8 sectors/track, dual side

FEh : 160K 5¼ floppy disk, 8 sectors/track, single side

FDh : 360K 5¼ floppy disk, 9 sectors/track, dual side

FCh : 180K 5¼ floppy disk, 9 sectors/track, single side

F9h : 1.2M 5¼ floppy *or* 720K 3½ disk[1]

F8H : fixed disk — any size[2]

1. To determine disk ID further, calculate Sectors / Sec__size / Clusters. *Hints:* A high-density (5¼) disk returns a value of one sector per cluster and 2371 (0943h) clusters; a 3½ disk returns two sectors per cluster and 713 (02C9h) clusters. Both return a sector size of 512 bytes (0200h). The number of clusters may vary if the disk surface had any physical defects when it was formatted (fewer valid clusters).

2. Sectors / Sec__size / Clusters returned are for fixed drive partition, not for physical drive size.

Errors: None

Get System Date   Interrupt 21h, Function 2Ah

Turbo 3.x: No equivalent

Turbo 4.0:   **GetDate**

Call: ```
Reg.DH := $2A;
msdos(dos.registers(Reg));
  year := Reg.CX; { 1980 – 2099 }
 month := Reg.DH; { 1 – 12 }
  date := Reg.DL; { 1 – 31 }
   day := Reg.AL; { day of week: Sunday = 0, etc }
```
```

Notes: Returns date and day of week from system clock.

Errors: None

Set System Date   Interrupt 21h, Function 2Bh

Turbo 3.x: No equivalent
Turbo 4.0: **SetDate**

Call:
```
Reg.AH := $2B;
Reg.CX := year;   { 1980 – 2099 }
Reg.DH := month; { 1 – 12 }
Reg.DL := date;   { 1 – 31 }
msdos(dos.registers(Reg));
result := Reg.AL;
```

Notes: Sets system-clock to specified date. AL register returns 00h if date set successfully; it returns FFh if date is invalid (not set).

Errors: None

Get System Time   Interrupt 21h, Function 2Ch

Turbo 3.x: No equivalent
Turbo 4.0: **GetTime**

Call:
```
Reg.AH := $2C;
msdos(dos.registers(Reg));
    hour := Reg.CH;   ( 0-23 )
```

```
  minutes := Reg.CL;   ( 0-59 )
  seconds := Reg.DH;   ( 0-59 )
 hundreds := Reg.DL;   ( 0-99 )
```

Notes: Not all systems have a clock with hundredths of a second resolution. Values returned by Reg.DL may be odd values only or may be discontinuous.

Errors: None

Set System Time   Interrupt 21h, Function 2Dh

Turbo 3.x: No equivalent
Turbo 4.0: **SetTime**

Call:
```
Reg.AH := $2D
Reg.CH := hour;      ( 0-23 )
Reg.CL := minutes;   ( 0-59 )
Reg.DH := seconds;   ( 0-59 )
Reg.DL := hundreds;  ( 0-99 )
msdos(dos.registers(Reg));
result := Reg.AL;
```

Notes: Sets system-clock to specified time. AL register returns 00h if time set successfully; it returns FFh if time is invalid (not set).

Errors: None

Set Verify Flag   Interrupt 21h, Function 2Eh

Turbo 3.x: No equivalent
Turbo 4.0:   No equivalent

Call: Reg.AH := $30;
         Reg.AL := $00; { turns verify off — 01h turns verify on }
         Reg.DL := $00; {required by DOS versions 1.x, 2.x only }
         msdos(dos.registers(Reg));

Notes: Duplicates DOS commands VERIFY OFF and VERIFY ON.

Errors: None

Get MSDOS Version Number   Interrupt 21h, Function 30h

Turbo 3.x: No equivalent
Turbo 4.0:   No equivalent

Call: Reg.AH := $30;
         msdos(dos.registers(Reg));
         major_version := Reg.AL;
         minor_version := Reg.AH;

Notes: Major_version number returns as integer (that is, DOS 3.2 = 3).
         Minor_version number returns decimal value (that is, 3.2 = 14h = 20).
         DOS version 1.0 may return a zero value.

Errors: None

Turbo 3.x: Use $C+ / $C–
Turbo 4.0: $C directive obsolete

Call: *Get Ctrl-Break Status*
```
Reg.AH := $30;
Reg.AL := $00;  { read status of Ctrl-Break flag }
msdos(dos.registers(Reg));
status := Reg.DL;
```
Set Ctrl-Break Status
```
Reg.AH := $30;
Reg.AL := $01;  { set status of Ctrl-Break flag }
Reg.DL := $00;  { 00h turns break checking off }
                { 01h turns break checking on }
msdos(dos.registers(Reg));
status := Reg.DL;
```

Notes: When Ctrl-Break checking is turned on, the keyboard is checked for Ctrl-Break or Ctrl-C when input or output is requested. When found, control is transferred to interrupt 23h (Ctrl-C handler).

Flag setting affects all programs; should be reset to default (on) before program exits.

Errors: None

Get Free Disk Space   **Interrupt 21h, Function 36h**

Turbo 3.x: No equivalent
Turbo 4.0: **DiskFree**

Call:
```
Reg.AH := $36;
Reg.DL := drive;  { 0 = default, 1 = A, 2 = B, etc }
msdos(dos.registers(Reg));
sectors per cluster := Reg.AX;  { see Notes }
```

```
available clusters := Reg.BX;
   bytes per sector := Reg.CX;
clusters per drive := Reg.DX;
```

Notes: Returns FFFFh in AX register if selected drive is invalid. (See also functions 1Bh and 1Ch.)

Errors: None

Get or Set Country   Interrupt 21h, Function 38h

Turbo 3.x: No equivalent
Turbo 4.0:   No equivalent

Get Country Information
```
var
    Data_Buffer = array[0..33] of byte;      { DOS version 3.x }
  { Data_Buffer = array[0..31] of byte; }    { DOS version 2.x uses two bytes less }
```

Call:
```
Reg.AH := $38;
Reg.AL := 00h;
Reg.DS := seg(Data_Buffer);
Reg.DX := ofs(Data_Buffer);
msdos(dos.registers(Reg));
country_code := Reg.BX;
if (Reg.Flags and FCarry <> 0)
    then error_code := Reg.AX
    else error_code := 0;
```

Notes: If the Carry Flag is returned set, the error_code is found in the AX register. Currently, only one error code is used: 2 = country code invalid. If no error has occurred, the Data_Buffer will contain the country information:

Byte	DOS version 3.x	Byte	DOS version 2.x
0..1	date format	0..1	date format (same as 3.x)
	0 = USA (m d y)	2	currency symbol
	1 = Europe (d m y)	3	zero
	2 = Japan (y m d)	4	thousands separator
2..6	currency symbol string,	5	zero
	null terminated	6	decimal separator
7	thousands separator char	7	zero
8	zero	8..31	reserved
9	decimal separator char		
10	zero		
11	date separator char		
12	zero		
13	time separator char		
14	zero		
15	currency format		
	bit 1 spaces following currency symbol (1 or 0)		
	bit 0 0 = symbol preceeds value		
	1 = symbol follows value		
16	digits following decimal in curency		
17	time format		
	bit 0,0 = 12 hour clock		
	1 = 24 hour clock		
18..21	case-map call address (see notes)		
22	data-list separator char		
23	zero		
24..33	reserved		

Set Country Information (DOS 3.x or Greater)

Call:
```
Reg.AH := $38;
Reg.AL := country_code;   { 01h..FEh or FFh }
{ if AL = FFh then
  Reg.BX := country__code; }  { 16-bit country code > = 255 }
Reg.DX  : = FFFFh;             { signals information being set }
msdos(dos.registers(Reg));
if (Reg.Flags and FCarry <> 0)
   then error_code := Reg.AX
   else error_code := 0;
```

Notes: The country code is normally the International Telephone Prefix code (check your local telephone book).

Case_Map Call is seg:ofs for a Far procedure, which executes country-specific lowercase to uppercase mapping for ASCII values 80h..FFh.

The 34-byte data buffer can be used for both DOS 2.x and 3.x. The smaller, 32-byte buffer is valid only for DOS 2.x.

Errors: If the Carry Flag is returned set, the error_code is found in the AX register. Currently, only one error code is used: 2 = country code invalid.

Create Subdirectory   Interrupt 21h, Function 39h

Turbo 3.x: **MkDir**
Turbo 4.0: **MkDir**

Call:
```
Reg.AH := $39;
Reg.DS := seg(path_spec);
Reg.DX := ofs(path_spec);
msdos(dos.registers(Reg));
if (Reg.Flags and FCarry <> 0)
   then error_code := Reg.AX
   else error_code := 0;
```

Notes: Function operates as per DOS MkDir (MD) command.

Path_spec is an ASCIIZ string, must contain complete pathname, and must terminate with a null (00h) character.

Errors: If the Carry Flag returns set (that is, is not zero), an error has occurred. Two error codes can be returned: error 3 — path not found; and error 5 — access denied (normally happens only on networks).

Failure occurs when any element of the path_spec except the new subdirectory does not exist (could be syntax error in creating path_spec); when a subdirectory with the specified path_spec already exists; or if the parent directory is the root directory and is already full.

Delete Subdirectory Interrupt 21h, Function 3Ah

Turbo 3.x: **RmDir**
Turbo 4.0: **RmDir**

Call:
```
Reg.AH := $3A;
Reg.DS := seg(path_spec);
Reg.DX := ofs(path_spec);
msdos(dos.registers(Reg));
if (Reg.Flags and FCarry <> 0)
    then error_code := Reg.AX
    else error_code := 0;
```

Notes: Function operates as per DOS **RmDir** (RD) command.

Path__spec is an ASCIIZ string, must contain complete pathname, and must terminate with a null (00h) character.

Errors: If the Carry Flag returns set (that is, is not zero), an error has occurred. Four error codes can be returned: error 3 — path not found; error 5 — access denied (normally happens only on networks); error 6 or 16 — specified directory is current (active) directory.

Failure occurs when any element of the path_spec except the new subdirectory does not exist (could be syntax error in creating path_spec; when the subdirectory named is the current (operating) subdirectory (see function 3Bh); or if the subdirectory specified is not empty (contains files or further subdirectories).

Set Current Directory Interrupt 21h, Function 3Bh

Turbo 3.x: **ChDir**
Turbo 4.0: **ChDir**

Call:
```
Reg.AH := $3B;
Reg.DS := seg(path_spec);
Reg.DX := ofs(path_spec);
```

```
msdos(dos.registers(Reg));
if (Reg.Flags and FCarry <> 0)
    then error_code := Reg.AX
    else error_code := 0;
```

Notes: Function operates as per DOS **ChDir** (CD) command.

Path__spec is an ASCIIZ string, must contain complete pathname, and must terminate with a null (00h) character. Wildcards are never allowed in path__spec.

(See function 47h to determine current directory/path.)

Errors: If the Carry Flag returns set (that is, is not zero), an error has occurred. Only one error code is returned: error 3 — path not found.

Failure occurs when any element of the path__spec except the new subdirectory does not exist (could be syntax error in creating path__spec).

Delete File   Interrupt 21h, Function 41h

Turbo 3.x: **Erase**
Turbo 4.0: **Erase**

Call:
```
Reg.AH := $41;
Reg.DS := seg(path_file_spec);
Reg.DX := ofs(path_file_spec);
msdos(dos.registers(Reg));
if Reg.Flags and FCarry <> 0)
    then error_code := Reg.AX
    else error_code := 0;
```

Notes: Path__file__spec is an ASCIIZ string, should provide the complete path and filename, and must terminate with a null character (00h). No wildcards are allowed.

When the specified file is deleted, the first byte of the filename in the disk directory is reset. This does not erase the file contents from the disk, but it does free the space allocated for reuse. As long as no new material has been written in this space, the file can be recovered by an UnErase utility.

Wildcards are not permitted in the filename — only unambiguous filenames. (See function 13h.)

Errors: If the Carry Flag returns set (that is, is not zero), an error has occurred and the file has not been deleted. Two error codes may be returned: 2 — file not found; or 5 — access denied. An error will occur if the path_file_spec is incorrect or if the file exists but is flagged as read/only. (See function 43h.)

Get or Set File Attributes   Interrupt 21h, Function 43h

Turbo 3.x: No equivalent
Turbo 4.0:   GetFAttr, SetFAttr

Call: *Get File Attributes*

```
Reg.AH := $43;
Reg.AL := $00;
Reg.DS := seg(path_file_spec);
Reg.DX := ofs(path_file_spec);
msdos(dos.registers(Reg));
attribute := Reg.CX;
if (Reg.Flags and FCarry <> 0)
   then error_code := Reg.AX
   else error_code := 0;
```

Set File Attributes

```
Reg.AH := $43;
Reg.AL := $01;
```

```
Reg.DS := seg(path_file_spec);
Reg.DX := ofs(path_file_spec);
Reg.CX := attribute;
msdos(dos.registers(Reg));
if (Reg.Flags and FCarry <> 0)
    then error_code := Reg.AX
    else error_code := 0;
```

Attrubute byte: 0   0 x^5 0   0 x^2 x^1 x^0

archive   system   hidden   read/only

Notes: Attribute flag bits 4 and 3 (subdirectory and volume label) cannot be changed by this function. Bits 6 and 7 are not used.

Errors: If the Carry Flag is returned set (that is, is not zero), four error codes may be returned in the AX register: 1 = function code invalid (AL register 00h or 01h only); 2 = invalid path (not found); 3 = path or file not found; 5 = attribute cannot be changed.

Get Current Directory   Interrupt 21h, Function 47h

Turbo 3.x: **GetDir**
Turbo 4.0: **GetDir**

Call:
```
Reg.AH := $4E;
Reg.DL := drive; { default = 0, A = 1, B = 2, etc }
Reg.DS := seg(path_spec);
Reg.SI := ofs(path_spec);
msdos(dos.registers(Reg));
if (Reg.Flags and FCarry <> 0)
    then error_code := Reg.AX
    else error_code := 0;
```

Notes: Path__spec is a 64-byte buffer that receives the complete pathname from root to current directory as an ASCIIZ string.

Errors: If the Carry Flag is returned set (that is, is not zero), the AX register returns the error code. Only one error code is returned here: 0Fh — drive specification invalid.

Find First Match   **Interrupt 21h, Function 4Eh**

Turbo 3.x: No equivalent
Turbo 4.0:   **FindFirst**

Call:
```
Reg.AH := $4E;
Reg.CX := attribute;                         { used in search }
Reg.DS := seg(path_name_name);
Reg.DX := ofs(path_name_spec);
msdos(dos.registers(Reg));
if (Reg.Flags and FCarry <> 0)
   then error_code := Reg.AX
   else error_code := 0;
```

Notes: Use function 1Ah to set data transfer address before calling 4Eh.

Wildcards (? or *) are allowed in filename specification only. The * character is expanded as ?s to fill blanks (that is, a filename specified as ABC*.D* is expanded to become ABC?????.D??).

Path__name__spec is an ASCIIZ string with a maximum length of 77 characters (including the terminating null character). The drive/path portion of the specification should not exceed 64 characters length.

Errors: If the Carry Flag is returned set (that is, is not zero), an error__code is returned in the AX register. Two error conditions are returned: 2 = path__spec invalid; 12h — no matching entry found.

Remember that match includes attribute specification, path_spec, and file_spec. Use Attribute value 3Fh to match all files, subdirectories, and so on.

Find Next Match   **Interrupt 21h, Function 4Fh**

Turbo 3.x: No equivalent
Turbo 4.0:   **FindNext**

Call:
```
Reg.AH := $4F;
msdos(dos.registers(Reg));
if (Reg.Flags and FCarry <> 0)
    then error_code := Reg.AX
    else error_code := 0;
```

Notes: Use function 4Eh to find first match; subsequent matches are made by repeated calls to function 4Fh.

Function 4Fh uses information in the data transfer address established by function 1Ah for file match. (See bytes 0–20 of DTA, page 96.)

Errors: If the Carry Flag is returned set (that is, is not zero), an error_code is returned in the AX register. Only one error condition is returned: 12h = no matching entry found.

Remember that match includes attribute specification, path_spec, and file_spec. Attribute value 3Fh matches all files, subdirectories, and so on.

Turbo 3.x: No equivalent
Turbo 4.0:   No equivalent

Call: Reg.AH := $54;
         msdos(dos.registers(Reg));
         verify_flag := Reg.AL;

Notes: Returns the current setting of the system verify flag (read after disk write). A value of 00h returns if the verify flag is off; 01h returns if the verify flag is set.

       DOS command **Verify On** and **Verify Off** or function 2Eh can be used to change the state of the verify flag.

Errors: None

Rename File   **Interrupt 21h, Function 56h**

Turbo 3.x: **Rename**
Turbo 4.0:   **Rename**

Call: Reg.AH := $56;
         Reg.DS := seg(**old_path_file_spec**);
         Reg.DX := ofs(**old_path_file_spec**);
         Reg.ES := seg(**new_path_file_spec**);
         Reg.DI := ofs(**new_path_file_spec**);
         msdos(dos.registers(Reg));
         if (Reg.Flags and FCarry <> 0)
           then **error_code** := Reg.AX;

Notes: Old_path_file_spec and new_path_file_spec are ASCIIZ strings.

Errors: If the Carry Flag returns set (that is, is not zero), the AX register returns an error code. Four errors are reported: 2 = file not found; 3 = path or file not found; 5 = access denied; 11h = device select error (that is, different drives were specified in old_path_file_spec and new_path_file_spec).

Wildcard characters are not allowed.

Failure may also occur if destination is root directory and root directory is already full or if a duplicate file already exists in the destination directory.

Get Extended Error Information   Interrupt 21h, Function 59h

Turbo 3.x: **IOresult**, etc.
Turbo 4.0: **IOresult**, etc.

Call:
```
Reg.AH := $59;
Reg.BX := $00;
msdos(dos.registers(Reg));
error_code   := Reg.AX;
error_class  := Reg.BX;
error_action := Reg.BL;
error_locus  := Reg.CH;
```

Notes: Returns extended error information following a previously unsuccessful call to any of the interrupt 21h functions *that return error information*. Possible corrective action and probable error location are also returned.

Error information is destroyed by this call — it cannot be retrieved again by subsequent calls.

Extended Error Codes 13h..1Fh correspond to error codes 00h..0Ch returned by interrupt 24h.

Future releases/versions of MS-DOS *will* include new error codes. Error recognition limited to specific error numbers will not be upwardly compatible with new releases.

Four tables showing error information messages follow: Error Codes, Error Class, Error Action and Error Locus. Extended Error Information usage is discussed in Chapter 12.

Results: Error__Codes

Errors in **boldface** correspond to Turbo 4.0 Runtime Error numbers shown at left in decimal format.

—	01	function number invalid
02	**02**	**file not found**
03	**03**	**path not found**
04	**04**	**too many files open**
05	**05**	**access denied**
06	**06**	**file handle invalid**
—	07	memory control blocks destroyed
—	08	insufficient memory
—	09	memory block address invalid
—	0A	environment invalid
—	0B	format invalid
12	**0C**	**access code invalid (12)**
—	0D	data invalid
—	0E	* reserved *
15	**0F**	**disk drive invalid**
16	**10**	**cannot remove current directory**
17	**11**	**cannot rename across drives**
—	12	no more files
150	**13**	**disk write-protected**
151	**14**	**unknown unit**
152	**15**	**drive not ready (not responding)**
153	**16**	**unknown command**
154	**17**	**data error (CRV — Cyclical Redundancy Check)**
155	**18**	**bad drive request structure length**
156	**19**	**disk seek error**
157	**1A**	**unknown media type (disk)**
158	**1B**	**sector not found (disk)**
159	**1C**	**printer out of paper**
101,160	**1D**	**device write fault**
100,161	**1E**	**device read fault**
162	**1F**	**general hardware failure (catch all)**
—	20	share violation (network)
—	21	lock violation (network)
—	22	disk change invalid
—	23	FCB (File Control Block) unavailable
—	24..4F	* reserved *
—	50	file already exists
—	51	* reserved *
—	52	cannot create directory
—	53	Interrupt 24h failure (Critical Error Interrupt)

* Error__Class

01	resource exhausted (storage or channels)
02	not error, temporary situation expected to change (might be locked region in file, etc.)
03	authorization problem
04	internal error in system software
05	hardware failure
06	system software failure not directly caused by active process (such as missing configuration files).
07	application program error
08	file or item not found
09	file or item has invalid format or type
0A	file or item interlocked
0B	wrong disk in drive / bad media / storage medium problem
0C	other error . . . .

* Error__Action

01	Retry some reasonable number of times, then prompt user for abort or ignore.
02	Retry some reasonable number of times with delay between tries, then prompt user for abort or ignore.
03	Prompt user for corrective information (such as correct drive or path/filename.)
04	Terminate program without haste — close files, etc.
05	Abort immediately! System is corrupted, cleanup actions would do more harm than good.
06	Ignore error . . .
07	Ask user for corrective intervention, then retry.

* Error__Locus

01	Unknown . . .
02	Block device — disk or disk emulator
03	Network related
04	Serial device
05	RAM problem

Appendix D
Turbo Pascal Version 3.x/Version 4.0

Turbo Pascal version 4.0 offers a number of new features that were not available in earlier versions. There are also a number of changes in variable types, in the ways certain data types are handled, and a few familiar procedures and functions have been replaced with different but similar handling procedures.

Borland has provided a utility, **UPGRADE.EXE**, to read a version 3.x source file, make changes, and insert change comments for conversion to 4.0 compatibility. In this process, some changes are made automatically; others are commented but will require changes to be entered by the programmer.

Two compatibility units, **Turbo3** and **Graph3**, are provided. They permit compilation of version 3.x programs with minimal revision.

UPGRADE is called from the command line, not from the Turbo Interactive Compiler/Editor. The syntax for calling UPGRADE is:

```
d:\path\UPGRADE [options] FILENAME
```

UPGRADE Options

Option	Description
/3	Uses **Turbo3** compatibility unit when required. This provides version 3.x handling for such features as **Kbd**, **CBreak**, **MemAvail**, **MaxAvail**, **LongFileSize**, **LongFilePos**, and **LongSeek**. The Turbo3 unit will be included by a `Uses` statement.
/J	Creates a detailed journal file showing changes, warning messages, revision messages, and so on. Each journal entry is numbered (corresponding to the revision messages in the source code) and contains text amplification concerning the revision.

Option	Description
/N	UpGrade makes all automatic changes to the source code but does not insert comments in the source. Generally this option should be combined with the /J or /U options.
/O [d:] [path]	Writes output file to new drive and/or path. The original source file is not changed. All output, including Journal file if active, is sent to a specified destination.
/U	Unitizes program according to .U switches in source code. This requires you to make some changes to the source code before using. The unit directives take the form {.U unitname}, where unitname must be a legal MS-DOS filename and must be a valid Pascal identifier, for example, {.U SUBPROG1}. This replaces the overlay feature used in version 3.x.

See your Turbo Pascal Manual for detailed information on UPGRADE restrictions; change, error and warning messages; and special handling suggestions.

Compiler Directives

The compiler directives A, B, C, D, F, G, P, U, W, and X are either no longer used or have changed meanings under Turbo version 4.0. Under Turbo Pascal version 4.0, most compiler options may be menu selected.

Table 4.1 Compiler Options

Version 3.x	Version 4.0	Option	Settings
$A+/−		Absolute Code	(CP/M-80)
$B+/−		I/O Mode Selection	on/off
	$B+/−	Boolean Evaluation	on/off
$C+/−		Control C and S	on/off
$D+/−		Device Checking	on/off
	$D+/−	Debug Information	on/off
$F##		Files Open	number
	$F+/−	Force Far Calls	on/off
$G##		Input File Buffer	size
$I+/−	$I+/−	I/O Error Handling	on/off
$I filename.ext		Include file directive	
$K+/−	$S+/−	Stack Checking	on/off
	$L+/−	Link Buffer	memory/disk
	$Msss,min,max	Memory Size	size
	$N+/−	Numeric Processing	hardware/software
$P##		Output File Buffer	size
$R+/−	$R+/−	Range Checking	on/off
	$T+/−	Map File Generation	on/off
$U+/−		User Interrupt	on/off

Version 3.x	Version 4.0	Option	Settings
$V+/−		Var-Parameter Checking	on/off
	$V+/−	Var-String Checking	on/off
$W##		Nested With Statements	(CP/M-80 only)
$X+/−		Array Optimization	(CP/M-80 only)

Differences Between Version 3.x and Version 4.0

The following partial list shows the differences between the two versions.

String References

Version 3.x	Version 4.0
length(StringRef);	ord(StringRef[0]);
copy(StringRef,I,1);	StringRef[I];
No equivalent	StringRef[X] := 'Y';

In version 4.0, elements of a string can be referenced as though the string were an array of char. The length of the string is found in the first element (0) as an ordinal value. The **copy** function is supported by version 4.0 and should still be used for string versus character references.

Version 3.x	Version 4.0
Ch := copy(Str,I,1);	Ch := Str[I];

Note: Version 4.0 does not allow mixing of string and char types as shown above for version 3.x. Also, this mix of string and char types is not detected by the **UpGrade** utility.

String variable types may be assigned array data as:

StrVar := ArrayVar

However, the reverse:

ArrayVar := StrVar

is not valid. Also, the variable declaration StrVar : string; is valid and declares a string variable of length 255.

Integer References

Version 3.x	Version 4.0
`Y := succ(Y);`	`inc(Y);`
`Y := pred(Y);`	`dec(Y);`
No equivalent	`Inc(Y,9);`

In version 4.0, the **inc** and **dec** functions are used in place of **succ** and **pred**. The first argument (Y) can be any ordinal type variable. Unlike the earlier procedures, a second integer argument can be used to specify the amount to increment or decrement. **Succ** and **pred** are still supported by version 4.0, but **inc** and **dec** generate tighter code.

Keyboard

Version 3.x	Version 4.0
`read(kbd,Ch);`	`Ch := ReadKey;`

The **kbd** device supported by version 3.x is not found in version 4.0. Instead, use the **ReadKey** function.

Local Variables for Loops

Version 4.0 requires integers for loop counters to be local to the procedure or function where they are used or to be pure global variables. A loop variable cannot be locally global (global to a group of procedures and subprocedures but not to the entire program).

Boolean Evaluation

Under Turbo version 3.x, evaluation of Boolean expressions is not short-circuited as it is under version 4.0. In other words, in version 3.x, the expression

```
if Boolean1 and Boolean2 then
```

would result in both expressions being evaluated. Under version 4.0, if Boolean1 evaluates as False, Boolean2 will not be tested.

In most circumstances, this makes little difference to the programmer. However, if the Boolean condition remaining untested leaves an error flag or error condition set that should have been cleared, a problem is likely to occur later, and it may be very difficult to troubleshoot. For example, `if Error1 and (IOresult) <> 0) then ...`

When **IOresult** is tested, the error condition flag is cleared. But, if `Error1` is false, **IOresult** will not be called and may continue to hold an error code generated by a previous I/O operation, leaving it to "appear" later as a new error.

UpGrade inserts a compiler directive, `{$B+}`, which forces full Boolean evaluation but does not detect any possible condition where short-circuited evaluation might produce an error. Exercise caution when changing the $B directive.

I/O Changes

The special device filenames **CON:**, **TRM:**, **AUX:**, and **USR:** provided under version 3.x are not supported by version 4.0. Likewise, the devices **LST:**, **CRT:**, and **KBD:** are no longer supported nor are the special filenames **INP:**, **OUT:**, and **ERR:**.

The Turbo3 unit can be used to support the **KBD:** device if desired. For **LST:**, use the **Printer Lst** file.

The `BufLen` restriction on **ReadLn** is no longer supported.

I/Oresult error codes have been changed to correspond (more or less) to DOS error codes. See Interrupt 21h, function 59h, Extended Error Information, in Appendix C.

Video Changes

HighVideo, **NormVideo**, and **LowVideo** perform differently under version 4.0. See also the `TextAttr` variable, which offers an alternative to the **TextColor** and **TextBackground** procedures.

Graphic video support is provided for CGA, EGA, Hercules, AT&T400, MCGA, 3270 PC, and VGA video cards.

Numerical Data Types

Under version 3.x, Integer data types were either `integer` or `byte`, and Real data types were either `reals` or BCD `reals`. Under version 4.0, Integer data types have been expanded to include `shortint`, `integer`, `longint`, `byte`, and `word`; and Real data types have been expanded to `real`, `single`, `double`, `extended` and `comp`.

Tables D-2 Integer Types and D-3 Real Types show the value ranges supported by version 4.0 data types.

Table D-2 Integer Types

Type	Range	Sign	Size (in bytes)
shortint	−128..127	signed	1
integer	−32768..32767	signed	2
longint	−2147483648..2147483647	signed	4
byte	0..255	unsigned	1
word	0..65535	unsigned	2

Table D-3 Real Types

Type	Range	Significant Digits	Size (in bytes)
real	$2.9 \times 10^{-39}..1.7 \times 10^{38}$	11-12	6
single	$1.5 \times 10^{-45}..3.4 \times 10^{38}$	7-8	4
double	$5.0 \times 10^{-324}..1.7 \times 10^{308}$	15-16	8
extended	$1.9 \times 10^{-4951}..1.1 \times 10^{4932}$	19-20	10
comp	$-2^{63}+1..2^{63}-1$	19-20	8*

*The comp type holds only integral values, no fractions.

All integer data types may be used on any system. The single, double, extended, and comp data types require the presence of a math coprocessor (8087, 80287, or 80387) and the inclusion of the {$N+} directive. The math coprocessor is required both for compiling and for the program to be executed.

Appendix E
Word Processing Memory Management

Pointer record structures were discussed in Chapter 7, together with a warning that the memory management techniques shown were not recommended for word processing applications. Although word processing per se is not within the intended scope of this book and a complete treatment of this subject would require an entire book or more, a few suggestions and approaches for memory management for word processing applications are covered here.

Small Text Models

Small text sizes — up to 100 lines of 80 characters width — are most conveniently handled by a variable array (1 . . 100] of string(80). Since the total memory requirement is not expected to exceed 8 Kbytes, even though this approach is essentially inefficient in terms of memory usage, the emphasis is more properly placed on convenience in programming rather than the machine's convenience in managing the data.

As long as the end user can access, correct, enter, and edit the text material (or whatever the application requires), memory efficiency is definitely secondary and there is little point in using complex programming in order to save small amounts of hypothetically wasted memory.

Medium Text Tools

Text arrays larger than 8 Kbytes and up to, for example, 50–60 Kbytes in size might be handled as arrays of strings, but these are beginning to reach the point where the 64K unit limit becomes important. In this range, the pointer functions detailed in Chapters 7 and 8 provide more efficient memory management than indexed arrays.

If indexing is required or desirable, an array of pointer indexes will provide direct access for sorting or other operations. Essentially, the only upper limit to the size of any pointer array is the amount of memory available in the system (up to 640 Kbytes unless Extended Memory Management is used) less the memory required by the operating system, program, and any resident services.

The only real drawback to the pointer structures previously shown is that each pointer record is a fixed size and, using a record of string(80), for example), even a blank text line will still occupy 80 bytes of memory.

If margins are set to 60 versus 80 characters, each line will have at least 20 extra bytes that are expanded memory but are not used. Further, if lines wider than 80 characters are desired, the programmer must set a new record size (line width).

Flexible (Large) Text Models

For larger and more flexible text applications, the prorammer is advised to begin by abandoning the basic concept of lines of text and to begin thinking in terms of storing arrays of characters, remembering that carriage returns and line feeds are also ASCII characters (0Dh and 0Ah, respectively), not merely line terminators. Two programming approaches are possible on this basis. First, the text data can be stored using pointer records consisting of records of arrays of characters (instead of strings). Second, the text data can be stored using direct memory management.

In the first instance, using arrays of characters, a line of text may be stored as block of characters terminated by a carriage return and/or line feed character. Alternately, screen lines may not be indicated. Instead, each paragraph might be terminated with a CR/LF (see Figure E-1) and the next text line begins with the next character position in the array. Thus a line may begin in one array record and extend into the next record.

Access to these records may be managed by an array of index pointers or by linked pointer records as previously demonstrated. The actual screen display, however, would be a "translation" re-created from the stored data.

In the second instance, using direct memory management, the program would use the GetMem and FreeMem procedures to create and dispose of dynamic variables in memory. This approach also uses pointers to access the data but places the onus on the prorammer of keeping track of memory usage, seeing that unused memory is properly released, and so forth. Again, the actual screen display would be a "translation" re-created from the stored data.

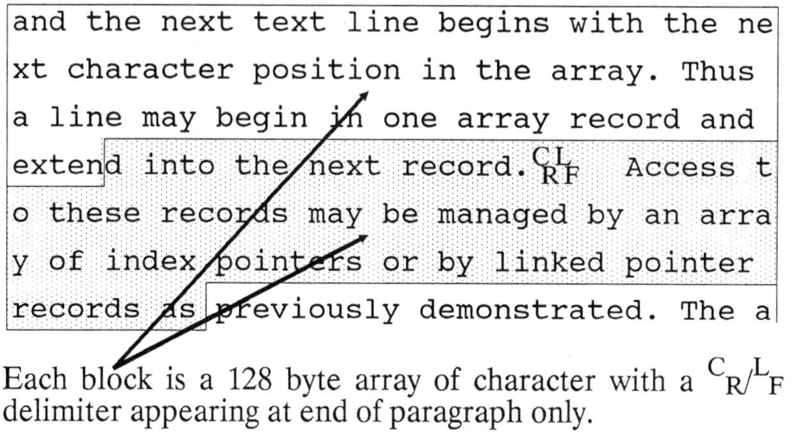

```
and the next text line begins with the ne
xt character position in the array. Thus
a line may begin in one array record and
extend into the next record. C L     Access t
                              R F
o these records may be managed by an arra
y of index pointers or by linked pointer
records as previously demonstrated. The a
```

Each block is a 128 byte array of character with a $^C_R/^L_F$ delimiter appearing at end of paragraph only.

Figure E-1 Text Memory Management

You may also wish to refer to MS-DOS interrupt 21h, function 48h, **Allocate Memory**; interrupt 21h, function 49h, **Release Memory**; interrupt 21h, function 4Ah, **Modify Memory Allocation**; and interrupt 21h, function 58h, **Get or Set Memory Allocation Strategy**. Also refer to the interrupt 67h functions, Lotus/Intel/Microsoft Expanded Memory Specifications which provide access to up to 8 Mbytes of bank-switched RAM.

Editing and Operating on Text Data

Using either of the suggested direct memory management techniques, a blank text line may be stored as either one or two bytes instead of an 80-byte record and any text line requires a maximum of two bytes (for the CR/LF characters) overhead.

Since the text is not stored in a format ready for immediate use/display — but can be written to disk simply as a file of character — the active display will require some manipulation. For this reason, most applications use a separate working buffer/image that holds a subset of the material that is actually being displayed/edited.

Particularly if the material is to be edited, this separate "work space" makes revisions, additions, and deletions much more convenient since the existing memory data (the big text stack) is only updated after editing is finished and the material is scrolled off the screen — not during a succession of minor alterations.

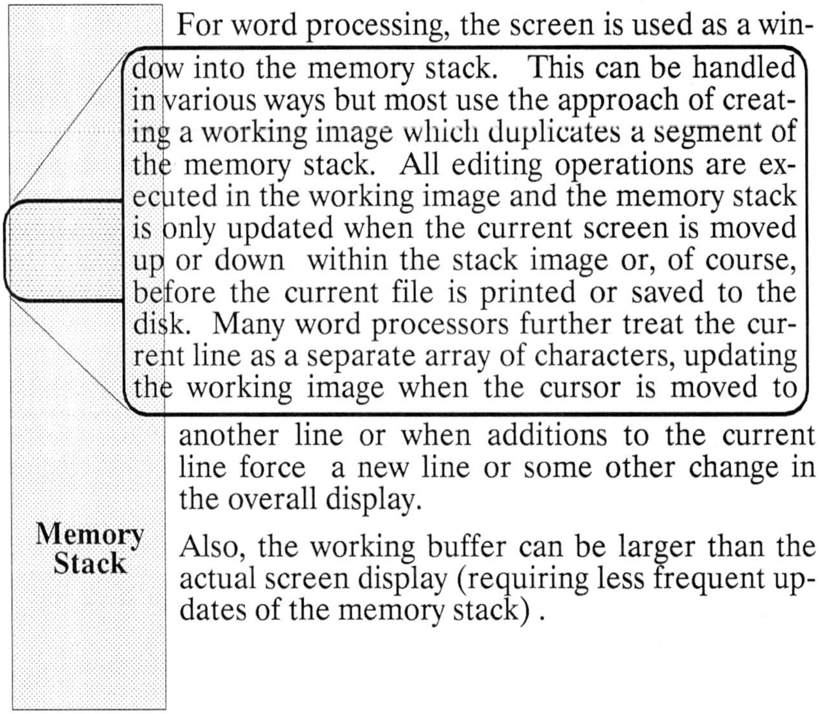

For word processing, the screen is used as a window into the memory stack. This can be handled in various ways but most use the approach of creating a working image which duplicates a segment of the memory stack. All editing operations are executed in the working image and the memory stack is only updated when the current screen is moved up or down within the stack image or, of course, before the current file is printed or saved to the disk. Many word processors further treat the current line as a separate array of characters, updating the working image when the cursor is moved to another line or when additions to the current line force a new line or some other change in the overall display.

Memory Stack

Also, the working buffer can be larger than the actual screen display (requiring less frequent updates of the memory stack) .

Figure E-2 The Display Window

As material is brought into the "work" buffer or returned to the main stack, two pointers are maintained; one to the main stack preceding the first active record and the second to the next record following the material in the work buffer. Nominally, the records transferred to the work area should be released from main memory, but some prefer to wait and only release these records when their contents are rewritten as a new memory record. Generally speaking, the first technique is easier to manage.

This "work" buffer might be an array of strings or a separate array of characters and its precise size can vary depending on your application and handling method. As a general rule, however, your work buffer should be at least the size of your edit display *plus* two record blocks (as used for your main storage). In many cases, larger would be helpful.

This extra space is not a luxury but is working room so that changes on screen do not force immediate and time-consuming updates to the main memory data stack.

For similar reasons, when reading data into the work area, it would also be advisable to leave a minimum of one record block free space in the work area. This way, when the reserve block becomes full from material "forced down" by editing insertions, the entire block (or several blocks) can be quickly dumped out to the main stack. Likewise, extensive deletions would bring new material "swapped in" from the stack, ready for access.

In both cases, memory should be swapped from work to storage as full record blocks whenever possible. Unfortunately, of course, "whenever possible" implies that it will not always be possible. Sometimes extensive memory swapping would be required to re-create continuous memory blocks after editing and it will probably be helpful to have some provision for maintaining partially filled blocks in main memory, for example, filling out a partial block with null characters (00h).

Other Considerations

The storage memory blocks may be virtually any size desired, but some practical consideration is suggested. If a block of 128 bytes is used (as shown in figure E-1), updates are relatively frequent. However, even partial records contain relatively little "wasted" memory. If a larger block — such as a one kilobyte block (1024 bytes) — is used, memory swapping is less frequent, but leaving partial records becomes more critical in terms of good memory management.

Back in the dark ages (say, 5 to 10 years ago), when 64 Kbytes was a memory maximum and many machines had 16 Kbytes (or less), efficient memory usage was critical and was also a chronic problem. One common method of "expanding" available working space was to use the disk (usually a floppy disk) as a memory extension, writing some portion of the material to a temporary disk file until needed. This practice resulted in slow access, and frequently keeping some part of the material swapped out to the extended memory produced other, more serious problems. This practice is not recommended except in extreme cases and is mentioned here simply because it did work if handled carefully and because a few situations may still arise where this approach could be helpful. Happily, with minimum 640 Kbyte memories standard and already being replaced by Megabyte and KiloMegabyte memories, such practices should not be common.

As mentioned earlier, this was not an attempt to cover word processing in any comprehensive detail. It is simply a few notes on memory management for extensive and irregular records. If you require a moderately sophisticated custom word cruncher within your application and do not wish to design your own, you might also consider Borland's *Turbo Pascal Editor Toolbox*.

Appendix F
How To Write a Bug Report

An anonymous computer-humorist once defined the ultimate computer program as three lines of instruction which would state:

```
READ MY MIND
    THEN
        DO WHAT I AM THINKING
```

Computers and programming languages are a very long way from reaching such a level of sophistication and, more important, computer programmers and computer users are also! Unfortunately, the computer users (our customers/friends/critics) too often regard their computer-knowledgeable programmer as some sort of a djinni who, abandoning the traditional brass lamp, now comes equipped with CRT, floppy drives, and keyboard.

Even if I (or the computer) could read your mind, just exactly what would result? Humans (Vulcans like Mr. Spock excepted) are, at our best, merely rational creatures, whereas computers (bless their silicon hearts) are only logical. As humans, we think in gestalts — images that contain a vast amount of information but do not detail the means by which this information is related or derived. Computers, in total contrast, are monotheorists. For example, a computer begins with fact A, proceeds through B to C and finally arrives at result Z but is never, under any circumstances, capable of jumping from F to X to M to T in the dizzying, vaulting intuitive leaps that are so thoroughly characteristic of human cognition.

As programmers, we are expected to act as interface between the rational (and intuitive) biomentality and the strictly logical (and linear) silicon computer. Unfortunately, we lack the omniscience that, ideally, would suit us to such a role, and to replace this lack, we must tediously question the end users of our programs either directly (if they are customers for specialty software) or indirectly (for general program design) by placing ourselves in the role of the user and imagining all the myriad possibilities that will later arise.

In this latter instance, our task is effectively impossible and we must rely on friends (and others) to provide Beta testing to uncover the unforeseen. Of course, some elements of the unforeseen will always remain after even the most rigorous testing and will be eventually reported by customers. But such are the vicissitudes of our professions/hobbies/avocations.

When designing custom software, however, the problem becomes much more intense. The customers know — or think they know — what they want. However, they also have the unconscious idea that you, the programmer, also know, in detail, what they have only imagined in gestalt and have *not* stated in detail. When the end result shows the flaws that lie between the perfect program (as it exists in their imaginations) and the real program resulting from the actual instructions offered coupled with your best efforts at implementation, disappointment is the result.

Because you are the computer-djinni (you've proved it by wresting miracles from a thing of plastic, silicon, and wires) but it wasn't the miracle they had imagined, they do not understand why! Quite likely, neither do you. You've put a lot of effort into your programming, you've worked virtual miracles, you've used tricks that only another computer-djinni could appreciate, you've surpassed yourself in so many ways — but it isn't what the customer expected.

Strictly speaking, most or all of the problems are not (I hope) truly bugs, that is, problems that cause incorrect answers or (horrors upon horrors) cause the program to abort or the system to crash. Most likely the problems will be gaps between what the customer actually told you and what they *imagined* you understood or even what *you* imagined you understood.

The primal cause of such problems is less important than how these can be corrected. Proper handling of "bug" reports will save you, the programmer, considerable time, effort, and aggravation. *More important*, it will save your cutomer time and *money*.

How To Write a Bug Report

Step One: Get it in writing! I am not talking about a document drawn by a lawyer (unless your client happens to be such) for ajudication in court, but you must insist that your customer write down *exactly* what the problem appears to be, *exactly* how or why it occurs, and how they think it should be corrected.

This is a complex requirement. Your client, most likely, does not understand the mechanism that produced the problem and therefore cannot describe in programming terms how to fix it. However, they can tell you, in simple English, "The figures in the right-hand column are not correctly aligned. Also, when an entry is zero, I do (or do not) want anything printed (and/or shown on the screen)."

Obviously, not all bugs are quite so easily described nor do these all appear *on screen*, but in my own experience the greatest portion of these do, and when they appear in another fashion, these instructions can be adapted accordingly.

If you (and your client) are using a PC-, XT-, or AT-type computer, you (and they) should use the PrtSc feature to produce a printed record of the screen display at the point where the error appears. On the printed copy, indicate where the error appears. Draw circles around entries, draw arrows, use highlighters, red ink, blue pencil — anything that will show *exactly* what and where the error appears.

If the problem is a discrepancy between what appears on one screen and does not on another, or appears at one time and does not earlier or later, print them both — paper is cheap!

If you are working with a system such as a Z-100 which has no inherent screen dump, a variety of software (consult the HUG library) is available to provide this important utility. Buy it! It's well worth the price!

Remember to date and number these comments and screen dumps! It will save a lot of confusion three weeks hence!

Step Two: Get it in writing! This is not an error. The duplication is intentional because, as I began by explaining, humans are merely rational and cogitate in gestalt images. When your customer takes pen in hand (or keyboard in lap) and writes down exactly what is needed, he or she is forced into a shifted state of communication in which their gestalt image must be "translated" into step-by-step instructions that *do* detail the needed results.

Because we can think so much faster than we speak, a verbal explanation almost always leaps from point to point as it tries to keep up with the thoughts behind the words — and fails! Important details are lost unconsciously but forgotten and omitted.

With pen or keyboard in hand, a permanent record is produced which can be reviewed, edited, and amended. Important points overlooked can be included, second thoughts can be appended, an incorrect phrase can be revised, and the end result should show precisely what is needed. Even if the results fall short of such a standard, the printed or written statement will provide a reference allowing you, the programmer, to ask the *correct* questions to clarify important points. Remember that this is for your client's benefit as well as your own!

Step Three: Put it in writing! Provide your client with a list of the corrections and changes you have made, and reference these to their original notes.

To do so, briefly restate the problem and, in complete sentences, describe the corrective action. Use terms that your customer can understand.

Step Four: Keep a record! Though you may hate being a file clerk, surely you can spare some small measure of the patience that anyone working with computers must have for the very important task of keeping a record of the evolution and changes in your program and, most important, the bug reports!

Your files needn't be elaborate. They might consist of no more than stapling your customer's problem report together with a copy of your fix record and dropping these into an empty paper box. This system is known as a FILO file (First In, Last Out), and it operates exactly like saving registers on a stack. Of course, you can always convert FILO to FIFO by turning the box over, but in any case *do it!*

Here you have it. The necessary instructions (and reasons) for generating proper bug reports and, although I have addressed this to you, the programmer, you are also invited to give a copy of this to your customer(s). After all, they are part of the process as well and, in many ways, the more important part!

Appendix G
Turbo Pascal Version 5.0

New with the release of version 5.0, Turbo Pascal's Integrated Development Environment (IDE) includes a debug utility which facilitates program testing and debugging by allowing step-by-line execution while displaying selected variables and values.

In Chapter 14 (Debugging), test lines were suggested to display selected factors with either a **delay** or **readln** to allow time for the information to be read — a time honored and reliable method of examining otherwise "invisible" variables to determine if, how, and why a bug might appear.

Now, the Integrated Development Environment offers similar debugging display capabilities but with several advantages over inserting display and pause instructions in your source code. First, the IDE debugger operates without requiring any direct alterations in your source code. Using the IDE facility, you can select which variables to display, trace these through all or only a selected portion of your program, and trace variables while controlling program execution on a step-by-line basis. Second, chosen variables can be conveniently discarded and new variables selected at virtually any point during a debug session. Third, using the IDE facility, you can step from your program output display to the Edit display (with an highlight bar showing the next program line to be executed), to the Watch display (showing variables and values), and back again, observing precisely what is happening at each point. Fourth, you can even "edit" variable values *while* the program is running, changing the contents of a variable while directly observing the effects of the revision on your program.

Sound impressive? Or too good to be true? Or like just what you've been waiting for?

I hope the last, because Turbo's Integrated Development Environment is not a magical solution to all your programming problems, but it is a useful — and very convenient — tool for tracing and debugging programs quickly.

Menu	Hot Key	Function
Run . . .	**Alt-R**	
/**R**un	*Ctrl-F9*	Executes program, uses **Make** if required.
/**P**rogram reset	*Ctrl-F2*	End debugging session, prepare for new start. Releases memory allocations, closes files.
/**G**o to cursor	*F4*	Executes program, halting when (or if) line indicated by **Edit** cursor is reached. Will initiate debugging session.
/**T**race into	*F7*	Executes current line; if procedure or function call occur in line, continues trace into the procedure or function if possible. Will initiate IDE debugging session.
/**S**tep over	*F8*	Executes current line but does not trace into called procedures or functions. Will initiate IDE debugging session.
/**U**ser screen	*Alt-F5*	Allows view of program output screen by toggling between Integrated Debugging Environment and program execution screen display.
Option/Compile . . .	**Alt-O**	
/**D**ebug information	‡	Enables source-level debugging; toggles *$D* directive. Use of *$D* within source code overrides **Option** setting.
/**L**ocal symbols	‡	Enables evaluation of local symbols; toggles +*L* directive. Use of *$L* within source code overrides **Option** setting.
Option/Environment . . .	**Alt-O**	
/**Z**oom windows	*F5*	Toggles ZOOM display on active window.
Debug . . .	**Alt-D**	
/**E**valuate	*Ctrl-F4*	Calls **Evaluate** box permitting direct evaluation of variables and experssions and modification of variable values.
/**C**all stack	*Ctrl-F3*	Shows current call stack; allows tracing back through procedures and functions. Valid only during debugging.
/**F**ind procedure	‡	Locates first source code line in procedure or function for display in **Edit** window.

Debug . . .	**Alt-D**	
/Integrated debugging	‡	Enables debugging in the Integrated Debugging Environment. When OFF, disables IDE debugging to release memory for program compile and execution.
/Stand-alone debugging	‡	Adds debug information to end of .EXE program, enabling stand-alone debugging using the Turbo Debugger.
/**D**isplay swapping	‡	Selects display swapping option: **Smart** (default),**Always** or **None**.
/**R**efresh display	‡	Recreates environment screen, removing any extraneous material.
Break/watch . . .	**Alt-B**	
/**A**dd watch	*Ctrl-F7*	Adds expression at **Edit** cursor to the **Watch** window. Can also be executed by selecting **Watch** window and entering *Ins* or *Ctrl-N* (when Display Swapping set to **None**).
/**D**elete watch	‡	Deletes current **Watch** expression from window. Can also be executed by selecting **Watch** window and entering *Del* or *Ctrl-Y.*
/**E**dit watch	‡	Edits current **Watch** expression. Can also be executed by selecting **Watch** window, selecting an item and pressing *Enter.*
/**R**emove all watches	‡	Clears **Watch** window of all expressions.
/**T**oggle breakpoint	*Ctrl-F8*	Toggles breakpoint setting on current line selection in **Edit** window.
/**C**lear all breakpoints	‡	Clears all breakpoint settings.
/**V**iew next breakpoint	‡	Displays next breakpoint without execution.
Other Hot Keys		
	F6	Toggles between **Edit** and alternate window (**Watch** or **Output**) in Integrated Debugging Environment.

Alt-F6   Switches window contents. If the **Edit** window is active, loads previous file (if any). If **Edit** window is not active, toggles between **Watch** and **Output** windows.

Bold hot keys select pull-down menus only. *Italic hot keys* activate features directly without requiring menu selection. ‡ indicates menu selection only.

Figure G-1 Turbo Pascal version 5.0 Integrated Debugging Commands

Using Turbo's Integrated Debugger

Turbo Pascal provides two principal debugging options: integrated or standalone, the latter requiring the separate Turbo Debugger (TD) but usable with either the IDE (TURBO.EXE) or the command-line Pascal compiler (TPC.EXE). For the moment, only the integrated debugging facility will be discussed.

With two exceptions (see Figure G-1) all of the debug options can be selected from the IDE pull-down menus and, more important to most applications, the principal debugging features can be called using predefined "hot keys." These features fall into three principal categories: **R**un options, **B**reak/watch options and **D**ebug options.

The **R**un Options

The following **R**un options can be selected from the Run menu (called with Alt-R) or selected directly using the hot keys. These are listed in approximate order of importance.

The *Run / Run* option. The Ctrl-F9 hot key, as with previous versions of Turbo Pascal, still executes the **R**un menu / **R**un option but does not initiate debugging.

The *Run / Trace into* option. To initiate debugging, the F7 hot key (**R**un / **T**race into) will recompile your program if necessary and begin a stepped (trace) execution of the program. Each time the F7 key is pressed, execution will advance one program (source) line with the Edit window showing the *next* source line to execute (see Figure G-2, top, where the code corresponding to the source line beginning `if( ( I div J )...` has just finished execution).

Please realize at this time that the source program is *not* being interpeted line by line as with a BASIC program. The source code has been compiled to memory but the debug facility is controlling execution, halting the program and switching to the Edit window display at the point corresponding to each program line. Also, lines which are broken in the source code, such as

```
if( ( I div J ) = ( I / J ) )
  then Result := false;
```

are treated as a single line by the debugger and the *if* portion of the source line is not executed separately from the *then Result* portion. If you combine several statements in a single line, the debugger will not halt execution between statements but only at the end of the line.

In summary, the **Run** / *Trace into* option allows you to step through your program one source line at a time, carrying the trace into called subprocedures and functions.

The **Run** / *Step* over option. Frequently, however, you do not want to trace execution through all the subprocedures and functions but only to look at the main procedures called. (This is the usual first step to decide where a problem lies before a more detailed examination is undertaken, see also the **Break** options).

For this purpose, the F8 hot key (**Run** / **Step** over) also initiates debugging, beginning with the current line (as shown in the Edit window), after recompiling if necessary, but does so without executing the trace through called subprocedures and functions. Naturally, the called subprocedures and functions are still executed but the program is not halted and the Edit window is not updated to show these procedures and functions.

The **Run** / *Go to cursor* option. A third hot key, F4 (**Run** / **Go** to cursor), also starts program execution but halts when (or if) the source line indicated by the Edit window cursor is reached. At this point, the debug facility has been initiated and the F7 or F8 options will begin a step-by-line execution of the remaining program.

The **Run** / *Program reset* option. Last, the Ctrl-F2 hot key (**Run** / **Program** reset) is provided either to end a debugging session or to prepare the program for a restart. This option includes resetting all variables, releasing allocated memory, closing open files and preparing the program for reinitialization.

The **B**reak Options

The **B**reak/watch options are found on the Break pull-down menu (called as Alt-B). These will be described under two categories: Break options and Watch options.

The Break options allow you to assign, clear and step to break points in your program. In a long or complex program, a step-by-line debug session could quickly become either an exercise in supreme patience or an exercise in frustration (when you accidently step past the point of interest). Instead, the Break point options offer a means of running a program quickly up to a desired point, then initiating a step-by-line debug session.

The *Break / Toggle breakpoint* option. The Ctrl-F8 hot key (**B**reak / **T**oggle breakpoint) toggles the breakpoint setting on the current line (shown by Edit window cursor). Multiple breakpoints can be set (but only the first point reached will activate a break) and each line with the breakpoint set will be indicated by highlight (or by color display) in the Edit window.

Once one or more breakpoints are set, the program can be run in the normal manner but will halt (switching to the Edit window) when the first breakpoint setting is encountered. At this point, Watch selections can be entered (see below), then the F7 (**R**un / **T**race into) or F8 (**R**un / **S**tep over) hot keys used to initiate a step-by-line debug session.

Other *Break* options. Two additional breakpoint options are included but are menu selected only: the *Break/watch / Clear all breakpoints* option which cancels all breakpoints set in the program and the *Break/watch / View next breakpoint* option which steps the Edit window display to the next breakpoint set but without further program execution.

The Watch Options

Also include in the **B**reak/watch menu are the Watch options which allow tracing (watching) the values of selected variables during a step-by-line debugging session.

The *Break/watch / Add watch* option. The first Watch option is called with the Ctrl-F7 (**B**reak/watch / **A**dd watch) hot key. If the Edit window cursor is positioned within any alphanumeric string or immediately following the string, the string will appear in the Add Watch box. That is, if the cursor is positioned on the word `sqrt` (in PRIME.PAS), then `sqrt` will appear in the Add Watch (popup) entry box.

```
   File     Edit    Run    Compile   Options   Debug    Break/watch
─────────────────────────────────── Edit ───────────────────────────────
    Line  16   Col 77   Insert Indent         Unindent   *   C:PRIME.PAS
      J, K : integer;  Result : Boolean;
  begin
     Result := true;
     K := trunc( sqrt( I ) + 0.5;
     for J := 1 to K do
        if( ( I div J ) = ( I / J ) )
             then Result := false;
     end;

  begin
     clrscr;
     for I := 1 to 100 do
        if TestPrime(I)
           then writeln(I:3);
     writeln('Done');  readln;
─────────────────────────────────── Watch ──────────────────────────────
  TestPrime: PTR(CSEG,$0)
  Result: TRUE
   I: 3
   K: 2

  F1-Help   F5-Zoom  F6-Switch  F7-Trace  F8-Step  F9-Make  F10-Menu
```

Figure G-2 Edit and Watch Window Displays

If you prefer, a different variable can be typed in directly (simply start typing) or the right arrow key can be used to copy additional text from the Edit window. Thus, beginning with the Edit cursor on sqrt, the right arrow key can be used to make this entry read sqrt(I), or an entirely different term can be typed in. When the desired entry is selected, press Enter and the appropriate item will appear in the Watch window (see Figure G-2, bottom window) together with a value (or with a comment such as UNKNOWN, etc).

If you have the Display Swapping option set to NONE, the **A**dd option can also be selected by switching directly to the Watch window and using the Ins or Ctrl-N keys.

As the step-by-line debug session executes, the values for the items appearing in the Watch window will be updated with each step, providing you with a readout of the selected variables.

However, if you run the debug facility using the PRIME.PAS with the watch items shown in Figure G-2, as you step through the program, notice that each time the program exits from the TestPrime subroutine, the variables K and Result appear with the label UNKNOWN. This occurs because these variables are local to the TestPrime procedure and do not have any values or references outside of TestPrime.

Further, note the Watch entry for TestPrime itself. Since TestPrime is a reference to a subprocedure rather than a variable, the Watch display shows the pointer address PTR(CSEG,$0) rather than a value returned by TestPrime.

And, last, also note the Watch entry for the variable K when the TestPrime procedure begins or the variable I before the first for loop begins. Initially, neither variable has been assigned a value and the Watch entries will show some indeterminate value. This is perfectly normal and is not a problem but is an element you should keep firmly in mind while using the debug facilities.

Three other Watch options — *Delete watch*, *Edit watch*, and *Remove all watches* — are provided but are only available from the **B**reak/watch menu or from the Watch window: no hot keys are assigned to these features.

The *Break/watch* / *Delete watch* option. The *Delete watch* option is used to remove a single entry from the Watch window. This can be menu selected or executed by going to the Watch window, selecting the item to remove and entering Ins or Ctrl-N.

The *Break/watch* / *Edit watch* option. The *Edit watch* option is exercised either by menu selection or by going to the Watch window, selecting an item and pressing Enter.

The *Break/watch* / *Remove all watches* option. The *Remove all watches* option is a menu selection only and removes all items from the Watch window.

The **D**ebug Options

Several features appear under the **D**ebug menu, two of which, *Evaluate* and *Call stack*, are called by hot keys. The *Find procedure*, *Integrated debugging*, *Stand-alone debugging*, *Display swapping* and *Refresh display* options are called from the Debug menu.

The *Debug* / *Evaluate* option. The *Evaluate* option (called by the Ctrl-F4 hot key) is a second method of examining a variable's value. Unlike the Watch options, however, the *Evaluate* option (see Figure G-3) pops up a box display with the cursor in the first box (**Evaluate**). As with the *Add watch* selection, the cursor position in the Edit window will select an entry or an entry can be typed in directly.

After the variable to be evaluated has been selected, press Enter and the current value will appear in the **Result** box.

At this point, you can also use the up and down arrow keys to move between the three display boxes and, by entering the **New Value** box, a specific value

```
┌──────────────────────── Evaluate ────────────────────────┐
│  ┌──                                                      │
│  │ DataArray[DataItem]                                    │
│  └──                                                      │
│  ┌─────────────────────── Result ───────────────────────┐│
│  │ 12345.6                                               ││
│  └──                                                      │
│  ┌────────────────────── New Value ─────────────────────┐│
│  │ 12478.5                                               ││
│  └──                                                      │
└──────────────────────────────────────────────────────────┘
```

Figure G-3 Evaluation Box Showing Display Example

can be assigned to the displayed variable. This feature can be used to observe the effects on your program, to force a test of a specific circumstance, to run limit tests, or to examine any other type of result.

Note: the **New Value** entry is not limited to constants. You can also enter the name of some other variable for assignment *as long as the second variable type is compatible* with the variable in **Evaluate** box. See your Turbo Pascal 5.0 manual for further details and restrictions.

The *Debug / Call stack* option. The *Call stack* option (use the Ctrl-F3 hot key) displays the current call stack, listing the procedures and function calls which are *currently active* on the stack. The current procedure or function will appear on the top of the stack list (with parameter values if and when practical) and procedures calling the present function or procedure appearing below in order.

Thus, if the *Call stack* option is executed from the procedure TestPrime with the arguement of 5, the call stack window would look something like this:

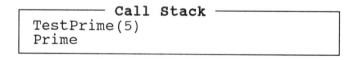

```
┌──────── Call Stack ────────┐
│ TestPrime(5)               │
│ Prime                      │
└────────────────────────────┘
```

Figure G-4 The Call Stack Display

With a more extensive source code, of course, the stack list could be longer. Remember, however, that only active references will appear on the stack list and, once a procedure or function has been completed, it is popped off of the stack and forgotten.

The *Debug / Find procedure* option. The *Find procedure* option pops up a window asking for the name of a procedure or function. After you enter an indentifying name and press Enter, the Edit window will locate the first executable source code line for the named procedure.

Note: the program must have been compiled before the *Find procedure* option is used.

This locator does not affect your current debugging state. If you are paused at another point during a step-by-line debugging session, the F7 key will resume execution at the previous location, not from the procedure or function located. Alternately, you can position the cursor, then call *Run / Go to cursor* (F4) to run the program down to the cursor line and begin step-by-line debugging from this point.

The *Debug / Integrated debugging* option. The *Integrated debugging* option enables debugging in the Integrated Development Environment. This option is on by default but can be turned off if more memory is required for compilation and execution of your program.

The *Debug / Stand-alone debugging* option. The *Stand-alone debugging* option adds debug information to the end of the .EXE file, allowing use of the stand-alone Turbo Debugger.

The *Debug / Display swapping* option. The *Display swapping* option allows you to select three display-swapping settings: **Smart**, **Always** or **None**. The default option is **Smart**.

The *Debug / Refresh display* option. The *Refresh display* option recreates the IDE screen, removing any extraneous information which might have been left on the screen by some other operation.

Switching Windows During Debug

With three windows active, facilities are required to step between windows. Two of the windows, the Watch and Edit windows, are normally displayed together on the same screen (but are separate windows and scroll independently) while the third, the program output window, is displayed as a separate screen.

The F6 key toggles between the Edit window and the Watch window, if active, or the Output window if Watch is inactive. Otherwise, the Alt-F5 hot key (or the *Run / User screen* option for menu selection) provides a toggle between the IDE display (the Edit and Watch windows) and the program display.

The Alt-F6 hot key switches the active window contents. If the Edit window is active, Alt-F6 loads the previously edited file (if any) or creates a blank edit screen (if no previous edit file). If either the Watch or Output windows are active, Alt-F6 toggles between these.

Other Debug Options

Option / Compile / Debug information. The *Option / Compile / Debug information* call toggles the generation of debug information for global identifiers and is also required for information for stand-alone debuggers. This can also be enabled by the {$D+} directive and use of the $D directive within your program overrides the option setting.

Option / Compile / Local symbols. The *Option / Compile / Local symbols* call enables the evaluation of local symbols, allowing the debugger to "remember" identifiers local to each procedure or function. Use of the $L directive within your program overrides the option setting.

Option / Enviroment / Zoom windows. The *Option / Enviroment / Zoom windows* call toggles the zoom display on the active window.

A Sample Debug Session

The program listing PRIME.PAS (source code following) is used to illustrate the IDE debugging facility. As you can easily discover, the listing shown contains two deliberate errors which have been provided for demonstration purposes.

```
program Prime;
{$D+,L+,R-}
uses Crt;
var
   I : integer;
   function TestPrime( I : integer ): Boolean;
   var
      J, K : integer; Result : Boolean;
   begin
        Result := true;
        K := trunc( sqrt( I ) + 0.5 );
        for J := 1 to K do
            if( ( I div J ) = ( I / J ) )
                then Result := false;
   end;
begin
   clrscr;
   for I := 1 to 100 do
      if TestPrime(I)
          then writeln(I:3);
   writeln('Done'); readln;
end.
```

Begin by entering the twenty-four line program as shown and using the **Compile** option (Alt-C) to identify any syntax errors which might have occured during entry.

With this done, use the F7 hot key (**Run / Trace into**) to initiate debugging. The screen should flicker, appearing with the Edit window highlighting the begin statement in the main program. If you hold the F7 key down, the screen will flicker as it alternates between the Edit window, where you will observe the highlighted bar moving though the program, and the Output window, where the program results are displayed.

When you release the F7 key, the display will show the Edit window. The Alt-F5 key (**Run / User screen**) will toggle between the Edit and Output displays.

At this point, you should observe (in the Output display) that **PRIME** is identifying all integers from 1 to 100 as prime numbers. That is, **PRIME** is listing all the tested integers — a obvious error.

Even if you have already recognised one error in the program, please follow along because the point of this exercise is to demonstrate a few aspects of using the debugger and, for the next step, you will need to be in the Edit window. If you are not, then use Alt-F5 to shift back to the IDE screen.

Since it is rather obvious that the function **TestPrime** is returning a Boolean 'true' for each integer tested, the first step in debugging would be assigning a watch to the local variable Result so that we can see precisely what is happening to this variable as the program is stepped.

This is done by moving the cursor in the Edit window to the word Result (anywhere in the listing is fine) and use the Ctrl-F7 key (Break/watch / **Add** watch) to select the Result variable, then press Enter.

And, as long as watches are being assigned, move down to the main program and repeat the same operation for the term TestPrime.

At this point, both terms should be visible in the Watch window. The term Result may appear initially as TRUE, FALSE or UNKNOWN depending on where the step-by-line execution was interrupted. For the moment don't worry about the initial values shown. What is important are the values shown as each step executes.

Oh, yes, the term TestPrime in the Watch window will probably show PTR(CSEG, $0) as a value. This is correct and, as mentioned earlier, when a Watch is assigned to a function or procedure, the reference shown is a pointer value with a pointer address, not a value returned by the function.

While this information is not particularly useful, you should be aware of what you will see and why. But more on this in a moment.

Now, repeat the step-by-line execution using the F7 key (if necessary, use the Ctrl-F2 key to restart execution from the top). As the program steps through execution, you should see the value of Result changing according to which line of the program has just been executed and what arguement was passed to the function **TestPrime**, and you should see Result being set to FALSE.

But the Output screen is still showing all the numbers tested as Primes. So, what's happening? In this case, the error is simply that the value Result, after the test loop completes, is never assigned to the function **TestPrime**, and **TestPrime** always returns the same value because it is never instructed differently.

And, this is the type of error which the debug facility can point out only indirectly. If the Boolean variable TestResult had been declared in the main program and the assigments

```
TestResult := TestPrime(I);
if TestResult
```

were used, then a watch could have been assigned to `TestResult` and the error — when `Result` and `TestResult` showed different values — might have been more immediately obvious. But this would also have been awkward programming and, remember, I didn't promise you that the debug facility would be a miracle cure for all your problems.

For the moment, however, simply correct this error by making the addition shown below and we'll look at the new results:

```
      ...then Result := false;
   TestPrime := Result;
end;
```

After entering the correction, press the F7 key. This time, instead of executing the next line of code, Turbo will pop up a message box instructing:

```
========= Verify =========
  Source modified, rebuild? (Y/N)
```

An affirmative response will recompile the source code before initiating step-by-line debugging, precisely as if the Ctrl-F2 (**R**un / **P**rogram reset) option had been used.

Next, hold the F7 key down and watch the value of `Result`.

But what's happening now? The value of `Result` is changing from TRUE to FALSE (with UNKNOWN appearing each time the function exits to the main program) but now nothing is appearing in the Output screen.

Now, instead of holding the F7 key down, press and release the F7 key several times, observing the Watch display for `Result` as the loop in the **TestPrime** function executes. Notice that each time the test loop for `J := 1 to K do` begins, the value of `Result` is immediately set to FALSE, and always on the first step through the loop.

If, at this point, the test error is not immediately obvious, you could add the variables *I* and *J* to the Watch window and continue with the step-by-line debug session, paying particular attention to the values of *I* and *J* at the point where `Result` first becomes FALSE.

Now what do you see? That all integers are evenly divisible by 1? And not exactly the best way to test for primes, either.

So, the second error in **PRIME.PAS** lies in running the test loop `for J := 1 to K do` instead of the correct `for J := 2 to K do`. Make this final change to the source code, then run debug once more.

This time, you should see the variable Result remain true for primes and return as false for all non-prime integers, with the appropriate integers appearing in the Output display.

And the current debug example is concluded.

Several of the basic features of the debug facility have been demonstrated but the best way to really become familiar with this facility is simply to experiment with it on your own programs. And, particularly, experiment with the *Debug / Evaluate* (Ctrl-F4) feature, because you may find this particular option one of the most useful of all.

Index

Disk to Accompany
Programming the IBM® User Interface
Using Turbo Pascal®

The Pascal source files listed in **Programming the IBM User Interface: Using Turbo Pascal** by Ben Ezzell are available on one 5 1/4" disk.

Equipment you will need:

Hardware: IBM® Personal Computer, or 100% IBM PC-compatible computer; 2 disk drives or one disk drive and a hard disk; DOS 2.0 or higher.

Memory: 640 K

Available by mail only. Use the postage-paid card below.

Please send me_____(quantity) Disks to accompany *Programming the IBM User Interface* by Ben Ezzell, at $19.95 each. ISBN 0-201-51748-5

____ Check enclosed (include your state sales tax; Addison-Wesley will pay postage and handling)

____ Charge to my Visa card #_____ Exp. date _____

____ Charge to my MasterCard #_____ Exp. date _____

Four digits above your name: _____

____Charge to my American Express card # _____ Exp. date _____

YOUR SIGNATURE:_____

Name:_____ Title: _____

Company (if applicable): _____

Address: _____

City: _____ State: _____ Zip: _____

BUSINESS REPLY CARD
FIRST CLASS   PERMIT NO. 11   READING, MA.

Postage Will Be Paid By Addressee

ADDISON-WESLEY
PUBLISHING COMPANY, INC.
Order Department
Reading, Massachusetts U.S.A. 01867-9984